MostUsedWords.com presents

French Frequency Dictionary

Essential Vocabulary

2500 Most Common French Words

Book 1

First Printing, 2018

Jolie Laide LTD
12/F, 67 Percival Street, Hong Kong

www.MostUsedWords.com

Contents

Why This Book?

Hello, dear reader.

Thank you for purchasing this book. We hope it serves you well on your language learning journey.

Not all words are created equal. The purpose of this frequency dictionary is to list the most used words in descending order, to enable you to learn a language as fast and efficiently as possible.

First, we would like to illustrate the value of a frequency dictionary. For the purpose of example, we have combined frequency data from various languages (mainly Romance, Slavic and Germanic languages) and made it into a single chart.

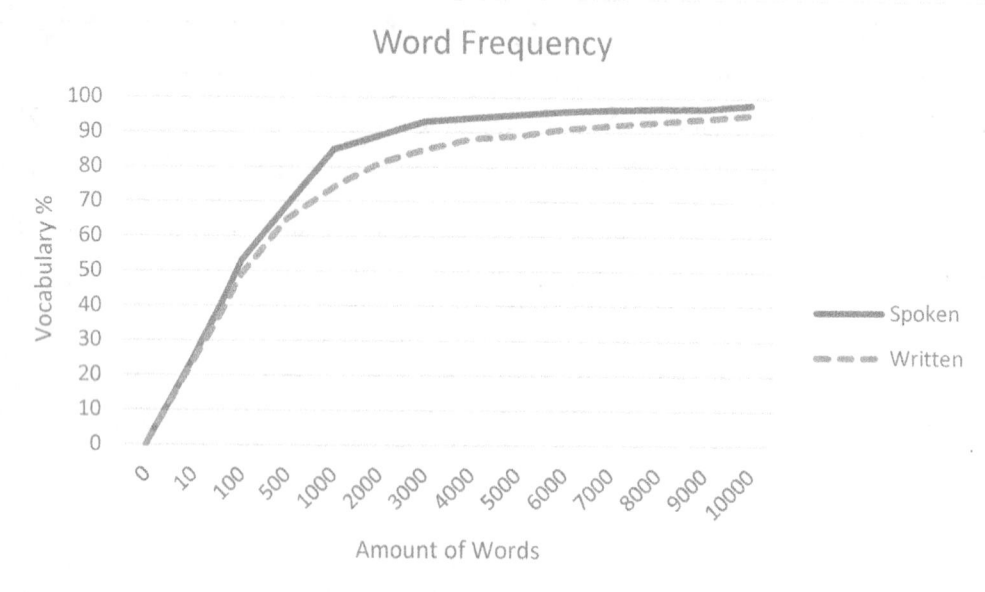

The sweet spots, according to the data seem to be:

Amount of Words	Spoken	Written
• 100	53%	49%
• 1.000	85%	74%
• 2.500	92%	82%
• 5.000	95%	89%
• 7.500	97%	93%
• 10.000	98%	95%

Above data corresponds with Pareto's law.

Pareto's law, also known as the 80/20 rule, states that, for many events, roughly 80% of the effects come from 20% of the causes.

In language learning, this principle seems to be on steroids. It seems that just 20% of the 20% (95/5) of the most used words in a language account for roughly all the vocabulary you need.

To put his further in perspective: The Concise Oxford Hachette French Dictionary lists over 175.000 words in current use, while you will only need to know 2.9% (5000 words) to achieve 95% and 89% fluency in speaking and writing. Knowing the most common 10.000 words, or 5.6%, will net you 98% fluency in spoken language and 95% fluency in written texts.

Keeping this in mind, the value of a frequency dictionary is immense. Study the most frequent words, build your vocabulary and progress naturally. Sounds logical, right?

How many words do you need to know for varying levels of fluency?

While it's important to note that it is impossible to pin down these numbers and statistics with 100% accuracy, these are a global average of multiple sources.

According to research, this is the amount of vocabulary needed for varying levels of fluency.

1. 250 words: the essential core of a language. Without these words, you cannot construct any sentence.
2. 750 words: those that are used every single day by every person who speaks the language.
3. 2500 words: those that should enable you to express everything you could possibly want to say, although some creativity might be required.
4. 5000 words: the active vocabulary of native speakers without higher education.
5. 10,000 words: the active vocabulary of native speakers with higher education.
6. 20,000 words: what you need to recognize passively to read, understand, and enjoy a work of literature such as a novel by a notable author.

Caveats & Limitations.

A frequency list is never "The Definite Frequency List."

Depending on the source material analyzed, you may get different frequency lists. A corpus on spoken word differs from source texts based on a written language.

That is why we chose subtitles as our source, because, according to science, subtitles cover the best of both worlds: they correlate to both spoken and written language.

The frequency list is based on analysis of roughly 20 gigabytes of French subtitles.

Visualize a book with almost 16 million pages, or 80.000 books of 200 pages each, to get an idea of the amount words that have been analyzed for this book. A large base text is vital in order to develop an accurate frequency list.

The raw data included over 1 million entries. The raw data has been lemmatized; words are given in their root form.

Some entries you might find odd, in their respective frequency rankings. We were surprised a couple of time ourselves. Keep in mind that the frequency list is compiled from a large amount of subtitle data, and may include words you wouldn't use yourself.

You might find non-French loanwords in this dictionary. We decided to include them, because if they're being used in subtitle translation, it is safe to assume the word has been integrated into the French general vocabulary.

We tried our best to keep out proper nouns, such as "James, Ryan, Alice as well as "Rome, Washington" or "the Louvre, the Capitol".

Some words have multiple meanings. For the ease of explanation, the following examples are given in English.

"Jack" is a very common first name, but also a noun (a jack to lift up a vehicle) and a verb (to steal something). So is the word "can" It is a conjugation of the verb "to be able" as well as a noun (a tin can, or a can of soft drink).

This skews the frequency rankings slightly. With the current technology, it is unfortunately not possible to rightly identify the correct frequency placements of above words. Luckily, these words are very few, and thus negligible in the grand scheme of things.

If you encounter a word you think you won't need in your vocabulary, just skip learning it. The frequency list includes 25 extra words to compensate for any irregularities you might encounter.

The big secret to learning language is this: build your vocabulary, learn basic grammar and go out there and speak. Make mistakes, have a laugh and learn from them.

We hope you enjoy this frequency dictionary, and that it helps you in your quest of speaking French.

How To Use This Dictionary

abbreviation	*abr*
adjective	*adj*
adverb	*adv*
article	*art*
auxiliary verb	*av*
conjunction	*con*
interjection	*int*
noun	*f(eminine), m(asculine)*
numeral	*num*
particle	*part*
phrase	*phr*
prefix	*pfx*
preposition	*prp*
pronoun	*prn*
suffix	*sfx*
verb	*vb*
singular	*sg*
plural	*pl*

Word Order

The most common translations are generally given first. This resets by every new respective part of speech. Different parts of speech are divided by ";".

Translations

We made the decision to give the most common translation(s) of a word, and respectively the most common part(s) of speech. It does, however, not mean that this is the only possible translations or the only part of speech the word can be used for.

International Phonetic Alphabet (IPA)

The pronunciation of foreign vocabulary can be tricky. To help you get it right, we added IPA entries for each entry. If you already have a base understanding of the pronunciation, you will find the IPA pronunciation straightforward. For more information, please visit www.internationalphoneticalphabet.org

French English Frequency Dictionary

Rank	French Part of Speech [IPA]	English Translation(s) French Example Sentence -English Example Sentence
1	**de** prp [də]	**of| from** Il existe de nombreux cas de recrutement et de licenciement inappropriés et de discrimination en matière de salaire, de conditions de travail et de sécurité de l'emploi. -There are many inappropriate cases in terms of hiring into and dismissing from the job, and providing salary, labour condition, as well as guaranteeing security.
2	**je** prn [ʒə]	**I** Je sais, je l'ai déjà dit, mais je ne pense pas que le gouvernement écoutait. -I know I mentioned this earlier but I do not think the government was listening.
3	**être** vb [ɛtʁ]	**be| exist** La personne concernée ne doit pas être définie comme telle pour la personne incitant. -The person addressed needs not to be determined as such for the inciting person.
4	**pas** adv; m [pa]	**not; step** Ce n'est pas que je suis antipathique, mais je ne peux pas vous aider. -It's not that I am unsympathetic, but I am not able to help you.
5	**le** art; prn [lə]	**the; it** Tout le monde aurait préféré qu'ils le fassent plus tôt, mais ils l'ont fait. -Everybody would have liked that to have occurred earlier, but it did happen.
6	**vous** prn [vu]	**you (form, pl)** Relancerez -vous cette dynamique institutionnelle, lui donnerez -vous une chance? -Will you revive the institutional dynamic, will you create that new chance?
7	**la** art; prn [la]	**the; it** La sous-commission est là pour faire rapport devant la commission qui l'a créée. -The purpose of a subcommittee is to report back to the main committee.
8	**tu** prn [ty]	**you (coll)** Si tu te débrouilles bien, tu pourras dire que tu as survécu à Jesse James. -Nelson, you do this right, you can say you've seen Jesse James and lived to tell the story.
9	**que** con; prn; prp; adj; adv [kə]	**that; that; than; which; how** Une lettre annonçant une vérification fiscale suscite le même niveau d'anxiété et de crainte que... -A tax audit letter evokes about the same level of emotion and fear as...
10	**un** art; adj; num; prn [ɛ̃]	**a; one; one; one** Un exploitait un pub et un bar, un autre, un salon de tatouage et de bronzage. -One runs a pub and a grill, and one runs a tattoo parlour and suntanning salon.
11	**il**	**he, it**

	prn [il]	Il a persévéré, il a servi et il a bâti, tant au gouvernement que dans l'opposition. -He persevered; he served; he built — from the government and the opposition benches.

12 et — **and**

con
[e]

J'ai besoin de pain et de lait.
-I need some bread and milk.

13 à — **to**

prp
[a]

Il a promis de rappeler à 17 heures, mais il a rappelé à 15 heures et a disparu.
-He promised to call back at 5 p.m. but he called back at 3 p.m. and then disappeared.

14 avoir — **have; asset**

vb; m
[avwaʁ]

Je suis désolé de vous avoir entraînées là-dedans.
-I'm sorry I have dragged you into this.

15 ne — **not**

adv
[nə]

Mais parfois, les patients ne ne se réveille pas de la chirurgie.
-But sometimes patients do not wake up from surgery.

16 ce — **this; that**

prn; adj
[sə]

Et alors que j'occupe ce bureau, je sais ce dont ce pays a besoin.
-And occupying this office, I know what the country needs.

17 en — **in; thereof**

prp; adv
[ɑ̃]

Elles savaient en quels périls ils se trouvaient.
-They knew how much danger they were in.

18 on — **we**

prn
[ɔ̃]

On dit: «On veut continuer, on veut continuer, on veut continuer.»
-It says ``We want to continue, we want to continue, we want to continue".

19 cela — **it| that**

prn
[səla]

Mes collègues de l'autre côté n'auront pas le courage de m'appuyer sur cela.
-My colleagues on the other side would not have the courage to support me on that.

20 pour — **for**

prp
[puʁ]

C'est mauvais pour Emma, pour moi et pour toi.
-It's bad for Emma, it's bad for me, it's bad for you.

21 moi — **me; ego**

prn; m
[mwa]

Je n'ai pas plus de cent yens sur moi.
-I have no more than one hundred yen with me.

22 qui — **which**

prn
[ki]

C'est décevant pour la Procureure et pour ceux d'entre nous qui soutiennent les Tribunaux.
-It is disappointing to the Prosecutor and to those of us who uphold the Tribunals.

23 nous — **we| us**

prn
[nu]

Pour nous, Européens, c'est tout bonnement inacceptable, c'est indigne de nous,...
-For us as Europeans, that is simply not acceptable, it is unworthy of us …

24 mais — **but; probably**

con; adv
[mɛ]

La plupart des cas font l'objet d'un diagnostic clinique, mais, même ainsi, on note des inexactitudes.
-Most of the cases are clinically diagnosed, but even so there are inaccuracies.

25 me — **me| myself**

	prn [mə]	Il répondit: "Je vais me réfugier vers un mont qui me protégera de l'eau". -He said: "I will betake myself to a mountain that will protect me from the waters!"
26	**dans** prp; adv [dɑ̃]	**in; aboard** Dans plusieurs paragraphes, on insiste sur la nécessité d'une large harmonisation fiscale. -In several paragraphs mention is made of the need for a long-term harmonisation of taxes.
27	**bien** adv; m; adj [bjɛ̃]	**well| very; good; right** Trois choses ne peuvent pas être cachées bien longtemps: le soleil, la lune et la vérité. -Three things cannot be long hidden: the sun, the moon, and the truth.
28	**elle** prn [ɛl]	**she| it** La Convention prime-t-elle le droit interne ou est-elle directement applicable ? -Does the Convention take priority over national laws and is it directly applicable?
29	**si** con; adv [si]	**if; so** Tout bien considéré, le règlement n'est pas si mauvais sur le plan du contenu. -In the final analysis there is not so much intrinsically wrong with the regulation.
30	**tout** adj; adv; m; prn [tu]	**all; all; all; all** Tu ne m'as pas tout conté. -You didn't tell me everything.
31	**plus** adj; adv; m [ply]	**more; more; plus** Notre société est plus urbanisée, plus mobile et plus anonyme que jamais. -Our society is more urban, more mobile, and more anonymous than ever before.
32	**non** adv; part [nɔ̃]	**not; no** Il me semble que la réponse à toutes ces questions est essentiellement non. -It would seem to me that the answer to all these questions is essentially no.
33	**mon** prn [mɔ̃]	**my** Un exemple frappant de l'empiétement du Conseil de sécurité concerne mon propre pays. -One vivid example of encroachment by the Security Council concerns my own country.
34	**te** prn [tə]	**you** Falk, je te le dis, elle te trompe, et tu es trop typhlotique pour le voir. -Falk, I'm telling you, she's cheating on you, and you're too typhlotic to see it.
35	**avec** prp [avɛk]	**with** Nous avons demandé à ces jeunes s'ils s'entendaient bien avec leurs parents. -We asked those young people how they got along with their moms and dads.
36	**oui** part; m [wi]	**yes; yea** Si je fais campagne pour le "oui" en Irlande, c'est néanmoins un "oui" critique. -I happen to be campaigning in Ireland for a "yes" vote but it is a critical "yes".
37	**aller**	**go| travel**

vb [ale]	Il avait les mains et les jambes attachées et ne pouvait pas aller aux toilettes. -His hands and legs had been tied, and he had not been allowed to visit a toilet.

38 toi — **you**

prn
[twa]

A défaut de toi-même... tu pourrais me respecter, moi qui me suis exténué sur toi.
-If you've no respect for yourself...... you at least might have some for me, who sweated over you.

39 faire — **do**

vb
[fɛʁ]

Elles ne le font pas parce qu'elles doivent le faire mais parce qu'elles veulent le faire.
-They do not do this because they have to, but because they want to.

40 se — **-self (reflexive marker)**

prn
[sə]

White Mike se déshabilla et se coucha sur le plancher pour se rafraîchir un peu.
-White Mike stripped to his shorts and lay down on the floor... so he felt a little cooler.

41 comme — **as; as; such as**

con; prp; adj
[kɔm]

Par conséquent, la Commission considère ces amendements comme non pertinents.
-For this reason the Commission does not consider these amendments to be appropriate.

42 sur — **on**

prp
[syʁ]

J'insisterais davantage sur cela que sur tout autre point de notre résolution.
-I would put more emphasis on that than on anything else in our resolution.

43 quoi — **what**

prn
[kwa]

Malgré les évidences, il n'apprécie pas qu'on lui dise quoi faire.
-It does not appreciate our telling it what to do, even when what is needed is obvious.

44 ici — **here**

adv
[isi]

Je projette de revenir ici dimanche soir et d'être ici du lundi au vendredi.
-My plans are to come back here on Sunday night and to be here Monday to Friday.

45 savoir — **know; knowledge**

vb; m
[savwaʁ]

Je pense que Jack est ici le seul à savoir où Jill habite.
-I think Jack is the only one here who knows where Jill lives.

46 lui — **him**

prn
[lɥi]

Ensuite, je lui demanderais de répondre à la question qui lui a été posée hier.
-Second, I would ask him to answer the question that was put to him yesterday.

47 vouloir — **want| wish**

vb
[vulwaʁ]

Vouloir protéger la santé des citoyens, vouloir protéger l'environnement, c'est quelque chose de fort louable.
-To want to protect human health, to want to protect the environment is quite worthy.

48 là — **there**

adv
[la]

La communauté internationale se heurte là à une tradition culturelle ancestrale.
-There the international community is facing a cultural and ancestral tradition.

49 rien — **nothing; anything; nix**

m; prn; adv
[ʁjɛ̃]
Ils n'auraient rien fait.
-They wouldn't have done anything.

50 **dire**
vb
[diʁ]
say| speak
Je vous demande tout simplement, si je veux dire quelques mots, que vous m'écoutiez.
-If I wish to say something, I would ask members to listen to what I have to say.

51 **où**
adv; prn; con
[u]
where; that; wherein
Je la laisse m'emmener où elle veut.
-So, I just let myself go and wherever music takes me, so be it.

52 **votre**
adj; prn
[vɔtʁ]
your; your
J'admire votre esprit hardi, votre humour pétillant, vos mains et vos accolades amicales.
-I admire your challenging mind, your sparkling humour, your hands and hugs of friendship.

53 **pourquoi**
adv; con
[puʁkwa]
why; wherefore
Pourquoi jouent-ils à ce jeu, pourquoi nous renvoient-ils de Pilate à Caïphe ?
-Why are they playing this game with us? Why is it being sent from pillar to post?

54 **quand**
adv; con
[kɑ̃]
when; when
Mais quand pourront -ils bénéficier du système démocratique occidental?
-But when are they going to reap the benefits of the Western democratic system?

55 **par**
prp; m
[paʁ]
by; par
Arrache la plante par les racines.
-Pull the plant up by the roots.

56 **son**
adj; m
[sɔ̃]
its; sound
Bill a été lourdé de son boulot la semaine dernière.
-Bill was canned from his job last week.

57 **ton**
adj; prn; m
[tɔ̃]
your; your; tone
J'ai tout lu à ton sujet.
-I've read all about you.

58 **pouvoir**
m; vb; av
[puvwaʁ]
power; can; might
La richesse génère le pouvoir.
-Wealth begets power.

59 **alors**
adv
[alɔʁ]
then
D'où viennent alors les armes à présent ?
-Where are the weapons coming from now then?

60 **comment**
adv
[kɔmɑ̃]
how
Le rapport a bien indiqué comment cela est fait et comment les ressources sont réunies.
-The report adequately describes how this is done and how the resources are secured.

61 **bon**
adj; m; adv
[bɔ̃]
good| well; voucher; then
Je suis du genre à devenir nerveux devant un public, donc je ne suis pas bon pour faire des discours.
-I'm the type who gets nervous in front of people, so I'm bad at speech making.

62 **ou**
con
[u]
or
De deux choses l'une, ou bien il existe un problème de santé publique ou bien il n'en existe pas.

-It is an either/ or situation: either there is a public health problem or there is not.

63 très
adv
[tʁɛ]

very

Les États membres sont en effet très attachés à leur souveraineté en la matière.
-Indeed Member States are extremely protective of their sovereignty in this area.

64 même
adj; adv
[mɛm]

same; even

Ce sont le même chef, la même politique discréditée, les mêmes extrémistes.
-It is the same leader, the same discredited policies, the same extremists.

65 merci
m; int
[mɛʁsi]

thanks; thanks

Merci vraiment.
-Thank you very much!

66 jamais
adv
[ʒamɛ]

never| ever

Les femmes ayant commis une faute disciplinaire ne sont jamais mises aux arrêts.
-Women soldiers are not given incarceration as a disciplinary punishment at all.

67 aussi
adv; con
[osi]

also| as; and

Le Conseil, lui aussi, investit plus, mais ses investissements sont aussi plus sélectifs.
-The Council is also investing more, but it is also investing more selectively.

68 voir
vb
[vwaʁ]

see| view

C'est exactement ce que j'ai dit au Parlement - que nous aimerions voir cela changer.
-This is exactly what I told Parliament - that we would like to see this change.

69 deux
num
[dø]

two

Il y a deux sorties en avant, deux sur les côtés et deux sorties en arrière.
-There are two exits in the front, two exits over the way and two in the back.

70 falloir
vb
[falwaʁ]

have to

Concrètement, cela signifie qu'il va falloir dire adieu aux combustibles fossiles.
-In specific terms, this means that we need to say goodbye to fossil fuels.

71 autre
prn; adj; adv
[otʁ]

other; another; else

Les décisions de celle-ci ne peuvent être réformées par aucune autre autorité.
-The decision of the Constitutional Court cannot be changed by any other authority.

72 maintenant
adv
[mɛ̃tnɑ̃]

now

Nous devons résoudre la crise maintenant et fournir les ressources maintenant.
-We must resolve the crisis now and provide the resources now.

73 encore
adv
[ɑ̃kɔʁ]

still| again

Il ne faut pas répéter encore et encore où nous allons, c'est bien là l'idée.
-We should not repeat again and again where we are going: that is the whole idea.

74 peu
adv; m; adj
[pø]

little; bit; few

Ces gens-là se sont acquittés de leurs fonctions comme bien peu savent le faire.

-These are a few of the individuals who did their job to a standard few can compare.

75	**vraiment**	**really| actually**
	adv	Je le veux vraiment. Mais si je le veux vraiment, je dois le rendre possible.
	[vʁɛmã]	-I really want it, but if I really want it then I have to make it possible.
76	**temps**	**time**
	m	Quel temps fera-t-il demain ?
	[tã]	-What'll tomorrow's weather be like?
77	**toujours**	**always| still**
	adv	Nous nous sommes engagés à collaborer toujours plus étroitement avec les Nations unies.
	[tuʒuʁ]	-We are committed to working ever more closely with the United Nations.
78	**notre**	**our**
	prn	Il s'agit de l'expression de la vocation pacifiste de notre pays et de notre Gouvernement.
	[nɔtʁ]	-This is the expression shown of our country's and our Government's vocation for peace.
79	**vie**	**life**
	f	Ce fut l'un des meilleurs moments de ma vie.
	[vi]	-It was one of the best experiences of my life.
80	**Oh!**	**Oh!**
	int	Oh ! monsieur ! votre maintien est trop arrogant et impérieux.
	[o!]	-O, sir, your presence here is too bold and peremptory.
81	**juste**	**just| fair; just**
	adj; adv	Mon gouvernement appuie la position juste de la République arabe syrienne, pays frère.
	[ʒyst]	-My Government supports the just position of the fraternal Syrian Arab Republic.
82	**sans**	**without**
	prp	Le terrorisme doit être combattu sans exception, sans hésitation et sans crainte.
	[sã]	-Terrorism must be fought without exception, without hesitation and without fear.
83	**quelque**	**some; about**
	adj; adv	Cela n'est acceptable, ni au Soudan, ni dans quelque pays du monde que ce soit.
	[kɛlk]	-That is not acceptable in Sudan or in any other country of the world.
84	**monde**	**world**
	m	Un monde plus sain ne peut qu'être un monde meilleur, plus sûr et plus juste.
	[mɔ̃d]	-A healthier world is a better world, a safer world and a more just world.
85	**accord**	**agreement| deal**
	m	Je suis d'accord avec toi sur ce point.
	[akɔʁ]	-I agree with you on this point.
86	**trop**	**too| too much**
	adv	Les procédures demeurent trop longues, trop lourdes et trop bureaucratiques.
	[tʁo]	-They remain essentially long, cumbersome and overly bureaucratic.
87	**venir**	**come**
	vb	Notre prix Sakharov, Leila Sana, n'a pas pu venir pour recevoir son prix.
	[vəniʁ]	-Our Sakharov prizewinner, Leyla Zana was unable to come here to collect her prize.
88	**croire**	**believe| think**

vb
[kʀwaʀ]

Un crucifix dans la salle de classe ne force personne à croire ou ne pas croire.
-A crucifix in the classroom does not force anyone to believe, or not to believe.

89 devoir
m; vb; av
[dəvwaʀ]

duty; have to; must

J'ai peut-être bien réussi le devoir surveillé d'hier, mais je ne connais pas encore les résultats.
-I might have done well on yesterday's test, but I do not know the results yet.

90 père
m
[pɛʀ]

father| dad

Mon père adore jouer de la guitare.
-My father loves to play the guitar.

91 dieu
m
[djø]

god

Personne ne connaît tant de contes que le dieu du sommeil.
-Nobody knows as many bedtime stories as the god of the dream.

92 homme
m
[ɔm]

man| person

Le Président Rugova était un homme digne, un homme de dialogue et de réconciliation.
-President Rugova was a man of dignity, a man of dialogue and a man of reconciliation.

93 sûr
adj
[syʀ]

sure| safe

En revanche, ce qui est sûr, c'est que les autorités actuelles sont des occupants.
-However, it was known for certain that the present authorities were occupiers.

94 leur
prn
[lœʀ]

their

Je tiens à leur dire à quel point j'ai apprécié leur coopération active et leurs commentaires utiles.
-I should like to express my appreciation for their active cooperation and sensible comments.

95 avant
adv; prp; adj; m
[avã]

before; before; front

Le futur aussi était mieux avant.
-The future was better before.

96 besoin
m
[bəzwɛ̃]

need

Ils ont besoin de sens, ils ont besoin de valeurs; ils ont besoin de reconnaissance de leurs droits.
-They need meaning, they need values, and they need recognition of their rights.

97 femme
f
[fam]

woman

Elle est la seule femme à son travail.
-She is the only woman at her job.

98 personne
f; prn
[pɛʀsɔn]

person; nobody

La personne concernée ne doit pas être définie comme telle pour la personne incitant.
-The person addressed needs not to be determined as such for the inciting person.

99 aimer
vb
[eme]

love| like

Comme nous le savons, de nombreux députés auraient aimer se prononcer sur le sujet.
-As we know, there are many members in the House who would like to speak on this matter.

100	**chez**	**in| by**
	prp	Le taux d'alphabétisme est de 42 % chez les femmes, et de 66 % chez les hommes.
	[ʃe]	-The literacy rate for females is 42 per cent, compared to 66 per cent for males.
101	**parce que**	**because**
	adv	Tant mieux parce que j'adore les Néerlandais.
	[paʁsə kə]	-Well, that's good, because I'm a big fan of the Dutch.
102	**vrai**	**true| real; right**
	adj; m	Le vrai est trop simple, il faut y arriver toujours par le compliqué.
	[vʁɛ]	-The truth is too simple, one can only go there by way of the complex.
103	**an**	**year**
	m	J'étais allée là-bas un an plus tôt, et j'ai été étonnée des progrès accomplis en un an.
	[ã]	-I was there a year earlier and was amazed at the progress made in one year.
104	**mal**	**evil| wrong; amiss; untimely**
	m; adv; adj	Le gouvernement protégera toujours la population de ceux qui lui veulent du mal.
	[mal]	-The government will always protect Canadians from those who wish to harm us.
105	**parler**	**speak| tell**
	vb	Comme le dit le tribunal de Waitangi pour décrire ses travaux: «Le Traité continue de parler».
	[paʁle]	-As the Waitangi Tribunal says to describe its work: "The Treaty is always speaking".
106	**après**	**after| next; after**
	adv; prp	Pour l'agrandir, il faudra poser pierre sur pierre ou plutôt pierre après pierre.
	[apʁɛ]	-In order to enlarge it stone must be laid on stone, or rather stone after stone.
107	**mort**	**dead; death**
	adj; f	Sami a été déclaré mort à neuf heures.
	[mɔʁ]	-Sami was pronounced dead at nine o'clock.
108	**mieux**	**better; adj**
	adv; adj	Si nous y parvenons, nous nous en trouverons peut-être mieux dans quelques années.
	[mjø]	-If we succeed in this then perhaps we will be better off in a few years ' time!
109	**petit**	**small| little; child**
	adj; m	Veux-tu un petit gâteau?
	[pəti]	-Do you want a small cake?
110	**beaucoup**	**many; much; much**
	prn; adj; adv	Beaucoup de recommandations ont été faites et beaucoup d'idées ont été avancées.
	[boku]	-There were a lot of recommendations and a lot of thoughts advanced.
111	**Monsieur**	**Mr.; sir**
	abr; m	Le monsieur est un économiste canadien.
	[məsjø]	-The gentleman is a Canadian economist.
112	**voilà**	**here**
	adv	Voilà pourquoi combiner économie et écologie est une idée astucieuse.
	[vwala]	-It is for that reason that combining economy and ecology here is a smart move.

113 depuis
adv; prp
[dəpɥi]
since; since
Les gens courageux de cette terre se sont aventurés à nouveau dans le monde depuis.
-The brave and bold of that land have ventured back out into the world ever since.

114 mère
f
[mɛʁ]
mother
« Cesse de me supplier pour avoir un biscuit, Tim », dit sa mère. « Rappelle-toi, les enfants qui demandent avec trop d'insistance sont exclus de la distribution de biscuits ».
-"Stop begging for a cookie, Tim," his mum said, "Remember, 'Children who ask get skipped.'"

115 quel
adj; prn
[kɛl]
what; what
Quel est le potentiel des futures mesures de réduction et quel en sera le coût ?
-What is the potential of future reduction measures and what will their costs be?

116 fille
f
[fij]
daughter| girl
C'est une fille riche.
-This is a rich girl

117 déjà
adv
[deʒa]
already
Comme il a déjà été mentionné, le changement climatique est déjà en cours ici.
-As has already been said, climate change is already happening here.

118 gens
mpl
[ʒã]
people
Peu de gens sont capables de comprendre ses théories.
-Few people are able to understand his theories.

119 donc
con; adv
[dɔ̃k]
therefore; consequently
Il est donc nécessaire de renforcer la coordination intergouvernementale.
-Thus, the need for strengthening intergovernmental coordination was also stressed.

120 jour
m
[ʒuʁ]
day
Demain est un jour férié.
-Tomorrow is a holiday.

121 soir
m
[swaʁ]
evening
Voudriez-vous aller voir un film, ce soir ?
-Would you like to go to a movie tonight?

122 ouais
part
[wɛ]
yeah
Ouais, ça veut aussi dire le range-chaussures.
-Yeah, that includes the hanging shoe sorter.

123 argent
m
[aʁʒã]
money
Il est donc très important que nous obtenions de l'argent pour démobiliser les combattants.
-It is therefore very important that we get the money for the purpose of demobilizing the combatants.

124 maison
f
[mɛzɔ̃]
house| home
Reste dans la maison.
-Stay in the house.

125 nom
m
[nɔ̃]
name
J'ai ouvert un compte au nom de ma fille.
-I opened an account in my daughter's name.

126 Bonjour!
Hello!

	int [bɔ̃ʒuːʁ!]	Monsieur le président Reid et distingués membres du sous-comité, bonjour. -Good afternoon, Chairman Reid, and distinguished members of the subcommittee.
127	**penser** vb [pɑ̃se]	**think| reflect** Il ne faut pas simplement le dire, il faut aussi le penser et le ressentir. -It is not enough to just say this; one must think it, one must feel it.
128	**nuit** f [nɥi]	**night** Comment ça s'est passé, cette nuit ? -How did it go last night?
129	**papa** m [papa]	**papa** À chaque fois que je tombe amoureux, Papa me dit que la fille est ma demi-sœur. -Every time I fall in love, Dad tells me the girl is my half sister.
130	**maman** f [mamɑ̃]	**mom** Maman est restée dans la voiture pendant que papa faisait les courses. -Mom remained in the car while Dad shopped.
131	**rester** vb [ʁɛste]	**stay| keep** La Constitution produite par la Convention doit rester largement inchangée. -The constitution produced by the Convention must remain largely intact.
132	**peur** f [pœʁ]	**fear| scare** Vous n'avez pas peur que ce soit peut-être un piège? -Aren't you scared it might be a trap?
133	**désoler** vb [dezɔle]	**distress| grieve** Nous avons dû constater des pertes civiles et nous sommes désolés pour chacune d'entre elles. -We have witnessed civilian casualties, and we grieve for each one of them.
134	**salut** m; int [saly]	**salvation; hi** Salut, pourriez-vous bouger? Nous allons tenir une réunion, ici. -Hi, could you move? We're about to have a meeting here.
135	**seul** adj; m; adv [sœl]	**only; only one; very** Un seul homme survécut. -Only one man survived.
136	**arriver** vb [aʁive]	**arrive| happen** D'arriver dans des conditions satisfaisantes au lieu de destination. -To arrive in satisfactory condition at the place of destination.
137	**vite** adv [vit]	**quickly| fast** Svilanovic était convaincu qu'en voulant aller trop vite, on risquerait de déstabiliser toute la région. -Svilanovic believed that "quick fixes" could jeopardize the situation in the region.
138	**prendre** vb [pʁɑ̃dʁ]	**take| have** Je conclurai donc en encourageant le député à prendre part à ce débat. -Therefore, I simply conclude by encouraging the hon. member to partake in this debate.
139	**regarder** vb [ʁəgaʁde]	**look| watch** C'est vrai aussi, je pense, qu'on doit regarder l'ensemble des institutions parlementaires. -It is also true, I think, that we must look at all parliamentary institutions.
140	**soit** con [swa]	**whether| either** Information disponible insuffisante (soit insuffisante soit trop générale). -Insufficient information available (either insufficient or too general).

141	**air**	**air**
	m	Soyez notre bouffée d'air frais.
	[ɛʁ]	-You'd be like a breath of fresh air.
142	**passer**	**pass| spend**
	vb	Cela n'aurait jamais dû se passer.
	[pase]	-That never should've happened.
143	**trois**	**three**
	num	En général, je déjeune avec Jack deux à trois fois par semaine.
	[tʁwa]	-I usually eat lunch with Jack two or three times a week.
144	**plaire**	**please**
	vb	Mais aucune politique, où que ce soit, ne peut plaire toujours et à tout le
	[plɛʁ]	monde.
		-But no politics anywhere can please all the people all the time.
145	**chose**	**thing**
	f	Je vis quelque chose.
	[ʃoz]	-I saw something.
146	**Ah!**	**Ha!**
	int	Ah! par pitié, écoutez-moi.
	[a!]	-Ah! For pity's sake, hear me.
147	**bas**	**low| base; bottom**
	adj; m	On fait profil bas pendant quelque temps.
	[ba]	-Well, we're keeping a low profile for a while.
148	**moins**	**less; minus; wanting**
	adv; m; prp	Tu aurais dû verrouiller toutes les portes, ou tout du moins les fermer.
	[mwɛ̃]	-You should have locked, or at least closed, all the doors.
149	**entre**	**between; between**
	adv; prp	L'Europe représente l'égalité entre les nations, entre les peuples, entre les
	[ɑ̃tʁ]	cultures.
		-Europe means equality between nations, between peoples, between
		cultures.
150	**passe**	**pass**
	f	Je n'arrive pas à atteindre ce bocal sur cette étagère. Passe-le-moi, s'il te
	[pas]	plaît.
		-I can't reach the jar on that shelf. Hand it down to me, please.
151	**Hé!**	**Hey!**
	int	Hé, Bain de Sang, si ma voiture est abîmée, je bouffe tes mômes !
	[e!]	-Hey, yo, Bloodbath, if there's one scratch on my ride, I'm gonna eat your
		children!
152	**demain**	**tomorrow; tomorrow**
	adv; m	Il est impatient que tu viennes demain.
	[dəmɛ̃]	-He is eager that you come tomorrow.
153	**appeler**	**call| appeal**
	vb	Tous les détenus peuvent appeler leur avocat au prix d'une communication
	[aple]	ordinaire.
		-All prisoners have the ability to call legal representatives at the standard
		call costs.
154	**grand**	**large| wide**
	adj	Il a été élevé par sa grand-mère.
	[gʁɑ̃]	-He was brought up by her grandmother.
155	**tête**	**head| top**

	f	Pourquoi elle fait la tête ?
	[tɛt]	-Why is she sulking?
156	**arrêter**	**stop| quit**
	vb	La vérité, c'est que très peu de jeunes arrêteront de fumer au cours de leur vie.
	[aʁete]	-The reality is that very few young people kick the habit of smoking during their lives.
157	**attendre**	**expect| wait for**
	vb	Nous croyons que nous devrions attendre leurs conclusions, que celles-ci soient positives ou négatives.
	[atɑ̃dʁ]	-We believe that we should await their conclusions, positive or negative.
158	**raison**	**reason| why**
	f	C'est la raison de ma présence, ici.
	[ʁɛzɔ̃]	-That's why I'm here.
159	**enfant**	**child**
	m	L'enfant attrapa le chat par la queue.
	[ɑ̃fɑ̃]	-The child caught the cat by the tail.
160	**assez**	**enough| quite**
	adv	Et donc, il me semble que cette redistribution-là est assez juste et assez efficace.
	[ase]	-I therefore feel that this form of redistribution is quite fair and quite efficient.
161	**moment**	**time| moment**
	m	That is not to say for a moment that this issue is not one of importance.
	[mɔmɑ̃]	-Cela ne veut pas dire pour autant que cette question est sans importance.
162	**amour**	**love**
	m	Mais faites-les déposer leurs armes avec votre amour.
	[amuʁ]	-But make them lay down their weapons with your love.
163	**heure**	**time**
	f	En une demie-heure sur ce tapis roulant, tu parviendras à un assez bon niveau de transpiration.
	[œʁ]	-With half an hour on this treadmill you'll work up a pretty good sweat.
164	**puis**	**then**
	adv	Ralentissez le train en périphérie, puis arrêtez-le complètement.
	[pɥi]	-Slow the train down outside of town, then come to a complete stop.
165	**tard**	**late**
	adv	Voici donc que l'Europe réagit; lentement, certes, mais mieux vaux tard que jamais.
	[taʁ]	-So Europe is reacting, albeit slowly, but better late than never.
166	**tuer**	**kill| murder**
	vb	N'y a -t-il pas là un paradoxe que de tuer des animaux pour en tuer «humainement» d'autres ?
	[tɥe]	-Is that not a paradox, to kill animals in order to 'humanely' kill other animals?
167	**partir**	**depart| leave**
	vb	Bonjour, quand part le prochain train pour Paris, s'il vous plaît ?
	[paʁtiʁ]	-Hello, when does the next train for Paris leave? Thank you.
168	**connaître**	**know**
	vb	Merete, en tant que vendeuse, doit connaître ses droits dans cette situation.
	[kɔnɛtʁ]	-Merete, as the seller, must know her rights in this situation.
169	**aider**	**help| support**

	vb	
	[ede]	

Ils trouveront sur place le meilleur moyen d'aider les blessés et leurs proches.
-They will determine how best to aid those injured in the attack and their families.

170 gars — **guy**
m
[ga]
Vous êtes un bon gars.
-You're a great guy.

171 chance — **chance| luck**
f
[ʃɑ̃s]
Tu n'auras peut-être pas autant de chance, la prochaine fois.
-You may not be as lucky next time.

172 combien — **how many**
adv
[kɔ̃bjɛ̃]
On va savoir combien attendent, mais je ne sais pas combien on va en guérir.
-We will know how many are waiting, but I do not know how many we will cure.

173 tant — **so such**
adv
[tɑ̃]
La protection des témoins devrait également être assurée en tant que de besoin.
-In the circumstances, adequate protection should also be provided for witnesses.

174 part — **share| part**
f
[paʁ]
Nous restons pour notre part fortement engagés.
-For our part, we continue to be strongly committed.

175 problème — **problem| issue**
m
[pʁɔblɛm]
Ce problème a tout naturellement attisé les discussions.
-That problem naturally invited discussion.

176 coup — **blow| shot**
m
[ku]
Je ne suis pas sûre de ce que c'était, mais cela a fait le bruit d'un coup de feu.
-I'm not sure what it was, but it sounded like a gunshot.

177 porte — **door| gate**
f
[pɔʁt]
En colère, il secoua bruyamment la porte fermée à clef.
-Being angry, he loudly rattled the locked door.

178 travail — **work**
m
[tʁavaj]
Je dois être au travail à 7h30.
-I need to be at work by 7:30.

179 famille — **family**
f
[famij]
Comment votre nom de famille s'écrit-il ?
-How is your surname written?

180 putain — **whore| bitch**
f
[pytɛ̃]
Tu es une putain d'idiote !
-You're a bitching moron.

181 idée — **idea**
f
[ide]
Toute l'argumentation est faite autour d'une idée, c'est l'idée du coût/efficacité.
-All the arguments are built around one idea, the idea of cost-effectiveness.

182 ni — **or; neither**
con; adv
[ni]
Elle ne devra être ni sélective, ni partielle, ni sectorielle, ni partisane,
-It must be neither selective nor partial, neither sectoral nor partisan.

183 contre — **against**
prp
[kɔ̃tʁ]
Ce serait une politique contre le respect de l'individu, contre la solidarité.
-That would be a policy against respect for the individual and against solidarity.

184	**revoir**	**revise**
	vb	Il sera donc peut-être nécessaire de revoir en conséquence le programme de travail.
	[ʁəvwaʁ]	-It might therefore be necessary to revise the programme of work accordingly.

185	**entendre**	**hear**
	vb	Nous devons pouvoir entendre les questions et nous espérons entendre les réponses.
	[ãtãdʁ]	-We must be able to hear the questions and I am hopeful we can hear the answers.

186	**comprendre**	**understand| include**
	vb	On peut comprendre que des documents fructueux doivent mûrir un peu avant d'être exposés à la lumière.
	[kɔ̃pʁãdʁ]	-There is a sense in which seminal papers must be allowed to sow the seeds of their ideas before they see the light of day.

187	**pendre**	**hang**
	vb	Ils vont pendre Jack.
	[pãdʁ]	-They're going to hang Jack.

188	**trouver**	**find| get**
	vb	Je crois que là, effectivement, nous pouvons trouver une ligne fondamentale d'accords.
	[tʁuve]	-I believe, in fact, that we can find a fundamental line of agreement on this.

189	**vieux**	**old| ancient; old man**
	adj; m	Comment ça va, mon vieux ?
	[vjø]	-How are you, old boy?

190	**attention**	**attention**
	f	Jack avait toute l'attention de Jill.
	[atãsjɔ̃]	-Jack had Jill's undivided attention.

191	**demander**	**request| seek**
	vb	Cela ne signifie pas que nous ne devons pas nous demander comment faire davantage.
	[dəmãde]	-At the same time, we must continually ask ourselves if we are doing enough.

192	**chercher**	**search| try**
	vb	Puis-je aller te chercher une boisson ?
	[ʃɛʁʃe]	-Can I go find you a drink?

193	**sous**	**under; underneath; cash**
	prp; adv; f	Le cambrioleur s'introduisit dans la maison sous couvert de la nuit.
	[su]	-The burglar broke into the house under the cover of night.

194	**voici**	**here is**
	prp	Ce projet de loi n'existe plus, mais voici certaines des dispositions que nous approuvions.
	[vwasi]	-It is no longer there, but these are some of the ideas we were supporting.

195	**sang**	**blood**
	m	Avec son sang et tes empreintes dessus.
	[sã]	-The one with her blood and your fingerprints all over it.

196	**histoire**	**history| story**
	f	Ils ont essayé de répéter l'histoire de Salvador Allende, l'histoire du Chili.
	[istwaʁ]	-They are trying to repeat the history of Salvador Allende, the history of Chile.

197	**sortir**	**exit| come out**

vb
[sɔʁtiʁ]

Il peut en sortir affaibli militairement, mais politiquement renforcé.
-Possibly it will come out debilitated militarily, but strengthened politically.

198 question
f
[kɛstjɔ̃]

question| issue

That question was in due course completely absorbed by the question of "crimes".
-Cette question a finalement été totalement absorbée par la question des «crimes».

199 frère
m
[fʁɛʁ]

brother

Mon frère a endommagé mon nouvel ordinateur.
-My brother damaged my new computer.

200 ville
f
[vil]

city

J'ai décidé de sortir et d'explorer la ville.
-I decided to go out and explore the town.

201 finir
vb
[finiʁ]

end| finish

Si nous ne prenons pas les produits de ces pays, nous allons finir par prendre leurs habitants.
-If we do not take the produce of these countries, we will end up taking their people.

202 nouveau
adj; m
[nuvo]

new| further; incoming

Dans l'état actuel des choses, une entreprise qui engage un nouveau travailleur est pénalisée.
-At present, any enterprise which recruits a new employee is penalized for doing so.

203 eux
prn
[ø]

them

Ils se sont désignés eux-mêmes pour tuer tous ceux qui ne pensent pas comme eux.
-They are self-appointed killers of any persons who think differently from them.

204 truc
m
[tʁyk]

thing| trick

Tu ne peux pas me tromper avec un truc comme ça.
-You can't fool me with a trick like that.

205 tenir
vb
[təniʁ]

hold| keep

Le SC.2 et le WP.24 devraient tenir une session commune sur cette question en avril 2001.
-- SC.2 and WP.24 should hold a common session on this issue in April 2001.

206 œil
m
[œj]

eye

Ce n'est pas du «oeil pour oeil, dent pour dent», c'est de la légitime défense.
-It is not a case of ``an eye for an eye, a tooth for a tooth", but a matter of self-defence.

207 laisser
vb
[lese]

leave| let

Je crois que nous devons agir et que nous ne pouvons pas laisser les choses comme elles sont.
-I think that we have to take action, that we cannot leave everything as it is.

208 mec
m
[mɛk]

guy| dude

Surtout ne lui achète rien : ce mec est un arnaqueur de première !
-Above all, don't buy anything from him: he's a blithering swindler.

209 longtemps
adv; adj
[lɔ̃tɑ̃]

for a long time; longtime

Enfin, on peut vivre longtemps sans manger, très longtemps.
-Final point...... people can live a long time without food, a very long time.

210 beau

beautiful| nice; beautiful

adj; m
[bo]

Le chien est beau.
-The dog is beautiful.

211 police police

f
[pɔlis]

La police a détenu plusieurs suspects pour interrogatoire.
-The police detained several suspects for questioning.

212 seulement only| just; only

adv; con
[sœlmɑ̃]

C'est là une question essentielle, pas seulement autrichienne, mais européenne.
-This is also a question of principle, not just Austrian, but European principle.

213 importer import

vb
[ɛ̃pɔʁte]

Pour importer de nouveaux pilotes, cliquez dans la boîte de dialogue des pilotes disponibles sur Importer.
-To import new drivers, click Import in the driver selection dialog.

214 eau water

f
[o]

Manque d'eau et d'hygiène : manque d'eau courante et de WC à chasse d'eau.
-Insufficient water and hygiene: flowing water and WC with water pipes, both insufficient.

215 car car

m
[kaʁ]

Il existait une liaison régulière par car avec Kapan en Arménie mais seulement un car par mois jusqu'à Latchine.
-There is a regular bus connection to Kapan, Armenia, but only a monthly bus to Lachin.

216 chaque each; either

adj; prn
[ʃak]

Il frappe chaque entreprise, chaque travailleur, chaque propriétaire et chaque famille aussi.
-It is hitting every business, every worker, every homeowner and every family too.

217 cas case| event

m
[ka]

Cette règle ne s'applique pas dans tous les cas.
-This rule does not apply in all cases.

218 terre earth| land

f
[tɛʁ]

Qui possède les biens corporels, en particulier la terre, et qui exploite la terre ?
-Who owns physical assets, particularly land, and who is farming the land?

219 placer place| put

vb
[plase]

Pourriez-vous placer la main sur la barrière.
-Would you please place your hand on the barrier.

220 main hand

f
[mɛ̃]

Institutions, Présidence, États membres: nous devons travailler main dans la main.
-The institutions, the Presidency and the Member States must all work hand in hand.

221 ensemble together; ensemble; collection

adv; m; f
[ɑ̃sɑ̃bl]

Je pense que si nous abordons ce problème ensemble, nous réussirons ensemble.
-I think that if we tackle the issue together, then together, we will be successful.

222 pardon forgiveness

	m [paʁdɔ̃]		Je vous demande pardon, monseigneur. Ce n'est pas de l'hébreu, c'est du latin. -I beg you pardon, milord. It's not Hebrew, but Latin.
223	**vers** prp; adv; m [vɛʁ]	**to| towards; about; verse**	Ils levèrent les yeux vers le ciel. -They looked up at the sky.
224	**aucun** adj; prn [okɛ̃]	**no; none**	Travaux de dragage Travaux de dragage pour lesquels aucun autre Sujet n'est applicable. -Exercises Exercises for which none of the other mentioned subjects are valid.
225	**guerre** f [gɛʁ]	**war**	On ne pense jamais qu'on ira à la guerre et qu'on finira par tomber sous un tir ami. -You never think you'll go to war and end up a victim of friendly fire.
226	**suite** f [sɥit]	**suite| sequence**	Tu devrais nettoyer cette coupure tout de suite, tu ne voudrais pas avoir une infection ! -You should clean that cut straight away, you don't want to get an infection!
227	**prier** vb [pʁije]	**pray**	Khalilov et son père se sont rendus à la mosquée pour prier. -Mr. Khalilov and his father went to pray in the town mosque.
228	**devant** adv; prp; m [dəvɑ̃]	**before| past; before; front**	Retrouvons-nous devant le théâtre. -Let's meet in front of the theatre.
229	**mettre** vb [mɛtʁ]	**put| apply**	Nous avons accumulé dans la zone une grande expérience, que nous pouvons mettre en application à l'avenir. -We have great experience in this area and we can apply it in the future.
230	**matin** m [matɛ̃]	**morning**	C'était un beau dimanche matin au bord de la mer Baltique. -It was a beautiful Sunday morning at the baltic sea.
231	**aide** f [ɛd]	**aid| relief**	En Allemagne, il y a une superstition comme quoi si on allume une cigarette à l'aide d'une chandelle, un marin mourra en mer. -In Germany, there's a superstition that if you light a cigarette off a candle, a sailor will die at sea.
232	**dessus** adv [dəsy]	**over**	Les partisans d'une ligne dure seraient-ils en train de prendre le dessus ? -Are the hardliner partisans on the way of taking over?
233	**genre** m [ʒɑ̃ʁ]	**kind| gender**	Les progrès de la science ne profitent pas toujours au genre humain. -Advances in science don't always benefit humankind.
234	**fin** f; adj [fɛ̃]	**end; fine**	La civilisation est la multiplication sans fin de besoins non nécessaires. -Civilization is the endless multiplication of unnecessary necessities.
235	**perdre** vb [pɛʁdʁ]	**lose| waste**	Je n'aurais pas dû perdre mon temps à lire ça. -I shouldn't have wasted my time reading that.
236	**jeune**	**young; youth**	

	adj; m [ʒœn]	Le jeune est alors complètement dépourvu de protection aux yeux de la loi. -Then, the young person is completely unprotected in the eyes of the law.
237	**chéri** adj; m [ʃeʁi]	**darling| precious; honey** Voulez-vous prendre le petit-déjeuner, chéri ? -Do you want some breakfast, darling?
238	**premier** adj [pʁəmje]	**first| prime** Remplacer l'expression « premier exercice » par l'expression « premier exercice financier ». -Replace the words "first budgetary period" with the words "first financial period".
239	**donner** vb [dɔne]	**give| yield** L'Union européenne doit se donner les moyens de relever cet épouvantable défi. -We in the European Union must empower ourselves to deal with this horrific challenge.
240	**droit** adj; m; adv [dʁwa]	**right; right; due** On a le droit de vote à vingt ans. -We are entitled to vote at the age of twenty.
241	**côté** m [kote]	**side** Ils sont partis chacun de leur côté. -They went their separate ways.
242	**loin** adv; adj [lwɛ̃]	**far; distant** Ces pays sont loin des yeux de l'Union, et ainsi loin de son contrôle. -These countries are far from the eyes of the Union, and therefore far from its control.
243	**feu** m [fø]	**fire** Ses joues étaient teintées de rouge par la chaleur du feu. -Her cheeks were tinged with red by the warmth of fire.
244	**jouer** vb [ʒwe]	**play| act** Aux 27 États membres maintenant de jouer le jeu. -Now it is up to the 27 Member States to play the game.
245	**train** m [tʁɛ̃]	**train** Je suis à la plage en train de jouer au volley-ball. -I'm on the beach playing volleyball.
246	**gros** adj; m [gʁo]	**large| fat; fat man** Il a de gros problèmes. -He has big problems.
247	**compter** vb [kɔ̃te]	**count| expect** Je sais que je peux compter sur votre collaboration pour respecter ce calendrier. -I know that I can count on your cooperation to make this timetable possible.
248	**mourir** vb [muʁiʁ]	**die| end** Combien d'autres femmes et d'enfants doivent mourir pour que ce massacre prenne fin ? -How many more women and children will have to die in order for the massacre to end?
249	**aura** f [ɔʁa]	**aura** Je pense qu'il s'agit davantage d'aura politique que de décorum. -I think we have to deal more with the political aura, rather than the superficial aura.

250 dernier — last| latter; last

adj; m
[dɛʁnje]

C'est le dernier changement apporté lors du dernier débat, donc elle a été incluse.
-This was the last change that was made at the last debate, so it has been included.

251 minute — minute

f
[minyt]

Il y a une minute qu'il est parti.
-He left a minute ago.

252 mari — husband

m
[maʁi]

Elle restait proche de son mari.
-She stood close to her husband.

253 enfin — finally| after all

adv
[ɑ̃fɛ̃]

Enfin, j'aimerais également adresser un mot au rapporteur principal, M.
-Finally, I would also like to address a few words to the principal rapporteur, Mr Casaca.

254 Madame — madame| Mrs

f
[madam]

Bonjour. Est-il possible que je parle à madame Johnson, s'il vous plait ?
-Hello. Is it possible to speak with Mrs Johnson please?

255 façon — way| method

f
[fasɔ̃]

Penses-tu que ma façon d'enseigner est mauvaise ?
-Do you think that my way of teaching is wrong?

256 film — film| cinema

m
[film]

Ce film a été inscrit à la Sélection officielle du Festival du Film de Montréal (Canada) en 2003.
-The film was part of the Official Selection at the 2003 Montreal (Canada) Film Festival.

257 fort — strong| loud; fort; highly

adj; m; adv
[fɔʁ]

Je m'attends à ce que tu travailles plus fort.
-I expect you to work harder.

258 écouter — listen| hear

vb
[ekute]

Toutefois, à cette occasion, nous devons écouter la population irlandaise, nous devons écouter la population.
-But on this occasion we must listen to the Irish people; we must listen to the people.

259 pays — country

m
[pei]

Les vaches sont plus utiles qu'aucun autre animal dans ce pays.
-Cows are more useful than any other animal in this country.

260 endroit — place| spot

m
[ɑ̃dʁwa]

Jack ne veut pas aller dans un endroit aussi dangereux.
-Jack doesn't want to go to such a dangerous place.

261 corps — body

m
[kɔʁ]

Pas de corps.
-No body.

262 fou — crazy; fool

adj; m
[fu]

Pensez-vous que je sois fou ?
-Do you think I'm crazy?

263 vivre — live

vb
[vivʁ]

Elle n'est plus heureuse depuis que son neveu, Louis, est venu vivre avec elle.
-She hasn't been happy since her nephew, Louis, came to live with her.

264 prêt — ready| willing; loan

adj; m
[pʁɛ]

C'est prêt.

-It's ready.

265 dont   **whose**

prn
[dɔ̃]

Le premier d'entre eux, bien sûr, est le Traité sur l'espace de 1967, dont je viens de parler.

-The first one, of course, is the Outer Space Treaty of 1967 of which I just spoke.

266 espérer   **hope| expect**

vb
[ɛspeʁe]

Un public bien informé est l'un des meilleurs garde-fous que nous pourrions espérer.

-A well-informed public is one of the greatest safeguards we could possibly hope for.

267 cause   **cause| case**

f
[koz]

Je ne veux pas que vous démissionniez à cause de moi.

-I don't want you to quit because of me.

268 point   **point| item**

m
[pwɛ̃]

Je voudrais simplement soulever un point.

-I would just bring up a small point..

269 dehors   **outside| out; outside**

adv; m
[dəɔʁ]

En restant dehors, ils s'affaiblissent et ils nous affaiblissent.

-By staying out they are weakening themselves and they are making us weaker.

270 hier   **yesterday; yesterday**

adv
[ijɛʁ]

Monsieur le Président, chers collègues, j'ai fait hier une remarque qui a été mal comprise.

-Mr President, ladies and gentlemen, yesterday I made a comment that was misunderstood.

271 boulot   **job| work**

m
[bulo]

Quand ils doivent élucider plein de mystères, ils ont du mal à faire leur boulot.

-With secrecy like this it is very difficult for them to do their job.

272 garçon   **boy| lad**

m
[gaʁsɔ̃]

Le garçon pouilleux se révéla être un prince déguisé.

-The dirty boy turned out to be a prince in disguise.

273 près   **near| by**

adv
[pʁɛ]

L'aide est en diminution et nous savons qu'elle n'est pas près d'augmenter.

-Aid is falling, and we know that it will not rise in the near future.

274 cinq   **five**

num
[sɛ̃k]

Cela coûtera au moins cinq dollars.

-It'll cost at least five dollars.

275 chef   **chief| leader**

m
[ʃɛf]

Leur chef de file, Kurti, ne se satisfera que d'une indépendance sans condition.

-Their leader, Kurti, will not settle for anything but unconditional independence.

276 ainsi   **thus| thereby; as**

adv; con
[ɛ̃si]

Les sanctions ainsi établies doivent être efficaces, proportionnées et dissuasives.

-The penalties thus provided for shall be effective, proportionate and dissuasive.

277 haut   **high; top; in heaven**

adj; m; adv
[o]

L'Iran a le taux le plus haut d'exécutions par habitant dans le monde.
-Iran has the highest rate of executions per head of population in the world.

278 **celui**

prn
[səlɥi]

that

Ils ont en moyenne 60 ans dans le cas des femmes et 53 ans dans celui des hommes.
-The average age of the holders is 60 in case of females and 53 in case of males.

279 **bébé**

m
[bebe]

baby| kid

Le bébé grandit.
-The baby is growing up.

280 **possible**

adj; m
[pɔsibl]

possible; possible

Et en rendant possible la connaissance, elle rend possible la liberté et le progrès.
-And insofar as it makes knowledge possible, it makes freedom and progress possible.

281 **école**

f
[ekɔl]

school

Pars tout de suite, ou tu seras en retard à l'école.
-Go at once, or you will be late for school.

282 **plein**

adj
[plɛ̃]

full| fraught

Au contraire, il est incohérent et plein de contradictions.
-Far from it; it is incoherent and riddled with contradictions.

283 **année**

f
[ane]

year

Je déteste être seule à cette époque de l'année.
-I hate being alone this time of year.

284 **manger**

vb
[mɑ̃ʒe]

eat| feed

On en parle maintenant après on pourra manger et apprécier le repas.
-I'll get it out of the way then we can eat and enjoy the meal.

285 **docteur**

m
[dɔktœʁ]

doctor

Jack est docteur.
-Jack is a doctor.

286 **tour**

m; f
[tuʁ]

turn; tower

Elle a également fourni des photos de matériel hydraulique pour la construction d'une tour.
-It also provided photographs of a hydraulic apparatus for tower construction.

287 **quatre**

num
[katʁ]

four

Ne faut-il pas faire de nos champs, de toute notre vie, une immense œuvre d'art à quatre dimensions ?
-Shouldn't we make our fields - our entire life - an immense work of art in four dimensions?

288 **plutôt**

adv
[plyto]

rather| quite

N'est-ce pas plutôt que la Conférence n'est plus en accord avec le monde réel ?
-Or is it that the Conference on Disarmament is out of tune with the real world?

289 **marcher**

vb
[maʁʃe]

walk| work

En tant que femmes, nous devrions marcher la tête haute, avec fierté et vigueur.
-We are meant to be women who walk tall, walk proud, and walk strong.

290 **semaine**

week

f
[səmɛn]

Nombre de sénateurs vont dans de petites agglomérations semaine après semaine.
-Many senators in this chamber travel to small communities week after week.

291 vérité — **truth**

f
[veʁite]

Je vous demande d'accepter d'insérer la "vérité": réconciliation avec vérité et mémoire.
-Please agree that 'truth' be inserted: reconciliation with truth and remembrance.

292 envier — **envy**

vb
[ɑ̃vje]

Le système britannique a -t-il quelque chose à envier aux autres États membres ?
-Is this any worse in Britain than in any other Member State?

293 capitaine — **captain**

m
[kapitɛn]

Il fera un bon capitaine.
-He will make a good team captain.

294 affaire — **case | matter**

f
[afɛʁ]

Es-tu décidée à faire affaire ?
-Are you willing to make a deal?

295 bientôt — **soon | almost**

adv
[bjɛ̃to]

Cette omission sera bientôt rectifiée et ceux-ci seront assimilés à des piétons.
-This issue will soon be corrected and they will be considered as pedestrians.

296 instant — **moment | while; urgent**

m; adj
[ɛ̃stɑ̃]

Pour l'instant, la Norvège ne compte aucun détenu dans ce type de quartier.
-At the moment, there are no prisoners in such a department in Norway.

297 essayer — **try | attempt**

vb
[eseje]

Je vais certainement essayer d'obtenir cette information, honorables sénateurs.
-I will certainly attempt to obtain the information, honourable senators.

298 tellement — **so**

adv
[tɛlmɑ̃]

Le projet de loi est tellement tordu, tellement obscur et tellement difficile à saisir.
-The bill itself is so convoluted; it is so misunderstood; it is so difficult to follow.

299 derrière — **behind; behind; behind**

adv; m; prp
[dɛʁjɛʁ]

Il a des yeux derrière la tête.
-He has eyes at the back of his head.

300 tomber — **fall | drop**

vb
[tɔ̃be]

Si elle ne peut être écoutée en entier, il faut « laisser tomber » l'appel.
-If it cannot be listened to in its entirety, the listener will "drop" the call.

301 presque — **almost; all but**

adv; adj
[pʁɛsk]

Les parcs sont gérés de façon que l'activité humaine ne les altère pas, ou presque.
-Parks are managed in such a way that they will remain essentially unaltered by human activity.

302 meilleur — **best; better**

m; adj
[mɛjœʁ]

Je pense que j'aimerais être un meilleur étudiant.
-I think I'd like to be a better student.

303 numéro — **number**

m
[nymeʁo]

Quel est le numéro de téléphone d'urgence ?
-What is the emergency telephone number?

304 journée — **day**

f
[ʒuʁne]

Il en sera question à mesure que la journée avancera, et la journée sera longue.
-We will hear about that as the day wears on and it will be a long day.

305 dollar — **dollar| greenback**

m
[dɔlaʁ]

Cette décision pourrait être d'adopter le dollar américain ou d'adopter un dollar panaméricain.
-It might decide we should adopt the American dollar or a pan-American dollar.

306 confiance — **confidence| faith**

f
[kɔ̃fjɑ̃s]

Tu ne devrais pas faire confiance à Jack.
-You shouldn't trust Jack.

307 garde — **custody| guard; guarding**

f; adj
[gaʁd]

Peu importe ce qui arrive, garde le sourire.
-No matter what happens, just keep smiling.

308 souvenir — **memory| souvenir**

m
[suvəniʁ]

C'est avec ce souvenir que je vous propose de faire vite, nous sommes pressés !
-It is with this in mind that I propose swift action. There is no time for delay.

309 dur — **hard| tough**

adj
[dyʁ]

Par ailleurs, nous avons l'homme dur, Herman Van Rompuy, qui a fait clairement savoir que le but de cette aventure libyenne est d'amener un changement de régime.
-On the other hand, we have got hard man Herman Van Rompuy, who has made it clear that regime change is the aim of this Libyan adventure.

310 bureau — **office| desk**

m
[byʁo]

Laisse-le simplement sur mon bureau !
-Just leave it on my desk.

311 abord — **first| start**

m
[abɔʁ]

Parlons d'abord des conséquences financières.
-Let us refer to the financial consequences first.

312 important — **important**

adj
[ɛ̃pɔʁtɑ̃]

Je pense que c'est là une conclusion très importante de cet important débat.
-I think that is a very important conclusion to this important debate.

313 peiner — **labor| pain**

vb
[pene]

Après une telle peine, il est extrêmement éprouvant de tenter de se réinsérer dans la société.
-It is absolutely devastating to try to reintegrate back into the community after such pains.

314 seigneur — **lord**

m
[sɛɲœʁ]

Je devrai bientôt embrasser le seigneur Sforza.
-I shall soon have to kiss the Lord Sforza.

315 suffire — **suffice**

vb
[syfiʁ]

Pour certains pays, il peut suffire de publier le rapport en anglais et en russe.
-For some countries it may suffice to provide the report in English and Russian.

316 route — **road| way**

		f	Cette route mène à la ville.
		[ʁut]	-This road goes to the city.
317	**cul**		**ass**
		m	Elle lèche le cul du prof.
		[ky]	-She sucks up to the teacher.
318	**Bonsoir!**		**Good evening!**
		int	Ruth Massie, grand chef, Conseil des Premières nations du Yukon : Bonsoir.
		[bɔ̃swaːʁ!]	-Ruth Massie, Grand Chief, Council of Yukon First Nations: Good evening.
319	**jeu**		**game**
		m	Je te prie de cesser de parler. Il me faut me concentrer sur mon jeu.
		[ʒø]	-Please stop talking. I need to concentrate on my game.
320	**ferme**		**farm; firm**
		f; adj	Vous avez été également un président ferme, certains diront très ferme,
		[fɛʁm]	pensant peut-être trop ferme.
			-You have also been a firm president - some would say very firm, perhaps meaning too firm.
321	**plaisir**		**pleasure**
		m	C'est un plaisir d'avoir un compatriote comme président de la séance de ce
		[pleziʁ]	soir.
			-It is a pleasure to have a compatriot in the chair for this evening's sitting.
322	**mot**		**word**
		m	Si vous placez le curseur dans un mot, la fonction est appliquée au mot
		[mo]	complet.
			-If the cursor is within a word, the function will be applied to the whole word.
323	**chien**		**dog**
		m	Ce chien est la mascotte de mon régiment.
		[ʃjɛ̃]	-This dog is our regimental mascot.
324	**calme**		**quiet| calm; calm**
		adj; m	Restez calme et donnez-moi votre adresse.
		[kalm]	-Okay, just stay calm and tell me your address.
325	**dedans**		**in; in; inside**
		adv; prp; m	Comment me suis-je fourré là-dedans ?
		[dədɑ̃]	-How did I get into this?
326	**mariage**		**marriage**
		m	Après l'enregistrement du mariage, les époux reçoivent un certificat de
		[maʁjaʒ]	mariage.
			-After the marriage is recorded, the spouses are issued a marriage certificate.
327	**entrer**		**enter**
		vb	Elle compte faire entrer ces modifications en vigueur dans les plus brefs
		[ɑ̃tʁe]	délais.
			-New Zealand intends to promulgate these amended Regulations as soon as possible.
328	**rentrer**		**return**
		vb	Il a dû faire de l'auto-stop à sa sortie de l'hôpital pour rentrer chez lui.
		[ʁɑ̃tʁe]	-He had to hitchike from his hospital bed to get back home.
329	**lit**		**bed**
		m	Après un passage sur le refroidissoir, les tôles rejoignent le lit d'inspection.
		[li]	-After cooling down on the cooling bed, the plates reach the inspection bed.
330	**autant**		**as far as**

con
[otã]

C'est d'autant plus incompréhensible que tous les États ne l'ont pas ratifiée.
-This is all the more bewildering since not all Member States have ratified it.

331 revenir
vb
[ʁəvəniʁ]

return| get back
Nous avons déclaré qu'il s'agissait uniquement d'un report et que nous allions revenir sur ce vote.
-We have said that it is just a deferral and we are going to come back to this vote.

332 parfait
adj
[paʁfɛ]

perfect
Nous ne vivons pas dans un monde parfait.
-We don't live in a perfect world.

333 cœur
m
[kœʁ]

heart| core
Les scaroles peuvent être présentées cœur à cœur ou couchées.
-Broad-leaved (Batavian) endives may be packed heart-to-heart or flat.

334 ceci
prn; adj
[səsi]

this; following
Ceci est important, car ceci complète l'objectif central de l'examen final.
-This is important, for it complements the central objective of the final review.

335 service
m
[sɛʁvis]

service| serving
Il est en service.
-He is in service.

336 téléphoner
vb
[telefɔne]

call
Aucun d'entre eux n'a été autorisé à quitter la maison ni à téléphoner.
-No family member was allowed to leave the house or to make phone calls.

337 pauvre
adj; m
[povʁ]

poor; poor person
Un enfant pauvre qui a reçu une éducation pendant moins de 12 ans restera probablement pauvre.
-A poor child with fewer than 12 years of education is likely to remain poor.

338 Mademoiselle
abr; f
[madmwazɛl]

Ms.; miss
Mademoiselle Klein fait passer un test chaque vendredi.
-Miss Klein gives a test every Friday.

339 drôle
adj
[dʁol]

funny
Madame le Président, je vois que certains s'amusent mais ce n'est absolument pas drôle !
-I know that some people are amused, but the matter is not funny.

340 parfois
adv
[paʁfwa]

sometimes
Parfois, il y a une erreur humaine, parfois, la nature réserve des surprises.
-Sometimes, there is human error and sometimes nature springs a surprise.

341 retour
m
[ʁətuʁ]

return
Il devrait être de retour à tout instant maintenant.
-He should be back any minute now.

342 verre
m
[vɛʁ]

glass
Installations destinées à la fabrication de verre, y compris de fibres de verre.
-Installations for the manufacture of glass including glass fibre.

343 six
num
[sis]

six
1994: Six bulletins de condamnations et six individus condamnés définitivement.
-1994: six notices of judgement and final sentencing of six individuals;

344 impossible
adj
[ɛ̃pɔsibl]

impossible
Chaque année, la mission impossible devient tout à fait impossible.
-Every year, mission impossible becomes ever more impossible.

345 **facile** | **easy| simple**
adj | Vraiment trop facile!
[fasil] | -Really very easy!

346 **maître** | **master| teacher**
m | J'ai fait confiance à mon maître.
[mɛtʁ] | -I trusted my teacher.

347 **mauvais** | **bad| ill; brute**
adj; m | Il n'y a rien de mauvais à cela.
[movɛ] | -There is nothing wrong with this.

348 **général** | **general; general**
adj; m | En général, les enfants aiment les glaces.
[ʒeneʁal] | -In general, kids like ice cream.

349 **doute** | **doubt**
m | Il n'y a aucun doute à ce sujet et le Conseil ferait bien lui aussi de s'en
[dut] | convaincre.
 | -There is no doubt about that and Council should be in no doubt about that whatsoever.

350 **prison** | **prison**
f | J'ai passé trois ans en prison.
[pʁizɔ̃] | -I spent three years in prison.

351 **adorer** | **worship**
vb | Pensez à lui et à adorer ce merveilleux mystère, grâce à Dieu pour cela et de
[adɔʁe] | la confiance à la Vierge les mains.
 | -Think of it and adore this wonderful mystery, thank God for it and trust to the Virgin's hands.

352 **faute** | **fault**
f | Tout ça est de ta faute.
[fot] | -This is all your fault.

353 **oublier** | **forget**
vb | J'ai le sentiment que tout le monde préférerait oublier ce rapport et ses
[ublije] | conclusions.
 | -My feeling is that everyone has chosen to forget this report and its conclusions.

354 **bras** | **arm**
m | Donnez-moi votre bras.
[bʁa] | -Give me your arm.

355 **exactement** | **exactly| accurately**
adv | On encourage tous les employés à remplir le questionnaire le plus
[ɛgzaktəmã] | exactement possible.
 | -Everyone is encouraged to complete the questionnaire as accurately as they can.

356 **fêter** | **celebrate| feast**
vb | Promets-moi de ne pas fêter mon anniversaire.
[fete] | -Promise me when my birthday comes, we don't celebrate it.

357 **café** | **cafe| coffee**
m | Il aime boire son café sans sucre.
[kafe] | -He likes drinking coffee without sugar.

358 **chérir** | **cherish**
vb | Mais la transparence est un principe que nous devons chérir dans cette
[ʃeʁiʁ] | situation.
 | -But transparency is a principle that we must hold dear in this context.

359 gentil
adj; m
[ʒɑ̃ti]

nice| kind; gentile
Je pense que Jack est un gamin vraiment gentil.
-I think Jack is a really nice kid.

360 valoir
vb
[valwaʁ]

be worth
Parce que le dollar aujourd'hui peut valoir 66¢ mais, dans un an, il en vaudra peut-être 64.
-Because the dollar can be worth 66 cents today and only 64 cents a year later.

361 lieu
m
[ljø]

place| venue
Ma première réunion avec elles aura lieu mardi prochain.
-My first meeting with the families will take place on Tuesday of next week.

362 malade
adj; m
[malad]

sick| invalid; patient
Il reste à nous assurer que le malade prend les remèdes et réagit comme attendu.
-What remains is to make sure that the patient takes the medicine and that the patient reacts as expected.

363 changer
vb
[ʃɑ̃ʒe]

change| switch
En deux mots, il est vrai qu'il faut changer la mobilité plutôt que la réduire.
-In short, it is true that mobility has to be changed rather than reduced.

364 roi
m
[ʁwa]

king
Brahe reçut une île nommée Hven de la part du roi.
-Brahe received an island called Hven from the king.

365 commencer
vb
[kɔmɑ̃se]

start| begin
La reforestation et la restauration des zones protégées doit commencer sur-le-champ.
-Reforestation and restoration of the protected areas must begin immediately.

366 président
m
[pʁezidɑ̃]

president
Le Président voulait une action immédiate.
-The president wanted immediate action.

367 travailler
vb
[tʁavaje]

work
Cette façon de travailler ne semble donc pas tenable dans le cas du CST.
-This way of working has not proved to be a sustainable method for the CST to do business.

368 partout
adv
[paʁtu]

everywhere| throughout
Or, on réclame précisément un peu partout le droit de recourir à ce moyen concurrentiel douteux.
-There are, however, calls far and wide to outlaw this improper competitive practice.

369 cher
adj; m
[ʃɛʁ]

expensive| dear; dear
Bonjour, mon cher.
-Hello, my dear.

370 rendre
vb
[ʁɑ̃dʁ]

render| restore
Le traité de Lisbonne va rendre possible une Europe militariste.
-The Lisbon Treaty will make a militaristic Europe possible.

371 écrire
vb
[ekʁiʁ]

write
Les citoyens peuvent écrire au Parlement et recevoir une réponse dans ces langues.
-Citizens can write to Parliament and receive a response in these languages.

372 équipe

team| crew

f
[ekip]

Nous devons équiper techniquement les véhicules pour que les piétons aient une chance.
-We have to equip vehicles technically in such a way that pedestrians have a chance.

373 **sinon**

con; adv
[sinɔ̃]

otherwise; or else

Sinon, l'histoire les jugera tous, moralement sinon légalement.
-Otherwise, all of them will be morally, if not legally, accountable before history.

374 **esprit**

m
[ɛspʁi]

mind| spirit

Il ne m'est jamais venu à l'esprit qu'il allait vraiment mettre sa menace à exécution.
-It never crossed my mind that he would actually carry out his threat.

375 **plan**

m; adj
[plɑ̃]

plan; plane

Le chef de service a modifié le plan.
-The section chief altered the plan.

376 **montrer**

vb
[mɔ̃tʁe]

show

Chacun, aujourd'hui, a pu montrer devant tous ce qu'il voulait et afficher ses choix.
-Each of us has today had the opportunity to indicate in full public view what he wanted and display his choices.

377 **boire**

vb
[bwaʁ]

drink

J'estime d'ailleurs que les enfants mais aussi les adultes devraient boire davantage de lait.
-In fact, I think that not only children but adults too should drink more milk.

378 **propre**

adj; m
[pʁɔpʁ]

own| clean; proper

Il a sa propre chambre.
-He has his own room.

379 **état**

m
[eta]

state| condition

La Corée du Nord a été traitée comme un État paria le plus clair de son existence.
-North Korea has been treated as a pariah state for most of its existence.

380 **bois**

m
[bwa]

wood| timber

Est-ce qu'un ours défèque dans les bois ?
-Does a bear shit in the woods?

381 **dès**

prp
[dɛ]

from| since

Nous devons dès lors les protéger de la concurrence déloyale des pays tiers.
-They therefore need to be protected from unfair competition from third countries.

382 **sembler**

vb
[sɑ̃ble]

seem| sound

Les règles ne sont pas aussi restrictives qu'elles peuvent sembler à première vue.
-The rules are not as restrictive as they might appear at first sight.

383 **dix**

num
[dis]

ten

Monsieur le Président, dix nouveaux commissaires pour dix nouveaux pays.
-Mr President, ten new countries and ten new Commissioners.

384 **génial**

adj
[ʒenjal]

great| brilliant

Ce qui est génial entre nous, c'est qu'on ne passe pas cette porte avec beaucoup de bagages.
-What's great about you and me... right here, this very moment, is that we don't come through that door with a lot of baggage.

385 **sécurité**

security

f
[sekyʁite]

La notion de sécurité englobe tant la sécurité de l'État que celle des individus.
-The concept of security includes both State security and the security of the individual.

386 tôt
adv
[to]

early| soon

La seule possibilité est donc de partir plus tôt, ce qui est alors fort tôt.
-So the only other option open to me is to return earlier, which will be very early indeed.

387 rêver
vb
[ʁeve]

dream

Ne nous endormons pas pour rêver, mais rêvons de faire de notre monde un monde meilleur.
-Let us thus not sleep to dream, but dream to change the world, for the better.

388 armer
vb
[aʁme]

arm

Ce ne fut pas un effort en vue d'armer l'UE afin qu'elle soit capable de s'élargir.
-But what they did not do was endeavour to equip the EU to pursue enlargement.

389 avis
m
[avi]

opinion| notice

Ne change pas d'avis.
-Don't change your opinion.

390 surtout
adv
[syʁtu]

mainly| above all

Ce sont surtout les attitudes qui alimentent la discrimination, surtout sur le marché du travail.
-It is mainly attitudes that fuel discrimination, especially in the labour market.

391 difficile
adj
[difisil]

difficult

C'est un homme avec qui il est difficile de traiter.
-He is a man with whom it is difficult to deal.

392 dormir
vb
[dɔʁmiʁ]

sleep

En outre, il est absurde de ne pas considérer le temps de garde qui peut être passé à dormir comme du temps de travail.
-It is, moreover, absurd, not to include on-call duty that can be spent asleep as working time.

393 ensuite
adv
[ãsɥit]

then| later

Elle examine ensuite la question de l'assistance internationale humanitaire.
-Then the question of international humanitarian assistance will be addressed.

394 pire
adj
[piʁ]

worse

Un traitement similaire, voire pire, est réservé aux enfants handicapés.
-Similar if not worse treatment is given to children with disabilities.

395 simple
adj
[sɛ̃pl]

simple; singles

Ils agirent selon la conviction toute simple que Dieu était avec eux.
-They acted on the straightforward and uncomplicated conviction that God was with them.

396 paix
f
[pɛ]

peace

Le président désire la paix, n'est-ce pas ?
-The President desires peace, doesn't he?

397 sujet
m; adj
[syʒɛ]

subject; prone

J'ai menti à mon petit ami au sujet de mon âge.
-I lied to my boyfriend about my age.

398	**retard**	**delay**
	m	Je vous assure que je ne serai pas en retard.
	[ʁətaʁ]	-I assure you that I won't be late.
399	**livre**	**book**
	m	Ne touche pas à ce livre.
	[livʁ]	-Don't touch that book.
400	**apprendre**	**learn| teach**
	vb	Michael Forrestall : Honorables sénateurs, je suis très heureux de
	[apʁɑ̃dʁ]	l'apprendre.
		-Hon. J. Michael Forrestall: Honourable senators, I am very pleased to hear that.
401	**saler**	**salt**
	vb	On dirait que quelqu'un est prêt à saler sa première margarita.
	[sale]	-I think someone's ready to salt his first margarita glass.
402	**souvent**	**often**
	adv	Elles ont souvent prêté à controverse; elles ont souvent été marquées par
	[suvɑ̃]	l'émotion.
		-They have often been controversial; they have often been emotional.
403	**sauf**	**except; safe; excepting; short of**
	prp; adj; con; adv	Le véhicule a été réquisitionné mais les enfants libérés sains et saufs.
	[sof]	-The bus was commandeered but the children were released unhurt.
404	**choix**	**choice| selection**
	m	J'ai eu le sentiment de ne pas avoir le choix.
	[ʃwa]	-I felt as if I had no choice.
405	**sûrement**	**surely**
	adv	Pendant le mois de novembre la situation a progressé lentement, mais
	[syʁmɑ̃]	sûrement.
		-November was a month of slow but substantial progress in Bosnia and Herzegovina.
406	**or**	**gold**
	m	L'activation de feuilles d'or : une feuille d'or peut réagir en présence de
	[ɔʁ]	neutrons.
		-Gold foil activation: gold foil is susceptible to activation by neutrons.
407	**visage**	**face**
	m	L'Europe a certes besoin d'un visage économique, mais aussi d'un visage
	[vizaʒ]	humain !
		-Europe does not just need an economic face, it also needs a human face.
408	**ordre**	**order**
	m	C'est renverser l'ordre logique des choses.
	[ɔʁdʁ]	-That's reversing the logical order of things.
409	**noir**	**black; black**
	adj; m	Nous associons souvent le noir à la mort.
	[nwaʁ]	-We often associate black with death.
410	**dîner**	**dinner; dine**
	m; vb	Au lieu de préparer un dîner aux chandelles, elle a mis son copain aux
	[dine]	enchères sur eBay.
		-Instead of preparing a dinner by candlelight, she put her boyfriend up for auction on eBay.
411	**âge**	**age**
	m	Auparavant, cet âge était de 18 ans pour les femmes et de 21 ans pour les
	[aʒ]	hommes.

-Regulations in force until then defined it as 18 years for women and 21 for men.

412	**chemin**	**path| road**
	m	Je pense que Jack a encore beaucoup de chemin à parcourir.
	[ʃəmɛ̃]	-I think Jack has a long way to go.
413	**bouillir**	**boil**
	vb	Crème d'asperges: faire bouillir les asperges dans l'eau salée, les égoutter et
	[bujiʁ]	les refroidir rapidement.
		-Asparagus sauce: boil the asparagus in salted water, drain and cool quickly.
414	**face**	**face| front**
	f	Le bateau fuyait face à la tempête.
	[fas]	-The ship scudded before a heavy gale.
415	**rue**	**street**
	f	Cette rue est beaucoup de choses.
	[ʁy]	-Now this street is a lot of things.
416	**inquiet**	**worried| concerned**
	adj	Je suis inquiet lorsque le gouvernement parle de protectionnisme culturel.
	[ɛ̃kjɛ]	-I am concerned when this government talks about cultural protectionism.
417	**photo**	**photo**
	f	Je n'ai pas pu me résoudre à jeter ta photo.
	[fɔto]	-I couldn't bring myself to throw your picture away.
418	**sérieux**	**serious; seriousness**
	adj; m	Sois sérieux.
	[seʁjø]	-Get serious.
419	**ciel**	**sky| heaven**
	m	Le ciel s'éclaircit.
	[sjɛl]	-The sky is getting brighter.
420	**honneur**	**honor| credit**
	m	Il est l'honneur de nos démocraties européennes et l'honneur de notre
	[ɔnœʁ]	Parlement.
		-It is an honour to our European democracies and an honour to our
		Parliament.
421	**force**	**force| power**
	f	Il n'a pas la force de dire la vérité.
	[fɔʁs]	-He hasn't the nerve to tell the truth.
422	**garder**	**keep| maintain**
	vb	Ils ont la clef de l'utilisation durable de l'eau et doivent jalousement garder
	[gaʁde]	les ressources en eau douce.
		-They hold the key to sustainable water use and must jealously guard
		freshwater supplies.
423	**tirer**	**take| draw**
	vb	Il faut amadouer les hommes ou s'en défaire, parce qu'ils se vengent des
	[tiʁe]	offenses légères et qu'ils ne sauraient se venger des grandes. De sorte que
		l'offense qu'on fait à l'homme lui doit être faite d'une manière qu'il n'en
		puisse tirer vengeance.
		-Men ought either to be well treated or crushed, because they can avenge
		themselves of lighter injuries, but of more serious ones they cannot.
		Therefore, the injury that is to be done to a man ought to be of such a kind
		that he cannot take revenge.
424	**million**	**million**

	m	Sami héritera d'un million de dollars en assurance-vie si ses parents décèdent
	[miljɔ̃]	-Sami will inherit a million dollars in life insurance if his parents are dead.
425	**grave**	**serious| grave**
	adj	La décision de la Russie a de graves implications humanitaires et politiques.
	[gʁav]	-Russia's decision has grave humanitarian and political implications.
426	**voix**	**voice**
	f	Vous incarnez aujourd'hui, ici, la voix des peuples, la voix des humbles.
	[vwa]	-You are the incarnation here today of the voice of the people, the voice of the humble.
427	**courant**	**current| running; current**
	adj; m	Percevant le danger, il s'enfuit en courant.
	[kuʁɑ̃]	-Sensing danger, he ran away.
428	**propos**	**talk**
	m	Nous avons l'intention de présenter une communication à ce propos au mois de juin de l'an 2000.
	[pʁɔpo]	-The plan is to present a report on this subject in June 2000.
429	**bateau**	**boat**
	m	Il n'y a aucun moyen d'atteindre l'île autre que le bateau.
	[bato]	-There is no way of reaching the island other than by boat.
430	**con**	**cunt| prick; bloody**
	m; adj	Il s'excuse pas assez d'être un gros con.
	[kɔ̃]	-Not sorry enough for being a fat cunt.
431	**gauche**	**left; left**
	adj; f	Tourne au deuxième feu à gauche !
	[goʃ]	-Turn left at the second traffic light.
432	**content**	**content| happy**
	adj	Je suis content que ce point soit également bien clair dans le rapport de M.
	[kɔ̃tɑ̃]	-I am glad that that is also stated very clearly in Mr Morillon's report.
433	**prix**	**price| prize**
	m	Pour les consommateurs, cela signifie des prix plus élevés et une moindre variété.
	[pʁi]	-For consumers, the costs are in terms of higher prices and less variety.
434	**rouge**	**red; red**
	adj; m	La robe a un joli contraste entre le rouge et le blanc.
	[ʁuʒ]	-The dress has a beautiful contrast between red and white.
435	**faim**	**hunger**
	f	Je préfère mourir de faim plutôt que de voler.
	[fɛ̃]	-I would rather starve than steal.
436	**avion**	**aircraft**
	m	Nous avons acheté nos billets d'avion deux mois à l'avance.
	[avjɔ̃]	-We bought our plane tickets two months in advance.
437	**devenir**	**become| be**
	vb	Les enfants sont son avenir, puisqu'elle prépare les femmes et les hommes en devenir.
	[dəvəniʁ]	-For the children is her future, since she prepares future men and women.
438	**prochain**	**next| upcoming; next**
	adj; m	L'Andorre est également un petit pays qui croit en la tolérance et au respect du prochain.
	[pʁɔʃɛ̃]	-Andorra is also a small country that believes in tolerance and respect for our fellow man.
439	**acheter**	**buy| take**

vb
[aʃte]

Les femmes, sans restriction, peuvent acheter, gérer et vendre des biens ou des marchandises.
-Women, without any restriction, may purchase, manage and sell property or goods.

440 voyage
m
[vwajaʒ]

travel| trip

Le premier voyage de retour et le dernier voyage aller d'une série de navettes ont lieu à vide.
-The first return journey and the last outward journey of a series of shuttles are made unladen.

441 sorte
f
[sɔʁt]

kind| manner

Ils verront dans ce genre d'initiative de la Commission une sorte de distraction.
-They will see this kind of initiative by the Commission as a distraction.

442 long
adj
[lɔ̃]

long

Je t'assure que l'honnêteté paie sur le long terme.
-I can assure you that honesty pays in the long run.

443 espèce
f
[ɛspɛs]

species| kind

Espèce de sale porc !
-You filthy pig!

444 idiot
m; adj
[idjo]

idiot; silly

Vous me prenez pour un idiot ?
-Do you take me for a fool?

445 gueuler
vb
[gœle]

yell

Je veux pas vous gueuler après.
-I don't mean to holler at ya.

446 début
m
[deby]

beginning| debut

Le début de ce nouveau millénaire est très différent du début du millénaire précédent.
-The beginning of this new millennium is very different from the beginning of the last.

447 bouger
vb
[buʒe]

move| budge

Monsieur le Président, le premier ministre dit que ça lui prend des consensus pour bouger.
-Mr President, the Prime Minister says he needs a consensus before he will budge.

448 continu
adj
[kɔ̃tiny]

continuous

Selon l'État partie, les violations alléguées n'ont pas un caractère continu et leurs effets ne sont pas constants.
-According to the State party, the alleged violations are not of a continuous nature and their effects are not persistent.

449 hôpital
m
[ɔpital]

hospital

L'hôpital Wismari de Tallinn fait partie de l'hôpital central ouest de Tallinn.
-Tallinn Wismari Hospital is since 2001 under Western Tallinn Central Hospital.

450 grâce
f
[gʁas]

grace| favor

Grâce! Grâce! grâce! Que me voulez-vous donc? Que vous ai-je fait?
-Mercy! Mercy! Mercy! What do you want from me? What have I done to you?

451 message
m
[mesaʒ]

message

J'ai reçu un message disant que vous vouliez me voir.
-I got a message that you wanted to see me.

452 certain   **certain**

adj
[sɛʁtɛ̃]

De l'avis d'un certain nombre de participants, c'était là une évolution positive.

-In the view of a number of participants, that was a positive development.

453 patron   **boss| patron**

m
[patʁɔ̃]

Le patron a un pouvoir sur ses salariés que ces salariés n'ont pas sur leur patron.

-The boss has a power over his employees that they do not have over him.

454 recevoir   **receive| take**

vb
[ʁəsəvwaʁ]

Si c'est le cas, le Comité souhaiterait recevoir une copie de la législation concernée.

-If so, the Committee would be grateful to receive a copy of the relevant legislation.

455 promettre   **promise**

vb
[pʁɔmɛtʁ]

Aucun homme politique, aujourd'hui, ne peut promettre des emplois. Ce ne serait pas sérieux.

-No politician can promise jobs today; to do so would be rash.

456 oncle   **uncle**

m
[ɔ̃kl]

J'ai un oncle qui vit à Kyoto.

-I have an uncle who lives in Kyoto.

457 Euh!   **Haw!**

int
[ø!]

Euh... était-ce, euh... sérieux, Madame Peach ?

-Er... was it, er... serious, Miss Peach?

458 occuper   **occupy| hold**

vb
[ɔkype]

La Caisse devrait pouvoir occuper les nouveaux locaux d'ici le mois de décembre 2004.

-It is expected that the Fund will occupy the new premises by December 2004.

459 camp   **camp**

m
[kɑ̃]

Ils sont arrivés en Rhodésie du Sud, et il y avait le choix entre un camp d'immigrés, fait de huttes en terre avec prise d'eau commune, ou un hôtel ; et ils ont choisi l'hôtel, s'agissant de ce que l'on pourrait appeler des nantis.

-They arrived in Southern Rhodesia, and there was a choice of an immigrants' camp, consisting of mud huts with a communal water supply, or a hotel; and they chose the hotel, being what are known as people of means.

460 manquer   **miss**

vb
[mɑ̃ke]

Faute de priorités clairement établies, le Conseil a tendance à manquer d'une vue d'ensemble.

-Lacking clear priorities, the Council is prone to "miss the forest for the trees".

461 soleil   **sun**

m
[sɔlɛj]

Il y avait du soleil hier.

-It was sunny yesterday.

462 cheveu   **hair**

m
[ʃəvø]

Le prélèvement peut se faire avec de la salive ou même un seul cheveu ou une goutte de sang.

-It can come from saliva or from a single hair or a drop of blood.

463 arme   **weapon**

f
[aʁm]

J'ai un permis pour cette arme.

-I have a permit for this gun.

464 salle   **room**

f
[sal]
Quand vas-tu enfin sortir de la salle de bains ?
-When will you eventually get out of the bathroom?

465 **bizarre**
adj
[bizaʁ]
weird| bizarre
Un d'entre eux aurait déclaré ce qui suit : "C'est une situation extrêmement bizarre.
-One was quoted as saying "It is an extremely bizarre situation.

466 **gagner**
vb
[gaɲe]
win| earn
Elle menace l'environnement et peut gagner des pays et régions limitrophes.
-It threatens the environment and may spread to adjacent countries and regions.

467 **fondre**
vb
[fɔ̃dʁ]
melt| merge
Des choses dans mon congélateur vont fondre.
-No, some of the stuff in my freezer might melt.

468 **sauver**
vb
[sove]
save
Il ne suffit pas de sauver le monde, nous devons également sauver ses habitants.
-It is not enough to save the world: we also have to save the people in it.

469 **pièce**
f; adv
[pjɛs]
piece| room; apiece
Quelles sont les dimensions de cette pièce ?
-What are the dimensions of the room?

470 **erreur**
f
[eʁœʁ]
error| mistake
J'ai pris son parapluie par erreur.
-I took his umbrella by mistake.

471 **ailleurs**
adv
[ajœʁ]
somewhere else
Si les causes sont ailleurs, la solution doit elle aussi être trouvée ailleurs.
-If the causes lay elsewhere, the solution must also be sought elsewhere.

472 **rapport**
m
[ʁapɔʁ]
report| ratio
Je doute de la véracité de ce rapport.
-I doubt the truth of the report.

473 **froid**
adj; m
[fʁwa]
cold| cool; cold
Nous venons du froid de Yalta, mais le climat en Europe devient froid et égoïste.
-We are coming from the cold of Yalta, but the climate in Europe is becoming chilly and egoistic.

474 **scène**
f
[sɛn]
scene
Il est sans aucun doute le metteur en scène de films le plus apprécié dans le monde.
-He is without doubt the most successful movie director in the world.

475 **secret**
adj; m
[səkʁɛ]
secret| covert; secret
Il s'agit de savoir si ce document était très secret, secret ou confidentiel.
-I think it is germane as to whether the document was top secret, secret or confidential.

476 **sac**
m
[sak]
bag| sack
Nous le prîmes la main dans le sac.
-We caught him red-handed (with the hand in the sack).

477 **second**
adj; m
[səgɔ̃]
second; second
En général, on en sait peu sur les équations différentielles non linéaires du second ordre.
-In general, little is known about nonlinear second order differential equations.

478 **cru**
vintage| raw; vineyard

	adj; m	L' année 2004 fut un bon cru pour l' économie mondiale.
	[kʁy]	-2004 was a vintage year for the world' s economy.
479	**Allô!**	**Hello!**
	int	Et moi je commande, allo oui, c'est pour emporter.
	[alo!]	-I'm ordering, Hello, yes, I wanted to put in an order, please, to pick up,
480	**battre**	**beat| fight**
	vb	Ce dernier aurait commencé à le battre puis l'aurait entraîné au site militaire.
	[batʁ]	-The latter allegedly began to beat him, then took him to the military base.
481	**hôtel**	**hotel**
	m	Je cherche un bon hôtel.
	[otɛl]	-I am looking for a good hotel.
482	**soirée**	**evening**
	f	Croyez-moi, ce fut une belle soirée, une soirée francophone mémorable.
	[swaʁe]	-Believe me, it was a wonderful evening; a memorable francophone evening.
483	**sœur**	**sister; sister**
	adj; f	Contrairement à sa sœur, il a préservé la foi religieuse dans laquelle ses parents l'avaient éduqué.
	[sœʁ]	-Unlike his sister, he has retained the religious faith his parents brought him up in.
484	**pied**	**foot| leg**
	m	Je suis allé à pied.
	[pje]	-I went on foot.
485	**carte**	**map| card**
	f	Je t'enverrai une carte postale de Boston.
	[kaʁt]	-I'll send you a post card from Boston.
486	**joli**	**pretty**
	adj	L'enseigne se distingue par le raffinement de son intérieur et sa jolie façade.
	[ʒɔli]	-The brand is being distinguished by its refined interior and its beautiful facade.
487	**groupe**	**group| band**
	m	Elle est arrivée avec un groupe à un concours de danse.
	[gʁup]	-She arrived with a group at a dance competition.
488	**monter**	**mount| climb**
	vb	Les chats peuvent monter aux arbres, mais pas les chiens.
	[mɔ̃te]	-Cats can climb trees, but dogs can't.
489	**agent**	**agent; cooperative**
	m; adj	The court held that the independent distributor was not an agent of the seller.
	[aʒɑ̃]	-Il a estimé que le distributeur indépendant n'était pas un agent du vendeur.
490	**effet**	**effect**
	m	Le remède n'a pas eu d'effet.
	[efɛ]	-The medicine had no effect.
491	**libre**	**free| open**
	adj	Le Gouvernement est libre d'engager des consultants pour rédiger son rapport, qui demeure néanmoins sous sa responsabilité.
	[libʁ]	-The Government was free to hire consultants to draft its report, which nevertheless remained under its responsibility.
492	**bordel**	**mess| brothel**
	m	Désolé pour le bordel, Charley.
	[bɔʁdɛl]	-I'm sorry about the mess, Charley.
493	**neuf**	**nine**

num
[nœf]

Neuf gouvernements européens et la communauté internationale soutiennent ce projet.
-Nine European Governments and the international community support the project.

494 faux   false| fake

adj
[fo]

Ça ce n'est pas totalement faux.
-That is not altogether false.

495 situation   situation

f
[sitɥasjɔ̃]

Deux étudiants de sexe masculin se partageant un parapluie ? Une situation assez étrange.
-Two male students sharing an umbrella? How strange.

496 taire   hush up

vb
[tɛʁ]

Les voix les plus tonitruantes de l'armée semblent se taire par loyauté mal placée.
-Misguided loyalty appears to be muting the military's strongest voices.

497 lumière   light| spotlight

f
[lymjɛʁ]

Il va dormir en laissant la lumière.
-He goes to sleep with the lights left on.

498 debout   standing

adj
[dəbu]

Et qui pourtant n'a cessé de se tenir debout face à l'Histoire et devant les hommes.
-And yet France has always stood upright in the face of history and before mankind.

499 Noël   Christmas

m
[nɔɛl]

À l'approche de Noël, le commerce a quelque peu repris.
-With the approach of Christmas, business improved somewhat.

500 cheval   horse

m
[ʃəval]

Ce cheval a de beaux grands yeux.
-This horse has beautiful big eyes.

501 intérieur   inside| interior; inside

adj; m
[ɛ̃teʁjœʁ]

Il y avait un ministre du commerce intérieur, mais il n'y avait pas de commerce intérieur.
-There was a Ministry of Internal Trade, but there was no internal trade.

502 loi   law

f
[lwa]

Je vais suivre la loi.
-I will follow the law.

503 incroyable   incredible| amazing

adj
[ɛ̃kʁwajabl]

Le sénateur Gustafson: Un nombre incroyable de personnes ont participé à l'événement.
-Senator Gustafson: The number of people who participated was unbelievable.

504 lettre   letter

f
[lɛtʁ]

La lettre de l'Iran était une réponse directe à la lettre des trois États.
-The letter from Iran was a direct response to the letter from the three States.

505 présent   present; present

adj; m
[pʁezɑ̃]

J'ai eu une bonne journée, jusqu'à présent.
-I've had a good day so far.

506 absolu   absolute| total

adj
[apsɔly]

Dieu est l'être absolu.
-God is the absolute being.

507	**dame**	**lady**
	f	Qui est cette dame ?
	[dam]	-Who is this lady?
508	**professeur**	**professor| teacher**
	m	Notre professeur a l'air d'être très jeune.
	[pʀɔfesœʀ]	-Our teacher looks very young.
509	**fric**	**money| cash**
	m	On a claqué notre fric.
	[fʀik]	-We shot our wad.
510	**retrouver**	**find| meet**
	vb	Les termes «expédition» et «voyage» devraient retrouver leur sens originel.
	[ʀətʀuve]	-The words 'travel' and 'voyage' should regain their original meanings.
511	**coin**	**corner| wedge**
	m	Quels sont les meilleurs points de vues du coin?
	[kwɛ̃]	-What are the main sights around here?
512	**colonel**	**colonel**
	m	Le colonel Collins est marié et a une fille. Quand elle a du temps libre, elle
	[kɔlɔnɛl]	aime courir, jouer au golf et camper.
		-Colonel Collins is married and has a daughter. When she has free time she likes to run, play golf and go camping.
513	**âme**	**soul**
	f	La mort n'a que douceur pour une âme chrétienne.
	[am]	-Death has but sweetness for a christian soul.
514	**dos**	**back| reverse**
	m	Je ne parle pas de vous derrière votre dos.
	[do]	-I don't talk about you behind your back.
515	**magnifique**	**magnificent**
	adj	Une table magnifique, de superbes chaises, une atmosphère agréable,
	[maɲifik]	comme toujours.
		-An exquisite table, magnificent chairs, a congenial atmosphere, as always.
516	**rencontrer**	**meet| encounter**
	vb	Je n'aimerais sûrement pas rencontrer de tels conducteurs sur les routes
	[ʀɑ̃kɔ̃tʀe]	d'Europe.
		-I certainly would not like to encounter such drivers on the roads of Europe.
517	**réussir**	**succeed| pass**
	vb	Je suis convaincu que nous pouvons réussir et que nous devons réussir tous
	[ʀeysiʀ]	ensemble.
		-I am convinced that we can succeed and that, all together, we must succeed.
518	**tranquille**	**quiet**
	adj	Trinquons donc à une réunion tranquille.
	[tʀɑ̃kil]	-Let's toast then to a quiet meeting.
519	**chaud**	**hot| warm**
	adj	On s'assurera que la bouche d'air chaud ne peut pas être obstruée par le
	[ʃo]	chargement.
		-It shall be ensured that the heating air outlet cannot be blocked by cargo.
520	**agir**	**act**
	vb	La Commission n'est pas un État et ne peut ni ne doit agir en une telle
	[aʒiʀ]	qualité.
		-It cannot and must not act as if it were one.
521	**doucement**	**gently| slowly**

	adv		La première étape consiste à dévisser doucement et lentement la bonde.
	[dusmã]		-The first step is to gently and slowly loosen the bung plug.

522 pareil — **such| similar; the same; equal**

adj; prn; m
[paʁɛj]

Jamais il n'était allé dans un endroit pareil.
 -Never has he been to such a place.

523 accident — **accident**

m
[aksidã]

Un terrible accident impliquant une collégienne...
 -A terrible incident happened to a high school girl…

524 appel — **call| appeal**

m
[apɛl]

Je viens d'avoir un appel de ton école.
 -I just got a call from your school.

525 anniversaire — **anniversary; anniversary**

adj; m
[anivɛʁsɛʁ]

Aujourd'hui, nous célébrons un anniversaire. Le 20e anniversaire de ce prix.
 -Today, we are celebrating an anniversary: the 20th anniversary of this prize.

526 blanc — **white| albescent; white**

adj; m
[blã]

Elle était vêtue tout de blanc pour la noce.
 -She was dressed all in white for the wedding.

527 risque — **risk| hazard**

m
[ʁisk]

C'est un risque que nous devrons prendre.
 -It's a risk we'll have to take.

528 moyen — **means| medium; medium**

m; adj
[mwajɛ̃]

Il n'y a aucun moyen de prévoir ce que tu rêveras cette nuit.
 -There's no way to predict what you will dream tonight.

529 terminer — **finish| conclude**

vb
[tɛʁmine]

L'Assemblée décide de terminer l'examen des points susmentionnés.
 -The Assembly decided to conclude its consideration of the aforementioned items.

530 complètement — **completely| fully**

adv
[kɔ̃plɛtmã]

Certaines méthodes jugées inacceptables doivent être complètement abandonnées.
 -Certain methods judged unacceptable must be completely abandoned.

531 clair — **clear| bright**

adj
[klɛʁ]

Cela est parfaitement clair pour nous, et j'espère que c'est également clair pour tous à présent.
 -This is perfectly clear to us, and I hope it is now as clear to everyone else.

532 meurtre — **murder**

m
[mœʁtʁ]

Sa mort a été qualifiée en meurtre.
 -His death was ruled a homicide.

533 toucher — **touch; touch**

m; vb
[tuʃe]

Non, mais cela va toucher les employés de la fonction publique fédérale.»
 -NO, this will not affect me, but it will affect employees of the federal public service".

534 déjeuner — **lunch; lunch**

vb; m
[deʒœne]

Je te dois un petit-déjeuner.
 -I owe you a breakfast. ("small-lunch")

535 envoyer — **send| forward**

vb
[ãvwaje]

It cooperated closely with the Quartet's Special Envoy for Disengagement.
 -Il a coopéré étroitement avec l'Envoyé spécial du Quatuor pour le désengagement.

536 lire — **read; lira**

		vb; f	Je n'ai aucun livre à lire.
		[liʁ]	-I have no books to read.
537	**avance**		**advance| lead**
		f	Tu es en avance.
		[avãs]	-You are early.
538	**détester**		**hate**
		vb	Nous détestons la violence et la guerre.
		[detɛste]	-We abhor violence and war.
539	**forme**		**form| shape**
		f	Je suis toujours en forme.
		[fɔʁm]	-I'm still in shape.
540	**bord**		**edge| board**
		m	En été, les gens se rendent en bord de mer.
		[bɔʁ]	-In the summer, people go to the seaside.
541	**décider**		**decide| choose**
		vb	Les municipalités peuvent décider d'exempter de ces frais les familles pauvres.
		[deside]	-Schools of general education can decide to organise free meals for children from poor families.
542	**mer**		**sea**
		f	La montagne est à 2000 mètres au-dessus du niveau de la mer.
		[mɛʁ]	-The mountain is 2000 meters above sea level.
543	**médecin**		**doctor; doctoral**
		m; adj	Le médecin a interdit à mon père de porter des choses lourdes.
		[medsɛ̃]	-The doctor didn't allow my father to carry heavy things.
544	**midi**		**noon; midday**
		m; adj	Est -ce que nous reportons à demain midi ou à jeudi midi ?
		[midi]	-Should we adjourn it until noon tomorrow or until noon on Thursday?
545	**porter**		**wear| carry**
		vb	J'ai essayé de porter des choses trop grandes pour que des gens puissent les porter.
		[pɔʁte]	-I tried to carry things too large for people to be able to carry.
546	**ignorer**		**ignore**
		vb	Nous ne pouvons tout simplement pas continuer de prétendre ignorer l'histoire.
		[iɲɔʁe]	-We cannot simply go on pretending that we do not know our history.
547	**silence**		**silence| pause**
		m	Elle garda le silence toute la journée.
		[silãs]	-She kept silent all day.
548	**diable**		**devil; wretched**
		m; adj	Qui diable es-tu ?
		[djabl]	-Who the hell are you?
549	**cadeau**		**gift**
		m	Pouvez-vous faire un emballage cadeau pour ceci, je vous prie ?
		[kado]	-Can you gift-wrap this, please?
550	**supposer**		**assume| suppose**
		vb	On peut intuitivement supposer qu'une telle relation positive existe bel et bien.
		[sypoze]	-It would be intuitive to assume that such a positive relationship exists.
551	**flic**		**cop**

	m	Pensez-vous que vous pourriez être flic ?
	[flik]	-Do you think you could be a cop?
552	**avocat**	**lawyer**
	m	Son ambition est de devenir avocat.
	[avɔka]	-His ambition is to be a lawyer.
553	**jurer**	**swear**
	vb	J'aurais pu jurer avoir vu quelqu'un.
	[ʒyʁe]	-I could have sworn I saw somebody.
554	**anglais**	**English; English**
	adj; m|mpl	Les Anglais aiment autant les lions que les licornes.
	[ãglɛ]	-The English love the unicorn as much as they love the lion.
555	**sept**	**seven**
	num	Les pirates naviguaient sur les sept mers.
	[sɛt]	-The pirates sailed the seven seas.
556	**moitié**	**half; half**
	adv; f	Les paupières de Jack étaient à moitié ouvertes.
	[mwatje]	-Jack's eyelids were half open.
557	**surprendre**	**surprise| catch**
	vb	Ni les vicissitudes ni la survie de l'ONU ne devraient surprendre quiconque.
	[syʁpʁãdʁ]	-Neither the variable fortunes nor the survival of the United Nations should surprise anyone.
558	**chacun**	**each; apiece**
	prn; adv	Au tout début, il y a 100 ans, chacun des ministères s'occupait de ses affaires.
	[ʃakɛ̃]	-At the very beginning, 100 years ago, each department managed its own affaires.
559	**exact**	**exact**
	adj	Si les coordonnées exactes de chaque endroit du secteur sont parfaitement connues, on peut décrire le relief avec précision.
	[ɛgzakt]	-The exact coordinates of each spot of the area being perfectly known, the relief can be precisely described.
560	**commander**	**order| command**
	vb	Le quartier général d'une mission complexe peut commander jusqu'à quatre états-majors de secteur.
	[kɔmãde]	-Mission headquarters can command up to four sector headquarters.
561	**télé**	**TV; telly**
	abr; f	Rends-moi la télécommande de la télé.
	[tele]	-Give the television remote control back to me.
562	**autour**	**around**
	adv	En tournant autour du pot, oui.
	[otuʁ]	-In a roundabout way, yeah.
563	**disparaître**	**disappear**
	vb	Ils sont petits et, sans cette mesure, ils sont voués à disparaître.
	[dispaʁɛtʁ]	-These newspapers are small and they will disappear without this assistance.
564	**ligner**	**line**
	vb	Un enfant est considéré comme une richesse, assurant la continuité de la lignée.
	[liɲe]	-A child is a treasure that ensures the continuity of the line.
565	**expliquer**	**explain**
	vb	les circonstances le justifient, auquel cas les tribunaux devront expliquer
	[ɛksplike]	-justify it, and courts will be required to explain these circumstances.

566	**simplement**	**simply**
	adv	Je voulais juste vous informer du fait qu'elle ne s'est pas simplement éclipsée.
	[sɛ̃pləmɑ̃]	-I simply wanted to inform you of the fact that she did not simply disappear.
567	**mission**	**mission| assignment**
	f	Elle a nié qu'on l'ait envoyée en mission.
	[misjɔ̃]	-She denied having been asked to go on an assignment.
568	**quitter**	**leave| quit**
	vb	Certaines de ces personnes abandonneront les soins en institution et d'autres quitteront les maisons où elles ont passé leur enfance.
	[kite]	-Part of them move away from institutional care and part from their childhood homes.
569	**selon**	**according to; as follows**
	prp; adv	Chacun donne selon ses capacités, chacun reçoit selon ses besoins.
	[səlɔ̃]	-From each according to his means, to each according to his needs.
570	**classe**	**class| classroom**
	f	Pourrais-tu, à l'instant, m'aider avec mon travail de classe ?
	[klas]	-Could you please help me with my schoolwork right now?
571	**pari**	**bet| betting**
	m	Jack a perdu son pari.
	[paʁi]	-Jack lost the bet.
572	**peuple**	**common people**
	m	Il serait, à mon sens, intéressant d'aller à Kiruna ou dans les Canaries afin de rencontrer les gens, le peuple.
	[pœpl]	-I think that it would be worth going to Kiruna or the Canary Islands to speak to the ordinary folk.
573	**habitude**	**habit**
	f	Fumer est une mauvaise habitude.
	[abityd]	-Smoking is a bad habit.
574	**voie**	**way| track**
	f	Mais il m'a montré la voie et...
	[vwa]	-But he did show me the way and..
575	**dangereux**	**dangerous**
	adj	Un scénario catastrophe a été élaboré pour chacun des principaux sites dangereux.
	[dɑ̃ʒʁø]	-For each major hazard establishment a worst-case scenario has been developed.
576	**pote**	**buddy**
	m	"Tu es là pour suivre mes ordres." "Dans tes rêves, mon pote !"
	[pɔt]	-"You're here to follow my orders." "In your dreams, pal!"
577	**contrôle**	**control| check**
	m	Elle a un bon contrôle de sa classe.
	[kɔ̃tʁol]	-She has good control over her class.
578	**honte**	**shame**
	f	C'est un contrôle qui doit être fait en plus du contrôle mathématique des chiffres.
	[ɔ̃t]	-This is a check to be done alongside the mathematical check on the figures.
579	**impression**	**printing| impression**
	f	Jack a fait mauvaise impression.
	[ɛ̃pʁesjɔ̃]	-Jack made a poor impression.
580	**suivre**	**follow**

	vb	Afin de suivre la cargaison (traçage), des récépissés resteront nécessaires.
	[sɥivʁ]	-Receipts will continue to be necessary for following up the cargo (tracing).
581	**retourner**	**return**
	vb	Beaucoup trop de personnes attendent encore de pouvoir retourner dans leurs foyers.
	[ʁətuʁne]	-There are also too many who are still waiting to return to their homes.
582	**offrir**	**offer| give**
	vb	Ces galeries sont une vitrine de ce que les artistes de Gibraltar peuvent offrir.
	[ɔfʁiʁ]	-These galleries serve as a showcase of what Gibraltar's artists have to offer.
583	**chanson**	**song**
	f	Je ne pouvais pas me rappeler le titre de cette chanson.
	[ʃɑ̃sɔ̃]	-I couldn't remember the title of that song.
584	**tant pis**	**too bad**
	adv	Je dirais tant pis, mais c'est dommage.
	[tɑ̃ pi]	-Too bad, but just the same, it is sad.
585	**poste**	**position; post**
	m; f	Nous aurons besoin d'une agence de chasseurs de têtes pour trouver l'homme qui convient à ce poste de cadre.
	[pɔst]	-We'll need a head hunting agency to find the right man for this executive position.
586	**huit**	**eight**
	num	Nous avons réservé pour dix-huit heures trente.
	[ɥit]	-We have a reservation for six-thirty.
587	**radio**	**radio**
	f	Vois-tu un inconvénient à ce que j'allume la radio ?
	[ʁadjo]	-Do you mind if I turn on the radio?
588	**ressembler**	**look like**
	vb	Nous devons nous demander aujourd'hui à quoi le marché transatlantique devra ressembler en 2020.
	[ʁəsɑ̃ble]	-We need to ask ourselves today what the transatlantic market place should look like in 2020.
589	**attaque**	**attack**
	f	Attaquer l'ONU c'est en attaquer tous les Membres.
	[atak]	-An attack on the United Nations is an attack on all its Members.
590	**baiser**	**kiss; fuck**
	m; vb	Monsieur le Président, le ministre est invité à baiser la bague du pape.
	[beze]	-Speaker, I invite the minister to kiss the Pope's ring.
591	**pourtant**	**yet| however; nevertheless**
	con; adv	Pourtant, la situation économique et financière s'est détériorée rapidement.
	[puʁtɑ̃]	-However, the economic and financial situations have deteriorated rapidly.
592	**réponse**	**response**
	f	Il doit exister une réponse à court terme et une réponse à long terme à cette question.
	[ʁepɔ̃s]	-There must be a short-term answer, as well as a long-term answer, to that question.
593	**connard**	**prick**
	m	Quel connard !
	[kɔnaʁ]	-What an asshole!
594	**pute**	**bitch**

52

f | Une petite pute friquée dans la caisse de papa.
[pyt] | -Litle rich bitch driving in her daddy's Escalade.

595 bande — **band| strip**

f | C'est une bande d'ineptes crétins agressifs.
[bɑ̃d] | -They are a bunch of inept and vulturous morons.

596 enfer — **hell**

m | Tais-toi, servante de l'enfer !
[ɑ̃fɛʁ] | -Shut up, servant of hell!

597 triste — **sad**

adj | C'est triste pour la politique agricole et triste pour le contribuable.
[tʁist] | -It is a sad day for agricultural policy, and a sad day for the taxpayer.

598 tel — **such**

adj | La communauté internationale devrait encourager et appuyer un tel
[tɛl] | programme.
 | -The international community should encourage and support such a programme.

599 Bravo! — **Bravo!**

int | Bravo à Terre-Neuve et au Labrador !
[bʁavo!] | -Kudos to Newfoundland and Labrador.

600 plusieurs — **several| divers**

adj | Il y a eu dans l'Antiquité plusieurs États sur le territoire de l'actuelle Géorgie.
[plyzjœʁ] | -In ancient times, there were several States within the territory of present-day Georgia.

601 exister — **exist**

vb | Nous devons parler de nouveau de l'ordre qui devrait exister entre les gens.
[ɛgziste] | -We must speak anew of the order that should exist between peoples.

602 rire — **laugh; laugh**

m; vb | Il savait rire, se moquer de lui-même - surtout se moquer de lui-même.
[ʁiʁ] | -He knew how to laugh, even at himself - especially how to laugh at himself.

603 compagnie — **company**

f | Guillaume et Lebas, ces mots ne feraient-ils pas une belle raison sociale ?
[kɔ̃paɲi] | On pourrait mettre et compagnie pour arrondir la signature.
 | -Guillaume and Lebas' will that not make a good business name? We might add, 'and Co.' to round off the firm's signature.

604 étrange — **strange**

adj | Ce processus n'a rien d'étrange au Canada, sauf à la Chambre des
[etʁɑ̃ʒ] | communes.
 | -That process is not a strange process in the land but it is strange in the House.

605 exemple — **example| sample**

m | L'exemple des chantiers navals en Croatie en constitue un bon exemple.
[ɛgzɑ̃pl] | -The example of the shipyards in Croatia is also a good example of this.

606 combat — **combat**

m | Les militaires ont engagé le combat avec l'ennemi, cinq kilomètres au sud de
[kɔ̃ba] | la capitale.
 | -The military engaged the enemy five kilometers south of the capital.

607 secours — **relief| help**

m | D'où proviendrons les secours et les renforts ?
[səkuʁ] | -Where are the relief or reinforcements going to come from?

608 connerie — **bullshit**

f
[kɔnʁi]

C'est tellement de la connerie.
-This is such bullshit.

609 visiter
vb
[vizite]

visit| view
Le sénateur Kinsella: Le premier ministre devrait visiter la région.
-Senator Kinsella: The Prime Minister should visit the area.

610 coucher
vb; m
[kuʃe]

sleep| lay down; sunset
Il me faut coucher ça sur le papier.
-I need to write that down.

611 imaginer
vb
[imaʒine]

imagine
Les destructions et les perturbations ont atteint une ampleur difficile à imaginer.
-There was destruction and disruption on a scale difficult to imagine.

612 merveilleux
adj
[mɛʁvɛjø]

wonderful
Il y a ensuite eu un merveilleux programme du Professeur Salter de l'Université d'Édimbourg.
-Then there was a marvellous programme from Professor Salter of Edinburgh University.

613 continuer
vb
[kɔ̃tinɥe]

continue
On dit: «On veut continuer, on veut continuer, on veut continuer.»
-It says ``We want to continue, we want to continue, we want to continue".

614 voler
vb
[vɔle]

fly| steal
Le premier ministre peut-il expliquer à ces gens pourquoi il continue de les voler ?
-Can the Prime Minister explain to these people why he continues to rip them off?

615 lune
f
[lyn]

moon
Mais elle a également eu sous la lune, la lune est sous ses pieds.
-But She also had the moon underneath, the moon was under Her feet.

616 bouche
f
[buʃ]

mouth
Ce n'est pas moi qui ai dit «le boucher du Liban», c'est l'interprétation qu'on lui donne.
-The term "butcher of Lebanon" is not mine, it is the interpretation ascribed to him.

617 sud
adj; m
[syd]

south; south
En Allemagne du Nord, il y a plus de landes qu'en Allemagne du Sud.
-There is more moorland in Northern Germany than in Southern Germany.

618 danser
vb
[dɑ̃se]

dance
Les jeunes veulent voyager et danser, mais les personnes âgées aussi veulent voyager et danser.
-Young people want to travel and dance, but old people also want to travel and dance.

619 ennui
m
[ɑ̃nɥi]

boredom| trouble
Nous ne voulons causer aucun ennui.
-We don't want to cause any trouble.

620 but
m
[by]

purpose| goal
Je peux voir que vous êtes occupé donc je vais aller droit au but.
-I can see you're busy, so I'll get right to the point.

621 hors
prp
[ɔʁ]

except
La plupart des enfants nés hors mariage vivent dans les campagnes (59% en 1996).

-Most of the children born out of wedlock are from the rural areas (59% in 1996).

622	**boîte**	**box| can**
	f	Ouf ! Quelle grosse boîte !
	[bwat]	-Wow! What a big box!
623	**vol**	**flight| theft**
	m	Cela te coutera 100$ pour un vol vers l'île.
	[vɔl]	-It will cost you $100 to fly to the island.
624	**public**	**public; public**
	adj; m	Ce rapport prône un service offert au public indépendamment du lieu
	[pyblik]	d'habitation.
		-It is a report which ensures a service to the public, irrespective of where they live.
625	**lieutenant**	**lieutenant**
	m	Sami est devenu lieutenant-colonel.
	[ljøtnɑ̃]	-Sami became a lieutenant-colonel.
626	**système**	**system**
	m	Le système d'éducation doit être plus flexible.
	[sistɛm]	-The education system needs to be more flexible.
627	**époque**	**time| age**
	f	Dans l'Empire Romain, le temps était marqué en référence au souverain de
	[epɔk]	l'époque.
		-In the Roman Empire, time was marked in reference to the ruler at the time.
628	**bête**	**beast| idiot; stupid**
	f; adj	Maintenant le monde pense aussi Messieurs Messieurs, il est en proie à la
	[bɛt]	bête.
		-Now the world also believe Gentlemen Gentlemen, it is plagued by this beast.
629	**vendre**	**sell**
	vb	En décembre 1991, il a pu en vendre quelques-unes, mais à perte.
	[vɑ̃dʁ]	-In December 1991, he was able to sell some of his shares but at a loss.
630	**avenir**	**future**
	m	Ces deux types d'éducation sont essentiels pour l'édification d'un avenir
	[avniʁ]	viable.
		-Within this vast challenge, certain issues should receive particular attention.
631	**santé**	**health**
	f	Sa mère l'empêchait de sortir car elle s'inquiétait pour sa santé.
	[sɑ̃te]	-His mother prevented him from going out because she was anxious about his health.
632	**amoureux**	**in love; lover**
	adj; m	Bien entendu, je l'ai déjà dit souvent, je ne suis pas amoureux du
	[amuʁø]	capitalisme.
		-Of course, I have said it often before, I am no lover of capitalism.
633	**cuisine**	**kitchen| cuisine**
	f	Tu devrais mettre ce micro-ondes dans la cuisine.
	[kɥizin]	-Mom, you should put this microwave in the kitchen.
634	**normal**	**normal**

adj
[nɔʁmal]
On pourrait penser que c'est parfaitement normal, mais cela n'était pas auparavant.
-That might be considered perfectly normal, but it was not normal before.

635 danger

m
[dɑ̃ʒe]
danger
Je suis très conscient du danger.
-I'm very much aware of the danger.

636 gouvernement

m
[guvɛʁnəmɑ̃]
government| ministry
Dans ce pays, le gouvernement contrôle les prix.
-In that country the government controls prices.

637 village

m
[vilaʒ]
village
Jack habite une maison à l'entrée du village.
-Jack lives in a house on the edge of the village.

638 poser

vb
[poze]
pose| rest
La cause des droits de l'homme serait sans aucun doute mieux servie, si les États-Unis, l'Australie et les délégations partageant leurs vues, cessaient de se poser en braves types.
-The cause of human rights would no doubt be better served if the United States, Australian and like-minded delegations stopped posturing as good guys.

639 ouvrir

vb
[uvʁiʁ]
open| start
La méthode de la Commission a ouvert la porte, mais il convient aussi d'ouvrir les fenêtres.
-The Commission's method has opened the door, but the window must also be open.

640 journal

m
[ʒuʁnal]
newspaper| journal
Il était trop fatigué pour lire le journal du soir.
-He was too sleepy to read an evening paper.

641 approche

f
[apʁɔʃ]
approach
Il y a deux approches: une approche technique et une approche institutionnelle.
-There are two approaches: a technical approach and an institutional approach.

642 dommage

m
[dɔmaʒ]
damage| pity
C'est dommage que tu ne puisses pas venir.
-It's a pity that you can't come.

643 peau

f
[po]
skin
Les carcasses et parties de dinde peuvent être commercialisées avec peau ou sans peau.
-Turkey carcasses and parts are available for trade with skin (skin-on) or without skin (skinless).

644 nez

m
[ne]
nose
Pour détecter de la drogue ou des explosifs cachés, aucune technologie ne peut rivaliser avec le nez d'un chien.
-For detecting drugs or hidden explosives, there's no technology that can match a dog's nose.

645 servir

vb
[sɛʁviʁ]
serve| help
Cela pourrait servir de modèle à des efforts semblables dans d'autres provinces.
-It could serve as a legislative template for similar efforts in other provinces.

646 sympa
friendly

	adj	
	[sɛ̃pa]	

T'es le genre de personne... avec qui c'est sympa d'être dans un nid.
-You're the kind of person that's it's nice to be in a foxhole with.

647 mille — **thousand**

num
[mil]

Es-tu prête pour l'an deux mille ?
-Are you ready for Y2K?

648 banque — **bank**

f
[bɑ̃k]

La banque a un programme excellent.
-The bank has an excellent program.

649 sergent — **sergeant**

m
[sɛʁʒɑ̃]

Qui va là ? cria le sergent d'une voix rauque.
-Who goes there? shouted the sergeant in a hoarse voice.

650 clé — **key; key**

adj; f
[kle]

Je cherche ma clé.
-I'm looking for my key.

651 nord — **north; northern**

m; adj
[nɔʁ]

Une nation qui annihile toutes les nations et cultures indigènes de deux continents entiers, l'Amérique du Nord et l'Australie, puis lâche deux bombes nucléaires sur une île densément peuplée, serait crainte même par les extra-terrestres.
-A nation that annihilates all native nations and cultures of two continents, North America and Australia, then drops two nuclear bombs on a densely populated island, would be feared even by aliens.

652 inspecteur — **inspector**

m
[ɛ̃spɛktœʁ]

Commence à penser comme un inspecteur.
-I want you to start to think like a detective.

653 liberté — **freedom| liberty**

f
[libɛʁte]

La liberté commence où l'ignorance finit.
-Freedom begins where ignorance ends.

654 salaud — **bastard; dirty**

m; adj
[salo]

Vous êtes vraiment un parfait salaud.
-You really and truly are a perfect bastard.

655 cour — **court**

f
[kuʁ]

Remplacer "Cour interaméricaine de justice" par "Cour centraméricaine de justice".
-Replace "Inter-American Court of Justice" by "Central American Court of Justice".

656 juge — **judge| beak**

m
[ʒyʒ]

Le juge l'a condamné à mort.
-The judge condemned him to death.

657 terrible — **terrible**

adj
[teʁibl]

There is a terrible backlog, especially in applications for certification.
-Il y a un terrible arriéré, surtout dans le cas des demandes d'accréditation.

658 paraître — **seem| appear**

vb
[paʁɛtʁ]

La conclusion la plus importante peut paraître simplette: le réseau Échelon existe bel et bien.
-The most important conclusion may appear simple: ECHELON does in fact exist.

659 crime — **crime**

m
[kʁim]

Selon l'enquête de police, Jack était sur les lieux du crime au moment de l'événement.

-According to the police investigation, Jack was at the scene of the crime at the time of the event.

660	**asseoir**	**sit**

vb
[aswaʁ]

Le Comité tchèque d'Helsinki a même noté qu'il était interdit de s'étendre ou de s'asseoir sur le lit (pour les détenus moins gravement malades).
-The Czech Helsinki Committee noted even the prohibition to lie or sit on the bed (in the case of lighter illnesses).

661	**thé**	**tea**

m
[te]

Sur la recommandation du Dr Keon, nous buvions tous les deux du thé décaféiné.
-Keon's instructions, we were both drinking decaffeinated tea.

662	**bonheur**	**happiness; welfare**

m; adj
[bɔnœʁ]

L'argent ne fait pas le bonheur.
-Happiness does not consist simply in wealth.

663	**tas**	**pile**

m
[ta]

Les bandes dessinées étaient posées en tas sur le bureau.
-The comic books were piled on the desk.

664	**travers**	**across**

m
[tʁavɛʁ]

Elle se précipita à travers la pelouse.
-She hurried across the lawn.

665	**stupide**	**stupid; stupid**

adj; m
[stypid]

J'espère également que l'étiquetage sous forme de «feux de signalisation» que l'on envisage encore actuellement n'est qu'une stupide blague.
-I also hope that the 'traffic light'-style labelling to which consideration is still being given is no more than a witless joke.

666	**blague**	**joke**

f
[blag]

Elle lui a raconté une blague, mais il ne l'a pas trouvée drôle.
-She told him a joke, but he didn't think it was funny.

667	**préférer**	**prefer; would rather**

vb; av
[pʁefeʁe]

Il y a une tendance à préférer des projets qui sont exécutés à l'échelle des pays.
-There is a tendency to prefer projects that are executed at the country level.

668	**conseil**	**board| council**

m
[kɔ̃sɛj]

Je lui ai donné un conseil auquel il n'a pas prêté attention.
-I gave him advice, to which he paid no attention.

669	**protéger**	**protect| safeguard**

vb
[pʁɔteʒe]

Le médecin devrait être tenu de protéger la confidentialité de cette information.
-The medical professional should maintain the confidentiality of the information.

670	**rêve**	**dream**

m
[ʁɛv]

Il s'est réveillé de son rêve.
-He woke up from his sleep.

671	**pitié**	**pity**

f
[pitje]

Nous implorons pitié pour les civils irakiens, les militaires et leurs familles.
-We pray for compassion towards the Iraqi people and soldiers and their families.

672	**vin**	**wine**

m
[vɛ̃]

Votre Munich viticole change la définition du vin, la nature du vin.
-Your Munich Agreement of the wine industry changes the definition of wine and the nature of wine.

673	**don**	**gift| donation**
	m	Jack ne s'intéressait pas uniquement au don musical de Jill.
	[dɔ̃]	-Jack was not just interested in Jill's musical abilities.
674	**sol**	**soil**
	m	Les plantes ne poussent pas dans ce sol.
	[sɔl]	-Plants don't grow in this soil.
675	**vent**	**wind**
	m	Le vent ne doit pas perturber l'arrosage de la piste (les pare-vent sont
	[vɑ̃]	autorisés).
		-The wind conditions shall not interfere with wetting of the surface (Wind-shields are permitted).
676	**club**	**club**
	m	Transco and the golf club sued the Council.
	[klœb]	-Transco et le Club de golf ont intenté une action contre la municipalité.
677	**gamin**	**kid; kiddy**
	m; adj	Un jour, quand j'étais à l'école primaire, un gamin était harcelé, et ça me
	[gamɛ̃]	chamboulait tellement que j'ai explosé de colère.
		-Once, when I was in primary school, a kid was being bullied and it bothered me so much that I exploded with anger.
678	**tante**	**aunt**
	f	Ma tante a vécu une vie réservée.
	[tɑ̃t]	-My aunt lived a happy life.
679	**bar**	**bar| bass**
	m	Allez au bar faire votre spécialité.
	[baʁ]	-Go to the bar and do what you do best.
680	**milieu**	**medium**
	m	Jack, comme à son habitude, traînait en début de phrase, tandis que Jill, déjà
	[miljø]	douze mots devant lui, se trouvait maintenant en son milieu.
		-Jack, as his usual, lagged at the beginning of the sentence, when Jill, already twelve words ahead of him, stood now in its middle.
681	**reine**	**queen**
	f	La Reine − le souverain en droit de la Nouvelle-Zélande − est le chef de
	[ʁɛn]	l'État.
		-The Queen - the Sovereign in right of New Zealand - is the Head of State.
682	**signer**	**sign**
	vb	L'auteur aurait été contraint de signer cette reconnaissance de responsabilité.
	[siɲe]	-The author was allegedly forced to sign the acknowledgement of responsibility.
683	**centre**	**center| focus**
	m	Ce tramway relie le centre-ville à la gare.
	[sɑ̃tʁ]	-This tramway connects the city centre with the railway station.
684	**probablement**	**probably**
	adv	Deux des professeurs m'ont répondu spontanément: «Probablement Wilfrid
	[pʁɔbabləmɑ̃]	Laurier».
		-However, two of the teachers spontaneously said it was probably Wilfrid Laurier.
685	**bière**	**beer**
	f	Jack a ouvert sa bière et a pris une gorgée.
	[bjɛʁ]	-Jack opened his beer and took a sip.
686	**dingue**	**crazy| wild; loon**

adj; m/f
[dɛ̃g]

Techniquement parlant, c'est un dingue.
-In technical terminology, he's a loon.

687 **inutile**

adj
[inytil]

unnecessary| useless

Il est tout à fait inutile d'agir comme si aucune décision ne devait être prise.
-There is absolutely no point in acting as if no decision needs to be made here.

688 **nul**

adj; m; prn
[nyl]

no| zero; zero; no one

Tout acte préjudiciable découlant de cette distinction doit être considéré comme nul et de nul effet.
-Any prejudicial act taken on the basis of such distinction shall be deemed null and void.

689 **sentir**

vb
[sɑ̃tiʀ]

feel

Ils doivent sentir l'opprobre et la répugnance des gens civilisés du monde entier.
-They must feel the opprobrium and repugnance of civilized people everywhere.

690 **différent**

adj
[difeʀɑ̃]

different

C'est un débat complètement différent portant sur un sujet différent.
-This is an entirely different debate on a different issue.

691 **emmener**

vb
[ɑ̃mne]

drive

L'équipe d'intervention d'urgence est alors arrivée pour l'emmener ailleurs.
-As a result, the Emergency Response team arrived to remove him from the unit.

692 **vêtement**

m
[vɛtmɑ̃]

garment

Je n'ai aucun chouette vêtement.
-I don't have any nice clothes.

693 **liste**

f
[list]

list

Laisse-moi voir cette liste !
-Let me see that list.

694 **unir**

vb
[yniʀ]

unite

Nous devons unir nos instruments au niveau européen avec des efforts nationaux coordonnés.
-We must combine our instruments at European level with coordinated efforts in the Member States.

695 **société**

f
[sɔsjete]

society| association

J'aimerais voler pour une société pétrolière en mer.
-I'd like to fly for an offshore oil company.

696 **soin**

m
[swɛ̃]

care| carefulness

Il convient donc de rédiger cet article avec beaucoup de prudence et de soin.
-Therefore, it should be done with great caution and carefulness.

697 **utiliser**

vb
[ytilize]

use

Un débat s'est instauré sur les méthodes que les pays pourraient utiliser pour mobiliser leurs diasporas.
-There was discussion of methods that countries could employ to engage their diasporas.

698 **lequel**

prn
[ləkɛl]

which

Ce nouveau développement dans lequel nous nous sommes engagés et sur lequel nous débattons est précieux.
-This is a valuable new development in which we are involved and which we are debating.

699 **parole**

word| speech

	f	
	[paʁɔl]	Nous sommes ici au Parlement européen et les temps de parole ne sont pas illimités.
		-This is the European Parliament, and the speaking times are not unlimited.

700 marier — **marry**

vb
[maʁje]

Dans certains pays, les filles sont mariées avant d'avoir atteint la puberté.
-Girls may be wed in some countries even before reaching puberty.

701 départ — **departure| starting**

m
[depaʁ]

Nous avons été contraints de différer notre départ.
-We were compelled to put off our departure.

702 ennemi — **enemy| hostile; inimical**

m; adj
[ɛnmi]

L'ennemi de mon ennemi est-il mon ami... ou mon ennemi ?
-Is the enemy of my enemy my friend... or my enemy?

703 spectacle — **show| spectacle**

m
[spɛktakl]

Avez-vous apprécié le spectacle ?
-Did you enjoy the show?

704 recherche — **research| search**

f
[ʁəʃɛʁʃ]

Le gouvernement canadien a coupé dans le financement de la recherche pour l'environnement.
-The Canadian governement has cut back funding for environmental research.

705 choisir — **choose**

vb
[ʃwaziʁ]

Wittgenstein a dit que choisir une langue, c'était choisir une manière de vivre.
-Wittgenstein told us that to choose a language is to choose a form of life.

706 intérêt — **interest**

m
[ɛ̃teʁɛ]

Un taux d'intérêt un peu plus bas peut épargner des milliers de dollars au cours de la durée d'un prêt immobilier.
-A slightly lower interest rate could save thousands of dollars over the life of a home loan.

707 intéresser — **interest**

vb
[ɛ̃teʁese]

Je m'explique mal comment nous pouvons nous intéresser à réformer le mode du scrutin.
-I have trouble seeing how we could be interested in reforming the voting method.

708 rôle — **role**

m
[ʁol]

Pour avancer, nous devons réévaluer votre rôle.
-But, moving forward, I think we need to reevaluate your role.

709 félicitation — **congratulation**

f
[felisitasjɔ̃]

Monsieur le Président, je vous remercie pour vos aimables paroles de félicitation concernant la candidature olympique de Londres.
-Mr President, thank you for your gracious words of congratulation on London's Olympic bid.

710 descendre — **descend| get off**

vb
[desɑ̃dʁ]

Ils nous ont vues alors qu'ils étaient en train de descendre du train.
-They saw us as they were getting off the train.

711 tourner — **turn| rotate**

vb
[tuʁne]

Ces deux "non" signifient-ils que nous devons tourner le dos à l'innovation technologique ?
-Do those two 'nos' mean that we must turn our back on technological innovation?

712 position — **position**

| | f
[pozisjɔ̃] | Place the thigh in a horizontal position and the torso in a vertical position.
-Placer la cuisse en position horizontale et le torse en position verticale. |

713 **blessé**
adj; m
[blese]

injured; casualty
Jack a-t-il été blessé dans l'accident d'hier ?
-Did Jack get hurt in the accident yesterday?

714 **humain**
adj; m
[ymɛ̃]

human; human
Rapport sur le développement humain : droits de l'homme et développement humain, PNUD, p. 89.
-Human Development Report 2000: Human Rights and Human Development, UNDP, p. 89.

715 **match**
m
[matʃ]

match| game
Monsieur le Commissaire, une équipe de football qui n'est pas compétitive perd match après match.
-A football team, Commissioner, that is not competitive loses game after game.

716 **coupable**
adj; m/f
[kupabl]

guilty; culprit
On y désigne très clairement le coupable, tout comme nous l'avions demandé.
-The guilty party has been clearly identified, as we asked.

717 **environ**
adv; prp; adj
[ɑ̃viʁɔ̃]

about; around; all but
Établissement et suivi du budget annuel (environ 14 millions de livres).
-Setting and monitoring of annual budget (circa £14 million).

718 **art**
m
[aʁ]

art
L'Italie possède quelques-unes des meilleures galeries d'art du monde.
-Italy has some of the best art galleries in the world.

719 **espoir**
m
[ɛspwaʁ]

hope
Penses-tu qu'il y ait un espoir ?
-Do you think there's a hope?

720 **mur**
m
[myʁ]

wall
Ne t'adosse pas à ce mur.
-Don't lean against this wall.

721 **église**
f
[egliz]

church
Elle n'a toutefois pas le statut d'«Église établie», comme l'Église d'Angleterre.
-It is not, however, an "established church" like the Church of England.

722 **salope**
f
[salɔp]

slut
T'approche pas de mon mari, salope!
-Stay away from my husband, you slut!

723 **beauté**
f
[bote]

beauty
Il est amusant de savoir que la beauté des jardins japonais ne se retrouve dans aucune autre culture.
-It is fun to know that the beauty of Japanese gardens can't be found in other cultures.

724 **lâche**
m; adj
[laʃ]

coward; cowardly
La Commission européenne condamne cet acte lâche et cruel avec la plus grande fermeté.
-The European Commission vigorously condemns this cruel and cowardly act.

725 **adresser**
vb
[adʁese]

address
Je vous rappelle que vous devez adresser vos questions à la présidence.
-I remind members to please address your questions to the Chair.

726 **sauter** **jump| skip**
vb
[sote]
Je peux sauter dans deux minutes.
-I can jump there inside of two minutes.

727 **colère** **anger| passion**
f
[kɔlɛʁ]
Ssa colère sans aucune retenue (ou, au contraire, que la colère devrait être dissimulée ou camouflée).
-Expression of anger is acceptable (or the opposite - that anger should be concealed or disguised).

728 **directeur** **director**
m
[diʁɛktœʁ]
Le directeur de l'école veut fermer la cantine et créer une nouvelle salle récréative pour les élèves.
-The director of the school wants to close the canteen and create a new recreation room for the students.

729 **adieu** **farewell**
m
[adjø]
Adieu!
-Farewell!

730 **parier** **bet| gamble**
vb
[paʁje]
Le bon côté est que cela facilite le jeu et permet de parier plus facilement.
-The upside is that it facilitates the punter and it makes it easier to get and to place a bet.

731 **tort** **wrong| harm**
m
[tɔʁ]
Franchement, vous avez tort.
-Frankly speaking, you are in the wrong.

732 **conduire** **lead| drive**
vb
[kɔ̃dɥiʁ]
Le SPT passe donc au crible tous les éléments susceptibles de conduire à la torture ou d'autres peines ou traitements cruels, inhumains ou dégradants.
-The SPT subjects to scrutiny any and all such factors which may conduce to torture or other cruel, inhuman or degrading treatment or punishment.

733 **américain** **American**
adj
[ameʁikɛ̃]
Il a été choisi comme joueur américain par excellence et joueur par excellence du circuit universitaire.
-He was selected as both the All-American and Academic All-American player.

734 **revenu** **income**
m
[ʁəvəny]
Je suis revenu de ce voyage enrichissant, rempli d'espoir de progrès durables.
-I returned from this rewarding visit feeling optimistic about longterm progress.

735 **justice** **justice| law**
f
[ʒystis]
Jill poursuivait sa propre mère en justice.
-Jill sued her own mother.

736 **soldat** **soldier**
m
[sɔlda]
Jack n'est pas un vrai soldat.
-Jack is not a true soldier.

737 **expérience** **experience**
f
[ɛkspeʁjɑ̃s]
Le Canada peut tirer des enseignements de l'expérience des autres et partager sa propre expérience.
-Canada can learn from the experience of others and share its own experience.

738 **cerveau** **brain| brains**

	m	La structure du cerveau est compliquée.
	[sɛʁvo]	-The structure of the brain is complicated.
739	**quartier**	**neighborhood| district**
	m	Un lieu moderne et fonctionnel pour vos réunions au coeur du nouveau
	[kaʁtje]	Quartier Européen.
		-The modern and functional meeting place in the heart of the European
		Quarter.
740	**prince**	**prince**
	m	Son Altesse royale le Prince Willem, Prince des Pays-Bas, s'adresse à la
	[pʁɛ̃s]	Commission.
		-His Royal Highness Prince Willem, Prince of the Netherlands, addressed
		the Commission.
741	**riche**	**rich; rich person**
	adj; m/f	Je préfère être un riche inconnu.
	[ʁiʃ]	-I'd rather be the rich guy that nobody knows about.
742	**fleur**	**flower**
	f	Tu connais la jolie petite fleur.
	[flœʁ]	-You were familiar with the pretty little flower.
743	**présenter**	**present| offer**
	vb	J'admire toujours ceux qui peuvent présenter quelque chose d'impossible à
	[pʁezɑ̃te]	présenter.
		-I always admire those who can introduce that which is unintroducible.
744	**presse**	**press**
	f	L'entreprise a publié un communiqué de presse.
	[pʁɛs]	-The company issued a press release.
745	**ridicule**	**ridiculous; ridicule**
	adj; m	C'est la chose la plus ridicule que j'aie jamais entendue.
	[ʁidikyl]	-That's the most ridiculous thing I've ever heard.
746	**preuve**	**evidence| proof**
	f	Or, la preuve testimoniale est la preuve naturelle des faits récents.
	[pʁœv]	-Now, testimonial evidence is the natural evidence of recent events.
747	**épouser**	**marry**
	vb	De plus, les veuves ne sont pas obligées d'épouser le frère du mari décédé.
	[epuze]	-Furthermore, widows are not obliged to marry the deceased husband's
		brother.
748	**intéressant**	**interesting**
	adj	Époque ô combien intéressante, et un effet secondaire intéressant pour notre
	[ɛ̃teʁesɑ̃]	rapport.
		-Interesting times, and an interesting side-effect to our report.
749	**gosse**	**kid| brat; kiddy**
	m/f; adj	Quel sale gosse !
	[gɔs]	-What a horrible brat!
750	**rose**	**pink; rose**
	adj; f	Nous regardions une belle rose.
	[ʁoz]	-We were looking at a beautiful rose.
751	**nature**	**nature**
	f	La nature ne fait rien en vain.
	[natyʁ]	-Nature does nothing in vain.
752	**vide**	**empty; empty**

	adj; m	Elle laisse un vide que la Commission doit combler, et non le Parlement.
	[vid]	-It leaves an emptiness to be filled not by this Parliament but by the Commission.
753	**responsable**	**responsible; person responsible**
	adj; m/f	Vous serez tenu pour responsable des irrégularités.
	[ʁɛspɔ̃sabl]	-Should there be any irregularities, you'll be held responsible.
754	**courage**	**courage**
	m	Je ne pouvais qu'admirer son courage.
	[kuʁaʒ]	-I could not but admire his courage.
755	**capable**	**capable| competent**
	adj	Personne n'a été capable de coordonner la procédure, et celle-ci a été abandonnée.
	[kapabl]	-No one was able to coordinate the proceedings and it was effectively broken up.
756	**cinéma**	**cinema**
	m	J'aime aller au cinéma.
	[sinema]	-I like going to the movies.
757	**décision**	**decision**
	f	C'est leur décision, une décision qui n'appartient qu'à eux et que nous respecterons.
	[desizjɔ̃]	-It is their decision, their decision alone and we will respect that decision.
758	**taxi**	**taxi**
	m	Prenez un taxi pour cette adresse.
	[taksi]	-All right, get a taxi, to that address.
759	**chanter**	**sing**
	vb	Mais pour chanter de belles choses... et les faire croire aux gens.
	[ʃɑ̃te]	-But to sing beautiful things... and make people believe them.
760	**excuser**	**excuse| forgive**
	vb	D'avance, je vous prie de m'excuser si parfois la traduction n'est pas parfaite.
	[ɛkskyze]	-So please excuse me if occasionally the translation is not perfect.
761	**fier**	**proud**
	adj	Il est devenu un fier Canadien tout en demeurant fier de son patrimoine italien.
	[fjɛʁ]	-He became a proud Canadian who remained equally proud of his Italian heritage.
762	**deuxième**	**second**
	num	L'incidence est la deuxième la plus élevée en Europe, la première étant en Italie.
	[døzjɛm]	-Incidence is the second highest in Europe, second to Italy which tops the list.
763	**appartement**	**apartment**
	m	Il m'a été très difficile de trouver ton appartement.
	[apaʁtəmɑ̃]	-It was very hard for me to find your appartment.
764	**contact**	**contact**
	m	Prenez contact avec moi dès que vous arrivez ici.
	[kɔ̃takt]	-Get in contact with me as soon as you arrive here.
765	**cacher**	**hide| conceal**
	vb	Ils veulent cacher la façon dont ils forcent les leurs à voter et à gouverner.
	[kaʃe]	-They want to hide the way they are forcing their MPs to vote and govern.
766	**répondre**	**answer**

	vb	
	[ʁepɔ̃dʁ]	Il reste du temps au ministre des Finances s'il veut répondre à la question. -The finance minister still has time if he would like to answer the question.
767	**manière**	**way| form**
	f	Les données à discuter ci-dessous ont été collectées de la manière suivante.
	[manjɛʁ]	-The data to be discussed below was collected in the following way.
768	**jambe**	**leg**
	f	Attendre au moins trente minutes entre deux essais consécutifs sur la même
	[ʒɑ̃b]	jambe. -Allow a period of at least 30 minutes between successive tests on the same leg.
769	**occasion**	**opportunity| occasion**
	f	J'ai trouvé ce livre par hasard dans une librairie qui vend des livres
	[ɔkazjɔ̃]	d'occasion. -I found this book by chance in a secondhand bookstore.
770	**défense**	**defense| prohibition**
	f	La vie du prisonnier et de sa fille sans défense est menacée par un infernal
	[defɑ̃s]	complot. -The life of the prisoner and of his defenceless daughter is threatened by a diabolical plot.
771	**longue**	**long**
	adj	La Colombie a une longue tradition de solutions négociées avec les groupes
	[lɔ̃g]	armés. -Colombia has had a generous tradition of negotiated solutions with armed groups.
772	**Jésus**	**Jesus**
	m	Jésus est comme Dieu le Père, et Dieu le Père est comme Jésus, le Fils.
	[ʒezy]	-Jesus is like God the Father and God the Father is like Jesus the Son.
773	**jeté**	**thrown**
	adj	Trois jours plus tard, il a été jeté dans l'océan par les services de sécurité.
	[ʒəte]	-After three days, he was thrown into the ocean by the security services.
774	**formidable**	**tremendous| fantastic**
	adj	Ne serait -il pas formidable de pouvoir faire la même chose avec les armes?
	[fɔʁmidabl]	-Would it not be marvellous if we could do the same with weapons?
775	**base**	**base| basis**
	f	Il fut condamné sur la base d'accusations inventées de toutes pièces.
	[baz]	-He was convicted on the basis of entirely made-up charges.
776	**glacer**	**glaze| freeze**
	vb	Speaker, yesterday Cape Bretoners gathered in Glace Bay.
	[glase]	-Monsieur le Président, hier, les habitants du Cap-Breton se sont réunis à Glace Bay.
777	**dent**	**tooth**
	f	Tu devrais aller chez le dentiste te faire extraire cette dent.
	[dɑ̃]	-You should go to the dentist and have that tooth pulled out.
778	**parmi**	**among**
	prp	Parmi les hommes, cette catégorie représente 84 % et parmi les femmes 81
	[paʁmi]	%. -Among men, this category of workers amounts to 84%, and among women 81%.
779	**immédiatement**	**immediately**
	adv	Ceux-ci ne seraient pas immédiatement rééligibles à l'expiration de leur
	[imedjatmɑ̃]	mandat.

-They would not be eligible for immediate re-election at the end of their terms.

780 paie — **pay| payroll**
f
[pɛ]
Les Canadiens devraient payer des impôts en fonction de leur capacité d'en payer.
-Canadians should pay taxes consistent with their capacity to pay.

781 machiner — **engineer**
vb
[maʃine]
Only specialized technicians and facilities should saw, machine, heat, melt or incinerate the material.
-Seuls des techniciens spécialisés, opérant dans des installations prévues à cet effet, doivent scier, usiner, chauffer, fondre ou incinérer ce matériau.

782 vacance — **vacancy**
f
[vakãs]
La vacance du poste de coordinateur anti-terroriste de l'Union est intolérable.
-The vacancy of the post of EU anti-terrorist coordinator is unacceptable.

783 monstre — **monster; monstrous**
m; adj
[mõstʁ]
L'être humain est un monstre.
-Humans are monsters.

784 tueur — **killer**
m
[tɥœʁ]
Jack est un tueur professionnel.
-Jack is a professional killer.

785 naître — **be born**
vb
[nɛtʁ]
Ces droits peuvent naître en cas d'insolvabilité de l'acheteur.
-Reclamation claims may arise in the case of the insolvency of the buyer.

786 français — **French; French**
adj; m|mpl
[fʁãsɛ]
Comme leur conversation était en français, je ne pouvais pas en comprendre un mot.
-As their conversation was in French, I could not understand a word.

787 course — **race| running**
f
[kuʁs]
La course spatiale fut une période excitante de l'histoire.
-The space race was an exciting time in history.

788 majesté — **majesty**
f
[maʒɛste]
Sa Majesté a-t-elle bien dormie ?
-Has her Highness slept well?

789 mien — **mine**
adj
[mjɛ̃]
Cependant, pour un pays comme le mien, ce document est d'une importance majeure.
-For a country like mine this document is, however, an extremely important one.

790 type — **type| guy**
m
[tip]
Ce type mérite une médaille.
-This guy deserves a medal.

791 certainement — **definitely**
adv
[sɛʁtɛnmã]
Il y a certainement quelques points qui méritent réflexion.
-There are certainly some points worth considering.

792 couper — **cut**
vb
[kupe]
Il est également possible de couper une lisière longitudinale.
-A longitudinal edge of the length of material can also be cut off.

793 Ha! — **Ha!**
int
[a!]
Ha! sur le genre de programmation déjà offerte par Radio-Canada ou TQS par exemple.

-Ha! might have had on the type of programming already available from Radio-Canada or TQS, for example.

794	**importance** f [ɛ̃pɔʁtɑ̃s]	**importance| significance** Ne perdez jamais de vue l'importance d'un beau lever de soleil, ou de regarder vos enfants dormir, ou de l'odeur de la pluie. Ce sont souvent les petites choses qui importent vraiment dans la vie. -Never lose sight of the importance of a beautiful sunrise, or watching your kids sleep, or the smell of rain. It's often the small things that really matter in life.
795	**ouest** adj; m [wɛst]	**west; west** Le Nord-Ouest, l'Ouest et la région de Shannon affichent la croissance la plus faible. -The north-west, the west and the Shannon regions are displaying the weakest growth.
796	**chat** m [ʃa]	**cat** Le chat est-il sur ou sous la chaise? -Is the cat on or under the chair?
797	**dégager** vb [degaʒe]	**free** En s'arrêtant, les bateaux doivent dégager le chenal autant que possible. -When stopping, vessels shall keep clear as far as possible of the channel.
798	**ravir** vb [ʁaviʁ]	**delight| ravish** Monsieur le Président, la peine de mort est immorale parce que des personnes ne peuvent ravir la vie à d'autres. -Mr President, the death penalty is unethical because it is wrong to ravish someone else's life.
799	**joie** f [ʒwa]	**joy** Il a partagé ma joie. -He shared in my happiness.
800	**prévu** adj [pʁevy]	**planned** S'agissant de l'industrialisation, le taux de croissance prévu en 2001 est de 3 %. -With regard to industrialization, a 3 per cent growth rate was projected for 2001.
801	**lorsque** prp [lɔʁsk]	**during** Facile, lorsque votre adversaire est un ancien terroriste. -Well, it helps when your only real rival is a convicted terrorist.
802	**superbe** adj [sypɛʁb]	**superb; stunner** Les Jeux enrichissent la civilisation humaine dans toute sa superbe diversité culturelle. -The Games have enriched human civilization in all of its beautiful cultural diversity.
803	**bain** m [bɛ̃]	**bath** Nous aimerions une chambre double avec bain. -We'd like a double room with a bath.
804	**horrible** adj [ɔʁibl]	**horrible** Monsieur le Président, 40 officiers et soldats ont assisté à ce spectacle horrible. -Mr President, 40 other officers and soldiers witnessed this horrible sight.
805	**court** adj; m [kuʁ]	**short| brief; court** La présente invention permet le mécanisme de notification de message court en itinérance.

-The present invention enables the short message notification mechanism in roaming.

806	**déranger**	**disturb| disrupt**
	vb	Pardon de vous déranger, mais il s'est passé une chose bizarre.
	[deʁɑ̃ʒe]	-I 'm sorry to bother you, but something rather odd just happened.
807	**bombe**	**bomb**
	f	Il faudra deux heures pour désamorcer la bombe.
	[bɔ̃b]	-It'll take Phelps' team two hours to dismantle that bomb.
808	**ramener**	**bring back**
	vb	Ramener sa consommation de bromure de méthyle de 11,1 tonnes ODP en 2004 à :
	[ʁamne]	-To reduce methyl bromide consumption from 11.1 ODP-tonnes in 2004 as follows:
809	**réalité**	**reality**
	f	Réalité statistique, elle n'est pas encore une réalité du quotidien des populations d'Afrique.
	[ʁealite]	-A statistical reality, it is not yet an everyday reality for Africa's populations.
810	**enquêter**	**investigate**
	vb	Puis-je demander à M. Füle de mener une enquête sur les crimes d'honneur en Turquie ?
	[ɑ̃kete]	-Can we ask Mr Füle to carry out an investigation into honour killings in Turkey?
811	**camion**	**truck| lorry**
	m	Le lapin se tenait au milieu de la route, hypnotisé par les phares du camion qui arrivait.
	[kamjɔ̃]	-The rabbit stood in the middle of the road, mesmerized by the lights of the oncoming truck.
812	**signifier**	**mean| imply**
	vb	Une politique économique coordonnée à l'échelle de l'Union ne saurait signifier la même politique économique.
	[siɲifje]	-A coordinated economic policy in the Union cannot mean the same economic policy.
813	**cent**	**cent| hundred**
	m; num	Elle détient dix pour cent des parts de l'entreprise.
	[sɑ̃]	-She has a 10 percent interest in the company.
814	**rencontre**	**meeting| match**
	f	Et une seule rencontre me suffit.
	[ʁɑ̃kɔ̃tʁ]	-And the one encounter was more than enough.
815	**excellent**	**excellent**
	adj	Notre rapporteur a fait un excellent travail et d'excellentes propositions.
	[ɛksɛlɑ̃]	-The rapporteur has done an excellent job and has produced some excellent proposals.
816	**respect**	**respect**
	m	Avec tout le respect que je vous dois, Monsieur le Président, vous êtes un trou du cul !
	[ʁɛspɛ]	-With all due respect, Mr. President, you are an asshole!
817	**terrain**	**field| ground**
	m	Un groupe de jeunes hommes jouent au handball sur le terrain de jeu.
	[teʁɛ̃]	-A group of young men are playing handball in the playground.
818	**projet**	**project**

m
[pʁɔʒɛ]

Je voudrais porter ce toast à tous ceux qui ont donné de leur temps à ce projet. Je les remercie chaleureusement.
-I would like to make this toast to all those who have given their time to this project. I thank them warmly.

819 **éviter**

vb
[evite]

avoid| save

Je préférerais éviter de parler politique.
-I'd rather avoid saying anything about politics.

820 **poisson**

m
[pwasɔ̃]

fish

Le saumon est mon poisson préféré.
-My favorite fish is salmon.

821 **empêcher**

vb
[ɑ̃peʃe]

prevent| stop

Le temps est enfin venu où l' imprimerie de l' État ne peut plus empêcher nos publications.
-At long last, the state printing office can no longer prevent our publications.

822 **envers**

m
[ɑ̃vɛʁ]

back| against

Appelons un chat un chat ; la politique d'Israël envers les Arabo-palestiniens n' est pas raciste.
-Let's call a spade a spade, and Israel's policies against Palestinian Arabs isn't racism.

823 **kilomètre**

m
[kilɔmɛtʁ]

kilometer

La densité de la population est estimée à plus de 300 habitants par kilomètre carré.
-Population density is estimated at over 300 persons per square kilometer.

824 **ange**

m
[ɑ̃ʒ]

angel

Le bébé qui dort dans la poussette est mignon comme un ange.
-The baby sleeping in the baby carriage is as cute as an angel.

825 **chaussure**

f
[ʃosyʁ]

shoe

Il faudrait donc satisfaire soit aux prescriptions «avec chaussure» soit aux prescriptions «sans chaussure».
-It should either meet "with shoe" requirements or "without shoe" requirements.

826 **dossier**

m
[dosje]

folder| file

Si tu pouvais regarder mon dossier.
-I'd like you to look at my case.

827 **animal**

adj; m
[animal]

animal; animal

En Inde, la vache est un animal sacré.
-In India, the cow is a sacred animal.

828 **langue**

f
[lɑ̃g]

language

Leur langue maternelle est le romani vlax et leur deuxième langue, le français.
-Their native language is Vlax Romanes, their second language is French.

829 **imbécile**

m/f; adj
[ɛ̃besil]

imbecile; stupid

Tue-le, imbécile !
-Kill him, you imbecile!

830 **princesse**

f
[pʁɛ̃sɛs]

princess

Il reste toutefois exclu que la Princesse Aiko puisse un jour devenir impératrice.
-There was, however, no possibility that Princess Aiko would one day become an empress.

831 **droguer**

drug

vb
[dʁɔge]

Elle déclare, dans son exposé des motifs - je cite - que "dans un monde idéal, personne n'aurait besoin de se droguer.
-She says in her explanation, and I quote: 'In an ideal world, people wouldn't need to drug themselves'.

832 charge
f
[ʃaʁʒ]

load| charge
Cette charge peut être en particulier un moteur asynchrone polyphasé.
-The load may, in particular, be a multi-phase asynchronous motor.

833 nourriture
f
[nuʁityʁ]

food| feed
La consommation de nourriture délicieuse est l'un des plaisirs de la vie les plus intenses et poignants.
-The eating of delicious food is one of the most intense and poignant pleasures of life.

834 pont
m
[pɔ̃]

bridge
Aucun d'entre nous ne put arriver au pont à temps.
-None of us could arrive at the harbor on time.

835 refuser
vb
[ʁəfyze]

refuse
Cela revient à refuser une Europe sociale, à refuser la politique commune pour les travailleurs.
-That is to refuse a social Europe, to refuse the common policy for the workers.

836 contraire
adj; m
[kɔ̃tʁɛʁ]

contrary; contrary
Ce serait contraire à l'éthique.
-That would be unethical.

837 enchanter
vb
[ɑ̃ʃɑ̃te]

enchant| rejoice
Avec ces spectacles et de nombreux autres, le festival a de quoi enchanter et divertir les amateurs de théâtre.
-The festival has these and many other plays to delight and enchant theatre buffs.

838 douleur
f
[dulœʁ]

pain
Ces enfants leur rappellent quotidiennement leur douleur et leurs souffrances.
-These children are a daily reminder of their pain and suffering.

839 politique
f; adj
[pɔlitik]

policy; political
On s'attend à ce que le président propose une nouvelle politique énergétique.
-The president is expected to put forward a new energy policy.

840 fait
m; adj
[fɛ]

fact; ripe
C'est plus que cela: il s'agit d'un fait établi et de la reconnaissance de ce fait.
-More than this, it is a known fact and recognition of this fact.

841 magasin
m
[magazɛ̃]

store| shop
Le petit magasin du coin ou du village fait partie de la qualité de vie européenne.
-The small shop on the corner or in a village is part of European quality of life.

842 entier
adj
[ɑ̃tje]

whole| full
Si 50 % de ce nombre ne correspondent pas à un nombre entier, le nombre entier de blocs immédiatement supérieur.
-If 50 per cent of that number of blocks is a whole number and a fraction, the next higher whole number of the blocks.

843 chapeau

hat

m

[ʃapo]

Ce chapeau est trop petit pour vous.

-It is too small a hat for you.

844 raconter

vb

[ʁakɔ̃te]

tell

L'un d'entre vous a raconté une anecdote, on pourrait en raconter beaucoup plus.

-One of you had a story to tell about this, and I am sure we could all tell more.

845 discuter

vb

[diskyte]

discuss

Si nous ne discutons pas de faits, nous devrons discuter de rumeurs.

-If we do not discuss facts then we will have to discuss rumours.

846 papier

m

[papje]

paper

Je veux votre papier sur mon bureau d'ici lundi.

-Have your paper on my desk by Monday.

847 action

f

[aksjɔ̃]

action| effort

Malheureusement, son action manque de résultats concrets.

-Sadly, however, her effort is short on specific achievements.

848 permettre

vb

[pɛʁmɛtʁ]

allow| enable

Nous devons permettre aux petites et moyennes entreprises de faire entendre leur voix.

-We must allow the voice of small and medium-sized businesses to be heard.

849 rapide

adj; m

[ʁapid]

fast| rapid; rapid

Elle est rapide en tout.

-She is quick at everything.

850 shérif

m

[ʃeʁif]

sheriff

On joue au cowboy et aux Indiens ? Je me proclame shérif et vous devez tous m'obéir.

-Shall we play cowboy and Indians? I declare myself a sheriff, and you all must obey me.

851 frais

mpl; adj

[fʁɛ]

costs; fresh

La vue du homard frais me donna de l'appétit.

-The sight of fresh lobster gave me an appetite.

852 réunion

f

[ʁeynjɔ̃]

meeting| reunion

Quand la réunion s'est-elle terminée ?

-When did the meeting end?

853 île

f

[il]

island

Si vous voulez aller sur la mer, sans aucun risque de chavirer, alors n'achetez pas un bateau : achetez une île !

-If you want to go at sea without any risk of capsizing, then don't buy a boat: buy an island!

854 toilette

f

[twalɛt]

toilet

Ma femme a l'étrange habitude de barboter des paquets de papier toilette des toilettes publiques.

-My wife has the strange habit of pilfering wads of toilet paper from public restrooms.

855 opération

f

[ɔpeʁasjɔ̃]

operation

Cette opération au Congo n'est pas uniquement une opération de maintien de la paix.

-This operation in the Congo is not just a peace-keeping operation.

856 spécial

special

adj
[spesjal]

La Sierra Leone est tout à fait en faveur de l'idée de créer un comité spécial.
-In that context, it fully supported the proposal to convene a special committee.

857 **planète** — planet

f
[planɛt]

En seulement huit ans, nous avons diminué de moitié notre dépendance au pétrole étranger; nous avons doublé notre énergie renouvelable; et nous avons mené le monde à un accord qui promet de sauver la planète.
-In just eight years, we've halved our dependence on foreign oil; we've doubled our renewable energy; we've led the world to an agreement that has the promise to save this planet.

858 **champ** — field

m
[ʃɑ̃]

Minimiser la circulation dans un champ.
-Minimize the amount of traffic on a field.

859 **couleur** — color

f
[kulœʁ]

De quelle couleur sont-ils?
-What color are they?

860 **pain** — bread

m
[pɛ̃]

Le pain a durci.
-The bread went hard.

861 **destin** — destiny

m
[dɛstɛ̃]

L' Europe ne peut être un jouet du destin, d' un destin dessiné par d' autres.
-Europe cannot be a plaything of destiny, a destiny plotted by others.

862 **découvrir** — discover

vb
[dekuvʁiʁ]

C'est bien entendu de découvrir l'intention des parties et non quelque chose d'autre.
-Surely, it is to discover the intention of the parties and not something else.

863 **puisque** — since

con
[pɥisk]

Le Japon préfère que l'article soit placé dans le chapitre premier de la première partie puisque « l'article 39 vaut pour l'ensemble du projet ».
-Japan is in favour of placing the article in Part One, Chapter I "[a]s article 39 is related to the draft articles as a whole".

864 **tailler** — cut| carve

vb
[taje]

Elle doit aussi se tailler une place sur le marché en expansion rapide des technologies de l'environnement.
-It must also carve itself a niche in the rapidly expanding market of environmental technologies.

865 **vaisseau** — vessel

m
[vɛso]

Ils se concentrent maintenant sur le vaisseau, sans résultat.
-They're now concentrating on the ship itself, so far with no results.

866 **sexe** — sex| gender

m
[sɛks]

La collecte des données par sexe et les données ventilées par sexe laissent à désirer;
-Data collection on gender as well as existing gender-specific data have their limitations.

867 **sacré** — sacred

adj
[sakʁe]

L'équipage qui aura accumulé les meilleurs temps sera sacré Champion de l'Odyssée.
-The team with the best cumulative time will be named sacred World Sky Champion.

868 **repas** — meal

m
[ʁəpa]

Comment éviter de grignoter entre les repas ?
-How do you avoid grazing between meals?

869 contrat

m
[kɔ̃tʁa]

contract

J'ai conclu le contrat.
-I made the deal.

870 nécessaire

adj
[neseseʁ]

necessary

Il est nécessaire qu'un tel ordre existe, comme il est nécessaire qu'il y ait des lois.
-It is necessary that such an order exist, just as it is necessary that there be laws.

871 client

m
[klijɑ̃]

customer| client

Vous avez attrapé le mauvais client !
-You've got the wrong client!

872 détruire

vb
[detʁɥiʁ]

destroy

Suggérer autrement, toutefois, pourrait détruire le message et le messager.
-To suggest otherwise, however, could destroy the message of the messenger.

873 lait

m
[lɛ]

milk

Jack boit du lait tous les matins.
-Jack drinks milk every morning.

874 mémoire

m; f
[memwaʁ]

dissertation; memory

Vous avez une bonne mémoire.
-You've got a great memory.

875 pleurer

vb
[plœʁe]

cry| mourn

Monseigneur, le temps viendra de pleurer Boromir mais pas maintenant.
-My lord, there will be a time to grieve for Boromir...... but it is not now.

876 copain

m; adj
[kɔpɛ̃]

boyfriend| buddy; pally

Je ne veux pas de petit copain.
-I don't want a boyfriend.

877 reste

m
[ʁɛst]

rest| remainder

Il ne nous reste que trois jours de plus.
-We've only got three more days remaining.

878 personnel

m; adj
[pɛʁsɔnɛl]

staff| personnel; personal

Les travailleurs étrangers représentent 30% du personnel de son entreprise.
-Foreign workers make up 30% of his company.

879 doubler

vb
[duble]

double

Let us double or triple the number of inspectors and open up more regional offices.
-Doublons, triplons le nombre des inspecteurs et ouvrons de nouveaux bureaux régionaux.

880 mignon

adj
[miɲɔ̃]

cute| sweet

Denny, tu es mignon en rose.
-Denny, you look pretty in pink.

881 couteau

m
[kuto]

knife

Il manque un couteau.
-There is a knife missing.

882 témoin

m
[temwɛ̃]

witness

Il a été témoin de l'accident.
-He witnessed the accident.

883 foi

faith

f
[fwa]

En effet, les uvres sont sa «foi agissante», tandis que sa parole est sa «foi éloquente».
-Actions, in fact, are his "active faith", while words are his "eloquent faith".

884 **remercier**

thank

vb
[ʁəmɛʁsje]

De ce point de vue, nous devons remercier le rapporteur pour son excellent travail.
-In this connection I have to thank the rapporteur for her excellent work.

885 **direction**

direction| management

f
[diʁɛksjɔ̃]

La flèche indique la direction de Tokyo.
-The arrow indicates the way to Tokyo.

886 **malin**

malignant| smart; evil

adj; m
[malɛ̃]

S'il est capable de foirer un truc pareil, c'est qu'il n'est pas bien malin.
-He can't be smart if he can screw up something like that.

887 **niveau**

level

m
[nivo]

Le niveau de la rivière s'est élevé.
-The river's water level has risen.

888 **remettre**

deliver| return

vb
[ʁəmɛtʁ]

Le Parlement espère le revitaliser, le renforcer et le remettre sur la bonne voie.
-Parliament hopes to reinvigorate and strengthen them and get them back on track.

889 **habiter**

live in| inhabit

vb
[abite]

Les groupes arabes continuent d'habiter cette région et d'y cultiver les terres.
-The Arab groups continue to inhabit and plant crops in the area.

890 **apporter**

bring

vb
[apɔʁte]

Telles sont, en somme, les expériences vécues que nous pouvons apporter au Conseil.
-These are, in a nutshell, the experiences we can bring before the Council.

891 **procès**

trial| process

m
[pʁɔsɛ]

A ce procès, le juge est très respecté.
-At this trial, the judge is very respected.

892 **doux**

soft| sweet

adj
[du]

Climat tempéré : printemps et automne doux, été chaud, hiver froid et neigeux.
-Moderate climate: mild spring and autumn, hot summer, cold, snowy winters.

893 **solution**

solution

f
[sɔlysjɔ̃]

Nous différions quant à la solution au problème.
-We differed as to the solution to the problem.

894 **fermer**

close

vb
[fɛʁme]

Des entreprises manufacturières et minières ont été complètement pillées et ont dû fermer.
-Manufacturing and mining concerns were severely looted, forcing them to close operations.

895 **goût**

taste| flavor

m
[gu]

C'est une question de goût et il en va de même pour tous les autres.
-It is a matter of flavour, and that goes for the others as well.

896 **amuser**

amuse| entertain

vb
[amyze]

Des grimaces pour amuser les enfants.
-Funny faces to amuse the children.

897 **différence**

difference

f
[difeʁɑ̃s]

La seule différence entre une mauvaise cuisinière et une empoisonneuse, c'est l'intention.
-The only difference between a bad cook and a poisoner is the intent.

898 stop | **stop**

m
[sto]

Nourrice je t'en prie, stop.
-Nurse, I pray you, stop.

899 réfléchir | **reflect| think**

vb
[ʁefleʃiʁ]

J'ajouterais "réflexion" car nous devons réfléchir avant d'effectuer toute expérience.
-I would add reflection - we ought to reflect before every experiment is carried out.

900 enceinte | **pregnant; enclosure**

adj; f
[ɑ̃sɛ̃t]

Il est interdit aux étudiants de fumer dans l'enceinte de l'école.
-Students are forbidden to smoke on the school grounds.

901 université | **university**

f
[ynivɛʁsite]

La bibliothèque de l'Université de Genève a une bonne salle de lecture.
-The Geneva University Library has a good reading room.

902 bleu | **blue; blue**

adj; m
[blø]

J'aime le bleu.
-I like blue.

903 mètre | **meter**

m
[mɛtʁ]

Le tissu de ma robe coûte 10 euros le mètre.
-The price of my dress' fabric is 10 Euros per meter.

904 mentir | **lie**

vb
[mɑ̃tiʁ]

Alors avant de mentir à propos du mensonge, du mensonge, du mensonge... de ton mensonge...
-Then before lying about the lie, of the lie, of the lie... of your lie...

905 courir | **run| race**

vb
[kuʁiʁ]

J'ai vu de petits animaux courir dans tous les sens.
-I saw some small animals running away in all directions.

906 arranger | **arrange**

vb
[aʁɑ̃ʒe]

Peut-être pouvons-nous arranger que la discussion d'aujourd'hui soit poursuivie mardi prochain.
-It may be possible to arrange for us to continue today's discussion next Tuesday.

907 officier | **officer**

m
[ɔfisje]

Un officier de police a subi des blessures mineures.
-One police officer suffered minor injuries.

908 espace | **space**

m
[ɛspas]

De l'espace, la Terre a l'air plutôt petite.
-From space, the earth looks quite small.

909 sourire | **smile; smile**

m; vb
[suʁiʁ]

Il reste là avec un grand sourire énigmatique chaque fois que nous abordons ce sujet.
-He sits over there with a big cheshire cat grin on his face every time we debate this.

910 mérite | **merit| worth**

m
[meʁit]

Le mérite vous en revient, il en revient à la Présidence française.
-That is to your credit, to the credit of the French Presidency.

911 accepter | **accept**

	vb [aksɛpte]	Nous ne pouvons accepter l'amendement 8 car nous avons accepté l'amendement 9. -We cannot accept Amendment No 8 because we accept Amendment No 9.
912	**failli** adj; m [faji]	**bankrupt** On aide le failli à retrouver son amour-propre et la détermination à retenter sa chance. -The bankrupt will be helped to recover his self-esteem and the determination to try again.
913	**Angleterre** m [ãglətɛʁ]	**England** L'Angleterre a évolué depuis lors - grand Dieu, même l'Angleterre a évolué ! -Britain has moved on since then – heavens, even England has moved on!
914	**vitesse** f [vitɛs]	**speed** Il y a de grosses différences de vitesse et de qualité de haut débit d'un pays à l'autre. -There are big differences in broadband speed and quality from country to country.
915	**caméra** f [kameʁa]	**camera** Par hasard, il a trouvé la caméra qu'il avait perdue. -He found his lost camera by chance.
916	**arbre** m [aʁbʁ]	**tree| shaft** Tu t'es caché derrière l'arbre. -You hid behind the tree.
917	**trésor** m [tʁezɔʁ]	**treasure| treasury** Les pirates ont enfoui leur trésor sous terre. -The pirates buried their treasure in the ground.
918	**énergie** f [enɛʁʒi]	**energy** Il s'est vidé de son énergie. -He has run out of his energy.
919	**énorme** adj [enɔʁm]	**huge| enormous** Certains ont parlé de montagnes, mais ils vont nous amener à des sommets à la manière d'un Sisyphe qui poussait un énorme rocher sur la montagne. -I heard people talking about mountains, but they are going to take us up mountains in the same way as Sisyphus pushing a great big rock up the mountain.
920	**appartenir** vb [apaʁtəniʁ]	**behove** La culture de la paix est globale, et il nous appartient à tous de trouver des manières d'apporter notre aide. -The culture of peace is all-embracing, and it behooves us all to find ways in which we can help.
921	**préparer** vb [pʁepaʁe]	**prepare| make** Cela permettra à nos forces de se préparer à assumer la sécurité de notre nation. -It will enable our forces to ready themselves to take on our nation's security.
922	**regretter** vb [ʁəgʁete]	**regret| miss** Voilà qui me fait d' autant plus regretter l' absence du commissaire à ce débat. -That is why I regret the Commissioner' s absence from this debate all the more.
923	**finalement**	**finally**

adv
[finalmɑ̃]

L'intérêt pour les questions européennes croît finalement un peu partout en Europe.
-There is clearly now at last an increasing interest in EU issues around Europe.

924 **inviter**

vb
[ɛ̃vite]

invite| ask

On aimerait t'inviter à déjeuner.
-We'd like to invite you to lunch.

925 **moindre**

adj
[mwɛ̃dʁ]

lesser

C'est la moindre des choses si nous voulons protéger et les patients et les travailleurs.
-That is the very least that is required in order to protect patients and workers.

926 **image**

f
[imaʒ]

image

Les conflits dans la région ont sapé l'image des femmes dans la mémoire collective.
-The conflicts in the region have undermined the image of women in the collective memory.

927 **justement**

adv
[ʒystəmɑ̃]

rightly| exactly

L'objectif consiste justement à obtenir un effet préventif de cette confrontation.
-It is precisely the intention that confrontation should have a preventive effect.

928 **enlever**

vb
[ɑ̃lve]

remove| take off

Car c'est leurs moyens de défense qu'on est en train de leur enlever un par un.
-For it is their very means of defence which are being eliminated one by one.

929 **chasse**

f
[ʃas]

hunting| chase

Le rire, c'est le soleil, il chasse l'hiver du visage humain.
-Laughter is the sun that drives winter from the human face.

930 **unique**

adj
[ynik]

unique

C'est un événement unique, une chance unique, et par conséquent une responsabilité unique.
-This is a unique event, a unique opportunity, and therefore a unique responsibility.

931 **arrêt**

m
[aʁɛ]

stop| stopping

Il est arrivé à l'arrêt, pour s'apercevoir que le car était parti.
-Getting to the bus stop, he found the bus had left.

932 **filer**

vb
[file]

spin| run

Suivez mon conseil et laissez filer.
-So take my advice and let this go.

933 **balle**

f
[bal]

ball| bullet

Nous gardons un œil sur la balle et nous suivrons la situation sur le terrain.
-We are keeping an eye on the ball and will follow the situation on the ground.

934 **dimanche**

m
[dimɑ̃ʃ]

Sunday

Dimanche prochain, le processus électoral parlementaire au Liban sera achevé.
-This coming Sunday, the parliamentary electoral process in Lebanon will be completed.

935 **lycée**

high school

	m	Quand j'étais au lycée, j'avais l'habitude de me faire de l'argent de poche en gardant des enfants.
	[lise]	-When I was in high school, I used to earn extra money babysitting.
936	**fil**	**thread| lead**
	m	J'ai besoin d'un nouveau fil USB.
	[fil]	-I need a new USB cable.
937	**morceau**	**piece| track**
	m	Je veux que chacun de vous prenne un morceau de papier et écrive ce qui s'est passé.
	[mɔʁso]	-I want each of you to take out a piece of paper and write down what happened.
938	**durant**	**during**
	prp	Durant le premier mandat, ceci s'est traduit par des résultats concrets.
	[dyʁɑ̃]	-Over the course of the first mandate this has translated into a number of concrete outcomes.
939	**casser**	**break| crack**
	vb	L'objectif recherché sur le fond est de casser les circonscriptions nationales.
	[kase]	-The intended objective of the content is to break up national constituencies.
940	**doigt**	**finger**
	m	Je n'ai jamais levé le petit doigt sur elle.
	[dwa]	-I never laid a finger on her.
941	**vérifier**	**check| verify**
	vb	Il est tout aussi important d'examiner et de vérifier les méthodes de travail du Conseil.
	[veʁifje]	-Equally importantly, we have to scrutinize and audit the working methods of the Council.
942	**appareil**	**apparatus**
	m	Elle lui acheta un appareil photo.
	[apaʁɛj]	-She bought him a camera.
943	**piste**	**track| runway**
	f	Vous êtes sur la bonne piste.
	[pist]	-You're on the right track.
944	**troisième**	**third**
	num	Le troisième est un rapport additionnel au second et au troisième rapports périodiques de la Tanzanie.
	[tʁwazjɛm]	-The third was a supplementary report to the second and third periodic reports of Tanzania.
945	**dépendre**	**depend**
	vb	L'approvisionnement de l'Europe en gaz ne peut dépendre des conflits entre la Russie et l'Ukraine.
	[depɑ̃dʁ]	-Gas supplies to Europe cannot depend on conflicts between Russia and Ukraine.
946	**programme**	**program| agenda**
	m	Ce projet de loi s'inscrit dans les politiques et le programme du gouvernement.
	[pʁogʁam]	-This bill is part of the government's policy and program.
947	**honnête**	**honest**
	adj	Il est tellement honnête que tout le monde lui fait confiance.
	[ɔnɛt]	-He is so honest that everybody trusts him.
948	**voiture**	**car| vehicle**

f
[vwatyʁ]

Je ne pense pas que mon père veuille nous prêter sa voiture.
-I don't think my father is willing to lend us the car.

949 **régler**
vb
[ʁegle]

adjust| settle

Il faudrait régler le problème du Moyen-Orient dans un esprit de réconciliation.
-The question of the Middle East should be resolved in a spirit of reconciliation.

950 **flinguer**
vb
[flɛ̃ge]

shoot| whack

Il va falloir flinguer notre serveur.
-Well you'll have to shoot our waiter.

951 **aveugle**
adj; m/f
[avœgl]

blinded; blind

Cela me permettait de recevoir une pension d'aveugle et m'autorisait à m'inscrire comme aveugle en Irlande.
-This qualified me for the blind person's pension and to be registered for blind in Ireland.

952 **présence**
f
[pʁezɑ̃s]

presence

Ne vous fiez pas aux gens qui font votre éloge en votre présence.
-Don't trust people who praise you in your presence.

953 **crise**
f
[kʁiz]

crisis| attack

Smith est mort d'une crise cardiaque.
-Smith died of a heart attack.

954 **amener**
vb
[amne]

bring| lead

C'est le prochain Parlement qui devra amener le processus à sa conclusion.
-It will be a matter for the next Parliament to bring the process to a conclusion.

955 **interdire**
vb
[ɛ̃tɛʁdiʁ]

prohibit| ban

Il s'agit d'interdire à l'avenir ce qu'on appelle l'abus de réformes juridiques.
-This is to do with future prohibition of what is termed the misuse of legal form.

956 **lever**
vb; m
[ləve]

lift| raise; rise

Ils leur manquent un idéal, une raison de se lever le matin.
-They lack an ideal, a reason to get up in the morning.

957 **obtenir**
vb
[ɔptəniʁ]

get| obtain

S'il pense qu'il peut obtenir mieux en conciliation, il n'a pas fini de penser !
-If it thinks it can get a better deal in conciliation, then it has another think coming!

958 **pluie**
f
[plɥi]

rain

La pluie ne déprime pas les gens qui aiment lire.
-Rain doesn't depress people who like reading.

959 **récupérer**
vb
[ʁekypeʁe]

recover

A-t-on l'intention d'essayer de récupérer l'argent au moyen de compensations ?
-Is there going to be any attempt to recover the money by way of compensation?

960 **prouver**
vb
[pʁuve]

prove

Auparavant, pour caractériser un délit, les femmes devaient prouver leur "honnêteté".
-Previously, in establishing a criminal act, a woman had to prove her "honesty".

961 **souris**

mouse

f
[suʁi]
Trois hommes ridiculisés par une souris.
-Three grown men... outsmarted by a mouse.

962 **restaurer** — **restore**

vb
[ʁɛstɔʁe]
Dans ce pays, il est virtuellement impossible de restaurer les édifices chrétiens.
-In that country, it is made virtually impossible to restore Christian buildings.

963 **regard** — **look| gaze**

m
[ʁəgaʁ]
Elle m'a lancé un regard significatif.
-She gave me a meaningful look.

964 **intention** — **intention| mind**

f
[ɛ̃tɑ̃sjɔ̃]
«Element of intent» est plus précis que «References to intent» (référence à l'intention).
-"Elements of intent" was more specific than "References to intent".

965 **cou** — **neck**

m
[ku]
Tu te casseras parfaitement le cou.
-And you'll get your neck exactly broken.

966 **proche** — **near; near; neighbor**

adj; adv; m
[pʁɔʃ]
Fakhreddin, important homme d'affaires, est un proche d'Omar Karamé, qui était alors Premier Ministre.
-Fakhreddin, a prominent businessman, is a close associate of then-Prime Minister Omar Karame.

967 **urgence** — **emergency**

f
[yʁʒɑ̃s]
Est-ce une urgence ?
-Is it an emergency?

968 **folie** — **madness| folly**

f
[fɔli]
Les hommes ne vous trouvent sage que lorsqu'on partage ou approuve leur folie.
-Men only think that you are wise when you share or approve of their folly.

969 **ancien** — **former| ancient; former; ex-**

adj; m; pfx
[ɑ̃sjɛ̃]
Ce droit ancien a résisté à l'épreuve du temps et existe encore aujourd'hui.
-This ancient right has stood the test of time and is very much alive today.

970 **relation** — **relation**

f
[ʁəlasjɔ̃]
Dan a eu une relation très tumultueuse avec Linda.
-Dan had a very stormy relationship with Linda.

971 **bouteille** — **bottle**

f
[butɛj]
Il a bu une bouteille de vin.
-He drank a bottle of wine.

972 **rejoindre** — **rejoin**

vb
[ʁəʒwɛ̃dʁ]
Ils ont vocation à nous rejoindre autant que l' Union a vocation à les intégrer.
-They are as destined to join us as the European Union is to integrate them.

973 **casse** — **case| breakage| robbery**

f
[kas]
Un autre P40 de la casse d'Oncle Sam.
-Another P-40 from Uncle Sam's junkyard.

974 **jardin** — **garden**

m
[ʒaʁdɛ̃]
Le mot « Garabagh » signifie en azerbaïdjanais « Jardin noir ».
-The word "Garabagh" is translated from Azerbaijani as "Black Garden".

975 **malgré** — **despite; all the same**

prp; adv
[malgʁe]
L'Afrique, malgré quelques avancées courageuses, malgré les efforts de beaucoup, s'enfonce.

-Africa, despite separate valiant achievements, despite the efforts of many, is going downhill.

976	**oiseau**	**bird**
	m	Le chat s'approcha sans bruit de l'oiseau qui ne se doutait de rien.
	[wazo]	-The cat sneaked up on the unsuspecting bird.

977	**frappé**	**hit| struck**
	adj	La tragédie a déjà frappé cet éden.
	[fʁape]	-I see tragedy has already struck this cactus Eden.

978	**nombre**	**number**
	m	Nombre correspond au nombre à arrondir au nombre entier immédiatement
	[nɔ̃bʁ]	inférieur.
		-Number is the number that is to be rounded down to the nearest integer.

979	**sentiment**	**feeling| sense**
	m	Tel est le sentiment de l'Europe et le sentiment de ce Parlement.
	[sɑ̃timɑ̃]	-That is the feeling in Europe, and that is the feeling in this Parliament.

980	**toit**	**roof**
	m	Elles se trouvent sous le même toit, mais elles constituent néanmoins des
	[twa]	entités distinctes.
		-They are under one roof, but under that one roof there are still distinct entities.

981	**lors**	**then| while**
	adv	La fenêtre ancrable du Styliste peut rester ouverte lors l' édition du
	[lɔʁ]	document.
		-The floating window of the Stylist can remain open while you edit a document.

982	**métier**	**trade| job**
	m	La distillation est un métier, un métier véritablement traditionnel.
	[metje]	-Distillation is a craft, a truly traditional craft.

983	**maladie**	**disease| illness**
	f	Comment savez-vous que le patient ne feint pas la maladie ?
	[maladi]	-How do you know that the patient is not feigning illness?

984	**pocher**	**poach**
	vb	Champagne... saumon poché avec des petits œufs de caille et... bien
	[pɔʃe]	crémeux, un vrai rêve de soufflé au citron.
		-Sparkling champagne and...... yummy poached salmon with little quail eggs and...... a creamy...... dreamy...... lemon soufflé.

985	**frapper**	**hit| knock**
	vb	Toutefois, la sanction doit frapper les dirigeants politiques et non pas les
	[fʁape]	citoyens.
		-The sanction must hit the political leaders, however, and not the citizens.

986	**succès**	**success**
	m	Le succès dans l'un de ces domaines débouche sur le succès dans les autres.
	[syksɛ]	-Success in addressing one of these issues leads to success in addressing another.

987	**dessous**	**beneath; underside; under it**
	adv; m; prp	Même aujourd'hui, le mercure est au-dessous de zéro.
	[dəsu]	-Even today, the temperature is below zero.

988	**théâtre**	**theater| stage**
	m	Nous nous sommes amusés au théâtre hier soir.
	[teatʁ]	-We had a good time at the theater last night.

| 989 | **chinois** | **Chinese; Chinese** |

adj; m
[ʃinwa]

Vous n'avez pas humilié les Chinois, ce sont les Chinois qui vous ont humilié !
-You have not humiliated the Chinese; it is the Chinese who have humiliated you.

990 **craindre** **fear**

vb
[kʁɛ̃dʁ]

L'Union ne doit pas craindre les menaces et les mesures de rétorsion américaines.
-The Union should not be afraid of American threats and retaliatory measures.

991 **gare** **station| train station**

f
[gaʁ]

Où est la gare la plus proche ?
-Where's the closest train station?

992 **billet** **ticket**

m
[bijɛ]

The billeting of its combatants has already begun in some provinces.
-Le cantonnement de ses combattants a déjà commencé dans certaines provinces du pays.

993 **remarquer** **notice| note**

vb
[ʁəmaʁke]

L'Union européenne pourrait subventionner le Kosovo pour toujours et le remarquer à peine.
-The European Union could subsidise Kosovo for ever and hardly notice it.

994 **paradis** **paradise**

m
[paʁadi]

Le paradis et l'enfer existent dans le cœur des hommes.
-Paradise and hell exist in the hearts of man.

995 **étranger** **foreign| overseas; foreigner**

adj; m
[etʁɑ̃ʒe]

Il a vécu à l'étranger la majeure partie de sa vie.
-He lived abroad for much of his life.

996 **campagne** **campaign**

f
[kɑ̃paɲ]

Sa mère vit seule à la campagne.
-Her mother lives in the country all by herself.

997 **alcool** **alcohol**

m
[alkɔl]

Les Verts seraient partisans d'une taxation de l'alcool selon le degré d'alcool.
-The Greens would prefer alcohol to be taxed according to its alcohol content.

998 **samedi** **Saturday**

m
[samdi]

En une occasion comme samedi, on est conscient d'être entouré par l'histoire.
-On an occasion such as Saturday's, one is conscious of being surrounded by history.

999 **produire** **produce**

vb
[pʁɔdɥiʁ]

Et quatrièmement, ils vont produire un avis conjoint sur les fonds structurels.
-And fourthly, they are going to produce a joint opinion on the structural funds.

1000 **répéter** **repeat| rehearse**

vb
[ʁepete]

Nous pouvons bien répéter l'histoire, mais nous ne devrions pas la répéter trop rapidement.
-We may repeat history, but we should not repeat current events.

1001 **souhaiter** **wish| hope**

vb
[swete]

[Autres dispositions de fond que le Groupe de travail pourra souhaiter ajouter.
-[Other substantive provisions that the Working Group may wish to include.

1002 **odeur** **smell| odor**

	f [ɔdœʁ]	Cette fleur a une odeur très forte, est-ce que tu la sens ? -This flower has a strong scent, can you smell it?
1003	**montagne** f [mõtaɲ]	**mountain** Il me semblait que la beauté était pareille à un sommet de pic de montagne ; une fois atteint il ne reste plus qu'à descendre. -It seemed to me that beauty was like the summit of a mountain peak; when you had reached it there was nothing to do but to come down again.
1004	**fantastique** adj [fãtastik]	**fantastic** C'est fantastique, et j'aurais souhaité qu'il en aille de même pour d'autres rapports. -This is marvellous and I wish it happened with other reports.
1005	**victoire** f [viktwaʁ]	**victory| win** Notre équipe remporta une grande victoire. -Our team gained a great victory.
1006	**carrière** f [kaʁjɛʁ]	**career** Il a décidé peu de temps après son retour en France d'abandonner sa carrière comme économiste pour se dédier à sa vraie passion, l'écriture, en Espagne. -Shortly after coming back to France, he decided to abandon his career as an economist in order to dedicate himself to his true passion: writing, in Spain.
1007	**fatiguer** vb [fatige]	**tire| stress** Ma stratégie consistait à le faire courir le plus possible pour le fatiguer. -My strategy was to place my shots all over the court so that I would tire him out.
1008	**rater** vb [ʁate]	**miss| fail** Nous ne devons pas rater ce test, c'est là que rédide le défi. -We must not fail that test and therein lies the challenge.
1009	**règle** f [ʁɛgl]	**rule** Je ne peux faire aucune exception à la règle. -I can except no one from the rules.
1010	**assurer** vb [asyʁe]	**ensure| insure** Je veux m'assurer que vous êtes ceux que vous dites être. -I want to make sure you are who you say you are.
1011	**queue** f [kø]	**tail| queue** Durant cette période, il y avait un moyen pour entrer dans le pavillon français sans avoir besoin de faire la queue : il fallait aller manger les produits à l'intérieur, mais c'était vraiment trop cher. -During this period, there was a way to get into the French clubhouse without standing in line: you had to eat the products inside, but it was really expensive.
1012	**viande** f [vjãd]	**meat** L'administrateur nous laisse chasser notre viande. -Here the agent lets us hunt for our meat.
1013	**rivière** f [ʁivjɛʁ]	**river** J'avais l'habitude de nager dans cette rivière. -I used to swim in this river.
1014	**suivant** adj; prp; adv [sɥivã]	**following; according to; as follows** Achève la saisie dans un champ et place le curseur dans le champ suivant. -Completes the input in the field and places the cursor into the next field.
1015	**obliger**	**force| oblige**

	vb [ɔbliʒe]	Que fait le Portugal pour obliger les parents à envoyer leurs enfants à l'école? -What was Portugal doing to oblige parents to send their children to school?
1016	**fusil**	**rifle**
	m [fyzi]	Le sentiment est donc que la solution aux problèmes continue d'être au bout du fusil. -Thus, the perception is that the solution to their respective problems remains the rifle.
1017	**passager**	**passenger; passing**
	m; adj [pasaʒe]	Un passager s'est évanoui, mais l'hôtesse l'a ranimé. -A passenger fainted, but the stewardess brought him around.
1018	**hasard**	**chance| accident**
	m [azaʁ]	Je ne joue plus aux jeux de hasard. -I'm not gambling anymore.
1019	**neige**	**snow**
	f [nɛʒ]	La colline était toute recouverte de neige. -The hill was all covered with snow.
1020	**parfaitement**	**perfectly| thoroughly**
	adv [paʁfɛtmɑ̃]	J'en suis parfaitement convaincu. -I'm utterly convinced of it.
1021	**échapper**	**escape**
	vb [eʃape]	Aucune institution financière, privée ou publique, ne doit échapper à la régulation. -No financial institution, be it public or private, should escape regulation.
1022	**plage**	**beach**
	f [plaʒ]	Les enfants construisirent un château de sable sur la plage. -The children built a sand castle on the beach.
1023	**signal**	**signal**
	m [siɲal]	Le signal "N'approchez pas" se compose d'un signal sonore et d'un signal lumineux. -The `Do not approach' signal consists of a sound signal and a light signal.
1024	**crétin**	**cretin; moronic**
	m; adj [kʁetɛ̃]	C'est un crétin absolu. -He's a total moron.
1025	**vidéo**	**video**
	f [video]	Finalement je me suis décidé et j'ai acheté ce nouveau jeu vidéo. -Finally, I made up my mind and bought the new video game.
1026	**coffrer**	**put away**
	vb [kɔfʁe]	Pour me sauver, elle a dû les faire coffrer. -So, in order to save me, he had to put them away.
1027	**pression**	**pressure**
	f [pʁesjɔ̃]	La pression se fait sentir sur lui. -The pressure is getting to him.
1028	**information**	**information**
	f [ɛ̃fɔʁmasjɔ̃]	Information économique, information sur le marché, statistiques et échange d'informations. -Economic information, market intelligence, statistics and information-sharing.
1029	**futur**	**future; future**
	adj; m [fytyʁ]	J'ignore tout du futur. -I don't know anything about the future.

1030	**univers**	**universe**
	m	Il connaît l'univers et ne se connaît pas.
	[yniveʁ]	-He knows the universe and doesn't know himself.
1031	**volonté**	**will**
	f	Tout dépend de la volonté politique et cette volonté politique semble exister !
	[vɔlɔ̃te]	-Everything depends on the political will and the political will does appear to exist!
1032	**attendu**	**expected**
	adj	L'accord sur le règlement est attendu dans la deuxième étape du plan.
	[atɑ̃dy]	-Agreement on the resolution is expected in the second phase.
1033	**excuse**	**excuse**
	f	C'est un jalon important, mais n'y voyons pas une excuse pour relâcher notre effort.
	[ɛkskyz]	-This is a significant milestone, but it is not an excuse for complacency.
1034	**faible**	**low| weak; weakling**
	adj; m	Jack a un faible pour Jill.
	[fɛbl]	-Jack has a soft spot for Jill.
1035	**fiston**	**son**
	m	Vous devriez faire attention, fiston.
	[fistɔ̃]	-You ought to be more careful, son.
1036	**van**	**van**
	m	Avez-vous déjà conduit un van ?
	[vɑ̃]	-Have you ever driven a van?
1037	**attraper**	**catch| seize**
	vb	Il mange des écureuils crus et tous les chats qu'il peut attraper.
	[atʁape]	-He eats raw squirrels and all the cats he can catch.
1038	**inquiéter**	**worry| alarm**
	vb	Nous avons vu les preuves scientifiques et il n'y a aucune raison de s'inquiéter.
	[ɛ̃kjete]	-We have seen the scientific evidence and clearly there is room there for worry.
1039	**cesser**	**stop| desist**
	vb	La construction continue de la "Forteresse Europe" doit cesser dès que possible.
	[sese]	-The continued construction of 'Fortress Europe' must cease as soon as possible.
1040	**gaffe**	**blunder**
	f	Or, le gouvernement a fait une gaffe.
	[gaf]	-It was only through a slip-up on the part of the government.
1041	**ministre**	**minister**
	m	Le Premier Ministre désigne les membres de son cabinet.
	[ministʁ]	-The prime minister appoints the members of his cabinet.
1042	**naissance**	**birth| rise**
	f	Les orangs-outans de Bornéo, espèce gravement menacée, donnent naissance tous les huit ans environ.
	[nɛsɑ̃s]	-Bornean orangutans, a critically endangered species, give birth approximately at every eight years.
1043	**utile**	**useful**

	adj [ytil]	Le taux de réponses positives («Très utile» + «Utile») est très élevé et atteint 92 %. -The rate of approval answers (Very useful + Useful) is very high, at 92%.
1044	**gaz** m [gaz]	**gas** Je suis certaine d'avoir fermé le gaz. -I'm sure I turned off the gas.
1045	**bataille** f [bataj]	**battle** Les soldats engagèrent une féroce bataille. -A fierce battle was fought by the soldiers.
1046	**voleur** m; adj [vɔlœʁ]	**thief; thievish** Le voleur a été attrapé ce matin. -The robber was nabbed this morning.
1047	**poids** m [pwa]	**weight** La glace craqua sous le poids. -The ice cracked under the weight.
1048	**discourir** vb [diskuʁiʁ]	**discourse** L'urgence appelle un discours marqué par la vérité, le courage ainsi que des résultats. -What is urgently needed is discourse characterised by truth, courage and results.
1049	**star** f [staʁ]	**star** Je vous présente votre nouvelle star. -Gentlemen, I bring you your next star.
1050	**gâteau** m [gato]	**cake** Nous continuons à ajouter des ingrédients au gâteau, mais celui-ci ne sort jamais du four. -We continue to add ingredients to the cake, but the cake never leaves the oven.
1051	**ventre** m [vãtʁ]	**belly| stomach** Avoir les yeux plus gros que le ventre. -The eye is bigger than the belly.
1052	**connaissance** f [kɔnɛsãs]	**knowledge| acquaintance** Ils ont connaissance de nos projets. -They know our plans.
1053	**vif** adj; m [vif]	**bright| lively; quick** Nous tremblions tous dans le froid vif. -We were all shaking from the bitter cold.
1054	**assassin** m; adj [asasɛ̃]	**assassin; bloodthirsty** À son avis, Shaka Sankofa n'était pas l'assassin. -In his opinion, Shaka Sankofa was not the killer.
1055	**vendredi** m [vãdʁədi]	**Friday** Habituellement, elles vont à l'école du lundi au vendredi. -They usually go to school from Monday to Friday.
1056	**couple** m [kupl]	**couple| pair** Le couple n'avait pas moins de sept enfants. -The couple have no less than seven children.
1057	**sérieusement** adv [seʁjøzmã]	**seriously| gravely** Commençons dès aujourd'hui à mettre sérieusement en œuvre ces recommandations. -Let this be the day when we begin implementing those recommendations in earnest.

1058	**militaire**	**military; soldier**
	adj; m	Il a étudié l'histoire militaire.
	[militɛʁ]	-He studied military history.
1059	**date**	**date**
	f	Ils ont annoncé la date de leur mariage dans le journal.
	[dat]	-They announced the date of their wedding in the newspaper.
1060	**titre**	**title| headline**
	m	Vérifies le titre du dernier chapitre.
	[titʁ]	-Check out the title of the last chapter.
1061	**génie**	**genius| genie**
	m	Cela prendra d'autant plus de temps au monde de trouver et de comprendre
	[ʒeni]	un homme, que son génie est grand.
		-The greater the genius, the longer it takes the world to find it out and
		understand it.
1062	**autrement**	**otherwise**
	adv	Nous aurions souhaité qu'il fût possible que ces changements aient lieu
	[otʁəmɑ̃]	autrement.
		-We had hoped that it would be possible for those changes to take place
		differently.
1063	**os**	**bone**
	m	Un cœur joyeux est un bon remède, mais un esprit abattu dessèche les os.
	[ɔs]	-A cheerful heart is good medicine, but a crushed spirit dries up the bones.
1064	**valeur**	**value| worth**
	f	La valeur de vérité d'une affirmation peut être une valeur de probabilité.
	[valœʁ]	-The truth value of an assertion may be a probability value.
1065	**puissant**	**powerful| strong**
	adj	Les mesures de confiance sont un instrument puissant pour susciter la
	[pɥisɑ̃]	confiance.
		-Confidence-building measures are a powerful instrument for generating
		trust.
1066	**vert**	**green| young; putting green**
	adj; m	Dans mon pays, les écoles font un travail fantastique dans le domaine du
	[vɛʁ]	drapeau vert.
		-In my own country the schools do fantastic work in the area of the green
		flag.
1067	**fortune**	**fortune| wealth**
	f	En dépit de toute sa fortune, elle n'est point heureuse.
	[fɔʁtyn]	-For all her riches, she's not happy.
1068	**major**	**adjutant| matiére principale**
	m	Degree in Naval Sciences (major in Oceanology), Portuguese Naval
	[maʒɔʁ]	Academy, Lisbon, 1984.
		-Diplôme de sciences navales (matière principale : océanologie), Académie
		navale portugaise, Lisbonne, 1984
1069	**poulet**	**chicken**
	m	Le poulet est trop cuit.
	[pulɛ]	-The chicken is overcooked.
1070	**embrasser**	**embrace| kiss**
	vb	Une telle conception doit, fondamentalement, embrasser et honorer la
	[ɑ̃bʁase]	diversité.
		-A key component of universal design is to embrace and honour diversity.
1071	**genou**	**knee**

	m [ʒənu]	Le «centre du genou» est défini comme étant le point de flexion effectif du genou. -The 'centre of the knee' is defined as the point about which the knee effectively bends.
1072	**célèbre** adj [selɛbʁ]	**celebrated| popular** Le Diwali est célébré en Inde de la même manière que Noël est célébré au Canada. -Diwali is celebrated in India as Christmas is celebrated in Canada.
1073	**cibler** vb [sible]	**target at** Les politiques et les stratégies nationales doivent cibler la population tout entière. -National policies and strategies must target the whole population.
1074	**cousin** m [kuzɛ̃]	**cousin** Son cousin vit aux États-Unis d'Amérique. -His cousin lives in America.
1075	**conscience** f [kɔ̃sjɑ̃s]	**consciousness| conscience** Prenons bien conscience de la gravité de la journée d'aujourd'hui, car aujourd'hui, dans les murs accueillants de Boulogne-sur-Mer, ne se réunissent pas des Français avec des Anglais, des Russes avec des Polonais, mais des hommes avec des hommes. -Let us be fully aware of all the importance of this day, because today within the generous walls of Boulogne-sur-Mer have met not French with English, nor Russians with Polish, but people with people.
1076	**prévenir** vb [pʁevəniʁ]	**warn| inform** On nous a dit que l'intention de l'article 24.2 est de prévenir la fraude. -We are told that the intent of section 24.2 is to prevent fraud.
1077	**article** m [aʁtikl]	**art** Cet article contient certaines idées vraiment nouvelles. -This article contains some genuinely new ideas.
1078	**étoile** f [etwal]	**star| blaze** Une étoile brille à l'heure de notre rencontre. -A star shines on the hour of our meeting.
1079	**reprendre** vb [ʁəpʁɑ̃dʁ]	**resume| retake** Cette garantie est assortie d'une responsabilité pour les banques de commencer maintenant à prêter aux entreprises et aux particuliers, afin de permettre aux économies de reprendre. -With that guarantee also comes the responsibility for banks to now start lending to businesses and to people, to allow the economies to pick up again.
1080	**mine** f [min]	**mine| lead** Jack a été tué par une mine. -Jack was killed by a land mine.
1081	**charmant** adj; m [ʃaʁmɑ̃]	**charming| lovely; cunning** Un jeune et charmant monsieur m'offrit un bonbon. -A young and charming gentleman offered me a candy.
1082	**reposer** vb [ʁəpoze]	**rest** Le détenu peut se reposer ou s'étendre en dehors des heures normales de sommeil. -Resting or lying down outside regular sleeping hours is permitted.
1083	**noter**	**note**

	vb [nɔte]	Note : Les données et renseignements relatifs à l'année 2002 n'ont pas tous été fournis. -Note: submissions for calendar year 2002 have not been complete d
1084	**agréable** adj [agʁeabl]	**pleasant| nice** Dans ce cas-ci, l'expérience a été en tous points satisfaisante et agréable. -This experience has been satisfactory and agreeable in every way.
1085	**château** m [ʃato]	**castle| chateau** Les titres étaient en dépôt au château d'Aich, résidence secondaire de la famille. -These stocks were deposited at the family's secondary residence at Aich Castle.
1086	**bal** m [bal]	**ball** Profitez de la soirée au bal. -Please enjoy yourself at the dance.
1087	**oreille** f [ɔʁɛj]	**ear** Elle joue du piano à l'oreille. -She plays the piano by ear.
1088	**apparemment** adv [apaʁamɑ̃]	**apparently** La mondialisation offre apparemment d'immenses possibilités de développement. -Globalization had apparently opened enormous opportunities for development.
1089	**zéro** m [zeʁo]	**zero| nobody** Nous allons commencer de zéro. -We'll start from scratch.
1090	**saint** adj; m [sɛ̃]	**saint; saint; St.** La plus ancienne république d'Europe se nomme Saint-Marin. -The oldest republic in Europe is named San Marino.
1091	**marrant** adj; m [maʁɑ̃]	**funny; funny guy** Tu penses que tu es assez marrant, non ? -You think you're pretty funny, don't you?
1092	**joue** f [ʒu]	**cheek** Aimez votre prochain, tendez l'autre joue ... -Love thy neighbor, turn the other cheek...
1093	**salon** m [salɔ̃]	**lounge** Nous nous sommes reposés dans le salon. -We relaxed in the living room.
1094	**levé** adj [ləve]	**survey; lifted** Je me suis levé de mauvais poil ce matin. -I got up on the wrong side of the bed this morning.
1095	**conversation** f [kɔ̃vɛʁsasjɔ̃]	**conversation| talk** Je viens d'avoir une conversation avec votre avocat. -I just had a talk with your lawyer.
1096	**piloter** vb [pilɔte]	**pilot** Ce n'est pas le moment d'avancer en pilote automatique. -This is not the time to navigate by autopilot.
1097	**fer** m [fɛʁ]	**iron** Il est dangereux de marcher le long des chemins de fer. -It's dangerous to walk on railway lines.
1098	**gorge**	**throat**

	f		Ma gorge me fait mal quand j'avale.
	[gɔʁʒ]		-My throat hurts when I swallow.
1099	**victime**	**victim**	
	f		On suppose que la victime a absorbé par erreur une grande quantité de poison.
	[viktim]		-The victim is thought to have taken a large quantity of poison by mistake.
1100	**détail**	**detail**	
	m		Les trois volets couverts par l'évaluation sont décrits plus en détail ci-dessous.
	[detaj]		-The three components included in the evaluation are described in detail below.
1101	**sexy**	**sexy**	
	adj		Alors sa petite amie, une Asiatique très sexy, se met à crier:
	[sɛksi]		-Then this guy's girlfriend, this real sexy Asian.. she starts screaming at him:
1102	**priver**	**deprive| deny**	
	vb		Madame la Commissaire, quelle est la raison de priver la Cour constitutionnelle et le médiateur de leurs droits acquis ?
	[pʁive]		-Commissioner, what is the underlying reason for divesting the constitutional court and the ombudsmen of their acquired rights?
1103	**violence**	**violence| force**	
	f		Le Mexique subit une violence sans précédent alors que les cartels de la drogue se disputent les routes de la distribution.
	[vjɔlɑ̃s]		-Mexico is experiencing unprecedented violence as drug cartels are battling over distribution routes.
1104	**nerveux**	**nervous**	
	adj		Êtes-vous nerveux ?
	[nɛʁvø]		-Are you nervous?
1105	**aéroport**	**airport**	
	m		Je l'ai vu à l'aéroport.
	[aeʁɔpɔʁ]		-I saw him off at the airport.
1106	**direct**	**direct; straight**	
	adj; adv		Procédé de traitement direct dirigé sur des sites pathologiques spécifiques.
	[diʁɛkt]		-A method for the direct treatment towards the specific sites of a disease is disclosed.
1107	**tribunal**	**court| courthouse**	
	m		Les questions fusèrent de la part du grand nombre de journalistes qui s'étaient assemblés à l'extérieur du tribunal.
	[tʁibynal]		-The questions came fast and furious from the large number of reporters who had gathered outside the courthouse.
1108	**in-**	**un-**	
	pfx		Cela serait incompatible avec le texte du Traité.
	[in-]		-This would be incompatible with the wording of the Treaty.
1109	**paquet**	**package| pack**	
	m		Je voudrais expédier ce paquet au Canada.
	[pakɛ]		-I'd like to mail this package to Canada.
1110	**fumer**	**smoke**	
	vb		Il ne faut pas fumer dans cette pièce.
	[fyme]		-Don't smoke in this room.
1111	**aise**	**pleased; pleasure**	

adj; f
[ɛz]

Les familles aisées et leurs proches peuvent aussi envoyer leurs enfants étudier dans des universités étrangères.
-Well-to-do families and their relatives may also send their children abroad for university education.

1112 joindre
vb
[ʒwɛ̃dʁ]

join| attach
Il reste à demander au premier ministre de se joindre à lui.
-Now all he has to do is ask the Prime Minister to join him.

1113 lance
f
[lɑ̃s]

lance| hose
Cette lance aurait transpercé un sanglier.
-That spear would have skewered a wild boar.

1114 usine
f
[yzin]

plant| factory
Elle a créé une usine pour la fabrication de deux modèles, la Hilux et la Corolla.
-TSA established a plant to manufacture two models, Hilux and Corolla.

1115 défendre
vb
[defɑ̃dʁ]

defend| uphold
Les États les plus exposés devraient les défendre et les utiliser conjointement.
-The most badly affected States should defend these means and pursue them jointly.

1116 forêt
f
[fɔʁɛ]

forest
Deux petits écureuils, l'un blanc et l'autre noir, vivaient dans une grande forêt.
-Two little squirrels, a white squirrel and a black squirrel, lived in a large forest.

1117 champion
adj; m
[ʃɑ̃pjɔ̃]

champion; champion
Il est vraiment notre champion, notre champion de la recherche en santé.
-He is indeed our champion, our champion of health research. Hon.

1118 horreur
f
[ɔʁœʁ]

horror
Ma copine n'aime pas les films d'horreur.
-My girlfriend doesn't like scary movies.

1119 test
m
[tɛst]

test
Ça devrait être examiné à travers un processus de test soigneusement conçu.
-It should be vetted through a well-designed testing process.

1120 désormais
adv
[dezɔʁmɛ]

henceforth
Pour visiter notre pays, les étrangers auront désormais besoin d'un visa spécial.
-In order to visit our country, foreigners will from now on need a special visa.

1121 extérieur
adj; m
[ɛksteʁjœʁ]

outside| exterior; outside
Tu peux, de l'extérieur.
-You can, from outside.

1122 désert
m
[dezɛʁ]

desert
La dernière partie de l'excursion fut un parcours à travers le désert.
-The last part of the trip was across the desert.

1123 intelligent
adj
[ɛ̃teliʒɑ̃]

intelligent
Sans aucun doute, un bâtiment intelligent doit prouver qu'il l'est sous tous les angles.
-There is no doubt that an intelligent building must show intelligence throughout.

1124 job

job

	m	J'espérais récupérer mon ancien job.
	[dʒɔb]	-I was hoping I'd get my old job back.
1125	**compte**	**account**
	m	Il a fait un compte-rendu de son voyage.
	[kɔ̃t]	-He gave an account of his trip.
1126	**mode**	**mode; fashion**
	m; f	Le rouge n'est plus à la mode.
	[mɔd]	-Red is out of fashion.
1127	**série**	**series| set**
	f	La colère du peuple explosa, entraînant une série d'émeutes.
	[seʁi]	-The anger of the people exploded, leading to a series of riots.
1128	**pis encore**	**even worse**
	adv	Pis encore, les membres des forces armées sont à l'abri de toute poursuite judiciaire.
	[pi ɑ̃kɔʁ]	-To make matters worse, members of the armed forces were immune from prosecution.
1129	**sage**	**wise; sage**
	adj; m	Tu es plus sage que tu n'en as conscience.
	[saʒ]	-You're wiser than you know.
1130	**concerner**	**concern**
	vb	La troisième : la politique doit concerner les peuples et eux seuls.
	[kɔ̃sɛʁne]	-Thirdly: our policy must concern the peoples, and only them.
1131	**grandir**	**grow| augment**
	vb	Piot : De manière idéale, les enfants devraient grandir dans un monde sans sida.
	[gʁɑ̃diʁ]	-Piot: Ideally, children would grow up in a world without AIDS.
1132	**pousser**	**push| drive**
	vb	Voudriez-vous voir votre époux se laisser pousser la barbe ?
	[puse]	-Would you like to see your husband grow a beard?
1133	**vache**	**cow; bitchy**
	f; adj	Elle a trait la vache.
	[vaʃ]	-She milked the cow.
1134	**repos**	**rest| pause**
	m	Un bon repos me fait sentir mieux.
	[ʁəpo]	-A sound sleep made me feel better.
1135	**ordinateur**	**computer**
	m	Je n'ai pas les moyens d'acheter un autre ordinateur.
	[ɔʁdinatœʁ]	-I can't afford to buy another computer.
1136	**rock**	**rock**
	m	Une soirée de pop rock originel.
	[ʁɔk]	-An evening of fresh and original pop rock.
1137	**russe**	**Russian; Russian**
	adj; m	Il sait parler et écrire le russe.
	[ʁys]	-He can both speak and write Russian.
1138	**minuit**	**midnight**
	m	Pour l'instant, un débat est prévu entre minuit et minuit trente.
	[minɥi]	-At the moment there is a debate scheduled between midnight and 12.30 a. m.
1139	**amusant**	**amusing**

adj
[amyzã]

C'était très amusant de la voir dans les tranchées tirer avec cette mitrailleuse.
-It was quite amusing to see her down in the trenches firing this machine gun.

1140 membre

m
[mãbʁ]

member

Membre de la Commission. - Je remercie l'honorable membre pour sa question.
-Member of the Commission. - I thank the honourable Member for the question.

1141 ouvert

adj
[uvɛʁ]

open

Elle a ouvert un centre de télédétection consacré à la solutions de divers problèmes, dont la désertification et l'épuisement des ressources en eau souterraine.
-It had opened a remote sensing centre to address various problems, including desertification and the depletion of unconfined groundwater.

1142 nombreux

adj
[nõbʁø]

numerous

De nombreux problèmes, de nombreux conflits d' intérêts subsistent.
-Numerous problems, numerous conflicts of interest have still not been resolved.

1143 également

adv
[egalmã]

also| equally

D'autres aspects du bien-être physique des enfants sont également pris en compte.
-Other aspects of children's physical well-being are being addressed as well.

1144 mince

adj
[mɛ̃s]

thin| slim

Les États-Unis marchent sur une glace très mince, disait l'un de nos experts.
-As one of our experts said, the United States is skating on very thin ice.

1145 page

f
[paʒ]

page

Assignez à la première page de votre document le style de page Page droite.
-Apply the Page Style Right Page to the first page of your document.

1146 essence

f
[esãs]

gasoline| essence

L'essence est utilisée comme combustible.
-Gasoline is used for fuel.

1147 maire

m
[mɛʁ]

mayor

J'ai envoyé au maire une pétition.
-I addressed a petition to the mayor.

1148 lundi

m
[lɛ̃di]

Monday

Elle répond à toutes les demandes de renseignements du lundi matin au mercredi après-midi.
-She answers requests for information from Monday morning to Wednesday afternoon.

1149 moteur

m; adj
[motœʁ]

engine; motor

Le test du nouveau moteur a lieu aujourd'hui.
-The test of the new engine takes place today.

1150 réparer

vb
[ʁepaʁe]

repair

Nous devons reconstruire leurs logements et réparer les infrastructures.
-We must reconstruct their homes and repair the infrastructure.

1151 franchement

adv
[fʁãʃmã]

honestly| openly

Alors, franchement, toutes ces questions sont mal informées et tendancieuses.
-So, frankly, all of these questions are ill-informed and tendentious.

1152 cigarette

cigarette

	f	Ça te dérange si j'allume une cigarette ?
	[sigaʁɛt]	-Does it bother you if I light up a cigarette?
1153	**partager**	**share| divide**
	vb	Devillers (Conseiller pour la Communauté européenne) a dit partager cet
	[paʁtaʒe]	avis.
		-This view was shareed by Dr. Devillers (Councillor for the European Community).
1154	**puissance**	**power| strength**
	f	NHI est le régime supérieur où la puissance est de 70 % de la puissance
	[pɥisãs]	maximale
		-NHI is the highest speed where the power is 70 per cent of maximum power.
1155	**hiver**	**winter**
	m	Alors que l'hiver approche en Afghanistan, il faut leur apporter une aide
	[ivɛʁ]	immédiate.
		-There is an urgent and immediate need for relief as the Afghan winter approaches.
1156	**épée**	**sword**
	f	Pourtant, l'exploitation des ressources naturelles est une épée à double
	[epe]	tranchant.
		-However, the exploitation of natural resources is a double-edged sword.
1157	**souffle**	**breath| blast**
	m	À peine arrivé à l'hôpital, il a rendu son dernier souffle.
	[sufl]	-Hardly had he arrived at the hospital when he breathed his last.
1158	**tenter**	**try| attempt**
	vb	Entre-temps, Madame la Commissaire, vos services peuvent tenter de
	[tɑ̃te]	clarifier la situation.
		-In the meantime, Commissioner, our services can attempt to clarify the situation.
1159	**vingt**	**twenty**
	num	Mon oncle a vécu jusqu'à l'âge de quatre-vingt-dix ans.
	[vɛ̃]	-My uncle lived to be ninety. (4x20+10)
1160	**miracle**	**miracle**
	m	Si cela n'est pas un miracle, qu'est-ce qu'un miracle ?
	[miʁakl]	-If this is not a miracle, then there is no such thing as a miracle.
1161	**apprécier**	**appreciate| appraise**
	vb	Le Tribunal continue d'apprécier la coopération des autorités rwandaises.
	[apʁesje]	-The Tribunal continues to appreciate the cooperation of the Rwandan authorities.
1162	**artiste**	**artist**
	m/f	À travers les uvres qu'il réalise, l'artiste parle et communique avec les autres.
	[aʁtist]	-Through his works, the artist speaks to others and communicates with them.
1163	**créer**	**create**
	vb	Si nous voulons réussir à Copenhague, nous devons créer le Fonds
	[kʁee]	d'adaptation.
		-If we want to achieve success in Copenhagen, we must create the Adaptation Fund.
1164	**lac**	**lake**
	m	Après avoir marché un moment, nous parvînmes au lac.
	[lak]	-After we walked for a while, we got to the lake.

1165	**sommeil**	**sleep| rest**
	m	Je bâille parce que j'ai sommeil.
	[sɔmɛj]	-I am yawning because I feel sleepy.
1166	**réveiller**	**wake| awake**
	vb	Les peuples neufs provoquent les vieilles sociétés, comme pour les réveiller
	[ʁeveje]	de leur lassitude.
		-The new nations provoke the old-established societies, as if to arouse them
		from their lassitude.
1167	**leçon**	**lesson**
	f	C'est personnellement la leçon que je tire de nombre de ces
	[ləsɔ̃]	recommandations.
		-This is the lesson that I personally learn from many of these
		recommendations.
1168	**fantôme**	**ghost; phantom**
	m; adj	Tu es pâle comme un fantôme.
	[fɑ̃tom]	-You look pale as a ghost.
1169	**acteur**	**actor**
	m	Je veux être acteur.
	[aktœʁ]	-I want to be an actor.
1170	**parc**	**park**
	m	Il y avait beaucoup de monde dans le parc.
	[paʁk]	-There were a lot of people in the park.
1171	**chair**	**flesh**
	f	J'ai la chair de poule.
	[ʃɛʁ]	-I got goosebumps.
1172	**reculer**	**back| retreat**
	vb	Ni les deux parties ni aucun d'entre nous ne doit reculer : nous devons
	[ʁəkyle]	préserver les acquis obtenus jusqu'ici.
		-Neither the two parties nor any of us must move backward; we must
		preserve the gains made so far.
1173	**japonais**	**Japanese; Japanese**
	adj; m|mpl	Est-ce que c'est un plat japonais ?
	[ʒapɔnɛ]	-Is it Japanese food?
1174	**coûter**	**cost**
	vb	L'autre point, c'est que les gens disent que cela va coûter trop cher.
	[kute]	-Another issue is that many people say that it will cost too much.
1175	**champagne**	**champagne**
	m	Mais nous pouvons oublier le champagne, que le taux zéro soit appliqué ou
	[ʃɑ̃paɲ]	non.
		-But we can safely leave the champagne at home, with or without its zero
		rate .
1176	**semblant**	**semblance**
	m	Il y a donc un semblant de logique à ce que l'IAPSO serve de secrétariat à
	[sɑ̃blɑ̃]	l'IAPWG.
		-There is thus a semblance of coherence in IAPSO serving as secretariat to
		IAPWG.
1177	**annoncer**	**announce| advertise**
	vb	Annoncer officiellement la création du Fonds et faire connaître ses objectifs.
	[anɔse]	-To officially announce the Fund's establishment and to publicize its
		objectives.
1178	**échange**	**exchange| swap**

m
[eʃɑ̃ʒ]

Je crois que c'est un échange utile, mais que ce n'est pas un échange pleinement satisfaisant.

-I think this is a useful initial exchange, but it is not a fully satisfactory exchange.

1179 payer — **pay**

vb
[peje]

Ce particulier devra payer cette taxe.

-This individual will have to pay that charge.

1180 débarrasser — **rid**

vb
[debaʁase]

C'est de ce genre de communications dont nous devons nous débarrasser.

-However, it is this type of communication that we really need to get rid of.

1181 fuir — **flee| escape**

vb
[fɥiʁ]

Toutes ces prothèses sont toujours mal scellées, de sorte qu'elles fuient.

-All such devices have the same leaky valves that cannot hold water.

1182 supplier — **beg| entreat**

vb
[syplije]

Me force pas à te supplier.

-Don't make me beg you.

1183 gouverneur — **governor**

m
[guvɛʁnœʁ]

C'est la charge de Reine, celle de Gouverneur général et celle de lieutenant-gouverneur.

-It is the office of the Queen, the Governor General, and the Lieutenant-Governor of a province.

1184 chauffeur — **driver| chauffeur**

m
[ʃofœʁ]

Jack est apparemment chauffeur de camion.

-Jack is apparently a truck driver.

1185 marquer — **mark| tag**

vb
[maʁke]

Il n'y avait qu'une simple croix blanche pour marquer la tombe du soldat.

-There was only a simple white cross to mark the soldier's tomb.

1186 rapidement — **quickly| rapidly**

adv
[ʁapidmɑ̃]

Tu dois choisir, mais rapidement.

-You have to choose, but do it quickly.

1187 unité — **unit| unity**

f
[ynite]

Un individu est la plus petite unité de la société.

-An individual is the smallest unit of the society.

1188 fesser — **spank**

vb
[fese]

Quand David était petit, son père lui donnait la fessée quand il se conduisait mal.

-Whenever David misbehaved as a young boy, his father would spank him.

1189 souci — **worry| care**

m
[susi]

Si vous suivez mon conseil, vous n'aurez aucun souci.

-If you follow my advice, you will have no trouble.

1190 manteau — **coat| mantle**

m
[mɑ̃to]

Place ton manteau sur le cintre.

-Put the coat on the hanger.

1191 allemand — **German; German**

adj; m|mpl
[almɑ̃]

Mon mot préféré en allemand est le mot pour «gant».

-My favorite word in German is the word for "glove".

1192 pantalon — **pants**

m
[pɑ̃talɔ̃]

Seuls ceux qui ne portaient pas de sous-vêtements pouvaient garder leur pantalon.

-Only persons who did not have underwear were allowed to keep their trousers.

1193	**policier**	**police officer**
	m	Le policier est dans la voiture.
	[pɔlisje]	-The policeman is in the car.
1194	**innocent**	**innocent; innocent**
	adj; m	C'est un châtiment cruel et humiliant auquel peut être condamné un
	[inɔsã]	innocent.
		-It is cruel and demeaning, and a punishment to which an innocent person can be sentenced.
1195	**véritable**	**true| real**
	adj	Il n'y a eu aucun véritable progrès dans l'examen des archives du
	[veʁitabl]	renseignement.
		-No concrete progress was achieved regarding the review of intelligence records.
1196	**caisse**	**fund| register**
	f	Les brigands ont demandé à avoir tout l'argent de la caisse.
	[kɛs]	-The bandits demanded all money in the register.
1197	**monnayer**	**monetize**
	vb	Il ne sera pas question de prendre une décision qui revienne à monnayer nos
	[mɔneje]	droits !
		-No decision will be taken here on the basis of an exchange of rights for money.
1198	**patient**	**patient; patient**
	adj; m	J'ai rafraîchi le patient avec de la glace.
	[pasjã]	-I cooled the patient's head with ice.
1199	**menteur**	**liar| lying; lying**
	m; adj	Tu es bon menteur.
	[mãtœʁ]	-You're a good liar.
1200	**perte**	**loss| waste**
	f	La perte de la diversité biologique va de pair avec la perte de la diversité
	[pɛʁt]	culturelle.
		-Loss of biological diversity goes hand in hand with loss of cultural diversity.
1201	**menace**	**threat**
	f	Ne me menace pas.
	[mənas]	-Don't threaten me.
1202	**émission**	**emission| transmission**
	f	Cette émission est diffusée de manière bihebdomadaire.
	[emisjɔ̃]	-This program is broadcast biweekly.
1203	**abandonner**	**abandon| give up**
	vb	Vous ne devriez pas abandonner l'espoir.
	[abãdɔne]	-You should not give up hope.
1204	**permission**	**permission**
	f	On m'a donné la permission d'utiliser cette voiture.
	[pɛʁmisjɔ̃]	-I was accorded permission to use the car.
1205	**front**	**front| forehead**
	m	Ils ont perdu la guerre sur le front de l'Est.
	[fʁɔ̃]	-They lost the war on the eastern front.
1206	**juif**	**Jewish**
	adj	Réfléchis-y, un Juif n'est jamais venu à ma porte pour essayer de me
	[ʒɥif]	convertir au judaïsme. Un point en leur faveur !

-Come to think of it, a Jew has never come to my door trying to convert me to Judaism. A point in their favor!

1207	**chouette**	**owl; neat**
	f; adj	Peux-tu recommander un chouette restaurant près d'ici ?
	[ʃwɛt]	-Could you recommend a nice restaurant near here?
1208	**chaise**	**chair**
	f	C'est une chaise.
	[ʃɛz]	-This is a chair.
1209	**sir**	**sir**
	m	Sir Wilfrid Laurier est arrivé au troisième rang, derrière sir John A.
	[siʁ]	-Sir Wilfrid Laurier came in third might I add behind Sir John A. Macdonald.
1210	**malheureusement**	**unfortunately| unhappily**
	adv	Malheureusement, certaines institutions ne suivent pas les recommandations.
	[maløʁøzmã]	-Unfortunately, there are institutions that do not comply with the recommendations.
1211	**chocolat**	**chocolate**
	m	Ils ne veulent pas d'ersatz de chocolat mais un vrai chocolat au beurre de cacao.
	[ʃɔkɔla]	-They do not want substitute chocolate, but genuine chocolate made from cocoa butter.
1212	**whisky**	**whiskey| Scotch**
	m	Je me suis servi un verre de whisky.
	[wiski]	-I poured myself a glass of whisky.
1213	**mouvement**	**movement| stir**
	m	Sans trembler, elle versa de l'eau dans le verre avec un mouvement élégant.
	[muvmã]	-Without shaking, she poured water in the glass with an elegant gesture.
1214	**identité**	**identity**
	f	As-tu ta carte d'identité sur toi ?
	[idãtite]	-Have you got your ID with you?
1215	**douche**	**shower**
	f	La « douche écossaise » a été rayée de la liste des mesures éducatives et coercitives autorisées.
	[duʃ]	-"Scottish shower" was excluded from the list of permitted educational and coercive measures.
1216	**chaleur**	**heat**
	f	Elles se cramponnèrent l'une l'autre pour conserver leur chaleur.
	[ʃalœʁ]	-They clung together for warmth.
1217	**lèvre**	**lip**
	f	Les expressions et les sourires changent comme ça par une simple application de rouge à lèvre et de poudre.
	[lɛvʁ]	-Expressions and smiles change like that just from applying rouge and lipstick.
1218	**étude**	**study**
	f	Du temps est imparti pour le travail, le loisir, et l'étude.
	[etyd]	-Time is allotted for work, recreation, and study.
1219	**faveur**	**favor**
	f	Je leur ai accordé une faveur.
	[favœʁ]	-I did them a favor.
1220	**Christ**	**Christ**

	m	« Avant le Christ et après le Christ », voilà la clef !
	[kʀist]	-"Before Christ and after Christ!" That is the key.
1221	**totalement**	**totally**
	adv	Les soins ne seraient pas totalement personnalisés.
	[tɔtalmã]	-The care would not be totally directed towards him
1222	**chou**	**cabbage**
	m	On peut manger le chou, cru.
	[ʃu]	-Cabbage can be eaten raw.
1223	**pause**	**break| rest**
	f	La durée de la pause est établie par le règlement intérieur du lieu de travail.
	[poz]	-The length of the break is established in the internal workplace regulations.
1224	**fini**	**finished| finite; finish**
	adj; m	J'en ai fini de t'écouter.
	[fini]	-I'm done listening to you.
1225	**côte**	**coast**
	f	L'île se situe à un mille de la côte.
	[kot]	-The island lies a mile off the coast.
1226	**mai**	**May**
	m	L'élection générale se tiendra en mai.
	[mɛ]	-A general election will be held in May.
1227	**soudain**	**suddenly; sudden**
	adv; adj	C'est là ce qui déclenche cet intérêt soudain pour la politique énergétique.
	[sudɛ̃]	-That is what really triggered this sudden interest in energy policy.
1228	**heureusement**	**fortunately| happily**
	adv	Heureusement, le sous-continent possède des ressources naturelles abondantes.
	[øʀøzmã]	-Fortunately, the African continent was endowed with abundant natural resources.
1229	**choc**	**shock**
	m	Elle récupèrera du choc bientôt.
	[ʃɔk]	-She will get over the shock soon.
1230	**note**	**note**
	f	Je vous ai laissé une note.
	[nɔt]	-I left you a note.
1231	**piéger**	**trap| ensnare**
	vb	Mais évitons de nous faire piéger: la croissance ne convient pas à tous les domaines.
	[pjeʒe]	-We do not to become trapped, though: growth is not appropriate for all areas.
1232	**malheur**	**misfortune**
	m	Un malheur est rarement agréable.
	[malœʀ]	-Misfortune is rarely pleasant.
1233	**attaquer**	**attack**
	vb	Il nous faut attaquer.
	[atake]	-We must attack.
1234	**mars**	**March**
	f	Le Programme est offert depuis mars 2004.
	[maʀs]	-The program has been available since March of 2004.
1235	**fonctionner**	**function**
	vb	Il va de soi qu'un système de santé ne peut fonctionner sans médecins.
	[fõksjone]	-It is obvious that a health system cannot function without physicians.

1236 portable — portable; portable
adj; m
[pɔʁtabl]
Il vérifie son téléphone portable.
-He's checking his cellphone.

1237 secrétaire — secretary
m/f
[səkʁetɛʁ]
Abréviations : SGA = Secrétaire général adjoint; SSG = Sous-Secrétaire général.
-Abbreviations: USG, Under-Secretary-General; ASG, Assistant Secretary-General.

1238 mensonge — lie
m
[mãsɔ̃ʒ]
Dis: "En vérité, ceux qui forgent le mensonge contre Allah ne réussiront pas".
-Say: "Surely those who fabricate falsehood in attribution to God will never prosper."

1239 nettoyer — clean| clear
vb
[netwaje]
On voit deux de ces casemates une fois nettoyées.
-You are looking at two of those sanitized bunkers.

1240 pistolet — gun| pistol
m
[pistɔlɛ]
Jack dégaina son pistolet.
-Jack pulled out his gun.

1241 gloire — glory| fame
f
[glwaʁ]
Comme dit la maxime: « Gloire aux vainqueurs, honneur aux vaincus ! »
-The saying goes: 'Glory to the victor, honour to the vanquished!'

1242 accès — access
m
[aksɛ]
Dans un accès de colère, je cognai le mur et cassai mon index.
-In a fit of anger I punched the wall and broke my index finger.

1243 changement — change| changing
m
[ʃãʒmã]
Changement économique, changement politique et changement dans la gestion de l'Union.
-Economic change and political change, and change in the government of the Union.

1244 poupée — doll| puppet
f
[pupe]
Elle me donna une jolie poupée.
-She gave me a pretty doll.

1245 bref — short| brief; in short
adj; adv
[bʁɛf]
En bref, à cause des calculs électoraux à court terme et de l'économie doctrinaire.
-The short answer is short-term electoral calculations and doctrinaire economics.

1246 réel — real| live; real
adj; m
[ʁeɛl]
Cependant, ils ne représentent pas suffisamment l'environnement opérationnel réel.
-However, it does not sufficiently replicate the actual operating environment.

1247 ballon — ball
m
[balɔ̃]
Le chat joue avec le ballon.
-The cat is playing with the ball.

1248 abri — shelter| shed
m
[abʁi]
D'autres projets importants tels qu'un centre d'activités et un abri pour les femmes
-Other capital projects such as a creativity centre and a shelter for women.

1249 corde — rope

	f	Oh, non. J'ai cassé une corde de ma raquette.
	[kɔʁd]	-Oh, no. I broke a string in my racket.
1250	**respirer**	**breathe**
	vb	Elle fut transportée à l'hôpital et mise sous respirateur pour l'aider à respirer.
	[ʁɛspiʁe]	-She was brought to a hospital and put on a respirator to help her breathe.
1251	**plat**	**flat; flat| dish**
	adj; m	Peut-être auriez-vous préféré un plat français.
	[pla]	-Perhaps you would have preferred a French dish.
1252	**emploi**	**employment**
	m	Cela découle évidemment de la nature contractuelle de son emploi.
	[ãplwa]	-This is undoubtedly a result of the contractual nature of her employment.
1253	**ennuyer**	**bore| annoy**
	vb	Cela nous surprend et nous ennuie, et cela doit nous inciter à agir.
	[ãnɥije]	-That surprises and annoys us, and it must call us into action.
1254	**attrape**	**catch**
	f	Mais contrôler ce n'est pas seulement attraper les prévaricateurs.
	[atʁap]	-But controls are not just to catch prevaricators.
1255	**fouler**	**tread**
	vb	Il m'a dit: "Lee, il y a une foule de gens qui se pressent autour de mon bureau aujourd'hui."
	[fule]	-He said to me: "There is a whole bunch of people milling around my office today."
1256	**larme**	**tear| drop**
	f	À chaque fois que j'écoute cette chanson, je verse une larme.
	[laʁm]	-I tear up whenever I hear that song.
1257	**siècle**	**century**
	m	Le XXe siècle entrera dans l'histoire comme un siècle de contradictions.
	[sjɛkl]	-The twentieth century will go down in history as a century of contradictions.
1258	**atteindre**	**reach| achieve**
	vb	Aussi estime-t-elle qu'il nous faut atteindre trois objectifs immédiats.
	[atɛ̃dʁ]	-Cuba therefore believes that we must achieve three immediate objectives.
1259	**veste**	**jacket**
	f	Lorsque nous taillons une nouvelle veste, nous devons veiller à ne pas confectionner une camisole de force.
	[vɛst]	-While stitching a new jacket, we should be careful that it does not become a straitjacket.
1260	**couverture**	**coverage| cover**
	f	Puis-je avoir un oreiller et une couverture ?
	[kuvɛʁtyʁ]	-Could I have a pillow and blanket?
1261	**fac**	**uni**
	abr	Mais Claude, un vieux camarade de la fac de droit, venait de sombrer dans une profonde dépression.
	[fak]	-But Claude, an old friend from law school, had just fallen into a severe depression.
1262	**mener**	**lead| carry on**
	vb	Cependant, avec l'injection de ces 20 millions, nous aurions pu mener une autre politique.
	[məne]	-However, we could have used those EUR 20 million to carry out another policy.
1263	**lancer**	**launch**

	vb	Les autorités ont décidé de lancer la chasse aux médicaments dangereux.
	[lãse]	-The authorities have decided to launch a hunt for dangerous drugs.

1264 piano — piano; piano

adv; m — Jack joue mieux du piano que Jill.
[pjano] — -Jack plays the piano better than Jill.

1265 source — source| spring

f — La répétition est la source de la mémoire.
[suʁs] — -Repetition is the mother of memory.

1266 camarade — comrade| fellow

m/f — Notre Président, le camarade R. G. Mugabe exerce son patronage sur le Conseil.
[kamaʁad] — -The President of my country, Comrade R. G. Mugabe, is the patron of the Council.

1267 couche — layer| bed

f — Je me couche à 11 heures.
[kuʃ] — -I go to bed at eleven.

1268 prêtre — priest

m — Il semblerait qu'il ait été tué, avec un prêtre, par un groupe de paramilitaires.
[pʁɛtʁ] — -He was killed, together with a priest, apparently by a group of paramilitaries.

1269 saison — season

f — Il a été dévasté par les deux pires ouragans de cette saison, Gustav et Ike.
[sɛzɔ̃] — -It was devastated by the two worst hurricanes of this season — Gustav and Ike.

1270 mesurer — measure

vb — Pour mesurer les résultats, il faut établir des indicateurs appropriés.
[məzyʁe] — -To measure results, it was necessary to establish appropriate indicators.

1271 entreprendre — undertake| initiate

vb — Le recensement est le plus vaste projet qu'un service de la statistique puisse entreprendre.
[ãtʁəpʁãdʁ] — -Census is the biggest project that a Statistical Office can undertake.

1272 supporter — support| bear; supporter

vb; m — Je n'arrive pas à supporter les menteurs.
[sypɔʁte] — -I can't stand liars.

1273 évidemment — obviously

adv — Une enquête est évidemment indispensable parce que les accusations sont très graves.
[evidamã] — -Naturally, an investigation is necessary because the accusations are very serious.

1274 distance — distance| range

f — J'ignore à quelle distance.
[distãs] — -I don't know how far.

1275 commettre — commit

vb — Article 253 (Conspiration pour commettre un acte relevant du droit fédéral).
[kɔmɛtʁ] — -Article 253 ("Plotting to commit a criminal act covered by the Federal Law").

1276 de là — thence| therefrom

adv — De là-bas, vous verrez la Terre comme un point dans l'espace, dont vous vous souviendrez avec amour.
[də la] — -From there, you will see the earth as a point in space that you remember with love.

1277 laver   **wash| launder**
vb
[lave]
Tu pourrais juste laver la chemise.
-Well, you could just wash the shirt.

1278 somme   **sum**
f
[sɔm]
Il essaya en vain de leur emprunter une grosse somme d'argent.
-He tried to borrow a large sum of money from them in vain.

1279 affreux   **frightful| dreadful**
adj
[afʁø]
À la télévision ce matin, c'était affreux, on n'a rien compris à l'humour de Chrétien.
-On television this morning, it was awful. Nobody understood Mr. Chrétien's humour.

1280 ours   **bear**
m
[uʁs]
« Je n'arrive pas à croire qu'ils dorment ensemble ! » « Pourquoi pas ? Il est parfaitement normal d'emmener un ours en peluche au lit avec soi. »
-"I can't believe that they sleep together!" "Why not? It's perfectly normal to take a teddy bear to bed with you."

1281 geste   **gesture| movement**
m
[ʒɛst]
Sans doute était-ce au XIXe siècle l'équivalent d'un geste grossier aujourd'hui.
-Presumably that was the 19th century equivalent of the offensive gesture.

1282 prisonnier   **prisoner; captive**
m; adj
[pʁizɔnje]
Le prisonnier a été remis en liberté hier.
-The prisoner was set at liberty yesterday.

1283 directement   **directly| right**
adv
[diʁɛktəmã]
Murphy pour qu'il m'accuse directement ou qu'il s'excuse.
-I would ask you to insist that Mr Murphy either accuse me outright or apologise.

1284 tableau   **table| picture**
m
[tablo]
Le tableau est presque terminé.
-The painting is all but finished.

1285 reconnaître   **recognize| admit**
vb
[ʁəkɔnɛtʁ]
Ken Geiser, du Toxics Use Reduction Institute a reconnu que le discours international sur la durabilité aborde peu la prévention de la pollution.
-Ken Geiser, Toxics Use Reduction Institute, acknowledged that there has been little attention to pollution prevention in the international discourse on sustainability.

1286 demi   **half; half**
adj; m
[dəmi]
Ça a pris une demi-heure.
-It took half an hour.

1287 commissaire   **commissioner**
m
[kɔmisɛʁ]
C'était pas moi, commissaire !
-It wasn't me, commissioner!

1288 alerte   **alert; alert**
adj; f
[alɛʁt]
Je t'ai obligée à être présente et alerte.
-I forced you to be to present and alert.

1289 plaisanter   **joke| fun**
vb
[plɛzãte]
Si je peux me permettre de plaisanter sur un sujet aussi important: et les rousses, Madame Roth ?
-And if I may joke about such an important subject: redheads, Mrs Roth?

1290 crier   **shout| shriek**

	vb	
	[kʁije]	

Nous avons commencé à crier, appelant Achraf, pour lui demander de sortir au plus vite.
-We began to scream, shouting to Ashraf to get out as soon as possible.

1291 lunettes   **glasses**

fpl
[lynɛt]

J'irai réclamer les lunettes demain.
-I could go in and claim the glasses tomorrow.

1292 prudent   **careful**

adj
[pʁydã]

Je crois que nous devons exercer un jugement prudent.
-Honourable senators, it is my belief that we exercise prudential judgment.

1293 ressentir   **feel| be affected by**

vb
[ʁəsãtiʁ]

C'est comme cela que nous devions le ressentir et nous l'avons ressenti comme cela.
-We could not help but feel that way, and we did.

1294 donné   **given**

adj
[dɔne]

L'annexe 2 du présent Règlement donne des exemples de marque d'homologation.
-Annex 2 to this Regulation gives examples of arrangements of the approval mark.

1295 convaincre   **convince**

vb
[kɔ̃vɛ̃kʁ]

Nous devons convaincre non seulement les jeunes, mais encore leurs parents.
-We not only must convince the youth, but we must convince their parents.

1296 aube   **dawn| blade**

f
[ob]

L'aube de mon éveil féministe.
-It was the dawn of my feminist awakening.

1297 propriétaire   **owner| landlord; proprietary**

m/f; adj
[pʁɔpʁijetɛʁ]

"Aimeriez-vous acheter un complet ?" demanda le propriétaire du magasin à Jack alors que ce dernier, en franchissant la porte, amenait avec lui les odeurs de la nuit précédente.
-"Would you like to buy a suit?" the shopkeeper asked Jack, who brought the smells of the previous night with him as he walked through the door.

1298 coincer   **jam| catch**

vb
[kwɛ̃se]

Avec l'effraction, on peut la coincer.
-With the break-in, we can nail her right now.

1299 ténu   **tenuous**

adj
[teny]

Monsieur le Président, le lien n'est pas aussi ténu que le ministre des Finances le dit.
-Speaker, the association is not nearly as tenuous as the finance minister said.

1300 bite   **cock| knob**

f
[bit]

C'était comme plonger ma bite dans de l'acide.
-And it was like sticking my dick in battery acid.

1301 frontière   **border| frontier**

f
[fʁɔ̃tjɛʁ]

Son village est juste de l'autre côté de la frontière.
-His village is just across the border.

1302 remonter   **ascend| reassemble**

vb
[ʁəmɔ̃te]

Je souhaite pouvoir remonter le temps.
-I wish I could turn back time.

1303 sec   **dry| dried**

adj
[sɛk]

Ils étaient en train de boire du vin blanc sec.
-They were drinking dry white wine.

1304 bosse   **bump| lump**
f
[bɔs]
Un chameau peut stocker une grande quantité d'eau dans la bosse de son dos.
-A camel can store a large amount of water in the hump on its back.

1305 diriger   **direct| run**
vb
[diʁiʒe]
Les sections des hommes et des femmes sont dirigées chacune par un «
capitaine général » du sexe concerné.
-The male and female sections are each run by a "captain-general" of the
sex concerned.

1306 soi   **self; self**
m; prn
[swa]
Aider les autres, c'est s'aider soi-même.
-To help others is to help yourself.

1307 facilement   **easily**
adv
[fasilmɑ̃]
Les réservoirs des différents circuits doivent être facilement reconnaissables.
-It must be possible to easily identify the reservoirs of the different circuits.

1308 porc   **pork| pig**
m
[pɔʁ]
On assiste à une chute des prix des céréales et de la viande, notamment du
porc.
-Grain and meat prices, especially hog prices, are dropping.

1309 vierge   **virgin; virgin**
adj; f
[vjɛʁʒ]
La vierge la plus ménagère d'elle-même est déjà assez prodigue si elle
démasque sa beauté aux regards de la lune.
-The chariest maid is prodigal enough if she unmask her beauty to the
moon.

1310 haïr   **hate**
vb
[aiʁ]
Il y a des êtres qui continueront de haïr et de tuer même si toutes les
injustices étaient réparées.
-There are those who will hate and who will kill even if every injustice is
ended.

1311 titrage   **titration**
m
[titʁaʒ]
L'invention concerne un procédé de titrage destiné à des quantités de liquide
extrêmement réduites.
-The invention relates to a titration method for small quantities of liquid.

1312 suspect   **suspect| dubious; suspect**
adj; m
[syspɛ]
L'auteur a été interrogé en tant que témoin, mais il a été identifié comme
suspect.
-The author was interrogated as a witness, but then he was identified as a
suspect.

1313 station   **station**
f
[stasjɔ̃]
Jack se tient sur le quai de la station de métro de Westminster.
-Jack stood on the platform in Westminster Underground Station.

1314 tromper   **deceive| mislead**
vb
[tʁɔ̃pe]
Désormais, il ne sera plus possible de les tromper avec un étiquetage
incorrect.
-From now on, it will no longer be possible to deceive them with incorrect
labelling.

1315 souffrir   **suffer| experience**
vb
[sufʁiʁ]
Il souffre trop et depuis trop longtemps; il ne doit plus souffrir.
-They have suffered too much for too long; they should not suffer any more.

1316 jean   **jeans**
m
[dʒin]
Je pense que j'ai l'air grosse, dans ce jean.
-I think I look fat in these jeans.

1317	**bagage**	**luggage**
	m	Dois-je faire enregistrer ce bagage ou peut-il être accompagné ?
	[bagaʒ]	-Do I have to check this luggage, or can it be carry-on?

1318	**protection**	**protection**
	f	Je n'ai pas besoin de ta protection.
	[pʁɔtɛksjõ]	-I don't need your protection.

1319	**tir**	**shot**
	m	C'est ton seul tir.
	[tiʁ]	-It's your only shot.

1320	**empereur**	**emperor**
	m	Exposition - Le Premier Empereur - guerriers enterrés de la Chine Jusqu'à ce
	[ãpʁœʁ]	que 13 mars 2011.
		-Exhibition - The First Emperor - China's entombed warriors until 13 March 2011.

1321	**océan**	**ocean**
	m	Laisse-moi t'emmener sur l'océan demain.
	[ɔseã]	-Let me take you out on the ocean tomorrow.

1322	**concert**	**concert**
	m	Voir un concert des Boston Rats.
	[kõsɛʁ]	-We went to see a concert of the Boston Rats.

1323	**immeuble**	**building; immovable**
	m; adj	Cet immeuble a cinq ascenseurs.
	[imœbl]	-This building has five elevators.

1324	**virer**	**transfer| turn**
	vb	On doit pouvoir virer les machines principales en toute sécurité.
	[viʁe]	-It shall be possible to turn the main machinery over in complete safety.

1325	**chaîne**	**chain| string**
	f	Vois-tu un inconvénient à ce que je change de chaîne ?
	[ʃɛn]	-Do you mind if I change the channel?

1326	**enfance**	**childhood**
	f	L'enfance est fragile, l'enfance est par essence fugitive.
	[ãfãs]	-Childhood is fragile, childhood is essentially transient.

1327	**maudire**	**curse**
	vb	Comme dit un proverbe américain «Mieux vaut allumer une chandelle que
	[modiʁ]	maudire l'obscurité».
		-As an American proverb says: "It is better to light a candle than to curse the darkness."

1328	**cauchemar**	**nightmare**
	m	Ils ont pris la décision de consentir les efforts nécessaires pour faire face à ce
	[koʃmaʁ]	cauchemar.
		-They took the decision to make the efforts required to cope with this nightmare.

1329	**amitié**	**friendship**
	f	J'espère que l'amitié règne dans cette région, l'amitié symbolisée par ce pont.
	[amitje]	-I hope that friendship prevails in this area, the friendship symbolised by this bridge.

1330	**magie**	**magic**
	f	Le problème a disparu comme par magie.
	[maʒi]	-The problem disappeared as if by magic.

1331	**nana**	**girl| babe**

	f	Je vous ai dit que j'ai une nana.
	[nana]	-I told you I have a girlfriend.
1332	**partenaire**	**partner**
	m	En ce moment, l'homme a-t-il une partenaire qui n'est pas la partenaire battue ?
	[paʁtənɛʁ]	-Does the man have a current partner that is different from the assaulted partner?
1333	**curieux**	**curious; onlooker**
	adj; m	Vous êtes curieux, n'est-ce pas ?
	[kyʁjø]	-You are curious, aren't you?
1334	**patte**	**tab| leg**
	f	Le vieil homme s'est fait un croche-patte à lui-même.
	[pat]	-The old man tripped over his own feet.
1335	**lendemain**	**next day**
	m	Le lendemain, l'archevêque est parti avec le nouvel administrateur apostolique.
	[lɑ̃dmɛ̃]	-The day after, the Archbishop left together with the new appointee.
1336	**souper**	**supper; sup**
	m; vb	Il était si furieux qu'il en oublia de souper.
	[supe]	-He was so mad that he forgot to eat dinner.
1337	**uniforme**	**uniform; uniform**
	adj; m	Je l'ai rencontrée à la station mais je ne l'ai pas reconnue en uniforme.
	[ynifɔʁm]	-I met her at the station, but I did not recognize her in uniform.
1338	**marine**	**navy**
	f	Zigler est pompier et ancien marine.
	[maʁin]	-ZIgler Is a firefighter and a former marine.
1339	**réserver**	**book| reserve**
	vb	On ne peut dès lors réserver aux seuls Américains le rôle de gendarme du monde.
	[ʁezɛʁve]	-So the role of world policeman cannot be reserved exclusively to the Americans.
1340	**Chine**	**China**
	f	Je suis en Chine depuis moins d'un mois.
	[ʃin]	-I've been in China for less than a month.
1341	**désir**	**desire| wish**
	m	Et le désir me talonne et me mord, car je vous aime, ô Madame la Mort .
	[deziʁ]	-And desire follows me at my heels and bites me, for I love you, o Lady Death.
1342	**objet**	**object**
	m	Le côté gauche de l' objet initial devient alors le côté droit de l' objet reflété.
	[ɔbʒɛ]	-The left side of the object will become the right side of the flipped object.
1343	**tracer**	**draw| mark**
	vb	Elle l'a regardé tracer un dessin.
	[tʁase]	-She watched him draw a picture.
1344	**recommencer**	**restart| start again**
	vb	Monsieur le Président, si je devais recommencer, ce serait par la culture.
	[ʁəkɔmɑ̃se]	-Mr President, if I could begin again, I would start with culture.
1345	**traverser**	**cross| pass through**
	vb	Faire traverser de la sorte la mer à des navires est aux antipodes de ces efforts.
	[tʁavɛʁse]	-Having ships cross the sea in this way is diametrically contrary to this.

1346	**humanité**	**humanity**
	f	Bien sûr, reconnaître notre humanité commune est seulement le commencement de notre tâche.
	[ymanite]	-Of course, recognizing our common humanity is only the beginning of our task.
1347	**lapin**	**rabbit**
	m	J'ai un lapin comme animal de compagnie.
	[lapɛ̃]	-I keep a rabbit as a pet.
1348	**sonner**	**ring| sound**
	vb	Aussi à l'avenir, je vous prie de faire sonner la sonnette plus fort et plus longtemps.
	[sɔne]	-So could you make sure they ring it longer and louder in future?
1349	**baguer**	**ring**
	vb	Si j'avais su, j'aurais acheté une bague à 18 ans et...
	[bage]	-If I'd known, I'd have bought a ring when I was 18 and saved myself...
1350	**survivre**	**survive**
	vb	Ce n'est que de cette façon que les petites distilleries pourront survivre dans l'UE.
	[syʁvivʁ]	-Only this will make it possible for small distilleries in the EU to survive.
1351	**bâtiment**	**building| vessel**
	m	C'est à côté de ce bâtiment.
	[batimã]	-It's next to that building.
1352	**chèque**	**check**
	m	Pouvez-vous encaisser ce chèque pour moi ?
	[ʃɛk]	-Can you cash this check for me?
1353	**palais**	**palace**
	m	Il me guida jusqu'au palais.
	[palɛ]	-He guided me to the palace.
1354	**valise**	**suitcase| case**
	f	Il a mal à l'épaule parce qu'il a porté une valise très lourde.
	[valiz]	-His shoulder hurts because he carried a very heavy suitcase.
1355	**charger**	**load| charge**
	vb	Laisse-moi me charger d'elle.
	[ʃaʁʒe]	-Let me deal with her.
1356	**haine**	**hatred; heating**
	f; adj	Votre Honneur, je suis hanté par cette haine et cette colère.
	[ɛn]	-Your Honor, I've become obsessed with this deep feeling of hate and anger.
1357	**mile**	**mile**
	m	These supertankers need half a mile to turn around and a whole mile to stop.
	[majl]	-Ces superpétroliers ont besoin d'un demi-mille pour tourner et d'un mille pour effectuer un arrêt.
1358	**assurance**	**insurance| assurance**
	f	Ne t'en fais pas. J'ai une assurance.
	[asyʁãs]	-Don't worry. I have insurance.
1359	**navire**	**ship**
	m	Ce navire est pourvu d'un treuil pour lever l'encre.
	[naviʁ]	-This ship is outfitted with a windlass to heave up the anchor.
1360	**foyer**	**home| fireplace**
	m	Attention aux braises qui sautent du foyer !
	[fwaje]	-Watch out for the sparks that are flying out of the fireplace!

1361	**printemps**	**spring**
	m	Le printemps vient après l'hiver.
	[pʁɛ̃tɑ̃]	-Spring comes after winter.

1362	**voiler**	**veil| mask**
	vb	Les champignons voilés, c'est-à-dire les champignons dont le chapeau et le
	[vwale]	pied sont reliés par un voile.
		-Veiled mushrooms, i.e. mushrooms the cap of which is connected to the
		stalk by the veil.

1363	**personnage**	**character| figure**
	m	Aujourd'hui, le personnage« Europe» est en scène dans son habit de
	[pɛʁsɔnaʒ]	communauté solidaire.
		-The character of Europe as a mutually supportive community is now at
		stake.

1364	**brave**	**brave| good; brave**
	adj; m	Un peu plus tôt ce soir, j'ai reçu un appel extraordinairement élégant du
	[bʁav]	Sénateur McCain. Le Sénateur McCain a combattu longuement et durement
		dans cette campagne. Et il a combattu plus longtemps et durement encore
		pour le pays qu'il aime. Il a enduré des sacrifices pour l'Amérique que la
		plupart d'entre nous ne peuvent commencer à imaginer. Nous nous portons
		mieux grâce au service rendu par ce leader, brave et désintéressé.
		-A little bit earlier this evening, I received an extraordinarily gracious call
		from Senator McCain. Senator McCain fought long and hard in this
		campaign. And he's fought even longer and harder for the country that he
		loves. He has endured sacrifices for America that most of us cannot begin to
		imagine. We are better off for the service rendered by this brave and selfless
		leader.

1365	**évident**	**obvious| evident**
	adj	Il est cependant évident que l'offre de tels ateliers ne répond pas à la
	[evidɑ̃]	demande.
		-It is apparent, however, that the supply of workshops does not meet the
		demand.

1366	**sale**	**dirty| nasty**
	adj	Elle a mis le linge sale dans le lave-linge.
	[sal]	-She put the dirty laundry in the washing machine.

1367	**roulé**	**rolled**
	adj	Dans une affaire, par exemple, un navire de 52 pieds a été mis sous
	[ʁule]	séquestre après que l'on eut trouvé de la poussière de cocaïne dans un billet
		de banque roulé.
		-In one case, for example, a 52-foot vessel was impounded because of
		cocaine dust found on a rolled up dollar bill.

1368	**extraordinaire**	**extraordinary**
	adj	Vanter publiquement les mérites de cet extraordinaire programme !
	[ɛkstʁaɔʁdinɛʁ]	-Obviously to canvass for this marvellous programme.

1369	**piger**	**understand| get**
	vb	Le risque de confusion est trop élevé, je ne dois sûrement pas être la seule, à
	[piʒe]	ne pas piger ça.
		-The risk of confusion is too high, I surely cannot be the only one who does
		not get this.

1370	**explosion**	**explosion| blast**
	f	Un groupe de personnes moururent dans l'explosion.
	[ɛksplozjɔ̃]	-A bunch of people died in the explosion.

1371 **sucrer**   **sweeten**

vb

[sykʁe]

Les grandes entreprises du café que sont Nestlé, Kraft, Sara Lee et Procter et Gamble ne peuvent pas continuer à se " sucrer " impunément.
-As major coffee companies, Nestlé, Kraft, Sara Lee and Procter and Gamble cannot continue to get away with lining their pockets.

1372 **procureur**   **prosecutor**

m

[pʁɔkyʁœʁ]

Pour commencer, il y a le requin gris ordinaire, nommé par les marins « procureur des mers ».
-To begin. There is the ordinary Brown Shark, or sea-attorney, so called by sailors.

1373 **opinion**   **opinion**

f

[ɔpinjɔ̃]

Tu as droit à ton opinion.
-You are entitled to your opinion.

1374 **davantage**   **further**

adv

[davɑ̃taʒ]

Elle rassembla finalement le courage pour lui demander davantage d'argent.
-She finally mustered up the courage to ask him for more money.

1375 **gardé**   **guarded**

adj

[gaʁde]

On entend par garde conjointe la garde physique conjointe et la garde légale conjointe.
-joint custody means joint physical custody and joint legal custody

1376 **net**   **net| sharp; outright**

adj; adv

[nɛt]

Excédent total net du régime de retraite des salariés.
-This is the total of net surplus related to employees' pension scheme.

1377 **vivant**   **living| alive; living**

adj; m

[vivɑ̃]

Si ce n'était pour le Soleil, aucun être vivant ne pourrait exister sur Terre.
-If it were not for the sun, no living creatures could exist on the earth.

1378 **compliqué**   **complicated| difficult**

adj

[kɔ̃plike]

C'est compliqué, veuillez m'en excuser, mais la vie est parfois compliquée.
-I am sorry that this is complicated, but life sometimes is complicated.

1379 **fiancé**   **fiance; engaged**

m; adj

[fjɑ̃se]

Elle a été rejetée par son fiancé, par la majeure partie de sa famille et par la société.
-She has been rejected by her fiancé, by most of her family and by society.

1380 **accuser**   **accuse| blame**

vb

[akyze]

When does one move from being the accuser to being a recognized victim?
-À quel moment cesse-t-on d'être l'accusateur et devient-on la victime reconnue ?

1381 **construire**   **build| erect**

vb

[kɔ̃stʁɥiʁ]

Aucun parti ne possède ne majorité seul, nous devons construire un consensus en Europe.
-No party has a majority alone, so we have to build a consensus in Europe.

1382 **sombre**   **dark| gloomy**

adj

[sɔ̃bʁ]

In reality, the portrait may well be more sombre than that painted here.
-Dans les faits, le portrait risque d'être nettement plus sombre que celui brossé ici.

1383 **hâte**   **haste| hastiness**

f

[at]

L'unité du Conseil de sécurité est ainsi la victime d'une hâte injustifiée.
-The unity of the Security Council has been sacrificed for the sake of undue haste.

1384 **amen**   **amen**

m

[amɛn]

Notre rôle doit -il se limiter à dire " Amen " aux propositions du Conseil ?

-Should our role be limited to saying " Amen " to the Council's proposals?

1385 voisin   **neighbor; neighboring**

m; adj

[vwazɛ̃]

Je déteste mon voisin.

-I hate my neighbour.

1386 lourd   **heavy**

adj

[luʁ]

Le long conflit en Afghanistan a imposé un lourd tribu à la population civile.

-The long-running conflict in Afghanistan has taken a heavy toll on civilians.

1387 prof   **prof**

m

[pʁɔf]

Résumé préparé par le Prof. Ulrich Magnus, Correspondant national, et Jan Lüsing

-Abstract prepared by Prof. Ulrich Magnus, National Correspondent and Jan Lüsing

1388 retirer   **withdraw| pull**

vb

[ʁətiʁe]

Je demanderais au député de Calgary-Nord-Est de retirer ses paroles.

-I would ask the hon. member for Calgary Northeast to withdraw those words.

1389 comte   **count**

m

[kɔ̃t]

Le comte et moi voyageons beaucoup.

-The count and I travel a great deal.

1390 contrôler   **control| monitor**

vb

[kɔ̃tʁole]

Or nous pouvons contrôler les émissions, mais nous ne pouvons pas contrôler ces facteurs.

-We can control emissions but we cannot control these factors.

1391 réputation   **reputation| name**

f

[ʁepytasjɔ̃]

Il a la réputation d'être intègre. Il ne serait jamais impliqué dans de la corruption.

-He has a reputation as being straight as an arrow. He'd never get involved in corruption.

1392 exploser   **explode**

vb

[ɛksploze]

C'est sur le point d'exploser !

-It's about to explode!

1393 créature   **creature| being**

f

[kʁeatyʁ]

Ce n'est ni une créature de principes ni une créature altruiste.

-It is neither a principled nor a altruistic creature.

1394 étudier   **study| examine**

vb

[etydje]

Hippocrate disait déjà que pour étudier la médecine, il fallait étudier le climat.

-Hippocrates once said that to study medicine you have to study the climate.

1395 brûler   **burn| burn off**

vb

[bʁyle]

Il serait préférable de brûler cet argent plutôt que de le donner aux libéraux.

-It would be better to burn that money than give it to the Liberals.

1396 surveiller   **monitor| watch**

vb

[syʁveje]

Pouvez-vous rester et surveiller les enfants ?

-Can you stay and watch the children?

1397 soif   **thirst**

f

[swaf]

Après des décennies de répression, ils ont soif d'informations produites en Iraq.

-After decades of suppression, there is a thirst for information originating in Iraq.

1398 égal — equal| even; equal

adj; m
[egal]

Il faut un partenariat égal mais celui-ci requiert une Europe forte et unie capable d'agir.
-Coequal partnership is needed, but it requires a strong and united Europe capable of action.

1399 sport — sport; sporting

m; adj
[spɔʁ]

Aujourd'hui, le sport n'est plus simplement du sport, c'est aussi un commerce.
-Sport today is not only sport, it is also business.

1400 résultat — result| product

m
[ʁezylta]

Dans l'ensemble, le résultat n'a pas été satisfaisant.
-On the whole, the result was unsatisfactory.

1401 siège — seat| siege

m
[sjɛʒ]

Regarde sous le siège.
-Look under the seat.

1402 adorable — adorable

adj
[adɔʁabl]

Adorable mini petite gentille mignonne...
-You adorable wittle itty bitty fuzzy wuzzy...

1403 cinglé — crazy

adj
[sɛ̃gle]

On rendait notre pote Kenny cinglé.
-We used to drive our friend Kenny crazy.

1404 canon — gun

m
[kanɔ̃]

Nous donnons un nouveau canon à l'armée.
-We are delivering on a new gun for the army.

1405 gardien — keeper| guardian

m
[gaʁdjɛ̃]

Il travaille comme gardien dans un entrepôt.
-He is working as a security guard at a warehouse.

1406 représenter — represent

vb
[ʁəpʁezɑ̃te]

Le Kadima et le parti travailliste pourraient représenter une opportunité.
-Kadima and the Labour Party might represent an opportunity.

1407 terme — term

m
[tɛʁm]

Elle n'est jamais arrivée à payer la facture au terme.
-She never managed to pay the bill on time.

1408 troupe — troop

f
[tʁup]

Cette actrice est l'étoile rayonnante de la troupe.
-That actress is the shining star in the company.

1409 théorie — theory

f
[teɔʁi]

La théorie est bonne, mais la pratique est désastreuse et n'a pas suivi la théorie du tout.
-The theory is good, but the practice has been awful and has not matched the theory at all.

1410 joueur — player

m
[ʒwœʁ]

Jack est un très bon joueur de tennis.
-Jack is a very good tennis player.

1411 région — region| district

f
[ʁeʒjɔ̃]

Ma région compte de nombreux chômeurs.
-We have a lot of unemployment in my area.

1412 commun — common| joint

adj
[kɔmɛ̃]

Des familles sans rapport peuvent être amenées à partager un espace de vie commun.
-Unrelated families may be required to share a communal living space.

1413	**tien**	**yours**
	prn	Mon plan est différent du tien.
	[tjɛ̃]	-My plan is different from yours.
1414	**médicament**	**drug| medication**
	m	Ce médicament soignera ton mal de ventre.
	[medikamã]	-This medicine will cure you of your stomach-ache.
1415	**crâne**	**skull| cranium**
	m	Le masque est obtenu à partir d'une tête par enlèvement d'un seul bloc de
	[kʁan]	tous les os (crâne).
		-The mask is derived from a head by the removal of all bone (skull) in one
		piece.
1416	**traduction**	**translation**
	f	L'original est infidèle à la traduction.
	[tʁadyksjɔ̃]	-The original is unfaithful to the translation.
1417	**studio**	**studio**
	m	Elle gère un studio de danse.
	[stydjo]	-She runs a dance studio.
1418	**libérer**	**release| liberate**
	vb	A l'évidence, il diffère du verbe « libérer » qui signifie rendre libre.
	[libeʁe]	-Obviously, too, it is not the same as "liberate", which means "to set free".
1419	**responsabilité**	**responsibility**
	f	Dans ce pays, les gens n'ont pas de sentiment de responsabilité.
	[ʁɛspɔ̃sabilite]	-In this country, people have no sense of responsibility.
1420	**délicieux**	**delicious**
	adj	La région de Finlande dont je proviens produit un délicieux fromage au lait
	[delisjø]	de chèvre.
		-The region that I come from in Finland produces a delicious goat's milk
		cheese.
1421	**trace**	**trace| track**
	f	L'action internationale pour identifier et tracer ces armes est une priorité.
	[tʁas]	-International action to identify and trace these weapons is a priority.
1422	**traiter**	**treat| deal**
	vb	Je propose donc à l'Assemblée de ne pas traiter l'accord avec le Mexique
	[tʁete]	cette semaine.
		-I therefore propose to the House that we do not deal with the agreement
		with Mexico this week.
1423	**modèle**	**model; model**
	adj; m	C'est un modèle plus ancien.
	[mɔdɛl]	-It's an older model.
1424	**cellule**	**cell**
	f	Il a confectionné un nœud coulant avec les draps de lit et s'est pendu dans sa
	[selyl]	cellule.
		-He fashioned a noose out of the bed sheets and hung himself in his cell.
1425	**gêne**	**discomfort| embarrasment**
	f	Et j'ai prescrit du propofol pour soulager la gêne.
	[ʒɛn]	-And I've prescribed propofol to help with any discomfort.
1426	**pêcher**	**fish; peach**
	vb; m	Il est illégal de pêcher près d'ici.
	[peʃe]	-Fishing is illegal around here.
1427	**poule**	**hen**

f — Qui de la poule ou de l'œuf est arrivé en premier ?
[pul] — -What came first? The egg or the hen?

1428 sénateur — senator
m — Il avait servi en tant que député et sénateur.
[senatœʁ] — -He had served as a congressman and senator.

1429 péché — sin| trespass
m — Mon péché mignon, c'est le chocolat.
[peʃe] — -My sweetest sin, I just can't resist chocolate.

1430 lentement — slowly| leisurely
adv — Pendant le mois de novembre la situation a progressé lentement, mais
[lɑ̃tmɑ̃] — sûrement.
-November was a month of slow but substantial progress in Bosnia and Herzegovina.

1431 empire — empire
m — Les États-Unis s'assument comme un empire.
[ɑ̃piʁ] — -The United States is acting as if it were an empire.

1432 débile — stupid; defective
adj; m/f — C'est tellement débile !
[debil] — -This is so retarded.

1433 top — top
m — Ce soir, je suis au top.
[tɔp] — -I feel first-class tonight.

1434 deviner — guess| divine
vb — J'ai tenté de deviner ce qu'il allait contenir.
[dəvine] — -But let me move on - I have had to guess at what the motion will contain.

1435 imagination — imagination
f — Il a une imagination fertile.
[imaʒinasjɔ̃] — -He has a rich imagination.

1436 liquide — liquid| wet; liquid
adj; m — On dit que le liquide amniotique est à peu près de la même composition que
[likid] — l'eau de mer.
-They say amniotic fluid has roughly the same composition as sea water.

1437 avancer — advance| forward
vb — Le terrorisme, sous quelque forme que ce soit, ne saurait avancer une cause
[avɑ̃se] — juste.
-Terrorism in any shape or form will not advance just causes.

1438 marin — marine; marine
adj; m — Le sous-marin dut sourdre au travers d'une fine couche de glace.
[maʁɛ̃] — -The submarine had to break through a thin sheet of ice to surface.

1439 humeur — mood| spirit
f — Tout le monde est de bonne humeur et veut collaborer avec le
[ymœʁ] — gouvernement.
-Everyone is in a good mood to cooperate with the government.

1440 auprès — nearby
adv — Toute personne ayant besoin de services hospitaliers est recommandée
[opʁɛ] — auprès des hôpitaux proches.
-Any person needing hospital services is recommended to the nearby hospitals.

1441 jaloux — jealous
adj — Il est très jaloux de cette indépendance et il a parfaitement raison.
[ʒalu] — -He is very jealous of his own independence, and properly so.

1442	**temple** m [tɑ̃pl]	**temple** Quand a été construit ce temple ? -When was this temple built?
1443	**physique** adj; f [fizik]	**physical; physics** Vous devez être en bonne condition physique. -You must be in good physical condition.
1444	**bosser** vb [bɔse]	**work** Je peux vivre sans être marié, mais je ne peux pas vivre sans bosser. -I can be happy without a marriage, but if you take away my work, that's different.
1445	**infirmier** m [ɛ̃fiʁmje]	**male nurse** Cinq membres du personnel infirmier se trouvent dans cinq autres régions sanitaires. -An additional five nursing officers are working in five other health regions.
1446	**secteur** m [sɛktœʁ]	**sector** Le secteur informatique vit une période de croissance. -The computer industry is enjoying a boom.
1447	**tâcher** vb [taʃe]	**try** L'organisation devrait alors examiner la plainte et tâcher de parvenir à un règlement. -The organization should then look into the complaint and attempt to resolve it.
1448	**cirque** m [siʁk]	**circus** Les éléphants sont l'attraction principale du cirque. -The elephants are the chief attraction at the circus.
1449	**particulier** adj; m [paʁtikylje]	**particular| individual; private person** Le renforcement de la coopération interministérielle constitue un souci particulier. -The strengthening of inter-ministerial collaboration was a particular concern.
1450	**engager** vb [ɑ̃ɡaʒe]	**engage** We need to engage and create the participatory functioning of the EU institutions. -Nous devons enclencher et créer le fonctionnement participatif des institutions de l'UE.
1451	**réaliser** vb [ʁealize]	**realize| achieve** Cette Assemblée semble ne pas réaliser ce qui préoccupe réellement les citoyens. -This House seems not to realise what really preoccupies the citizens back home.
1452	**Chut!** int [ʃy!]	**Hush!** Chut, Scout ! -Hush, Scout.
1453	**vision** f [vizjɔ̃]	**vision** Porter des lunettes devrait corriger ta vision. -Wearing glasses should correct your vision.
1454	**clocher** m [klɔʃe]	**bell tower** Jade, dans les limites d'une ligne reliant le phare de Schillighörn et le clocher de Langwarden. -Jade, inside a line linking the Schillighörn cross light and Langwarden church tower.

1455 **empreindre**   **stamp**

vb

[ɑ̃pʁɛ̃dʁ]

La feuille (40) à empreindre présente au moins une couche (20) de motifs ou de couleur et une couche (22) de fusion.

-The stamping foil (40) has at least one design or colour layer (20) and one melting layer (22).

1456 **croix**   **cross**

f

[kʁwa]

Les églises sont marquées par une croix sur la carte.

-Churches are designated on the map with crosses.

1457 **vente**   **sale**

f

[vɑ̃t]

La vente sera terminée dans deux jours.

-The sale will be over in two days.

1458 **démon**   **daemon**

m

[demɔ̃]

Le seigneur démon perdit enfin connaissance et tomba au sol avec un bruit sourd.

-The demon lord finally lost conciousness and fell to the floor with a thud.

1459 **barrer**   **bar| get ouy**

vb

[baʁe]

Tu dois vraiment te barrer d'ici.

-You do have to get out of here.

1460 **aventure**   **adventure**

f

[avɑ̃tyʁ]

Cette aventure tient beaucoup du mythe et, en fait, il s'agit de notre aventure.

-There is much myth in this adventure and in fact it is our adventure.

1461 **taule**   **slammer| nick**

f

[tol]

Quiconque a volé l'argent devrait être interpellé, être obligé à le rembourser et aller en taule.

-Whoever stole the money should be caught, made to pay it back, and go to jail.

1462 **matériel**   **equipment| material; material**

m; adj

[mateʁjɛl]

On reconnaît qu'un ordinateur constitue du matériel nécessaire.

-There is recognition that a computer is a necessary piece of equipment.

1463 **surface**   **surface**

f

[syʁfas]

Unité de mesure: La surface (km2) et le pourcentage des terres agricoles touchées.

-Measurement unit: Area (km2) and percentage of agricultural land area affected.

1464 **télévision**   **television**

f

[televizjɔ̃]

As-tu regardé la télévision hier soir ?

-Did you watch TV last night?

1465 **jaune**   **yellow; yellow**

adj; m

[ʒon]

La porte du bureau est jaune.

-The door of the office is yellow.

1466 **veiller**   **watch**

vb

[veje]

Elle doit être protégée par l'État qui doit veiller à sa santé physique et morale.

-It shall be protected by the State which shall take care of its physical health and moral.

1467 **rare**   **rare**

adj

[ʁaʁ]

Il est très rare qu'un sursis d'application ne soit pas ordonné en pareil cas.

-It was extremely rare for a stay of enforcement not to be ordered in such cases.

1468 **journaliste**   **journalist| reporter**

m/f
[ʒuʁnalist]

Ce sont les mots qu'a employés le journaliste pour décrire les propos de l'ambassadeur.
-Those are the reporter's words, characterizing the ambassador's comments.

1469 magique

adj
[maʒik]

magic

La péréquation n'a rien de magique, rien de politique, rien de déterminé arbitrairement.
-There is nothing magical about equalization payments, nothing arbitrarily determined.

1470 rat

m
[ʁa]

rat

Si ça marche comme un rat, parle comme un rat et sent comme un rat, c'est probablement un rat.
-If it walks like a rat, talks like a rat and smells like a rat, it is probably a rat.

1471 cri

m
[kʁi]

cry| scream

C'est le cri de Rome, le cri de Constantinople, le cri de Moscou.
-It is the cry of Rome, of Moscow, of Constantinople.

1472 patience

f
[pasjɑ̃s]

patience

On manque parfois de patience avec les personnes âgées.
-We sometimes lack patience with old people.

1473 ménage

m
[menaʒ]

household| housework

Un ménage compte en moyenne 7,4 personnes.
-The average number of people per household in Afghanistan is 7.4.

1474 comité

m
[kɔmite]

committee| panel

Lors de la discussion au congrès du rapport de synthèse du comité central du PCUS, il a été noté que, sous la direction du Parti Communiste et en étroite coopération avec tous les pays socialistes, le peuple soviétique a fait des progrès remarquables dans la lutte pour l'établissement d'une société communiste en URSS et dans celle pour la paix mondiale.
-During the discussion of the summary report of CC CPSU in the congress, it was noted that, under the guidance of the Communist party, in close cooperation with all the Socialist countries, the Soviet people have made great progress in the struggle for building a Communist society in the USSR and in that for world peace.

1475 baisser

vb
[bese]

lower| fall

De même, le coût des liaisons de télévision de qualité professionnelle devrait également baisser.
-However, the cost of broadcast quality television links is likely to decrease too.

1476 combattre

vb
[kɔ̃batʁ]

combat| fight

D'où l'importance de tout ce qui revient à combattre ce sentiment d'insécurité.
-Hence the importance of any measures that can combat this feeling of insecurity.

1477 Japon

m
[ʒapɔ̃]

Japan

Au 1er octobre 1998, la densité de population du Japon était de 339 habitants par km2.
-As of 1 October 1998, the population density was 339 people per square kilometre.

1478 romantique

adj; m/f
[ʁɔmɑ̃tik]

romantic; romantic

La question que je soulève n'est pas vraiment romantique.
-The issue I have brought forward is not a terribly romantic one.

1479 port

port| harbor

m
[pɔʁ]

Tu pourras voir une forêt de mâts dans le port.
-You will see a forest of masts in the harbor.

1480 crédit   **credit**

m
[kʁedi]

Pour sauver son crédit, il faut cacher sa perte.
-To save your credit, you must conceal your loss.

1481 abrutir   **stupefy**

vb
[abʁytiʁ]

Ce serait pas mieux de l'anesthésier, de l'abrutir, de la détruire de ne pas avoir à vivre avec la douleur de se battre pour elle pour la garder pure ?
-Might it not be best to anaesthetize it, to deaden it, to destroy it, to not have to live with the pain of struggling towards it and trying to keep it pure.

1482 promesse   **promise**

f
[pʁɔmɛs]

Elle ne peut pas avoir rompu sa promesse.
-She cannot have broken her promise.

1483 inconnu   **unknown; unfamiliar**

m; adj
[ɛ̃kɔny]

Un changement d'opinion est quelque chose de presqu'inconnu chez un vieux militaire.
-A change of opinions is almost unknown in an elderly military man.

1484 ambulance   **ambulance**

f
[ãbylãs]

Les services d'urgence (ambulance) fournissent un service similaire dans les régions.
-The Emergency Services (Ambulance) provide similar service in the regions.

1485 cependant   **however| yet; though**

con; adv
[səpãdã]

Cependant, elle ne porte pas interdiction particulière des châtiments corporels.
-However, it does not specifically mention a prohibition of physical punishment.

1486 panique   **panic; panic**

adj; f
[panik]

Je ne me panique pas.
-I'm not panicking.

1487 criminel   **criminal; criminal**

adj; m
[kʁiminɛl]

Le criminel doit toujours conserver son statut de criminel, et la victime, celui de victime.
-The criminal should always remain a criminal and the victim a victim.

1488 sauvage   **wild; savage**

adj; m
[sovaʒ]

La peine de mort est la sentence la plus inhumaine et la plus sauvage qui soit.
-The death penalty is the most inhuman and savage punishment.

1489 royaume   **kingdom**

m
[ʁwajom]

Si un royaume est divisé contre lui-même, ce royaume-là ne peut subsister.
-If a kingdom is divided against itself, that kingdom cannot stand.

1490 complet   **full| complete; suit**

adj; m
[kɔ̃plɛ]

Je porte un complet, mais pas de cravate.
-I wear a suit, but not a tie.

1491 centaine   **hundred**

num
[sãtɛn]

Lorsque j'étais très petit, nous habitions dans une maison à Utsunomiya, à une centaine de kilomètres au nord de Tokyo.
-When I was very small, we lived in a house in Utsunomiya, about a hundred kilometres north of Tokyo.

1492 scénario   **scenario**

m
[senaʁjo]
Considérez le scénario suivant.
-Consider the following scenario.

1493 principal **main; principal**
adj; m
[pʁɛ̃sipal]
Le kébab est l'aliment principal dans plusieurs restaurants turcs.
-In various Turkish restaurants, shishkabob is the main food.

1494 jus **juice**
m
[ʒy]
Elle versa du jus de citron dans son thé.
-She dropped lemon juice into her tea.

1495 détective **detective**
m
[detɛktiv]
Je suis détective.
-I'm a detective.

1496 pot **pot| jar**
m
[po]
Arrête de tourner autour du pot et dis-nous ce que tu penses réellement.
-Stop beating around the bush and tell us what you really think.

1497 divorcer **divorce**
vb
[divɔʁse]
A judge who administers divorce case is obliged to fill out a divorce form.
-Dans une affaire de divorce, le juge responsable doit remplir un formulaire de divorce.

1498 cochon **pig| swine; dirty**
m; adj
[kɔʃɔ̃]
Ce n'est pas un cochon ; c'est un singe.
-It's not a pig; it's a monkey.

1499 cadavre **corpse| body**
m
[kadavʁ]
Les policiers soupçonnaient qu'il existait un lien entre la voiture abandonnée et le cadavre trouvé trois kilomètres plus loin.
-The police suspected there was a connection between the abandoned car and the dead body found three miles away.

1500 tapir **tapir**
m
[tapiʁ]
Pour beaucoup, il s'agit d'espèces rares, menacées et en voie d'extinction, comme l'aigle harpie, le jaguar ou encore le tapir.
-Many of these species, such as the harpy eagle, the jaguar and the tapir, are considered rare and endangered species at risk of extinction.

1501 révolution **revolution**
f
[ʁevɔlysjɔ̃]
La prospérité et la satisfaction générales sont la meilleur dissuasion à la révolution.
-General prosperity and satisfaction are the best deterrents to revolution.

1502 existence **existence| life**
f
[ɛgzistãs]
Existence de ressources suffisantes; Existence d'un réseau commercial de distribution adapté.
-Existence of sufficient resources; existence of a suitable commercial distribution network.

1503 accompagner **accompany| follow**
vb
[akɔ̃paɲe]
On peut se demander comment un document électronique peut accompagner la marchandise.
-It is questionable how an electronic document can accompany the goods.

1504 lien **link| connection**
m
[ljɛ̃]
-Permettez-moi un lien avec le développement régional.
-I would like to make a link with regional development.

1505 fromage **cheese**
m
[fʁɔmaʒ]
Je vais préparer une salade de tomates et fromage.
-I will prepare a salad of tomatoes and cheese.

1506 période **period| term**

	f	Cette coutume remonte à la période Edo.
	[peʁjɔd]	-This custom dates from the Edo period.
1507	**profond**	**deep| profound; deep**
	adj; m	Ce lac est profond.
	[pʁofɔ̃]	-This lake is deep.
1508	**malheureux**	**unfortunate| unhappy; unfortunate**
	adj; m	En dépit de ses richesses il était malheureux.
	[maløʁø]	-For all his wealth, he was still unhappy.
1509	**nommer**	**appoint| name**
	vb	La Réunion décide de nommer un des Commissaires aux comptes recommandés par le Tribunal.
	[nɔme]	-The Meeting decided to appoint one of the auditors recommended by the Tribunal.
1510	**roman**	**novel; Romance**
	m; adj	Je me souviens avoir lu ce roman auparavant.
	[ʁɔmɑ̃]	-I remember reading this novel before.
1511	**poussière**	**dust**
	f	Tu dois préserver cette machine de la poussière.
	[pusjɛʁ]	-You must keep this machine free from dust.
1512	**passion**	**passion**
	f	L'art de reconnaître les champignons matsutake est devenu ma passion, culminant par l'écriture d'un livre sur le sujet.
	[pasjɔ̃]	-The art of recognizing matsutake mushrooms became my passion, culminating in my writing a book on it.
1513	**récemment**	**recently**
	adv	Le système de télécommunications internationales a été récemment libéralisé.
	[ʁesamɑ̃]	-The international telecommunications system was recently liberalized.
1514	**lutte**	**fight| struggle**
	f	Jack a dit à Jill qu'il n'était pas le chef de l'équipe de lutte.
	[lyt]	-Jack told Jill that he wasn't the captain of the wrestling team.
1515	**briser**	**break| shatter**
	vb	Ses efforts pour briser les clivages politiques ont suscité de vives louanges.
	[bʁize]	-His efforts to build shatter the cliffs of the political divide were widely applauded.
1516	**quiconque**	**whoever**
	prn	La violence contre les femmes, les enfants ou quiconque dans la société ne sera pas tolérée.
	[kikɔ̃k]	-Violence against women, children or anyone in society will not be tolerated.
1517	**cap**	**cape| course**
	m	Nous devons changer radicalement de cap.
	[kap]	-There is a need for a fundamental change of course.
1518	**version**	**version**
	f	Y a-t-il la version sous-titrée ?
	[vɛʁsjɔ̃]	-Is there the subtitled version?
1519	**entraînement**	**training**
	m	Jack a encore besoin d'entraînement.
	[ɑ̃tʁɛnmɑ̃]	-Jack still needs more training.
1520	**mardi**	**Tuesday**

m
[maʁdi]

Quant à savoir quel jour de la semaine nous sommes, c'est aujourd'hui mardi, un point c'est tout.
-As to what day of the week it is today, a Tuesday is a Tuesday is a Tuesday is a Tuesday.

1521 indien
adj
[ɛ̃djɛ̃]

Indian
En effet, c'est l'océan Indien qui structure les zones économiques de la région.
-After all, it was the Indian Ocean that defined the economic zones of the area.

1522 meurtrier
m; adj
[mœʁtʁije]

murderer; murderous
Il semble que la victime ait tenté d'écrire le nom du meurtrier avec son propre sang.
-It appears that the victim tried to write the murderer's name with his own blood.

1523 examen
m
[ɛgzamɛ̃]

examination| review
C'est en première lecture que l'examen du projet d'arrêt est le plus approfondi.
-The discussion of the draft judgment for first reading was the most thorough one.

1524 septembre
m
[sɛptɑ̃bʁ]

September
La deuxième phase devrait être exécutée entre septembre 2001 et septembre 2002.
-The timeframe for the implementation of phase II is September 2001-September 2002.

1525 élever
vb
[elve]

raise| elevate
Aider à élever la conscience de leurs droits et de leurs responsabilités citoyennes.
-Helping raise the awareness of their civil rights and responsibilities.

1526 profiter
vb
[pʁɔfite]

benefit| avail
Ensuite, la nécessité de profiter de la reprise pour consolider le budget.
-Secondly, the need to take advantage of recovery for budgetary consolidation.

1527 serpent
m
[sɛʁpɑ̃]

snake
Le tronc de chêne est-il vénéneux parce que le serpent s'y abrite ?
-Is the trunk of the oak poisonous because a snake hides in it?

1528 bouton
m
[butɔ̃]

button
Appuyer sur ce bouton fera pivoter l'objet sur l'axe des ordonnées.
-Pushing that button will make the object pivot around the y axis.

1529 piscine
f
[pisin]

swimming pool
Elle a plongé dans la piscine.
-She dived into the pool.

1530 courrier
m
[kuʁje]

mail| courier
J'ai du courrier à traiter.
-I have some correspondence to deal with.

1531 logique
f; adj
[lɔʒik]

logic; logical
Le cours d'analyse commence avec les notions fondamentales de la logique mathématique, des techniques de démonstration importantes et la construction des nombres réels et complexes.
-Courses in analysis begin with the fundamental notions of mathematical logic, important proof techniques, and the construction of real and complex numbers.

1532	**rythmer**	**rhythm**
	vb	Parce que nous sommes tous d' accord qu' il faut bien faire rythmer élargissement et approfondissement.
	[ʁitme]	-It is because we all agree that we need to bring the enlargement and the deepening of the Union into step with each other.
1533	**cancer**	**cancer**
	m	Le cancer du sein est la deuxième forme de cancer la plus répandue, après le cancer du poumon.
	[kɑ̃sɛʁ]	-Breast cancer is the second most common type of cancer after lung cancer.
1534	**proposer**	**propose| offer**
	vb	Je regrette, mais à ce stade-ci du débat, le député ne peut proposer de motion.
	[pʁɔpoze]	-I am afraid at this point the member is not permitted to propose a motion.
1535	**jeudi**	**Thursday**
	m	Elles auront lieu le jeudi 23 juin, le mardi 28 juin, le jeudi 30 juin et le jeudi 7 juillet.
	[ʒødi]	-They will take place on Thursday 23 June, Tuesday 28 June, Thursday 30 June and Thursday 7 July.
1536	**courageux**	**courageous| brave**
	adj	Nous rendons hommage aux courageux efforts des organisations humanitaires.
	[kuʁaʒø]	-We pay tribute to the courageous efforts of the humanitarian agencies.
1537	**boss**	**boss**
	m	I am the absentee boss of a very small enterprise, our family business in London.
	[bɔs]	-Je suis le chef absent d'une très petite entreprise familiale établie à Londres.
1538	**hall**	**lobby| lounge**
	m	Il y avait cent personnes dans le hall.
	[ol]	-There were a hundred people in the hall.
1539	**figurer**	**figure**
	vb	L'autorité compétente peut spécifier l'ordre dans lequel ces mentions doivent figurer.
	[figyʁe]	-The Competent Authority may choose to specify the order in which they appear.
1540	**ascenseur**	**elevator| lifter**
	m	Prenez l'ascenseur jusqu'au 5e étage.
	[asɑ̃sœʁ]	-Take the elevator to the fifth floor.
1541	**garage**	**garage**
	m	Le Comité a examiné les procédures et pratiques existantes de l'administration du garage.
	[gaʁaʒ]	-The Board reviewed the existing procedures and practices in Garage Administration.
1542	**approcher**	**hang over**
	vb	Les forces gouvernementales ont reçu l'ordre de ne pas s'approcher de territoires en litige.
	[apʁɔʃe]	-The Government forces were instructed not to approach disputed areas.
1543	**traitement**	**treatment| processing**
	m	Pouvez-vous me dire comment utiliser ce logiciel de traitement de texte ?
	[tʁɛtmɑ̃]	-Could you tell me how to operate this word processor?
1544	**sein**	**breast| fold**

	m	Y compris mammographies et autres examens du sein, appareillage orthopédique, orthèse, etc.
	[sɛ̃]	-Includes breast cancer and other breast screenings, orthopaedics, orthotics etc.

1545 nation — nation

f

[nasjɔ̃]

Éliminer l'identité d'une nation revient à éliminer cette nation elle-même.

-To eliminate the identity of a nation is the same as eliminating that nation itself.

1546 propriété — property

f

[pʁɔpʁijete]

La propriété privée désigne la propriété individuelle comme la propriété en association.

-Private property includes individual ownership and in association with others.

1547 labo — lab

m

[labo]

Je les apporterai au labo moi-même.

-I'll take them to the lab myself.

1548 machine — machine

f

[maʃin]

Tout professeur qui peut être remplacé par une machine devrait l'être.

-Any teacher that can be replaced by a machine should be.

1549 pub — pub; advertising

m; f

[pyb]

Mais je crois qu'on va augmenter le volume de pubs.

-Um, but I think we 're gonna get ad pages up here.

1550 sabler — sand

vb

[sable]

Ça te tente-tu de me sabler ça?

-Could you sand this for me?

1551 commission — commission| board

f

[kɔmisjɔ̃]

J'obtiens une commission de trois pour cent sur tout ce que je vends.

-I get a three percent commission on anything I sell.

1552 section — section

f

[sɛksjɔ̃]

Il y a sept hommes et quatre femmes dans ma section.

-There are seven men and four women in my section.

1553 nager — swim

vb

[naʒe]

On en arrive au point d'employer sur des navires des marins qui ne savent même pas nager.

-We will be staffing ships with sailors who do not know how to swim, next.

1554 pratique — practice; practical

f; adj

[pʁatik]

Il change une pratique, mais cette pratique doit changer.

-It seeks to change a practice, but that practice must be changed.

1555 écran — screen

m

[ekʁɑ̃]

Le but de ce jeu est de faire exploser toutes les bombes sur l'écran.

-The aim of this game is to explode all the bombs on the screen.

1556 chuter — tumble

vb

[ʃyte]

Les nations s'élèvent pour chuter.

-Nations rise, only to fall.

1557 ceinture — belt| waistband

f

[sɛ̃tyʁ]

Elle a débouclé sa ceinture.

-She unbuckled her belt.

1558 briller — shine| sparkle

vb

[bʁije]

Les Africains ont décidé de faire briller la lumière de la prospérité sur eux-mêmes.

-Africans have decided to shine the light of prosperity on themselves.

1559	**miel**	honey
	m	La Commission propose d'ajouter une nouvelle catégorie de miel, le miel
	[mjɛl]	filtré.
		-The Commission proposes adding a new category of honey, filtered honey.
1560	**crever**	die| burst
	vb	Va crever !
	[kʁəve]	-Go to hell!
1561	**estomac**	stomach
	m	N'attrape pas mal à l'estomac en mangeant trop.
	[ɛstɔma]	-Don't get a stomachache by eating too much.
1562	**salaire**	salary
	m	Le salaire sera augmenté à partir d'avril.
	[salɛʁ]	-The salary will be raised from April.
1563	**inventer**	invent| make up
	vb	Je suis incapable d'inventer des sornettes pareilles.
	[ɛ̃vɑ̃te]	-I've got no imagination, I'd never be able to invent such lies.
1564	**étonner**	surprise| wonder
	vb	Je suis toujours étonné du nombre de passagers qui disparaissent dans les
	[etɔne]	aéroports !
		-It never ceases to amaze me the number of passengers that go missing in
		airports!
1565	**nourrir**	feed| nourish
	vb	Le pays a commencé à nourrir la guerre au lieu de nourrir sa population.
	[nuʁiʁ]	-The land began to fuel the war rather than to feed the people.
1566	**incendie**	fire
	m	L'incendie se déclara après que les employés fussent rentrés chez eux.
	[ɛ̃sɑ̃di]	-The fire broke out after the staff went home.
1567	**pur**	pure| clean
	adj	Dans votre réponse, vous mentionnez le programme "Air pur pour l'Europe"
	[pyʁ]	(CAFE).
		-In your reply you mentioned the Clean Air for Europe programme: CAFE.
1568	**refaire**	redo| repair
	vb	En quoi lui est-ce si difficile de refaire les études françaises et allemandes ?
	[ʁəfɛʁ]	-How difficult can it be for them to try to redo the French and German
		studies?
1569	**prénom**	first name
	m	Sami s'est donné comme deuxième prénom Farid.
	[pʁenɔ̃]	-Sami gave himself the middle name Farid.
1570	**invité**	guest
	m	Notre prochain invité est père célibataire.
	[ɛ̃vite]	-Now, our next guest is a single parent.
1571	**idéal**	ideal; ideal
	adj; m	Le compromis obtenu grâce à la conciliation n'est pas idéal, mais il est
	[ideal]	acceptable.
		-The compromise reached by conciliation is not ideal, but it is acceptable.
1572	**condition**	condition
	f	C'est une condition nécessaire, mais ce n'est pas une condition suffisante.
	[kɔ̃disjɔ̃]	-That is a necessary condition, but it is not a sufficient condition.
1573	**élève**	student
	m/f	Le CAR comprenait le nombre le plus élevé d'étudiantes, soit environ 72 %
	[elɛv]	des boursiers de la région.

-CAR posted the most number of female scholars comprising about 72% of the total IP scholars in the region.

1574	**douze** num [duz]	**twelve** Nous les répartîmes en douze tribus, (en douze) communautés. -We divided Moses' people into twelve tribes, forming them into communities.
1575	**virus** m [viʁys]	**virus** Mon anti-virus a laissé passer un virus. -My anti-virus let a virus through.
1576	**poil** m [pwal]	**hair** Un poil blanc dans sa barbe naissante. -In his slowly growing beard, there's one white hair.
1577	**jeunesse** f [ʒœnɛs]	**youth** Le vieil homme repense souvent à sa jeunesse. -The old man often looks back on his youth.
1578	**ordinaire** adj; m [ɔʁdinɛʁ]	**ordinary; ordinary** Ce n'est pas un homme ordinaire. -He is no ordinary man.
1579	**agence** f [aʒɑ̃s]	**agency** La Corée a reçu une inspection de l'Agence Internationale de l'Énergie Atomique. -Korea received an inspection from the International Atomic Energy Agency.
1580	**revolver** m [ʁevɔlvɛʁ]	**revolver** Présentement, la seule arme qu'a l'officier de la marine, c'est un revolver. -At the moment, the only weapon a fishery officer can carry is a revolver.
1581	**loup** m [lu]	**wolf** J'ai une faim de loup ; où puis-je trouver quelque chose à manger ? -I'm hungry like a wolf; where can I find something to eat?
1582	**naturel** adj; m [natyʁɛl]	**natural; nature** Le champ de gaz naturel de South Pars / North Dome, partagé entre l'Iran et le Qatar, a plus de réserves récupérables que tous les autres gisements de gaz combinés, et le monde se dirige donc vers la guerre pour voler des trillions de dollars. -The South Pars/North Dome natural gas field, shared between Iran and Qatar, has more recoverable reserves than all other gas fields combined, and, thus, the world is headed for war to steal this field worth trillions of dollars.
1583	**autrefois** adv [otʁəfwa]	**once| in the past** Après tout, ces personnes étaient rangées autrefois parmi les psychopathes. -After all, such people were once classed as psychopaths.
1584	**équipage** m [ekipaʒ]	**crew** Tous les membres de l'équipage espèrent que volerez à nouveau avec eux. Nous vous souhaitons une belle journée. -From all of us in the crew, we look forward to your flying with us again. We hope you have a nice day.
1585	**tempête** f [tɑ̃pɛt]	**storm** C'est le calme avant la tempête. -This is the calm before the storm.
1586	**central** adj [sɑ̃tʁal]	**central** Le noyau comprend un noyau central et au moins une couche noyau entourant ledit noyau central.

-The core includes a center core component and one or more core layers enclosing the center core component.

1587	**forcément**	**necessarily**
	adv	Mais cela nécessitera forcément d'énormes ressources internationales.
	[fɔʀsemɑ̃]	-But it will inevitably require substantial international funding too.

1588	**calmer**	**calm| soothe**
	vb	Nous appuyons également une médiation internationale pour calmer la
	[kalme]	situation.
		-We also support international mediation to calm the situation.

1589	**miroir**	**mirror**
	m	Vous vous regardez dans le miroir et vous vous sentez comme une personne
	[miʀwaʀ]	minable.
		-You look in the mirror and feel like a shitty person.

1590	**chic**	**chic| stylish; chic**
	adj; m	C'est un chic type, assurément, mais pas très malin.
	[ʃik]	-He is a nice person, to be sure, but not very clever.

1591	**jury**	**jury**
	m	Le jury est divisé.
	[ʒyʀi]	-The jury is hung.

1592	**pardonner**	**forgive| pardon**
	vb	Je pense que les Timorais ont montré qu'ils sont très tolérants et qu'ils sont
	[paʀdɔne]	prêts à pardonner.
		-I believe the Timorese have shown they are very tolerant and willing to
		forgive.

1593	**affronter**	**confront**
	vb	La réconciliation et la tolérance mutuelle dépendent de la volonté d'affronter
	[afʀɔ̃te]	le passé.
		-Reconciliation and mutual tolerance depend on a willingness to face the
		past.

1594	**lâcher**	**release| drop**
	vb	Mais voulez-vous bien lâcher Helga, qu'elle puisse retourner au travail ?
	[laʃe]	-But could you release Helga so she can get back to work?

1595	**cérémonie**	**ceremony**
	f	Avez-vous regardé la cérémonie de clôture des Jeux olympiques?
	[seʀemɔni]	-Did you watch the Olympics closing ceremony?

1596	**tasse**	**cup**
	f	J'aimerais une tasse de café, s'il te plaît.
	[tas]	-I'd like a cup of coffee, please.

1597	**absence**	**absence**
	f	Son absence a été causée par une maladie.
	[apsɑ̃s]	-His absence was due to illness.

1598	**comportement**	**behavior**
	m	Le comportement de Jack m'a exaspéré.
	[kɔ̃pɔʀtəmɑ̃]	-Jack's behavior infuriated me.

1599	**correct**	**correct; alright**
	adj; adv	Ça, c'est grammaticalement correct.
	[kɔʀɛkt]	-Now, see, that's grammatically correct.

1600	**récompenser**	**reward**
	vb	Celle-là va bientôt récompenser les investisseurs.
	[ʀekɔ̃pɑ̃se]	-That one's going to reward shareholders soon.

| 1601 | **national** | **national; national** |

adj; m
[nasjɔnal]

Nos frontières nationales sont bien connues, d'un océan à l'autre.
-Our national boundaries are well known from coast to coast to coast.

1602 masque

m
[mask]

mask

Il portait un masque, de telle manière que personne ne pourrait le reconnaître.
-He wore a mask so no one would recognize him.

1603 raisonnable

adj
[ʁɛzɔnabl]

reasonable

On essaie de paraître raisonnable, mais l'inaction est inadmissible.
-There is an attempt to appear reasonable but the inaction is unconscionable.

1604 bijou

m
[biʒu]

jewel

Jill n'a porté aucun bijou.
-Jill didn't wear any jewelry.

1605 mystère

m
[mistɛʁ]

mystery

Le mystère de sa mort ne fut jamais résolu.
-The mystery of her death was never solved.

1606 cabine

f
[kabin]

cabin| cab

Le personnel de cabine est le seul personnel de sécurité ayant une double responsabilité.
-Cabin crew are the only safety professionals with dual responsibilities.

1607 étudiant

adj; m
[etydjã]

student; student

Je l'ai rencontré une fois quand j'étais étudiant.
-I met him once when I was a student.

1608 parfum

m
[paʁfɛ̃]

perfume| fragrance

Nous sommes devant un plat sec, froid, qui a perdu tout son goût et tout son parfum.
-We have before us a dried-up, cold dish that has lost all its flavour and all its aroma.

1609 avouer

vb
[avwe]

confess| admit

Cette situation est à l'évidence plus dangereuse que beaucoup ne veulent se l'avouer et elle se détériore avec chaque heure qui passe.
-Certainly, this situation is more dangerous than many can bring themselves to avow and is getting more out of hand by the hour.

1610 vengeance

f
[vãʒãs]

vengeance

C'est une vengeance aveugle.
-It is indiscriminate revenge.

1611 nu

adj
[ny]

naked

Le gendarme l'a battu avec une cordelette, frappant son corps nu, ses bras, ses genoux et sa tête.
-The gendarme beat him with a "cordelette" on his naked body, arms, knees and head.

1612 presser

vb
[pʁese]

press| squeeze

Il est très facile d'atteindre et de presser ce bouton; cela ne devrait être difficile pour aucun député.
-It is very easy to reach out and press this button, it should not be difficult for any Member.

1613 qualité

f
[kalite]

quality

Elle peut perdre cette qualité dans diverses circonstances.
-It may be deprived of that quality by a variety of circumstances.

1614 couvert

adj; m
[kuvɛʁ]

covered; place

Le Canada, pays couvert de neiges et de glaces huit mois de l'année, habité par des barbares, des ours et des castors.

-Canada, a country covered with snows and ices eight months of the year, inhabited by barbarians, bears and beavers.

1615	**couloir**	**corridor| hallway**
	m	Dégagez le couloir !
	[kulwaʁ]	-Clear the corridor!
1616	**tape**	**slap**
	f	J'aimerais que ce bruit cesse. Ça me tape sur les nerfs.
	[tap]	-I wish that noise would stop. It gets on my nerves.
1617	**réaction**	**reaction**
	f	À chaque action correspond une réaction égale et opposée.
	[ʁeaksjɔ̃]	-For every action there is an equal and opposite reaction.
1618	**doué**	**gifted| capable**
	adj	Il est doué de grandes qualités et de grandes valeurs humaines.
	[dwe]	-He is gifted with great qualities and human values.
1619	**attenter**	**attempt**
	vb	Une guerre sera toujours sale puisque son objet est d'attenter à la vie
	[atɑ̃te]	humaine.
		-War is always dirty because its objective is to attack human life.
1620	**nôtre**	**our**
	prn	Il s'agit de la sauvegarde de notre espèce, de notre écosystème.
	[notʁ]	-It is a question of the preservation of our own species, of our own
		ecosystem.
1621	**race**	**race| breed**
	f	Accouplé un pure race avec un autre pure race garde les choses... pure.
	[ʁas]	-Mating a purebred with another purebred keeps things... pure.
1622	**bêtise**	**foolishness**
	f	Maintenant, pourquoi irais-tu commettre une telle bêtise ?
	[betiz]	-Now why would you go and do a stupid thing like that?
1623	**moquer**	**mock**
	vb	Il savait rire, se moquer de lui-même - surtout se moquer de lui-même.
	[mɔke]	-He knew how to laugh, even at himself - especially how to laugh at
		himself.
1624	**colle**	**glue**
	f	N'utilisez pas trop de colle.
	[kɔl]	-Don't use too much glue.
1625	**poitrine**	**chest| bosom**
	f	De nombreux hommes sont dotés de davantage de poitrine que les femmes.
	[pwatʁin]	-Many men have larger breasts than women.
1626	**enterrement**	**burial| funeral**
	m	Je vous rembourserai pour l'enterrement.
	[ɑ̃tɛʁmɑ̃]	-I will pay you back for this funeral.
1627	**installer**	**install| set**
	vb	D'autres doivent protéger les périmètres et installer des barrières de sécurité.
	[ɛ̃stale]	-Others have been asked to install perimeter barriers and security gates.
1628	**noble**	**noble; noble**
	adj; m/f	Ca vient du domaine d'un riche noble.
	[nɔbl]	-It came from the estate of a wealthy nobleman.
1629	**large**	**wide| large**
	adj	Cette veste est beaucoup trop large pour vous.
	[laʁʒ]	-That jacket is way too big for you.

1630 urgent
adj
[yʁʒɑ̃]

urgent
Il est urgent de mettre un terme à la pêche industrielle dans la mer Baltique.
-There is a pressing need for industrial fishing in the Baltic Sea to be stopped.

1631 poindre
vb
[pwɛ̃dʁ]

dawn
C'est très inquiétant et la stagflation semble également poindre à l'horizon.
-This is very worrying, and stagflation also seems to be dawning on the horizon.

1632 digne
adj
[diɲ]

worthy
Cette transformation est donc digne de reconnaissance et de commémoration.
-So this transformation is worthy of recognition and commemoration.

1633 uniquement
adv
[ynikmɑ̃]

only
Le financement versé à cet organisme ne provenait pas uniquement du gouvernement.
-The funding for that organization was not solely provided by the government.

1634 riz
m
[ʁi]

rice
Le prix du riz augmenta de plus de trois pour cent.
-The price of rice rose by more than three percent.

1635 plaisant
adj
[plɛzɑ̃]

pleasant
Même s'il n'est guère plaisant de le dire, je le dis devant cette Assemblée.
-Even if it is not nice to say as much, I say it here.

1636 condamner
vb
[kɔ̃dane]

condemn| convict
De ce fait, le Conseil ne doit pas se limiter à condamner les actes de violence.
-Therefore, the Council must not confine itself to condemning acts of violence.

1637 puce
f; adj
[pys]

chip| flea; puce
Une puce peut sauter deux cents fois sa propre taille.
-A flea can jump 200 times its own height.

1638 ex-
pfx
[ɛks-]

ex-
Voilà deux ans que les images des atrocités en ex- Yougoslavie parcourent le monde.
-It has been two years since the images of atrocities in former Yugoslavia spread around the world.

1639 origine
f
[ɔʁiʒin]

origin
Un certificat d'origine est obligatoire pour les marchandises contingentées.
-A certificate of origin is required for goods subject to quota restrictions.

1640 attitude
f
[atityd]

attitude| outlook
Nous devons avoir une attitude plus rigoureuse.
-We have to be more rigorous in our behaviour.

1641 absurde
adj; m
[apsyʁd]

absurd; absurd
Ta méthode d'enseigner l'anglais est absurde.
-Your method of teaching English is absurd.

1642 union
f
[ynjɔ̃]

union
Our European Union is not just a union of states, it is a union of citizens.
-L'Union européenne n'est pas seulement une union d'États, c'est une union de citoyens.

1643 bagnole

wagon| wheel

	f	Il y a un cadavre dans le coffre de la bagnole.
	[baɲɔl]	-There's a body in the trunk of the car.
1644	**maximum**	**maximum; maximum**
	adj; m	Mon travail ne durera que deux ans au maximum.
	[maksimɔm]	-My job will only last two years at most.
1645	**effort**	**effort| stress**
	m	This effort — this huge effort — will require both political will and public support.
	[efɔʁ]	-Cet effort, un effort énorme, nécessitera volonté politique et appui de l'opinion publique.
1646	**chambre**	**room**
	f	Je n'ai pas à nettoyer ma chambre.
	[ʃɑ̃bʁ]	-I don't have to clean my room.
1647	**vélo**	**bike**
	m	Le vélo de qui voulais-tu emprunter ?
	[velo]	-Whose bicycle did you want to borrow?
1648	**esclave**	**slave; enslaved**
	m; adj	Donc, puisque l'esclave peut être libre, il devient soudain un travailleur.
	[ɛsklav]	-Since the slave can be free, he or she suddenly becomes a worker rather than a slave.
1649	**foot**	**football**
	m	Jack a joué au foot avec les enfants du coin.
	[fut]	-Jack played soccer with the local children.
1650	**éducation**	**education| upbringing**
	f	Les racines de l'éducation sont amères, mais son fruit est doux.
	[edykasjɔ̃]	-The roots of education are bitter, but the fruit is sweet.
1651	**réellement**	**actually| true**
	adv	Nous devons donc lancer une politique réellement rigoureuse et transparente.
	[ʁeɛlmɑ̃]	-We must therefore launch a policy which is genuinely rigorous and transparent.
1652	**pair**	**even; peer**
	adj; m	L'amour et la jalousie vont de pair.
	[pɛʁ]	-Love and jealousy go hand in hand.
1653	**moche**	**ugly**
	adj	Tu me trouves moche, n'est-ce pas ?
	[mɔʃ]	-You think I'm ugly, don't you?
1654	**blond**	**blond; blonde**
	adj; m	Elle a teint ses cheveux en blond.
	[blɔ̃]	-She dyed her hair blonde.
1655	**boule**	**ball**
	f	C'est une boule de nerfs.
	[bul]	-He's a nervous wreck.
1656	**déclaration**	**declaration**
	f	L'observateur de l'Égypte a fait une déclaration au sujet de la déclaration de la Slovénie.
	[deklaʁasjɔ̃]	-A statement was made by Egypt with regard to the statement made by Slovenia.
1657	**chasser**	**hunt| expel**
	vb	Si les citoyens de certains États membres souhaitent chasser, ils peuvent
	[ʃase]	continuer.

-If people in any of our Member States wish to hunt, they can still continue to hunt.

1658	**site**	**site**
	m	MapSite se compose de deux services : MapSite du citoyen et MapSite du professionnel.
	[sit]	-MapSite is composed of two services: Citizen's MapSite and Professional's MapSite.

1659	**scientifique**	**scientific; scientist**
	adj; m/f	Chercheur scientifique principal à l'Institut roumain d'études internationales.
	[sjãtifik]	-Senior Researcher in the Romanian Institute of International Studies.

1660	**traître**	**traitor; treacherous**
	m; adj	Y aurait-il un traître parmi nous ?
	[tʁɛtʁ]	-Would there be traitor among us?

1661	**traîner**	**drag| trail**
	vb	Jack est quelqu'un avec qui j'aime vraiment traîner.
	[tʁene]	-Jack is someone I really enjoy hanging out with.

1662	**cave**	**cellar; hollow**
	f; adj	Ce gentil manager m'a remonté le tableau... de la cave.
	[kav]	-This nice manager brought me the nutrition wall chart... from the basement.

1663	**cassette**	**cassette**
	f	Écoutons cette cassette.
	[kasɛt]	-Let's listen to the tape.

1664	**essai**	**test| testing**
	m	J'en ferai l'essai.
	[esɛ]	-I'll give it a try.

1665	**minable**	**shabby| pathetic; piddling**
	adj; m/f	T'es un vrai minable.
	[minabl]	-You're such a bummer.

1666	**sommet**	**top| vertex**
	m	J'ai réussi à atteindre le sommet de la montagne.
	[sɔmɛ]	-I succeeded in reaching the top of the mountain.

1667	**blesser**	**hurt| cut**
	vb	En outre, cette loi interdit de tenir des propos susceptibles de blesser la sensibilité de tel ou tel groupe religieux, politique ou social.
	[blese]	-Moreover, it prohibits the use of language in a manner likely to offend against sensitivities of religious, political or other social groups.

1668	**aile**	**wing| blade**
	f	L'aile de l'oiseau était cassée.
	[ɛl]	-The bird's wing was broken.

1669	**bagarre**	**fight| brawl**
	f	J'ai vu la bagarre.
	[bagaʁ]	-I saw the fight.

1670	**production**	**production**
	f	Modifier les modes de production et de consommation (production/consommation).
	[pʁɔdyksjõ]	-Changing production and consumption patterns (production/consumption).

1671	**rang**	**rank| row**
	m	J'ai eu l'honneur de m'asseoir au premier rang.
	[ʁã]	-I had the honor to sit in the first row.

1672	**Bible**	**Bible**

| | f | «Tu aimeras ton prochain comme toi-même » est une citation de la Bible. |

f
[bibl]   «Tu aimeras ton prochain comme toi-même » est une citation de la Bible.
-"Love your neighbour as yourself" is a quotation from the Bible.

1673 **livrer** — **deliver**
vb
[livʁe]
Lenzing devait livrer des machines, des appareils et des matériaux.
-Lenzing was to deliver machines, apparatus and materials.

1674 **venger** — **revenge**
vb
[vɑ̃ʒe]
Ils cherchent maintenant à se venger du coup porté à leurs intérêts.
-They are now seeking to avenge their hurt interests.

1675 **show** — **show**
m
[ʃo]
C'est un show à l'américaine.
-It's a dog and pony show.

1676 **flotter** — **float| hover**
vb
[flɔte]
Nous devons aussi interrompre collectivement le flot d'armes classiques vers de tels groupes.
-We must also collectively stop the flow of conventional weapons to such groups.

1677 **humour** — **humor**
m
[ymuʁ]
Dernièrement, j'ai lu dans un journal français un article intitulé «Humour britannique».
-I read a story in a French paper recently entitled, "British Humour."

1678 **naturellement** — **naturally**
adv
[natyʁɛlmɑ̃]
Naturellement, les procédures doivent être simplifiées, directes et flexibles.
-Naturally, the procedures must be simplified, straightforward and flexible.

1679 **résoudre** — **solve| resolve**
vb
[ʁezudʁ]
Les hommes ont causé la crise et les femmes doivent la résoudre.
-The men caused the crisis and the women will have to resolve it.

1680 **commandement** — **command**
m
[kɔmɑ̃dmɑ̃]
Les militaires ont une chaîne de commandement très stricte.
-The military has a very strict chain of command.

1681 **remplacer** — **replace| change**
vb
[ʁɑ̃plase]
Remplacer l'annexe à la résolution 4/4 par l'annexe figurant à la page suivante.
-Replace the annex to resolution 4/4 with the annex set out on the following page.

1682 **mandat** — **mandate| warrant**
m
[mɑ̃da]
Nous avons un mandat de perquisition.
-We have a search warrant.

1683 **milliard** — **billion**
num
[miljaʁ]
La population mondiale a atteint un milliard pour la première fois en dix-huit-cent-quatre.
-The world population reached one billion for the first time in 1804.

1684 **fruit** — **fruit**
m
[fʁɥi]
Le succès est le fruit de tes efforts.
-The success resulted from your efforts.

1685 **plaindre** — **complain| pity**
vb
[plɛ̃dʁ]
à quel moment cesse-t-on de le plaindre?
-At what point do we cease to feel sorry for him?

1686 **partage** — **sharing| division**
m
[paʁtaʒ]
Je partage vraiment tes sentiments.
-I do sympathize with you.

1687 **bourse** — **scholarship**

	f	Selon des sources bien informées, X Ltd. se prépare à rejoindre la première section de la bourse de Tokyo.
	[buʁs]	-According to informed sources, X Ltd. is preparing for the move up to the first section of the Tokyo Stock exchange.

1688 jungle — **jungle**

f

[ʒɛ̃gl]

Nous ne sommes pas dans la jungle.

-We're not in the jungle.

1689 aimable — **friendly| kind**

adj

[ɛmabl]

Il était aimable, mais je me suis senti comme un guérisseur de bas étage.

-He was very nice about it, but he made me feel like a third-class witch doctor.

1690 guider — **guide| steer**

vb

[gide]

Un multilatéralisme efficace, avec l'ONU en son centre, devrait guider nos efforts.

-Effective multilateralism, with the United Nations at its heart, should guide our effort.

1691 gâcher — **spoil| ruin**

vb

[gaʃe]

Les libéraux fédéraux ont gâché le transfert de l'aéroport à la ville de Penticton dès le départ.

-The federal Liberals bungled the transfer of the airport to the city of Penticton from the beginning.

1692 adulte — **adult; adult**

adj; m/f

[adylt]

Les besoins des enfants sont souvent exprimés par l'intermédiaire d'un adulte.

-What children need is usually conveyed through an adult person's point of view.

1693 pomme — **apple**

f

[pɔm]

Sénateur Whelan, je vous donne une belle pomme verte et une belle pomme rouge.

-Senator Whelan, I give to you a beautiful green apple and a beautiful red apple.

1694 auteur — **author**

m

[otœʁ]

Cet auteur ne comprend pas du tout pourquoi un homme et une femme qui ne peuvent devenir amants deviendraient amis.

-This author doesn't understand at all why a man and a woman who can't become lovers would become friends.

1695 jugement — **judgment| trial**

m

[ʒyʒmɑ̃]

Le jugement lui était défavorable.

-The judgement was against him.

1696 organisation — **organization| setup**

f

[ɔʁganizasjɔ̃]

Le résultat est calculé selon la grille de correspondance type créée par l'Organisation Mondiale de la Santé (OMS) - identique pour les hommes et les femmes indépendamment de l'âge.

-The result is calculated according to general reading table created by World Health Organization (WHO) - the same for male and female regardless the age.

1697 Ô! — **Oh!**

int

[o!]

Ô ! Jour malheureux !

-O, what a heavy day!

1698 vague — **wave; vague**

f; adj
[vag]
Ce n'est pas en effet le début de la prochaine vague, mais bien la fin de la cinquième.
-It is not the beginning of the next wave but, in reality, the end of the fifth wave.

1699 **légende** **legend| caption**
f
[leʒɑ̃d]
Pour attribuer une légende à un objet sélectionné, vous utiliserez la commande Insertion - Légende....
-The captioning of a selected object can be done by using the command Insert - Caption....

1700 **botter** **kick**
vb
[bɔte]
Si nous le sommes alors, franchement, nous méritons de nous faire botter l'arrière-train !
-If we really think that, frankly, we need our butts kicked!

1701 **barbe** **beard**
f
[baʁb]
T'es-tu déjà laissé pousser la barbe ?
-Have you ever grown a beard?

1702 **territoire** **territory**
m
[teʁitwaʁ]
Il tente de s'immiscer sur mon territoire et d'obtenir une part du gâteau.
-He's trying to muscle in on my territory and get a piece of the action.

1703 **blessure** **injury**
f
[blesyʁ]
La blessure lui laissa une cicatrice sur le bras.
-The wound left a scar on her arm.

1704 **géant** **giant; giant**
adj; m
[ʒeɑ̃]
Le géant économique qu'est l'Union européenne doit également devenir un géant en matière de marketing.
-The economic giant, the EU, has to be a marketing giant as well!

1705 **moto** **motorcycle**
f
[mɔto]
Jack a balancé son argent sur une moto.
-Jack blew all his money on a motorcycle.

1706 **communauté** **community; community**
adj; f
[kɔmynote]
Les policiers font partie de cette communauté et la communauté fait partie du corps policier.
-And the police are part of the community and the community is part of the police.

1707 **cage** **cage| shaft**
f
[kaʒ]
Tu devrais libérer les animaux de leur cage.
-You should free those animals from the cage.

1708 **désirer** **desire| wish**
vb
[deziʁe]
Conformément à l'article 13, les deux conjoints doivent désirer se marier.
-According to article 13, both spouses should desire to get married.

1709 **rayon** **radius| ray**
m
[ʁɛjɔ̃]
Y a-t-il un rayon pour les enfants ?
-Do you have a children's department?

1710 **sorcier** **sorcerer**
m
[sɔʁsje]
J'abandonne. Qu'ont en commun un prêtre irlandais et un sorcier africain ?
-I give up. What do an Irish priest and Congolese witch doctor have in common?

1711 **pile** **battery| pile**
f
[pil]
Jack apparut pile au bon moment.
-Jack showed up at just the right moment.

1712 **kilo** **kilo**

m
[kilo]

China would propose that the package or kilo limitation in the Hague-Visby Rules be maintained.

-La Chine propose que la limite par colis ou par kilogramme des Règles de La Haye-Visby soit maintenue.

1713 **écrivain**

m
[ekʁivɛ̃]

writer

Elle est écrivain, journaliste et enseignante et soutient plus particulièrement cette cause.

-She is a writer, a journalist and a teacher, and particularly supports this cause.

1714 **forcer**

vb
[fɔʁse]

force| compel

Pourrait-on la forcer à trouver une solution qui n'existe peut-être pas encore ?

-Could they force them to find the solution when the solution may not be there?

1715 **respecter**

vb
[ʁɛspɛkte]

respect| observe

Le patronat et le Gouvernement doivent respecter les dispositions du Code du travail.

-Management and the Government must respect the provisions of the Labour Code.

1716 **limite**

f
[limit]

limit

Sa paresse excède la limite de la patience.

-His laziness is past the margin of endurance.

1717 **orange**

adj
[ɔʁɑ̃ʒ]

orange

C'est une réussite pour l'Ukraine, tant pour le camp orange que pour le camp bleu.

-This is an achievement of Ukraine, both on the orange and on the blue side.

1718 **associer**

vb
[asɔsje]

associate

Nous devons continuer à associer l'Ukraine à la structure européenne de sécurité.

-We must continue to associate Ukraine with the European security framework.

1719 **bénir**

vb
[beniʁ]

bless

Le Seigneur n'arrêtera pas de bénir par des fruits abondants la générosité de votre dévouement.

-The Lord will not fail to bless with abundant fruits the generosity of your commitment.

1720 **quinze**

num
[kɛ̃z]

fifteen

Quinze États ont indiqué qu'ils pouvaient extrader leurs ressortissants.

-Fifteen States indicated that they were able to extradite their nationals.

1721 **posséder**

vb
[pɔsede]

have| rejoice

Chaque époux a néanmoins le droit de posséder des biens en son nom propre.

-Nevertheless each spouse is entitled to own property in his/her own name.

1722 **conseiller**

m; vb
[kɔ̃seje]

advisor| counselor; advise

Il est le conseiller le plus proche du roi.

-He's the king's most trusted advisor.

1723 **ligne**

f
[liɲ]

line| design

L'enseignant mit les enfants en ligne par ordre de taille.

-The teacher lined the children up in order of height.

1724 **escalier**

staircase| stairs

136

	m [ɛskalje]	vi) Rez-de-chaussée (bâtiment des conférences) : descendez au 1er sous-sol par l'escalier No 6. -(vi) First floor (Conference Building): proceed down one flight of stairs in stairway No. 6 to the first basement.
1725	**explication** f [ɛksplikasjɔ̃]	**explanation| explication** Mon explication était très simple et suffisamment plausible, comme la plupart des fausses théories ! -Very simple was my explanation, and plausible enough—as most wrong theories are!
1726	**voyager** vb [vwajaʒe]	**travel** Les citoyens, comme leurs représentants politiques, veulent pouvoir voyager librement. -The citizens, like their politicians, want to be able to travel freely.
1727	**attirer** vb [atiʁe]	**attract| bring** Vous avez du toupet de m'attirer ici sous de faux prétextes. -You've got a lot of nerve bringing me here under false pretenses.
1728	**poursuivre** vb [puʁsɥivʁ]	**continue| pursue** Et, pourtant, je crois qu'il faut poursuivre nos efforts dans deux directions. -I believe nevertheless that we should pursue our efforts in two directions.
1729	**professionnel** adj; m [pʁofesjɔnɛl]	**professional; professional** Les magistrats sont classés en deux grandes catégories: professionnel et non-professionnel. -Magistrates are classified into two main categories; professional and lay.
1730	**incident** adj; m [ɛ̃sidɑ̃]	**incident; incident** L'incident est survenu suite à l'admission par Al-Qaïda, dans une déclaration de l'organisation, de sa responsabilité dans une attaque qui a visé le palais républicain dans la ville d'Al-Mukalla au sud du Yémen et qui a provoqué la mort de 30 officiers et soldats. -The incident came in the wake of Al-Qaeda's admission of responsibility, in a statement published by the organization, for an attack that targeted the republican palace in the city of Al-Mukalla in southern Yemen and resulted in the deaths of 30 officers and soldiers.
1731	**colline** f [kɔlin]	**hill** J'ai acheté une petite maison sur une colline dans le sud de la France et j'ai l'intention d'y bâtir une maison de retraite. -I bought a small lot on the hillside in Southern France where I plan to build a retirement home.
1732	**junior** m [ʒynjɔʁ]	**junior** Je me souviens que cette équipe démolissait l'équipe junior A locale, les Porcupine Combines. -I can remember them running roughshod over the local home Junior A team, the Porcupine Combines.
1733	**autorisation** f [ɔtɔʁizasjɔ̃]	**authorization| permission** Zone d'Accès Contrôlé : Entrée interdite sans autorisation. -Controlled Access Zone: No entry without permission.
1734	**assassiner** vb [asasine]	**murder** En 1993, l'Iraq a essayé d'assassiner l'Émir du Koweït et un ancien Président des États-Unis. -In 1993, Iraq attempted to assassinate the Emir of Kuwait and a former American President.
1735	**ministère**	**ministry**

m
[ministɛʁ]
Le dossier a été adressé au ministère.
-The record was sent to the ministry.

1736 exprès   **express; on purpose**

adj; adv
[ɛkspʁɛs]
Est-ce qu'un secteur donné ferait exprès pour se donner du trouble ?
-Would a given sector deliberately set out to cause itself problems?

1737 football   **football**

m
[futbol]
Demain, elle jouera au football.
-She's playing football tomorrow.

1738 rond   **round; round**

adj; m
[ʁɔ̃]
Notre homme est aussi rond que grand.
-Our target's as round as he is tall.

1739 exercice   **exercise| fiscal year**

m
[ɛgzɛʁsis]
Mon père fait de l'exercice chaque jour pour sa santé.
-My father exercises every day for his health.

1740 fichu   **damn| rotten; scarf**

adj; m
[fiʃy]
Elle a fichu son petit ami à la porte.
-She kicked her boyfriend out of the house.

1741 vote   **vote| polling**

m
[vɔt]
Chacun devrait exercer son droit de vote.
-Everyone should exercise their right to vote.

1742 domaine   **field| domain**

m
[dɔmɛn]
L'intelligence artificielle est un vaste domaine qui englobe de nombreuses techniques et applications.
-Artificial intelligence is a broad field encompassing numerous technologies and applications.

1743 retenir   **retain| hold**

vb
[ʁətəniʁ]
Il serait également préférable de retenir un critère alternatif et non cumulatif.
-It would also be preferable to take an alternative and not a cumulative approach.

1744 religion   **religion**

f
[ʁəliʒjɔ̃]
Toutefois, la religion catholique, apostolique et romaine était la religion d'État.
-However, the apostolic Roman Catholic religion was the religion of the State.

1745 clairement   **clearly**

adv
[klɛʁmã]
Ces pays doivent faire connaître clairement leurs intentions à l'égard du Traité.
-Those countries need to make their intentions with regard to the Treaty extremely clear.

1746 furieux   **furious; madman**

adj; m
[fyʁjø]
Je ne dis rien, ce qui le rendit plus furieux.
-I said nothing, which made him more furious.

1747 pisser   **piss**

vb
[pise]
Au vu de son manque total de gratitude, après tous les efforts que j'ai faits pour elle, je me dis que j'aurais mieux fait de pisser dans un violon.
-Given her complete lack of gratitude after all that I had done for her, I told myself that I would have done better by banging my head against the wall.

1748 bol   **bowl; circumstance**

m; m
[bɔl]
J'en ai vraiment ras le bol de cette chaleur.
-I'm really fed up with this heat.

1749 excellence   **excellence**

	f [ɛksɛlɑ̃s]	Le Conseil entend des exposés de Son Excellence M. Addo et de Son Excellence M. -The Council heard briefings by His Excellency Mr. Addo and His Excellency Mr.
1750	**cimetière** m [simtjɛʁ]	**graveyard** Il faut bouger le cimetière vers une nouvelle situation dans le sud de la ville. -The cemetery needs to be moved to a new location south of the town.
1751	**classique** adj; m [klasik]	**classic| standard; classic** Au total, 220 élèves malvoyants ont pu intégrer des écoles de la filière classique. -A total of 220 visually impaired pupils were mainstreamed into ordinary schools.
1752	**baron** m [baʁɔ̃]	**baron** Tu deviens un baron de la pègre. -You're becoming a crime lord.
1753	**arrestation** f [aʁɛstasjɔ̃]	**arrest| detention** Vous êtes en état d'arrestation ! -You're under arrest!
1754	**taper** vb [tape]	**type| beat** J'ai une dernière histoire à taper, avant de l'envoyer. -Well, I have one more story to type before I send it.
1755	**cabinet** m [kabinɛ]	**cabinet** Jack est allé à son cabinet de travail et a verrouillé la porte. -Jack went to his study and locked the door.
1756	**comédie** f [kɔmedi]	**comedy** La comédie est bien plus près de la vie réelle que le drame. -Comedy is much closer to real life than drama.
1757	**bond** m [bɔ̃]	**leap| jump** It is more than a rule; it is a bond, a friendship, a sacred bond that unites us forever. -En fait, c'est plus qu'une loi, c'est un lien, c'est l'amitié, le lien sacré qui nous unit pour toujours.
1758	**tunnel** m [tynɛl]	**tunnel** Sa voiture rasa les murs du tunnel. -His car shaved the wall of the tunnel.
1759	**amant** m [amɑ̃]	**lover** As-tu un amant ? -Do you have a lover?
1760	**incapable** adj [ɛ̃kapabl]	**unable| incapable** L'actuel gouvernement intérimaire est incapable de contrecarrer ces menaces. -The present interim government is unable to counter any of these threats.
1761	**drapeau** m [dʁapo]	**flag** Les Chinois ont un grand drapeau et un petit livre rouges. -Chinese people have a big red flag and a little red book.
1762	**do** m [do]	**do** Commençons par la gamme en do majeur. -We'll start with the C Major scale.
1763	**échouer**	**fail| defeat**

vb
[eʃwe]
Si les demandes de financement ont échoué, il est clair qu'ils n'ont pas d'argent.
-If they have been unsuccessful, there are obviously no funds.

1764 **auparavant**   **before**
adv
[opaʁavɑ̃]
Les politiques sociales et économiques s'entrecoupent comme jamais auparavant.
-Today's social and economic policies intersect like they never have before.

1765 **risquer**   **risk| venture**
vb
[ʁiske]
L' adopter, c' est risquer l' augmentation de l' insécurité ferroviaire.
-If this is adopted, there is a risk that rail safety will be jeopardised.

1766 **magazine**   **magazine**
m
[magazin]
At least one of the issues of the magazine will tackle disasters and conflicts.
-Au moins un des numéros du magazine traitera des catastrophes et des conflits.

1767 **remplir**   **fill| fill in**
vb
[ʁɑ̃pliʁ]
Pour vous donner un exemple, un agriculteur peut remplir incorrectement un formulaire.
-To give you an example, a farmer may fill out a form incorrectly.

1768 **précieux**   **precious| valuable**
adj
[pʁesjø]
La sécurité est un bien précieux, surtout pour les plus vulnérables d'entre nous.
-Safety is an important commodity, especially for the most vulnerable amongst us.

1769 **éternité**   **eternity| lifetime**
f
[etɛʁnite]
Je ne t'ai pas vu depuis une éternité.
-I haven't seen you for ages.

1770 **citer**   **quote| mention**
vb
[site]
The Commentary should cite examples of the various natural characteristics.
-Le commentaire devrait citer des exemples des diverses caractéristiques naturelles.

1771 **huiler**   **oil**
vb
[ɥile]
Huile d'olive raffinée: huile d'olive obtenue par le raffinage d'huiles d'olive vierges.
-Refined olive oil: olive oil obtained by refining virgin olive oils.

1772 **proposition**   **proposal| proposition**
f
[pʁɔpozisjɔ̃]
Votre proposition mérite qu'on la considère.
-Your proposal is worthy of being considered.

1773 **soutien**   **support**
m
[sutjɛ̃]
J'aimerais remercier sincèrement le premier ministre de son soutien indéfectible.
-I would like to sincerely thank the Prime Minister for his unwavering support.

1774 **hauteur**   **height| pitch**
f
[otœʁ]
Les mots inscrits au-dessus de la porte du théâtre faisaient un mètre de hauteur.
-The words above the door of the theatre were a metre high.

1775 **échec**   **failure| check**
m
[eʃɛk]
Il fut brisé par l'échec de son affaire.
-He was broken by the failure of his business.

1776 **fâcher**   **upset**

vb
[faʃe]

Elle a fâché les Nord-Coréens, qui ont suspendu l'aide humanitaire, laquelle n'a repris qu'il y a quelques mois.

-The resolution angered the North Koreans, who suspended the humanitarian aid, which was only resumed a few months ago.

1777 culture — **culture**

f
[kyltyʁ]

J'ai appris des choses sur la culture grecque.

-I learned about Greek culture.

1778 précis — **precise; abstract**

adj; m
[pʁesi]

Le «numéro CAS» renvoie à l'identificateur précis du Chemical Abstracts Service.

-The "CAS number" is the precise identifier of the pollutants in the Chemical Abstracts Service.

1779 langage — **language**

m
[lãgaʒ]

L'acquisition du langage demande de la créativité.

-Language acquisition requires creativity.

1780 objectif — **objective; goal**

adj; m
[ɔbʒɛktif]

D'un point de vue objectif, son argument était loin d'être rationnel.

-From an objective viewpoint, his argument was far from rational.

1781 onze — **eleven**

num
[ɔ̃z]

Écoute, Angel, je t'en donne onze cents.

-Look, Angel, I'll give you eleven cents for it.

1782 profondément — **deeply| heavily**

adv
[pʁɔfɔ̃demã]

Malheureusement la situation sécuritaire en Iraq reste profondément préoccupante.

-Unfortunately, the security situation in Iraq is still deeply troubling.

1783 souffrance — **suffering**

f
[sufʁãs]

Encore combien de souffrance peuvent-ils endurer ?

-How much more suffering can they endure?

1784 gang — **gang**

m
[gãg]

Un autre membre du gang serait sûrement moins héroïque.

-Anybody else on that crew got sick, I'm guessing they'd be a little more self-serving.

1785 pétrole — **oil| kerosene**

m
[petʁɔl]

Le Japon dépend d'autres pays pour son pétrole.

-Japan depends on other countries for oil.

1786 entièrement — **entirely| quite**

adv
[ãtjɛʁmã]

Il s'agit d'une version entièrement réécrite et restructurée du premier document.

-It is a completely-rewritten and reorganized version of the earlier Draft Proposal.

1787 épreuve — **test| trial**

f
[epʁœv]

Mettons-le à l'épreuve !

-Let's put it to the test!

1788 copier — **copy; copying**

vb; adj
[kɔpje]

Ils auraient peut-être intérêt à copier et à voir ce qui se fait au Québec actuellement.

-They would perhaps do well to look at what Quebec is doing and follow its example.

1789 bibliothèque — **library**

f
[biblijɔtɛk]
L'Autriche a une bibliothèque extrêmement précieuse, la Bibliothèque nationale autrichienne.
-Austria has a very, very valuable library, the Austrian National Library.

1790 énerver — **annoy| fret**
vb
[enɛʁve]
Les libéraux semblent s'énerver lorsque l'opposition les surprend en train de dormir.
-They seem to get excited when the opposition over here catches them sleeping.

1791 altesse — **highness**
f
[altɛs]
Après tout, je suis altesse Sérénissime.
-I am His Serene Highness, am I not?

1792 trente — **thirty**
num
[tʁɑ̃t]
Le bus peut transporter trente personnes.
-The bus is capable of carrying thirty people.

1793 électrique — **electric**
adj
[elɛktʁik]
Batterie de traction (pour véhicule électrique pur ou véhicule électrique hybride)
-Traction battery (for pure electric vehicle or hybrid electric vehicle)

1794 ranger — **ranger; put away**
m; vb
[ʁɑ̃ʒe]
Je dois ranger mon appartement.
-I have to clean up my apartment.

1795 enterrer — **bury| shelve**
vb
[ɑ̃teʁe]
L'autoroute, telle qu'elle est actuellement planifiée, "enterrera" ce site avant la réalisation de fouilles archéologiques.
-The motorway, as currently planned, will bury this site before an archaeological dig has been carried out.

1796 assister — **assist**
vb
[asiste]
De plus, des experts agréés devraient assister aux opérations et donner leur aval.
-Additionally, certified experts should witness and approve this work.

1797 vallée — **valley**
f
[vale]
Le scientifique cherchait des squelettes de dinosaures dans la vallée.
-The scientist searched for the bones of the dinosaurs in the valley.

1798 pizza — **pizza**
f
[pidza]
Pour faire passer le caractère un peu indigeste de la pizza dont parlait M.
-To wash down the rather indigestible nature of the pizza that Mr Ford mentioned.

1799 golf — **golf**
m
[gɔlf]
Membre du Saujana Golf and Country Club, du Royal Selangor Golf Club et du Sri Morib Golf Club.
-Member of Saujana Golf & Country Club, Royal Selangor Golf Club and Sri Morib Golf Club.

1800 las — **tired**
adj
[la]
Je suis las des musées, — cimetières des arts.
-I'm tired of museums, - graveyards of the arts.

1801 soigner — **treat**
vb
[swaɲe]
Les scientifiques ne savent pas encore soigner le cancer.
-Scientists haven't found a cure for cancer yet.

1802 loyer — **rent**

	m		Propriété du gouvernement hôte avec paiement de loyer, et montant du loyer.
	[lwaje]		-Host Government ownership with rent, and amount of such rent.
1803	**producteur**		**producer**
	m		Maximo et le producteur seront enchantés.
	[pʁɔdyktœʁ]		-Both Maximo and the producer will be thrilled.
1804	**quart**		**quarter**
	m		J'ai mangé le quart du gâteau.
	[kaʁ]		-I ate a quarter of a cake.
1805	**critique**		**critical; review**
	adj; f		Qu'est-ce que la pensée critique ?
	[kʁitik]		-What is critical thinking?
1806	**acte**		**act| certificate**
	m		J'aimerais revoir l'éclairage au second acte.
	[akt]		-I'd like to go over the light cues with you in the second act.
1807	**cardiaque**		**cardiac; heart patient**
	adj; m/f		Un cardiaque veut savoir qu'une salle d'opération est disponible 24 heures par jour.
	[kaʁdjak]		-A heart patient wants to know that there is an operating room available 24 hours a day.
1808	**plateau**		**tray**
	m		Ce spécialiste de la conception de jeux classifie les jeux sur plateau selon le nombre de pièces à jouer.
	[plato]		-This game design specialist classifies board games by the number of player pieces.
1809	**auto**		**auto**
	f		Laissez-moi au coin et ramenez cette auto volée.
	[oto]		-Don't talk nonsense, I left a note saying I was taking the car.
1810	**concernant**		**concerning; concerning**
	adv; prp		Nos préoccupations concernant la CPI portent sur les moyens, non sur les fins.
	[kɔsɛʁnã]		-Our concerns about the ICC are concerns about means, not about ends.
1811	**conférence**		**conference; lecturing**
	f; adj		S'il devait arriver tard, vous pouvez commencer la conférence sans lui.
	[kɔfeʁãs]		-If he should arrive late, you may start the conference without him.
1812	**baby**		**baby**
	m		J'ai oublié de te dire le nom de la baby-sitter.
	[babi]		-I forgot to tell you the babysitter's name.
1813	**charmer**		**charm| delight**
	vb		Me voilà obligé de les charmer tout seul.
	[ʃaʁme]		-Anyway, now I am stuck having to charm them all by myself.
1814	**fièvre**		**fever**
	f		Vous n'avez pas de fièvre.
	[fjɛvʁ]		-You have no fever.
1815	**réception**		**reception| desk**
	f		Je t'ai laissé une note à la réception.
	[ʁesɛpsjɔ̃]		-I left you a message at the front desk.
1816	**duc**		**duke**
	m		Le duc m'a toujours apprécié.
	[dyk]		-The Duke has always been partial to me.
1817	**italien**		**Italian; Italian**

adj; m

[italjɛ̃]

Le voleur étant italien, c'est un policier italien qui doit le poursuivre.

-That thief was Italian: an Italian policeman should have been chasing him.

1818 **amiral** **admiral**

m

[amiʁal]

Je vourais être amiral avante mourir.

-I'd like to make admiral before I die.

1819 **fenêtre** **window**

f

[fənɛtʁ]

Le pare-brise est la grande fenêtre en verre à l'avant d'un véhicule.

-The windscreen is the large glass window at the front of a vehicle.

1820 **couvrir** **cover| coat**

vb

[kuvʁiʁ]

Notre politique de cohésion et de consolidation doit couvrir toutes les régions européennes.

-Our cohesion and consolidation policy must cover all European regions.

1821 **cervelle** **brain| brains**

f

[sɛʁvɛl]

Soit tu nous donnes ce qu'on veut, soit je répands sa cervelle dans toute la pièce.

-Either you give us what we want, or I blow her brains all over you right now.

1822 **moral** **moral; morale**

adj; m

[mɔʁal]

Il importe d'améliorer leur statut, leur moral et leur professionnalisme.

-It is important to enhance their status, morale and professionalism.

1823 **supérieur** **upper; superior**

adj; m

[sypeʁjœʁ]

Le nombre de personnes sur Facebook est supérieur à la population des États-Unis d'Amérique.

-The amount of people on Facebook is greater than the population of the United States of America.

1824 **personnellement** **personally**

adv

[pɛʁsɔnɛlmã]

Personnellement, toutefois, je serais partisan de reporter les deux.

-Personally speaking, however, I would be in favour of postponing both.

1825 **tendre** **tender; tender**

adj; vb

[tãdʁ]

Il leur est également essentiel de tendre la main à un public non musulman.

-It is also essential for them to reach out to non-Muslim audiences as well.

1826 **discussion** **discussion| debate**

f

[diskysjɔ̃]

Il se leva et partit au milieu de la discussion.

-He got up and left in the middle of the discussion.

1827 **sandwich** **sandwich**

m

[sãdwiʃ]

Est-ce ce que nous voulons pour pouvoir manger une tranche de salami dans notre sandwich?

-Are we prepared to tolerate that for the sake of a slice of salami in our sandwich?

1828 **alarmer** **alarm**

vb

[alaʁme]

Ceci devrait nous alarmer sérieusement, mais nous ne voulons pas l'entendre.

-That should ring serious alarm bells, but we are turning a deaf ear.

1829 **ivre** **drunk**

adj

[ivʁ]

On dit que le roi était ivre, et qu'on a décapité le Baptiste pour lui faire plaisir.

-They say the king was drunk and cut off the Baptist's head to satisfy him.

1830 **héler** **hail**

vb

[ele]

Pour braquer un country club... ou héler un taxi.

-You wanna rip off a country club, or somebody needs to hail a cab.

1831 **gagnant** **winner; winning**

m; adj
[gaɲã]

Il prononça le nom du gagnant.
-He called out the name of the winner.

1832 beurre   **butter**

m
[bœʁ]

Un autre projet porte sur la production artisanale de beurre de karité.
-Another of their projects is for the hand crafted production of karite butter.

1833 commercer   **trade| deal**

vb
[kɔmɛʁse]

Continuerons-nous à commercer avec ce pays exactement comme maintenant ?
-Will we continue to trade with Lebanon in exactly the same way we do now?

1834 fleuve   **river| stream**

m
[flœv]

C'est le troisième plus grand fleuve d'Europe après la Volga et le Danube.
-It is the third largest in Europe (after the River Volga and the River Danube).

1835 appétit   **appetite**

m
[apeti]

Jill avait un appétit d'oiseau.
-Jill had the appetite of a bird.

1836 nerf   **nerve**

m
[nɛʁ]

Elle hurle à peine on lui touche le nerf ulnaire.
-She screams if you even touch her funny bone.

1837 séparer   **separate| part**

vb
[sepaʁe]

Il est impossible de séparer les riches des pauvres ou de séparer les différents groupes ethniques.
-There is no way to separate the rich from the poor or to separate different ethnic groups.

1838 assis   **seated**

adj
[asi]

Nous n'allons pas continuer la séance tant que vous ne vous serez pas assis et calmés.
-We are not going to continue the sitting until you sit down and be quiet.

1839 employer   **use| employ**

vb
[ãplwaje]

Le droit d'autrui d'employer ou de s'abstenir d'employer une personne quelconque;
-Another person's right to employ or refrain from employing any individual.

1840 liaison   **link| affair**

f
[ljɛzõ]

Avez-vous une liaison ?
-Are you having an affair?

1841 document   **document**

m
[dɔkymã]

Je vous ai dit de signer le document.
-I told you to sign the document.

1842 place   **square| spot**

f
[plas]

Il faut savoir assumer sa place de privilégié.
-Sometimes one has to embrace one's place in society.

1843 nuage   **cloud**

m
[nyaʒ]

Une grande préoccupation existe quant aux effets du nuage de cendres sur le secteur du tourisme.
-There is huge concern for the effects of the volcanic cloud on the tourist industry.

1844 fiancer   **betroth| fiance**

vb
[fijãse]

J'ai été fiancé il y a quelques années mais un malheur m'a ravi ma jeune promise.

145

-I was betrothed some years ago...... but tragedy snatched my young bride away.

1845 guitare — guitar
f
[gitaʁ]
Cette guitare est tellement chère que je ne peux pas l'acheter.
-That guitar is so expensive that I can't buy it.

1846 final — final| ultimate; finale
adj; m
[final]
Je voulais te piquer au moment final.
-No. I wanted to ease you into his final moments.

1847 robot — robot
m
[ʁɔbo]
Un androïde est une sorte de robot.
-An android is a kind of robot.

1848 brise — breeze| breath
f
[bʁiz]
Ces mesures sont indispensables pour briser le cycle actuel de désespoir et d'exploitation.
-These measures are necessary to break the present cycle of despair and exploitation.

1849 réseau — network| grid
m
[ʁezo]
On attend beaucoup du Réseau, considéré comme un modèle de réseau de sûreté nucléaire.
-High expectations have been placed on the Network, as a nuclear safety network model.

1850 prière — prayer
f
[pʁijɛʁ]
Il va sans dire que les travaux préparatoires de la prière est la prière.
-It goes without saying that the preparatory work of prayer was prayer.

1851 réalisateur — director
m
[ʁealizatœʁ]
Il était également réalisateur de films et photographe professionnel.
-He was a film director and certified still photographer.

1852 poison — poison
m
[pwazɔ̃]
Une goutte de poison est suffisante pour tuer 160 personnes.
-One drop of the poison is enough to kill 160 people.

1853 surveillance — surveillance
f
[syʁvɛjɑ̃s]
Finalement, il fut décidé que les magasins seraient équipés de caméras de surveillance.
-Eventually it was decided that the stores be equipped with surveillance cameras.

1854 épauler — support
vb
[epole]
Nous devons épauler les citoyens de nos collectivités.
-We have to support the citizens who live in our communities.

1855 médecine — medicine
f
[medsin]
Il s'est dévoué à l'étude de la médecine.
-He devoted himself to the study of medicine.

1856 placard — cupboard
m
[plakaʁ]
Hé, as-tu entendu ? Suzanne a un polichinelle dans le placard.
-Hey, did you hear? Susan has a bun in the oven.

1857 mercredi — Wednesday
m
[mɛʁkʁədi]
La Commission adoptait la proposition de directive mercredi dernier seulement.
-The Commission only adopted the proposal for a directive last Wednesday.

1858 chiffre — figure| number
m
[ʃifʁ]
Le chiffre indiqué est 48 103 216, alors que le chiffre correct est 63 103 216.
-The figure given is 48 103 216, whereas the correct figure is 63 103 216.

1859 **lampe**   **lamp**

f

[lãp]

Cette lampe consomme relativement peu de mercure.

-The lamp has a comparatively low mercury consumption.

1860 **expert**   **expert; expert**

adj; m

[ɛkspɛʁ]

Je ne suis pas expert.

-I'm not an expert.

1861 **autorité**   **authority**

f

[ɔtɔʁite]

Je ne voulais pas remettre en cause votre autorité.

-I didn't mean to challenge your authority.

1862 **destruction**   **destruction**

f

[dɛstʁyksjɔ̃]

Avez-vous un code d'auto-destruction ?

-Do you guys have a self destruct code?

1863 **congrès**   **conference**

m

[kɔ̃gʁɛ]

Le Congrès refusa d'agir.

-Congress refused to act.

1864 **poudrer**   **powder**

vb

[pudʁe]

Ne fait-il que jeter de la poudre aux yeux ou dispose-t-il de renseignements précis ?

-Is this just dust thrown up in the air or does he have real information?

1865 **juillet**   **July**

m

[ʒɥijɛ]

Il a été condamné en juillet 1995 et son appel a été rejeté en juillet 1996.

-In July 1995, he was sentenced, with the appeal being disposed of in July 1996.

1866 **moderne**   **modern**

adj

[mɔdɛʁn]

Cela répond aux exigences d'un multilatéralisme moderne et efficace.

-That is a response to the demands of a modern-day and effective multilateralism.

1867 **stade**   **stage**

m

[stad]

Nous voulons amener les outils linguistiques au stade suivant. Nous voulons voir de l'innovation dans le paysage de l'apprentissage des langues. Et cela ne peut pas arriver sans des ressources linguistiques libres, qui ne peuvent être construites sans une communauté, qui elle-même ne pourra contribuer sans plates-formes efficientes.

-We want to bring language tools to the next level. We want to see innovation in the language learning landscape. And this cannot happen without open language resources which cannot be built without a community which cannot contribute without efficient platforms.

1868 **serment**   **oath**

m

[sɛʁmã]

Cela aurait donné tout son sens au serment d'allégeance, au serment de citoyenneté.

-That would have made the oath of allegiance, the oath of citizenship, meaningful.

1869 **dette**   **debt**

f

[dɛt]

Notre dette est supérieure à ce que nous pouvons payer.

-Our debt is more than we can pay.

1870 **dragon**   **dragon**

m

[dʁagɔ̃]

L'animal en haut à gauche est censé être un dragon.

-The animal in the top left-hand corner is meant to be a dragon.

1871 **entraîner**   **train| drive**

vb
[ɑ̃tʁene]
Il ne dit rien non plus sur la revalorisation des salaires qu'il devrait entraîner.
-Furthermore, there is no mention of the salary increases that it will bring about.

1872 **sensible** **sensitive**
adj
[sɑ̃sibl]
J'ai soumis la candidature de Max parce qu'il est très sensible et très prévenant.
-I nominated Max because he is a very sensitive person and he's entirely approachable.

1873 **ajouter** **add**
vb
[aʒute]
Ajouter le mascarpone, mélanger et ajouter la crème semi-fouettée.
-Add the mascarpone, mix and add the partially whipped cream.

1874 **expression** **expression**
f
[ɛkspʁesjɔ̃]
L'expression « politicien honnête » est antinomique.
-The phrase 'honest politician' is an oxymoron.

1875 **métro** **subway**
m
[metʁo]
Veuillez m'excuser. Pourriez-vous m'indiquer la station de métro la plus proche ?
-Excuse me. Can you direct me to the nearest subway station?

1876 **foncer** **charge**
vb
[fɔ̃se]
Un projet financé par le Gouvernement danois prévoit de fournir à cette juridiction une caméra et une paroi de verre foncé pour protéger les victimes lorsqu'elles déposent.
-Under a project funded by the Government of Denmark, the Court will be provided with a camera and darkened glass to protect the victims when they give testimony.

1877 **durer** **last**
vb
[dyʁe]
L'instabilité et la violence actuelles ne peuvent et ne doivent pas durer indéfiniment.
-The present instability and violence cannot and must not continue indefinitely.

1878 **balance** **balance**
f
[balɑ̃s]
Une balance analytique s'entend d'une balance sensible au dixième de mg le plus proche.
-Analytical balance means a balance capable of weighing to the nearest 0.1 mg.

1879 **lion** **lion**
m
[ljɔ̃]
Le prophète Isaïe a prédit qu'un jour, le lion et l'agneau vivraient ensemble.
-The Prophet Isaiah foresaw a day when the lion and the lamb would live together.

1880 **extrêmement** **extremely**
adv
[ɛkstʁɛmmɑ̃]
C'est un acte extrêmement important, extrêmement fort, de cette institution.
-This is an extremely significant and extremely strong act on the part of this institution.

1881 **séance** **meeting| session**
f
[seɑ̃s]
Un billet pour la séance de dix-neuf heures s'il vous plait.
-Please give me a ticket for the seven o'clock show.

1882 **collier** **necklace**
m
[kɔlje]
J'ai donné un collier de perles à ma sœur pour son anniversaire.
-I gave my sister a pearl necklace on her birthday.

1883 **alliance** **alliance**

f
[aljɑ̃s]

Sami a mis son alliance.
-Sami put on his wedding ring.

1884 congé   **leave**

m
[kɔ̃ʒe]

J'ignorais que vous aviez eu une semaine de congé le mois dernier.
-I didn't know you had a week off last month.

1885 portefeuille   **portfolio| wallet**

m
[pɔʁtəfœj]

Il a perdu son portefeuille dans la rue. Il ne contenait pas d'argent, mais tous ses documents étaient à l'intérieur.
-He lost his wallet in the street. It didn't contain any money, but all of his documents were inside.

1886 trahir   **betray**

vb
[tʁaiʁ]

Lequel est le pire: trahir un ami ou trahir Rome ?
-Which is worse: to betray a friend or to betray Rome herself?

1887 repartir   **restart| redivide**

vb
[ʁəpaʁtiʁ]

Le Comité consultatif recommande de mettre en recouvrement et de répartir entre les États Membres le montant de 59 038 300 dollars.
-The Advisory Committee recommends that the amount of $59,038,300 be assessed and apportioned among Member States.

1888 terroriste   **terrorist**

m/f
[teʁɔʁist]

Le terroriste demandeur d'asile ne bénéficie donc pas d'une telle protection.
-If a terrorist has applied for asylum, that person will not be given protection.

1889 clan   **clan**

m
[klɑ̃]

Mais son clan lui arrangeait un mariage.
-But his clan was arranging a marriage for him.

1890 exécution   **execution| implementation**

f
[ɛgzekysjɔ̃]

On a tous pensé que mettre le plan à exécution a été difficile.
-We all thought it difficult to execute the plan.

1891 pourrir   **rot| decay**

vb
[puʁiʁ]

Oh, les gens mettent des années à pourrir.
-Oh, it takes years for people to rot.

1892 juger   **judge| assess**

vb
[ʒyʒe]

Il faut également un mécanisme pour juger qui tient et qui ne tient ses engagements en vertu de ces accords.
-It also needs a mechanism to arbitrate on who is meeting, and who is not meeting, their commitments under any such arrangements.

1893 invitation   **invitation**

f
[ɛ̃vitasjɔ̃]

Jack a décliné l'invitation.
-Jack declined the invitation.

1894 électricité   **electricity**

f
[elɛktʁisite]

Les câbles transmettent l'électricité.
-Wires transmit electricity.

1895 admettre   **admit| allow**

vb
[admɛtʁ]

Nous sommes tous d'accord pour admettre la vitalité et la vigueur du marché.
-We accept that, we accept the vitality and the vigour of the market.

1896 Hop!   **Poof!**

int
[ɔp!]

Et hop, des milliards de personnes sont invitées à se faire vacciner.
-Hey presto, thousands of people are invited to be vaccinated.

1897 avril   **April**

m
[avʁil]

Calendrier indicatif: Lundi 20 avril, après-midi - mercredi 22 avril, après-midi.
-Tentative timing: Monday, 20 April, afternoon - Wednesday, 22 April, afternoon

1898 acier   **steel**

m
[asje]

On estime que la production d'acier atteindra les 100 millions de tonnes cette année.
-Steel production is estimated to reach 100 million tons this year.

1899 promener   **promenade**

vb
[pʁɔmne]

Il nous suffit de nous promener dans les rues de cette ville miraculeuse qu'est New York.
-We have only to wander through the streets of this miraculous city of New York.

1900 sourd   **deaf| dull**

adj
[suʁ]

Lorsqu'un anglophone s'aperçoit que son interlocuteur étranger n'a pas compris une de ses phrases, il la répète, à l'identique, mais plus fort, comme si son interlocuteur était sourd.
-When an English speaker realises that a foreign person they are speaking to doesn't understand one of their sentences, they repeat it, the same way, but louder, as though the person were deaf.

1901 sire   **sire**

m
[siʁ]

Choisissez-en donc un de votre lignée sire.
-Then choose someone of your own descent, sir.

1902 degré   **degree**

m
[dəgʁe]

Ce travail exige un haut degré de compétence.
-This work calls for a high degree of skill.

1903 instruction   **instruction| education**

f
[ɛ̃stʁyksjɔ̃]

De la lecture de bons livres on peut tirer du plaisir, de l'amitié, de l'expérience et de l'instruction.
-From reading good books we can derive pleasure, friendship, experience and education.

1904 injuste   **unfair| wrong**

adj
[ɛ̃ʒyst]

Il s'agit d'une pratique injuste tant pour les jeunes que pour la collectivité.
-This is unfair to the kids and unfair to the community.

1905 division   **division| split**

f
[divizjɔ̃]

Le terrorisme est le plus important facteur de division d'un pays et de création de régions autonomes.
-Terrorism is the most important factor for the division of a country and the creation of autonomous regions.

1906 fierté   **pride**

f
[fjɛʁte]

Elle a ravalé sa fierté.
-She swallowed her pride.

1907 exprimer   **express| voice**

vb
[ɛkspʁime]

Ces groupes régionaux vous indiqueront la position que vous pourrez exprimer ici.
-Those regional groups will give you the position that you can express here.

1908 fidèle   **faithful| loyal; stalwart**

adj; m/f
[fidɛl]

C'est, en réalité, un sujet avec lequel le spectateur, le fidèle, entre dans un dialogue sans mots, par la vue.
-Indeed, it is a subject with which the viewer, the worshipper, enters into wordless dialogue through the sense of sight.

1909	**causer**	**cause| chat**
	vb	L'Espagne connaît bien la cruauté du terrorisme et la souffrance qu'il peut
	[koze]	causer.
		-Spain knows well the cruelty of terrorism and the grief that it can cause.
1910	**mamie**	**granny| nanny**
	f	Ma mamie est devenue très vieille.
	[mami]	-My grandma has gotten very old.
1911	**couler**	**flow| cast**
	vb	Sommes-nous en train de couler ?
	[kule]	-Are we sinking?
1912	**renseignement**	**inquiry**
	m	J'ai obtenu de lui un renseignement utile.
	[ʁɑ̃sɛɲmɑ̃]	-I got a useful piece of information out of him.
1913	**total**	**total| overall; total**
	adj; m	Combien d'argent as-tu dépensé au total ?
	[tɔtal]	-How much money did you spend in total?
1914	**réservé**	**reserved**
	adj	Un siège non permanent serait réservé aux États membres du Groupe des
	[ʁezɛʁve]	États d'Asie.
		-One non-permanent seat will be allocated to Member States of the Asian
		Group.
1915	**espagnol**	**Spanish; Spanish**
	adj; m|mpl	J'ai décidé d'écrire 10 phrases en espagnol chaque jour. Je suis sûre que
	[ɛspaɲɔl]	Rocío sera très contente de me les corriger.
		-I have decided to write ten sentences in Spanish each day. I'm sure that
		Rocío will be very happy to correct them.
1916	**solide**	**solid; solid**
	adj; m	Un certain nombre de pays se sont dotés de solides plans d'adaptation ou
	[sɔlid]	sont en train d'y mettre la dernière main.
		-A number of countries have well-developed adaptation plans or are in the
		process of finalizing them.
1917	**avantage**	**advantage**
	m	Celui qui est amoureux de soi a au moins l'avantage de ne point avoir trop de
	[avɑ̃taʒ]	rivaux.
		-He who is enamored of himself will at least have the advantage of being
		inconvenienced by few rivals.
1918	**habitant**	**inhabitant; resident**
	m; adj	Nul ne peut entrer dans un domicile contre la volonté de son habitant, sauf
	[abitɑ̃]	dans les cas prévus par la loi. »
		-No one can enter a domicile against the will of the dweller, except when
		the law prescribes such an entry.
1919	**rage**	**rage| rabies**
	f	Il était fou de rage.
	[ʁaʒ]	-He was bursting with fury.
1920	**neveu**	**nephew**
	m	Le grand-père du requérant est le neveu de la mère d'Abdullah Öcalan.
	[nəvø]	-The complainant's grandfather is a nephew of Abdullah Öçalan's mother.
1921	**emprunter**	**borrow**
	vb	En outre, les étudiants doivent subvenir à leurs besoins; ils doivent
	[ɑ̃pʁɛ̃te]	emprunter simplement pour subsister.

-As well the students have to stay alive; they have to borrow money to simply live.

1922 ouverture — **opening**
f
[uvɛʁtyʁ]
Dan fut tué deux jours avant l'ouverture du procès.
-Dan was killed just two days before the trial began.

1923 blé — **wheat**
m
[ble]
Le pain est produit à partir de blé.
-Bread is made from wheat.

1924 munition — **munition**
f
[mynisjõ]
Ce mécanisme a l'inconvénient de laisser intacte la munition non explosée.
-The disadvantage of SN is that the unexploded munitions is still intact.

1925 écraser — **crush| overwrite**
vb
[ekʁaze]
Ainsi, cela ne vise pas à écraser quelque minorité que ce soit.
-So, this is not to stamp down on any minority.

1926 juin — **June**
m
[ʒɥɛ̃]
The Caymanian Compass, 28 juin 2001 et 29 juin 2001; The Royal Gazette, 29 juin 2001.
-The Caymanian Compass, 28 June 2001, 29 June 2001; The Royal Gazette, 29 June 2001.

1927 dégoûter — **disgust| cause disgust**
vb
[degute]
Je ne dirai rien de plus, mais je suis dégoûtée - nous devons tous être dégoûtés - par cette barbarie.
-I will say no more, but I am disgusted - we must all be disgusted - at this savagery.

1928 démarrer — **start| get started**
vb
[demaʁe]
Or, celle-ci vient de démarrer aujourd'hui, et je n'ai toujours pas de réponse.
-The first day of that has now arrived, and I have still not received a reply.

1929 louer — **rent| let**
vb
[lwe]
Mais avant tout, nous devons louer les Timorais pour leurs efforts remarquables.
-But, above all, we must laud the Timorese for their great efforts.

1930 bâton — **stick| baton**
m
[batõ]
La langue est un bon bâton.
-The tongue wounds more than a lance.

1931 timide — **shy**
adj
[timid]
Le député devrait savoir que le premier ministre n'a pas la réputation d'être très timide.
-The hon. member should know that this Prime Minister is not known as a very shy person.

1932 fermé — **closed| sealed**
adj
[fɛʁme]
Il a toujours exprimé son ferme appui et son désir de coopérer avec le Tribunal.
-He has repeatedly expressed his strong support for cooperation with the Tribunal.

1933 caractère — **character| nature**
m
[kaʁaktɛʁ]
Le caractère Tilde est placé devant le caractère apparaissant souligné dans le menu final.
-The tilde character stands for the character that will be shown underlined in the finished menu.

1934 célibataire — **single| bachelor; single**

adj; m/f
[selibatɛʁ]
Avec tous les avantages auxquels peut goûter un célibataire nanti.
-Surrounded myself with all of the advantages of a wealthy bachelor.

1935 **pasteur**
m
[pastœʁ]
pastor| shepherd
Le pasteur portait des vêtements ternes.
-The vicar wore drab clothing.

1936 **progrès**
m
[pʁɔgʁɛ]
progress
Sans progrès social, les ressorts du progrès économique s'épuisent tôt ou tard.
-Without social progress, economic progress will run out of steam sooner or later.

1937 **ordure**
f
[ɔʁdyʁ]
filth| trash
Le cinéma avait déjà tiré la sonnette d'alarme avec le film "Le père noël est une ordure".
-The cinema has already sounded the alarm bells with the film 'Le père noël est une ordure'.

1938 **matière**
f
[matjɛʁ]
material
Désolée, mais vous avez tort en la matière.
-Sorry, but you're in the wrong here.

1939 **puits**
m
[pɥi]
well
Nous n'éprouvons jamais la valeur de l'eau jusqu'à ce que le puits tarisse.
-We never know the worth of water till the well is dry.

1940 **bonté**
f
[bɔ̃te]
goodness
Celui de garder confiance dans la bonté du genre humain.
-We are challenged to maintain our faith in the goodness of the human person.

1941 **déposer**
vb
[depoze]
deposit| file
En outre, les migrants rencontrent des difficultés pour déposer ou laver leurs effets personnels.
-It is also difficult for migrants to deposit or wash their personal belongings.

1942 **mondial**
adj
[mɔ̃djal]
global
Mme Ursula Wyndhoven (Bureau du Pacte Mondial) a donné un aperçu du Pacte mondial.
-Ursula Wyndhoven (Global Compact Office) presented an overview of the Global Compact.

1943 **intelligence**
f
[ɛ̃teliʒɑ̃s]
intelligence| intellect
L'intelligence se trouve dans la capacité à reconnaître les similitudes parmi différentes choses, et les différences entre des choses similaires.
-Intelligence is found in the capacity to recognize similarities among different things and differences between similar things.

1944 **généreux**
adj
[ʒeneʁø]
generous| liberal
Tout cela favorise l'absence de délais ou alors la fixation de délais généreux.
-care, all of which militates in favour of no time limits or very long time limits.

1945 **gérer**
vb
[ʒeʁe]
manage| run
Le rapporteur l' a évidemment accepté, d' où le fait qu' il parle de " gérer les migrations ".
-I believe that he has succeeded in this, but unfortunately not entirely, because others have presented all kinds of distracting amendments.

1946 **température**
f
[tɑ̃peʁatyʁ]
temperature
Température ambiante: La température ambiante doit être comprise entre 0 et 40 °C.

-Ambient temperature: The ambient temperature shall be between 0 °C and 40 °C.

1947	**fête**	**party**
	f	Il était malade, de telle sorte qu'il n'a pas pu assister à la fête.
	[fɛt]	-He was sick, so he couldn't attend the party.

1948	**saloperie**	**rubbish**
	f	Cette saloperie déconnecte le système nerveux et fait coaguler le sang.
	[salɔpʁi]	-Well, this junk zaps the nervous system, and it clogs the blood.

1949	**bonbon**	**candy**
	m	Je veux un bonbon.
	[bɔ̃bɔ̃]	-I want a piece of candy.

1950	**rapporter**	**report| relate**
	vb	C'est un investissement qui rapporterait vraiment.
	[ʁapɔʁte]	-That is an investment that really would pay dividends.

1951	**filmer**	**film| shoot**
	vb	Voilà pourquoi vous vouliez filmer un vrai dragon.
	[filme]	-I can see why you would want to film a real dragon.

1952	**tension**	**voltage| tension**
	f	La tension monte entre les deux pays.
	[tɑ̃sjɔ̃]	-Tensions are growing between the two countries.

1953	**serviette**	**towel| napkin**
	f	Il avait également été frappé sur les reins avec une serviette mouillée.
	[sɛʁvjɛt]	-He was also beaten on his kidneys with a wet towel.

1954	**guérir**	**cure| recover**
	vb	Le paludisme est pourtant une maladie que l'on peut prévenir, traiter et guérir.
	[geʁiʁ]	-Malaria is, however, is a disease that is preventable, treatable and curable.

1955	**rouler**	**roll**
	vb	Gideon Levy a ajouté que leur taxi avait roulé très doucement en direction du bureau.
	[ʁule]	-Levy said their taxi drove very slowly until they were 150 metres from the office.

1956	**passeport**	**passport**
	m	Le passeport étranger doit être retiré lors de la délivrance du passeport saoudien.
	[paspɔʁ]	-That the foreign passport is withheld when the Saudi passport is granted;

1957	**suffisamment**	**enough**
	adv	Une évolution se produit, mais elle n'est ni suffisamment rapide, ni suffisamment coordonnée.
	[syfizamɑ̃]	-We are seeing developments, but they are not fast enough or adequately coordinated.

1958	**échelle**	**scale| ladder**
	f	Il perdit l'équilibre et tomba de l'échelle.
	[eʃɛl]	-He lost his balance and fell off the ladder.

1959	**cercle**	**circle| ring**
	m	Il fait toujours partie du cercle.
	[sɛʁkl]	-He's still a part of the circle.

1960	**exiger**	**require| demand**
	vb	La communauté internationale doit continuer d'exiger leur arrestation.
	[ɛgziʒe]	-It is important that the international community continue to insist on their arrest.

1961 **citoyen**   **citizen**

m
[sitwajɛ̃]   Un citoyen mieux informé est un citoyen qui vote en connaissance de cause.
-A better informed citizen is a citizen who votes in full knowledge of the facts.

1962 **pervers**   **perverse**

adj
[pɛʁvɛʁ]   Je n'ai jamais vu de terroristes pervers qui meurent avec leurs victimes.
-I have not seen terrorists who are perverts and who die with their victims.

1963 **tentative**   **attempt| bid**

f
[tãtativ]   Elle a réussi sa tentative.
-She was successful in the attempt.

1964 **fan**   **fan**

m
[fan]   Description of the fan and its drive mechanism:
-Description du ventilateur et de son mécanisme d'entraînement:

1965 **règlement**   **settlement| regulation**

m
[ʁɛɡləmã]   Nous devrions en finir avec ce règlement.
-We should do away with this regulation.

1966 **immense**   **immense| great**

adj
[imãs]   Cet immense effort financier a atténué les effets les plus graves de la crise.
-This huge fiscal effort is alleviating the most serious effects of the crisis.

1967 **comté**   **county**

m
[kɔ̃te]   Sami vivait dans un comté très rural.
-Sami lived in a very rural county.

1968 **crainte**   **fear**

f
[kʁɛ̃t]   Ce garçon ne montra aucune crainte.
-That boy displayed no fear.

1969 **plaquer**   **stick| tackle**

vb
[plake]   Car il ne s'agit pas de plaquer sur l'Afghanistan une solution toute faite, conçue à l'extérieur.
-There is no question of imposing on Afghanistan some ready-made solution concocted by outsiders.

1970 **réunir**   **gather| reunite**

vb
[ʁeyniʁ]   Le Conseil consultatif peut se réunir en deux formations distinctes.
-The Advisory Board may assemble in two different compositions.

1971 **manuel**   **manual; manual**

adj; m
[manɥɛl]   Si seulement j'avais pris le temps de lire le manuel d'instructions !
-If I'd only taken the time to read the instruction manual!

1972 **cruel**   **cruel**

adj
[kʁyɛl]   La surpopulation carcérale constitue un traitement cruel, inhumain et dégradant.
-Overcrowded prisons constitute cruel, inhuman and degrading treatment.

1973 **octobre**   **October**

m
[ɔktɔbʁ]   La situation concernant le Sahara occidental (20 octobre 1975; 31 octobre 2007).
-The situation concerning Western Sahara (20 October 1975; 31 October 2007).

1974 **méchant**   **wicked| bad; naughty child**

adj; m
[meʃã]   Barroso, l' avocat de la solidarité européenne, en bon shérif, et le Premier ministre Tony Blair endosse le rôle du méchant.
-The film we are currently watching features Mr Barroso, the advocate of European solidarity, as a good sheriff, and Prime Minister Blair as a baddie.

1975 **bétail**   **livestock| cattle**

	m	Le bétail se nourrit d'herbe.
	[betaj]	-Cattle feed on grass.
1976	**dessin**	**drawing| design**
	m	Jack est doué pour le dessin.
	[desɛ̃]	-Jack is excellent at drawing.
1977	**Inde**	**India**
	f	Le cas de l'Inde: Mme Shashi Sareen, Conseil d'inspection des exportations, Inde
	[ɛ̃d]	-The case of India: Ms. Shashi Sareen, Export Inspection Council, India
1978	**dé**	**un-| in-**
	pfx	Existe-t-il un moyen de "dé-rétrécir" un T-shirt qui a rétréci ?
	[de]	-Is there any way you can un-shrink a T-shirt that has shrunk?
1979	**demeurer**	**remain| dwell**
	vb	La lutte contre la pauvreté doit demeurer au coeur de notre effort collectif.
	[dəmœʁe]	-The battle against poverty must remain at the heart of our collective effort.
1980	**léger**	**light| lightweight**
	adj	Ceux pour l'Europe enregistrent un léger recul (96 % contre 100%) (voir fig.
	[leʒe]	-Europe showed a small decline, from 100 per cent to 96 per cent (see figure II).
1981	**diamant**	**diamond**
	m	Le diamant était évalué à cinq milles dollars.
	[djamɑ̃]	-The diamond was valued at 5,000 dollars.
1982	**dalle**	**slab| flagstone**
	f	Une lourde dalle de pierre fut descendue sur la tombe.
	[dal]	-A heavy stone slab was lowered over the grave.
1983	**emporter**	**take| take away**
	vb	Ils ont emporté des documents, coupé les téléphones et la menace demeure d'une action en justice.
	[ɑ̃pɔʁte]	-Documents were taken away, the telephones were cut off and threats of legal action remain.
1984	**asile**	**asylum**
	m	La société est un asile dirigé par les patients.
	[azil]	-Society is an insane asylum run by the inmates.
1985	**organiser**	**organize| arrange**
	vb	Par ces questions, nous essayons de voir comment nous pouvons organiser notre travail.
	[ɔʁganize]	-Through these questions, we are attempting to find out how we can organize our work.
1986	**sou**	**cent**
	m	Si j'avais eu un sou à chaque fois qu'une femme m'a rejeté, je serais un homme riche !
	[su]	-If I had a cent for everytime a woman has turned me down, I'd be a rich man!
1987	**oser**	**dare**
	vb	Ce silence pesant ne doit plus exister aujourd'hui; oser en parler, c'est déjà agir.
	[oze]	-To dare to talk about mental health problems is already to have taken action.
1988	**tournage**	**shooting| turning**
	m	Quelques images du tournage de notre prochain clip.
	[tuʁnaʒ]	-Here are a few pictures from the shooting of our forthcoming video.

1989 nucléaire — **nuclear**
adj
[nykleɛʁ]
La non-prolifération nucléaire et le désarmement nucléaire sont complémentaires.
-Nuclear non-proliferation and nuclear disarmament complement each other.

1990 populaire — **popular**
adj
[pɔpylɛʁ]
C'est, en dernière analyse, l'affaire du mouvement populaire.
-In the final analysis, this is a matter for the populair movement.

1991 orchestrer — **orchestrate**
vb
[ɔʁkɛstʁe]
Il y a quatre ans de cela, Fuse a commencé à utiliser Avid Interplay Production pour orchestrer les tâches de montage.
-Four years ago, Fuse began using Avid Interplay Production to help orchestrate its editing function.

1992 couronne — **crown**
f
[kuʁɔn]
Mayuko portait une couronne de fleurs.
-Mayuko wore a flower crown.

1993 vedette — **star| launch**
f
[vədɛt]
Jacques Brel était une grande vedette.
-Jaccques Brel was a big star.

1994 renvoyer — **return| send**
vb
[ʁɑ̃vwaje]
Mon pays n'éprouve aucun problème à renvoyer des Roms vers leur pays d'origine.
-My country sees no problem in sending the Roma back to their countries of origin.

1995 garce — **bitch**
f
[gaʁs]
T'es une petite garce rapace.
-I think you are a rapacious little bitch.

1996 formation — **training| formation**
f
[fɔʁmasjɔ̃]
La formation (formation initiale et recyclage) doit être systématique et permanente.
-Training needs to be systematic and ongoing - initial training and re-training.

1997 Canada — **Canada**
f
[kanada]
Le Japon est plus petit que le Canada.
-Japan is smaller than Canada.

1998 audience — **audience**
f
[odjɑ̃s]
L'audience fut profondément affectée.
-The audience was deeply affected.

1999 participer — **participate| involve**
vb
[paʁtisipe]
Ainsi, la communauté desservie par la station peut participer à toutes ses activités.
-In this way, the community served can participate at all levels.

2000 procédure — **procedure**
f
[pʁɔsedyʁ]
Vous ne comprenez pas la procédure.
-You don't understand the procedure.

2001 brancher — **connect**
vb
[bʁɑ̃ʃe]
Le projet vise aussi à brancher les écoles du pays.
-Another goal is to connect the nation's schools.

2002 influencer — **influence**

vb
[ɛ̃flyɑ̃se]
Les directions imbriquées peuvent influencer la concurrence de diverses façons.
-Interlocking directorships can affect competition in a number of ways.

2003 salade — **salad**
f
[salad]
La salade de pommes-de-terre manque d'œufs durs.
-The potato salad wants boiled eggs.

2004 mouche — **fly| spot**
f
[muʃ]
Ne jamais utiliser de canon pour tuer une mouche.
-Never use a cannon to kill a fly.

2005 conséquence — **consequence**
f
[kɔ̃sekɑ̃s]
Ils sont sans conséquence.
-They're of no consequence.

2006 grouper — **group**
vb
[gʁupe]
Sélectionnez les objets à grouper à l' aide de la souris, puis choisissez Grouper dans le menu contextuel.
-Select the objects to be grouped using the mouse and then select Group from the context menu.

2007 espion — **spy**
m
[ɛspjɔ̃]
Mettez cet espion au cachot.
-Put that spy in the dungeon.

2008 Aie! — **Ouch!**
int
[ɛ!]
Aie ! Je me suis mordu l'intérieur de la lèvre...
-Ouch! I just bit the inside of my lip.

2009 objection — **objection**
f
[ɔbʒɛksjɔ̃]
Une objection tardive même si elle n'était pas valide était toujours une objection.
-A late objection, even if it was not valid, was always an objection.

2010 éteindre — **turn off| put out**
vb
[etɛ̃dʁ]
Éteindre les flammes d'un conflit entre des parties belligérantes ne suffit pas.
-Extinguishing the flames of conflict between warring parties is not enough.

2011 bouffer — **eat**
vb
[bufe]
Amène-toi, on va chercher à bouffer.
-Come on, let's get something to eat.

2012 allumer — **turn on| light up**
vb
[alyme]
Les feux de croisement doivent s'allumer et s'éteindre automatiquement.
-Dipped-beam headlamps shall be switched ON or OFF automatically.

2013 obéir — **obey**
vb
[ɔbeiʁ]
Au cours des premières années, les parents commandent et les enfants doivent obéir.
-During the early years the parents are in control and the children are expected to obey.

2014 chevalier — **knight**
m
[ʃəvalje]
Jack est chevalier.
-Jack is a knight.

2015 sabrer — **cut**
vb
[sabʁe]
Ils vont sabrer le financement des projets environnementaux.
-They are going to slash funding to environmental projects.

2016 sain — **healthy**
adj
[sɛ̃]
Nous pouvons avoir un environnement dynamique et sain ainsi qu'une économie dynamique et saine.

-We can have a vibrant and healthy environment and a vibrant and healthy economy.

2017	**tradition**	**tradition**
	f	Cette vieille tradition a disparu.
	[tʁadisjɔ̃]	-That old tradition has disappeared.
2018	**décevoir**	**disappoint| deceive**
	vb	Je dois décevoir tous ceux qui ont une conception romantique des jeux d'argent.
	[desəvwaʁ]	-If anyone has a romantic notion of gambling, then I have to disappoint them.
2019	**département**	**department**
	m	Veuillez vous rendre au département Chirurgie.
	[depaʁtəmã]	-Please go to the Surgery Department.
2020	**résister**	**resist**
	vb	Parallèlement, des initiatives se développent pour résister à cette tendance.
	[ʁeziste]	-At the same time, initiatives have been developing to resist this trend.
2021	**impressionnant**	**impressive| awesome**
	adj	Il a été impressionnant de voir le spectacle de ce référendum, impressionnant!
	[ɛ̃pʁesjɔnã]	-This referendum was an impressive sight, really quite impressive!
2022	**accusation**	**charge| accusation**
	f	L'audience de lecture de l'acte d'accusation d'aujourd'hui offre au prévenu sa première occasion d'exposer son cas en personne.
	[akyzasjɔ̃]	-Today's arraignment hearing offers the defendant his first opportunity to state his case personally.
2023	**disque**	**disk| discus**
	m	Avant de pouvoir écrire des données sur un disque, vous devez d'abord créer une partition, ensuite un système de fichiers par dessus, et finalement monter ce système de fichiers.
	[disk]	-Before being able to write data on a hard disk, you first need to create a partition, then to create a filesystem on it, and finally to mount this filesystem.
2024	**piquer**	**prick| sting**
	vb	Je me suis fait piquer par une abeille.
	[pike]	-I was stung by a bee.
2025	**entretien**	**maintenance| conversation**
	m	Une cravate classique est préférable à une cravate criarde pour un entretien d'embauche.
	[ãtʁətjɛ̃]	-A conservative tie is preferable to a loud one for a job interview.
2026	**accueillir**	**welcome| host**
	vb	Les Bahamas sont heureuses d'accueillir Tuvalu en tant que nouveau Membre de l'ONU.
	[akœjiʁ]	-The Bahamas is pleased to welcome Tuvalu as the newest Member of this Organization.
2027	**chasseur**	**hunter; gunner's**
	m; adj	Aucun homme ne peut les connaître, aucun chasseur ne peut leur tirer dessus avec de la poudre ou du plomb - Les pensées sont libres !
	[ʃasœʁ]	-No man can know them, no hunter can shoot them, with powder and lead - Thoughts are free!
2028	**examiner**	**examine**

	vb [ɛgzamine]	Nous aurons l'occasion de l'examiner, d'en débattre et de poser des questions. -We will have the chance to scrutinise, to debate, to question.
2029	**solitaire** adj; m/f [sɔlitɛʁ]	**solitary; loner** Elle a vécu une vie solitaire. -She lived a lonely life.
2030	**goutter** vb [gute]	**drip** L'eau de condensation ne doit pas goutter sur l'échantillon. -No condensate shall drip on to the sample.
2031	**micro** f; pfx [mikʁo]	**mike; micro-** Je lui ai donné le micro-micro. -I handed the mini-mike to him.
2032	**technologie** f [tɛknɔlɔʒi]	**technology** Haute technologie, grand naufrage. -Hi tech, big wreck.
2033	**original** adj; m [ɔʁiʒinal]	**original; original** Il a comparé la copie à l'original. -He compared the copy with the original.
2034	**ranch** m [ʁɑ̃ʃ]	**ranch** Il y a bien des années, j'avais été invité au ranch. -Years ago, I was invited to go to the ranch.
2035	**patrie** f [patʁi]	**country| homeland** Les idées n'ont pas véritablement de patrie sur terre, elles flottent dans l'air entre les peuples. -Ideas don't really have a home on the ground, they float in the air between people.
2036	**tuyau** m [tɥijo]	**pipe| hose** Le tuyau est de préférence un tuyau en polymère enroulable. -The pipe is preferably spoolable polymer pipe.
2037	**clinique** adj; f [klinik]	**clinical; clinic** Ce n'est pas une maison de fous. C'est une clinique pour les personnes mentalement instables. -It's not a madhouse. It's a clinic for the mentally unstable.
2038	**régime** m [ʁeʒim]	**regime| diet** Jill a suivi un régime l'année dernière et a perdu 20 kg! -Jill went on a diet last year and lost 20kg!
2039	**album** m [albɔm]	**album** Album on the latest Soviet studies of Arab and Islamic civilization. -Album sur les dernières études soviétiques de la civilisation arabo-islamique.
2040	**suprême** adj; m [sypʁɛm]	**supreme; supreme** La Cour Suprême se trouve près du Palais Impérial. -The Supreme Court is located near the Imperial Palace.
2041	**sincère** adj [sɛ̃sɛʁ]	**sincere| genuine** Rien de ceci ne pourra se réaliser sans un engagement sincère des acteurs nationaux. -But none of this can be achieved without genuine commitment of national actors.
2042	**pipe** f [pip]	**pipe** Il était assis là et fumait sa pipe. -He sat there smoking a pipe.

2043	**ça**	**it**
	prn	Parce que ça va changer tout ça, et chacun de ces téléphones a sa sonnerie
	[sa]	unique.
		-' Cause it 's gonna change all of that and each one of these phones has its
		own unique ring.

2044	**violent**	**violent| severe**
	adj	Le projet de loi fait une distinction entre le crime violent et le crime non
	[vjɔlɑ̃]	violent.
		-The bill tries to segregate violent and non-violent crimes.

2045	**émotion**	**emotion**
	f	La population québécoise suit avec émotion cette lutte des Franco-Ontariens.
	[emɔsjɔ̃]	-The people of Quebec followed the struggle of the franco-Ontarians with
		emotion.

2046	**coucou**	**cuckoo; cuckoo; hello**
	adj; m; int	Le dîner vient de me remonter faire coucou.
	[kuku]	-My dinner just came back up to say hello.

2047	**franc**	**frank; franc**
	adj; m	« Pour être franc, j'ai le vertige » « Tu es un trouillard ! »
	[fʁɑ̃]	-"To be frank, I am scared of heights." "You are a coward!"

2048	**remarque**	**remark| observation**
	f	Je remarque que les prix de vente sont écrits à l'encre rouge.
	[ʁəmaʁk]	-I notice the sale prices are written in red ink.

2049	**quatrième**	**fourth**
	num	Mon quatrième et dernier commentaire portera sur la révision du règlement
	[katʁijɛm]	OLAF.
		-My fourth and last comment will be on the revision of the OLAF
		regulation.

2050	**excitant**	**exciting; upper**
	adj; m	C'était excitant.
	[ɛksitɑ̃]	-It was exciting.

2051	**sel**	**salt**
	m	Ajoutez une pointe de sel.
	[sɛl]	-Add a tiny pinch of salt.

2052	**canapé**	**couch**
	m	Allonge-toi sur le canapé !
	[kanape]	-Lay down on the couch.

2053	**abattre**	**down| slaughter**
	vb	Les auteurs de ces lettres anonymes se disent capables d'abattre des
	[abatʁ]	appareils.
		-The authors of the letters claimed that they had the capacity to shoot down
		aircraft.

2054	**déclarer**	**declare**
	vb	Je veux simplement déclarer que je t'aime.
	[deklaʁe]	-I just want to say I love you.

2055	**splendide**	**splendid**
	adj	Il a fait un travail splendide et il est normal que le Parlement le reconnaisse.
	[splɑ̃did]	-He has done a splendid job and it has rightly been recognised by
		Parliament.

2056	**promotion**	**promotion**
	f	Ton père a été gratifié d'une promotion.
	[pʁɔmɔsjɔ̃]	-Your father got a promotion.

2057	**scandale**	**scandal**
	m	Ce fut un scandale, et un scandale que personne n'a dénoncé ou identifié.
	[skãdal]	-It was a scandal, and a scandal that no one has put their finger on or identified.
2058	**cran**	**notch**
	m	Descendons d'un cran !
	[kʁã]	-Let's take it down a notch.
2059	**mêler**	**mix| mingle**
	vb	Ils ont eu la possibilité de se mêler à la société iranienne et de travailler.
	[mele]	-They have had the opportunity to blend in with Iranian society and to work.
2060	**élément**	**element**
	m	Le plomb est un élément chimique symbolisé par Pb.
	[elemã]	-Lead is a chemical element symbolised by Pb.
2061	**arracher**	**snatch| extract**
	vb	D'aucuns veulent nous arracher un morceau, le plus « juteux » possible, d'autres leur prêtent la main.
	[aʁaʃe]	-Some want to wrest from us "a bigger piece of the pie", and others are helping them.
2062	**interroger**	**question| examine**
	vb	Il faut en effet s'interroger sur le contexte dans lequel s'inscrivent ces actes.
	[ɛ̃tɛʁɔʒe]	-The context in which these acts are carried out therefore needs to be examined.
2063	**efficace**	**effective| efficacious**
	adj	Enfin, une conception efficace doit trouver une expression efficace.
	[efikas]	-Finally, effective design is conveyed through the use of effective language.
2064	**événement**	**event**
	m	Cet événement l'a rendu célèbre.
	[evɛnmã]	-The event made him famous.
2065	**personnalité**	**personality; VIP**
	f; abr	Cela constitue dès lors notre personnalité, notre personnalité la plus authentique.
	[pɛʁsɔnalite]	-It is therefore our personality, our most genuine personality.
2066	**gentleman**	**gentleman; gentlemanly**
	m; adj	Ses manières ne sont pas celles d'un gentleman.
	[dʒɛntləman]	-His manners aren't those of a gentleman.
2067	**rumeur**	**rumor**
	f	Cette rumeur était l '? uvre du FSB et du service de contre-information russe.
	[ʁymœʁ]	-This rumour was put about by the FSB and the Russian counter-intelligence service.
2068	**parking**	**parking**
	m	Il n'y a pas de parking sur place.
	[paʁkiŋ]	-There are no parking facilities available at the Convention Center.
2069	**divin**	**divine**
	adj	Quelqu'un a finalement remarqué que la Commission européenne n'avait rien de divin.
	[divɛ̃]	-Finally someone paid attention to the difference between the European Commission and gods.
2070	**dégât**	**damage**
	m	Le dispositif a été neutralisé et on ne signale aucun blessé, ni aucun dégât.
	[dega]	-The explosive device was neutralized, and no injury or damage occurred.
2071	**négatif**	**negative; negative**

	adj; m [negatif]	Ces pratiques ont toutes un impact négatif sur la préservation de la biodiversité. -These practices all have a negative impact on the preservation of biodiversity.
2072	**éclater** vb [eklate]	**burst| erupt** La guerre va éclater entre l'Azerbaïdjan et l'Arménie à la fin de l'été ? -Will war break out between Azerbaijan and Armenia at the end of the summer?
2073	**viser** vb [vize]	**aim for** La science nous dit que nous devrions viser une réduction de 20, voire 40 %. -Science tells us that we should aim for a reduction of 25% and even 40%.
2074	**invisible** adj [ɛ̃vizibl]	**invisible** « Widowhood: invisible women, secluded ou excluded », Women 2000 (décembre 2001). -"Widowhood: invisible women, secluded or excluded", Women 2000 (December 2001).
2075	**signature** f [siɲatyʁ]	**signature** Ma parole a autant de valeur qu'une signature. -My word is as good as a signature.
2076	**user** vb [yze]	**use** À ce rythme, nous allons finir par user nos pantalons aux genoux. -At this rate we are going to wear out the knees of our pants.
2077	**insister** vb [ɛ̃siste]	**insist** Alors, répondez-nous: à la CIG, vous allez insister pour qu'il y ait publicité complète ? -Please answer us, therefore: at the IGC are you going to insist on full publicity?
2078	**autoriser** vb [ɔtɔʁize]	**authorize** Mon ministère n'a reçu aucune demande visant à autoriser un tel envoi au pays. -My department has had no request to authorize such a shipment into this country.
2079	**canard** m [kanaʁ]	**duck** La vache meugle, le coq chante, le cochon grouine, le canard cancane, et le chat miaule. -The cow goes "moo," the rooster goes "cock-a-doodle-doo," the pig goes "oink, oink," the duck goes "quack, quack" and the cat goes "meow."
2080	**stylo** m [stilo]	**pen** Découvrez toutes les possibilités de personnalisation et créez votre stylo ! -Discover all the customisation possibilities and create your Prodir pen!
2081	**possibilité** f [pɔsibilite]	**possibility** Comme il n'avait aucune possibilité de faire du feu, il mangea le poisson cru. -As he had no way of making fire, he ate the fish raw.
2082	**réveil** m [ʁevɛj]	**alarm clock** Règle l'heure pour faire sonner le réveil. -Set the time on the alarm.
2083	**pleuvoir** vb [pløvwaʁ]	**rain** Au moment où je parle, les bombes continuent de pleuvoir sur l'Afghanistan. -As I speak here, bombs are still falling over Afghanistan.
2084	**ère**	**era**

f
[ɛʁ]

L'humanité est passée de l'ère du bois à l'ère du charbon, puis à l'ère du pétrole.
-Humanity has gone from the wood age to the coal age, then to the oil age.

2085 **conclure**

vb
[kɔ̃klyʁ]

conclude

À court terme, bien sûr, nous devons conclure le train de mesures sur l'asile.
-In the short term, we, of course, need to conclude the asylum package.

2086 **étape**

f
[etap]

step| stage

La première étape est achevée.
-The first stage is complete.

2087 **contacter**

vb
[kɔ̃takte]

contact

Ce conseil consiste souvent à contacter un membre du réseau européen des médiateurs.
-Often, such advice is to contact a member of the European network of Ombudsmen.

2088 **identifier**

vb
[idɑ̃tifje]

identify

Les auteurs de ces attaques sont souvent difficiles à identifier avec certitude.
-Those responsible for these attacks are often hard to identify with certainty.

2089 **attacher**

vb
[ataʃe]

attach| fasten

Elle lui conseilla d'attacher sa ceinture.
-She advised him to fasten his seat belt.

2090 **prime**

f; adj
[pʁim]

premium; incentive

Ces garçons sont dans leur prime jeunesse.
-Those boys are in the first flush of youth.

2091 **publicité**

f
[pyblisite]

advertising| publicity

Quelle est ta publicité préférée ?
-What's your favourite advert?

2092 **Zut!**

int
[zy!]

Heck!

Zut! Je croyais que c'était ouvert.
-Darn, I thought they kept this open.

2093 **séjour**

m
[seʒuʁ]

stay| visit

Une règlementation spéciale régit l'enregistrement du séjour des étrangers.
-There are special regulations as to the registration of the stay of aliens.

2094 **tabac**

m
[taba]

tobacco

Elle lui conseilla de diminuer le tabac.
-She advised him to cut down on smoking.

2095 **chaos**

m
[kao]

chaos

À chaque fois qu'il arrive, c'est le chaos !
-Every time he arrives, it's chaos!

2096 **enfermer**

f; vb
[ɑ̃fɛʁme]

lock; confine

Je te ferai enfermer.
-I'll have you committed.

2097 **tarte**

f
[taʁt]

pie

Voudriez-vous un autre part de tarte ?
-Would you like another piece of pie?

2098 **frigo**

m
[fʁigo]

fridge

Il était temps de nettoyer le frigo !
-Sooner or later, somebody's gonna clean out the fridge.

2099 **traîne**

f
[tʁɛn]

train

Mettons en valeur cette belle traîne.
-Make the most of this beautiful train.

2100	**câbler**	**wire**
	vb	Il est ici pour câbler les cinémas locaux pour le son.
	[kable]	-He's here to wire the local cinemas for sound.
2101	**rarement**	**rarely| hardly**
	adv	C'est une chose qui arrive rarement dans la vie politique canadienne, trop
	[ʁaʁmã]	rarement.
		-This is something that happens rarely in Canadian politics, too rarely I
		might say.
2102	**goûter**	**taste**
	vb	Les enfants prennent le goûter après l'école.
	[gute]	-Children have a snack after school.
2103	**disputer**	**compete| fight**
	vb	Il doit être possible de disputer à nos concurrents des parts du marché
	[dispyte]	international dans le cadre d'une concurrence juste et équitable.
		-It must be possible to compete for markets worldwide on fair competitive
		terms.
2104	**impliquer**	**involve| implicate**
	vb	Il doit être nommé en vertu d'un processus ouvert qui doit impliquer le
	[ɛ̃plike]	Parlement européen.
		-The appointment must be by open process and must involve the European
		Parliament.
2105	**remarquable**	**remarkable**
	adj	Scott était un remarquable membre du Cabinet et un remarquable solliciteur
	[ʁəmaʁkabl]	général.
		-Scott was an outstanding cabinet minister and an outstanding Solicitor
		General.
2106	**exception**	**exception**
	f	À l'exception de Jack, toute la famille écoutait la télévision en silence.
	[ɛksɛpsjɔ̃]	-Except for Jack, the family was all watching TV in silence.
2107	**gant**	**glove**
	m	Dolly c'est une femme qui a une main de fer dans un gant de velours.
	[gã]	-Dolly is a woman with a hand of iron in a velvet glove.
2108	**ennuyeux**	**boring| annoying**
	adj	Il en résulte que cela nous semble inintéressant et parfois même ennuyeux.
	[ãnɥijø]	-The result is that people find it uninteresting and sometimes downright
		annoying.
2109	**ouvrier**	**worker**
	m	Le plus grand ouvrier de la nature est le temps.
	[uvʁije]	-Nature's greatest worker is time.
2110	**être à la traîne**	**fall behind**
	vb	Notre pays est à la traîne.
	[ɛtʁ a la tʁɛn]	-Our country is lagging behind.
2111	**record**	**record**
	m	Il a battu le record.
	[ʁəkɔʁ]	-He has broken the record.
2112	**délirer**	**rave**
	vb	À un moment, il s'est mis à délirer et a fini par perdre conscience.
	[deliʁe]	-He became delirious at some point and eventually lost consciousness.
2113	**enseigne**	**sign**
	f	Vous pourriez mettre une enseigne devant.
	[ãsɛɲ]	-At least you could put a sign out front.

2114	**angle**	**angle| corner**
	m	Ne t'en fais pas, j'ai couvert chaque angle.
	[ãgl]	-Don't worry, I have every angle covered.
2115	**instinct**	**instinct**
	m	Suis ton instinct.
	[ɛ̃stɛ̃]	-Go with your instinct.
2116	**impôt**	**tax**
	m	Nous devons payer l'impôt.
	[ɛ̃po]	-We must pay the tax.
2117	**rompre**	**break| break up**
	vb	Cela permettrait de rompre la dépendance vis-à-vis de l'aide extérieure de deux manières.
	[ʁɔ̃pʁ]	-Such a process would help to break up aid dependency in two ways.
2118	**rattraper**	**catch up| make up**
	vb	Ces mesures aideront les PMA à rattraper leur retard par rapport aux nations développées.
	[ʁatʁape]	-These measures will help LDCs to catch up with the rest of the developing nations.
2119	**vilain**	**ugly; villein**
	adj; m	Comme tu es vilain ! Arrête de m'ennuyer !
	[vilɛ̃]	-How naughty you are! Stop bothering me!
2120	**complexe**	**complex; complex**
	adj; m	La consommation excessive d'alcool peut endommager le complexe amygdalien.
	[kɔ̃plɛks]	-Binge drinking can damage the amygdala.
2121	**méthode**	**method**
	f	Elle élabora une bonne méthode pour faire de l'argent sur Internet.
	[metɔd]	-She thought of a good way to make money on the Internet.
2122	**suggérer**	**suggest| imply**
	vb	Ils semblent suggérer des limitations inacceptables et devraient être rejetés.
	[syɡʒeʁe]	-They seem to suggest limitations which are unacceptable and should be rejected.
2123	**motel**	**motel**
	m	Anthony Motel pendant 10 ans.
	[mɔtɛl]	-Anthony Motel for a period of 10 years.
2124	**tragédie**	**tragedy**
	f	C'est une tragédie humaine.
	[tʁaʒedi]	-This is a human tragedy.
2125	**torture**	**torture**
	f	Pendant encore combien de temps va durer cette torture ?
	[tɔʁtyʁ]	-How long is this torture gonna continue?
2126	**industrie**	**industry**
	f	Le ministre de l'Industrie devrait se faire le défenseur de cette industrie.
	[ɛ̃dystʁi]	-The Minister of Industry should be an advocate for this industry.
2127	**population**	**population**
	f	Nos gouvernements sont devenus des androïdes vivant parmi une population humaine.
	[pɔpylasjɔ̃]	-Our governments have become space aliens living among a human population.
2128	**adaptation**	**adaptation**

f

L'adaptation est la clé pour survivre.

[adaptasjɔ̃]

-Adaptation is the key to survival.

2129 **admirer**   **admire**

vb

Je ne peux qu'admirer l'hypocrisie opportuniste de mes collègues conservateurs.

[admiʁe]

-I can only admire the opportunistic hypocrisy of my Tory colleagues.

2130 **autoroute**   **highway**

f

J'ai pris l'autoroute 58.

[otoʁut]

-I took Highway 58.

2131 **pro**   **pro**

m/f

Mewes sort ses répliques comme un pro... avec le peu de répétition passe dessus.

[pʁo]

-Mewes whips through all his dialogue like a pro...... with the tiny bit of rehearsal we did.

2132 **obscurité**   **darkness| obscurity**

f

As-tu peur de l'obscurité ?

[ɔpskyʁite]

-Are you afraid of the dark?

2133 **fabuleux**   **fabulous**

adj

J'ai toujours trouvé cela fabuleux.

[fabylø]

-I always thought it was a fabulous thing.

2134 **linge**   **washing**

m

La quantité de linge et la saleté influencent elles aussi le dosage.

[lɛ̃ʒ]

-The amount of laundry and how soiled it is also affects dosage.

2135 **illégal**   **illegal**

adj

"m" Mentionne expressément les pratiques illégales et le commerce international illégal.

[ilegal]

-"m" Refers specifically to illegal practices and illegal international trade.

2136 **rigole**   **channel**

f

La rigole de lubrifiant (5) est avantageusement réalisée en matière plastique.

[ʁigɔl]

-The lubricant channel (5) advantageously comprises plastic.

2137 **opérer**   **operate| carry out**

vb

Ils pourront alors opérer dans le même fuseau horaire et la même zone géographique.

[ɔpeʁe]

-They will then be able to operate in the same time zone and geographical area.

2138 **fauteuil**   **armchair**

m

Le sénateur Dennis Glen Patterson (président suppléant) occupe le fauteuil.

[fotœj]

-Senator Dennis Glen Patterson (Acting Chairman) in the chair.

2139 **vendeur**   **seller| dealer**

m

"Puis-je vous aider?" demanda le vendeur.

[vɑ̃dœʁ]

-"How may I help you?" the sales clerk asked.

2140 **novembre**   **November**

m

Des grèves sont déjà prévues pour novembre en Italie et pour le 24 novembre au Portugal.

[nɔvɑ̃bʁ]

-Strikes are already planned for November in Italy, and for 24 November in Portugal.

2141 **collection**   **collection**

f

Ce musée dispose d'une fascinante collection d'objets celtes.

[kɔlɛksjɔ̃]

-This museum displays a fascinating collection of Celtic objects.

2142 **tonner**   **thunder**

	vb	Les canons peuvent bien tonner, il faut quand même moissonner les champs.
	[tɔne]	-The guns may thunder, but the fields must still be harvested.
2143	**bonhomme**	**fellow| old man**
	m	Elle n'a pas épousé le bonhomme.
	[bɔnɔm]	-She did not marry the man.
2144	**accent**	**accent**
	m	J'espère qu'il s'agissait d'une réflexion sur mon débit, et non sur mon
	[aksã]	accent.
		-I hope it was a reflection on my speed and not my accent.
2145	**déplacer**	**move| travel**
	vb	De nouveaux conflits continuent de déplacer des centaines de milliers de
	[deplase]	personnes.
		-Eruption of conflict continues to displace hundreds of thousands of people.
2146	**serrer**	**tighten| clamp**
	vb	Laissez-moi vous serrer dans mes bras.
	[seʁe]	-Let me give you a hug.
2147	**plastique**	**plastic; plastic**
	adj; m	L'agrafe en plastique transparent ton sur ton sert de surface de
	[plastik]	personnalisation.
		-A clip of transparent plastic serves as a surface for personalisation options.
2148	**marche**	**walking**
	f	Ils font frénétiquement marche arrière.
	[maʁʃ]	-They are frenetically backpedaling.
2149	**révérend**	**reverend**
	m	Tout ce pourquoi le Révérend Martin Luther King avait travaillé si dur
	[ʁeveʁã]	semblait perdu.
		-Everything Rev. Martin Luther King had worked so hard for seemed lost.
2150	**commande**	**order**
	f	La commande de passage en faisceaux de croisement doit commander
	[kɔmãd]	simultanément l'extinction du ou des feux-route.
		-The control for changing over to the passing beam(s) shall switch off the
		driving beam(s) simultaneously.
2151	**caporal**	**lance corporal**
	m	Ce refus de faire la lumière sur l'état de santé du caporal Shalit est très
	[kapɔʁal]	préoccupant.
		-The refusal to provide details regarding corporal Gilad Shalit's condition is
		greatly alarming.
2152	**lot**	**lot| prize**
	m	J'ai tiré le gros lot.
	[lo]	-I hit the jackpot.
2153	**trahison**	**treason**
	f	Je ne peux, quant à moi, Monsieur le Président, m'associer à cette trahison.
	[tʁaizõ]	-Personally, Mr President, I will not associate myself with such betrayal.
2154	**sensation**	**sensation| feeling**
	f	J'aimerais te décrire cette sensation.
	[sãsasjõ]	-God, I wish I could describe the feeling to you.
2155	**résistance**	**resistance| strength**
	f	Il était parfaitement détendu et n'opposa aucune résistance mais me lança un
	[ʁezistãs]	regard si hideux que cela me fit transpirer à grosses gouttes.
		-He was perfectly cool and made no resistance, but gave me one look, so
		ugly that it brought out the sweat on me like running.

2156	**mesure**	**measure| step**
	f	Sont-ils en mesure de me voir ?
	[məzyʁ]	-Can they see me?

2157	**chanceux**	**fortunate; lucky man**
	adj; m	Les plus chanceux mendient ou gagnent quelques sous en nettoyant des
	[ʃɑ̃sø]	pare-brise.
		-The lucky ones might end up begging for change or squeegeeing car
		windows.

2158	**boue**	**mud**
	f	Les pneus de la voiture étaient couverts de boue séchée.
	[bu]	-The car's tires were caked with dried mud.

2159	**merveille**	**wonder| marvel**
	f	Construite il y a plus d'un siècle, cette merveille d'ingénierie enjambe des
	[mɛʁvɛj]	canyons et des cols.
		-This an engineering marvel built at the turn of the last century over the
		canyons of the mountain passes.

2160	**poing**	**fist**
	m	Le lâche est le premier à lever le poing.
	[pwɛ̃]	-The coward is the first to raise his fist.

2161	**sacrifice**	**sacrifice**
	m	Il était prêt à faire le sacrifice ultime.
	[sakʁifis]	-He was ready to make the ultimate sacrifice.

2162	**communication**	**communication**
	f	Veuillez accuser réception de cette communication dès sa réception.
	[kɔmynikasjɔ̃]	-Kindly acknowledge the receipt of this communication immediately after
		the same has reached you.

2163	**appuyer**	**support| press**
	vb	Nous sommes fiers d'appuyer ces programmes en Afghanistan, et maintenant
	[apɥije]	en Iraq.
		-We are proud to be supporting those programmes in Afghanistan and, now,
		in Iraq.

2164	**chagrin**	**grief| heartache**
	m	Nous partageons le chagrin du peuple américain et des familles des victimes.
	[ʃagʁɛ̃]	-We share the grief of the American people and of the families of the
		victims.

2165	**concentrer**	**focus| concentrate**
	vb	Je pense que c'est sur ce domaine en particulier que nous devons nous
	[kɔ̃sɑ̃tʁe]	concentrer.
		-I think it is in this particular area that we need to focus.

2166	**drogue**	**drug**
	f	Il sera chancelant pour quelques heures encore, jusqu'à ce que la drogue se
	[dʁɔg]	dissipe.
		-He'll be groggy for another few hours until the drug wears off.

2167	**gratuit**	**free**
	adj	L'enseignement primaire est obligatoire et gratuit et l'enseignement
	[gʁatɥi]	secondaire est gratuit.
		-Primary education is mandatory and free, whereas secondary education is
		free.

2168	**britannique**	**British**
	adj	Le ministre de Sa Majesté britannique chargé des affaires européennes est
	[bʁitanik]	avec nous.

-Her Britannic Majesty's Minister with responsibility for European affairs is with us.

2169	**social**	**social**
	adj	Nous devons réinstaurer une véritable politique de logement social.
	[sɔsjal]	-What the government needs to do is reintroduce a real social housing policy.
2170	**coach**	**trainer**
	m	Un jeune coach comme toi nous serais très utile.
	[kɔaʃ]	-We could really use a good young coach like you.
2171	**coïncidence**	**coincidence**
	f	Je souhaitais simplement faire remarquer la coïncidence arithmétique frappante.
	[kɔɛ̃sidɑ̃s]	-I merely wanted to remark on the striking arithmetical coincidence.
2172	**halte**	**stop| stopover**
	f	Aux portes de ce Parlement, d'immenses bannières aux couleurs de l'UE proclament: Halte à la pauvreté !
	[alt]	-Outside the doors of this Chamber, huge banners with EU logos proclaim: Halt poverty.
2173	**août**	**August**
	m	Nous venons de vivre le matin d'août le plus froid en vingt ans.
	[ut]	-We've just had our coldest August morning for twenty years.
2174	**malédiction**	**curse**
	f	Et ils sont poursuivis par une malédiction ici-bas et au Jour de la Résurrection.
	[malediksjɔ̃]	-And a curse was made to pursue them in this world, and on the Day of Resurrection.
2175	**pension**	**pension**
	f	Les gens d'au moins 65 ans reçoivent une pension du gouvernement.
	[pɑ̃sjɔ̃]	-People of 65 and above get a pension from the government.
2176	**vampire**	**vampire**
	m	Il y a un nouveau vampire à Brooklyn, et il s'appelle Julius Jones !
	[vɑ̃piʀ]	-There's a new vampire in Brooklyn and his name's Julius Jones.
2177	**phase**	**phase**
	f	Il comprend deux phases, une phase préparatoire et une phase d'exécution.
	[faz]	-It consists of two phases, a preparatory phase and an implementation phase.
2178	**noix**	**nut; walnut**
	f; adj	Alex arrive à nommer des objets comme "noix", "papier" ou "maïs".
	[nwa]	-Alex names objects, like "walnut," "paper" and "corn".
2179	**toast**	**toast**
	m	J'aime tartiner du miel sur mon toast le matin.
	[tost]	-I like to spread honey on my toast in the morning.
2180	**Boum!**	**Bang!**
	int	Une petite bombe atomique qui ferait " boum ".
	[bum!]	-Then you'd have a small atomic bomb going " boom. "
2181	**sexuel**	**sexual**
	adj	L'abus sexuel d'enfants (art. 172); L'abus sexuel de majeurs dépendants (art173).
	[sɛksɥɛl]	-Sexual abuse of children (art. 172); Sexual abuse of dependent adults (art. 173).
2182	**honnêtement**	**honestly**

	adv	Le travail se fera équitablement et honnêtement et toujours dans les règles.
	[ɔnɛtmɑ̃]	-It will be business and it will be fair and square and above board at all times.
2183	**défi**	**challenge**
	m	Je me sens prêt à relever le défi.
	[defi]	-I feel ready for the challenge.
2184	**oublié**	**forgotten**
	adj	Avec ce jeu de substitution, ce terme qui était dans le paragraphe original a été oublié.
	[ublije]	-Thanks to this substitution, the term found in the original paragraph has been left out.
2185	**estimer**	**estimate**
	vb	Par la suite, il devient difficile d'estimer l'impact du dispositif mis en place.
	[ɛstime]	-Subsequently, it becomes difficult to estimate the impact of the system introduced.
2186	**désastre**	**disaster**
	m	C'est un désastre.
	[dezastʁ]	-This is a disaster.
2187	**éliminer**	**eliminate**
	vb	Il a affirmé qu'il faut éliminer les subventions des pays développés.
	[elimine]	-He said that the developed countries must eliminate their subsidies.
2188	**reconnaissant**	**grateful**
	adj	Le peuple éthiopien est reconnaissant de cette manifestation de solidarité.
	[ʁəkɔnɛsɑ̃]	-The people of Ethiopia are grateful for this demonstration of solidarity.
2189	**particulièrement**	**particularly**
	adv	Ceci est particulièrement important pour les personnes âgées ou handicapées.
	[paʁtikyljɛʁmɑ̃]	-This is particularly important for the elderly and persons with disabilities.
2190	**bâtard**	**bastard; bastard**
	adj; m	La brioche est comme l'enfant bâtard de la génoise et du pain, mais la sensation qu'elle procure sous la langue est la meilleure sous les cieux.
	[bataʁ]	-The brioche is like the bastard child of sponge cake and bread, but its feeling under the tongue is the best under the heavens.
2191	**solitude**	**solitude| loneliness**
	f	Cette femme connaît non seulement le déracinement, mais aussi la solitude.
	[sɔlityd]	-Their feelings of being uprooted go together with feelings of loneliness.
2192	**débrouiller**	**untangle**
	vb	Laissez-moi m'en débrouiller.
	[debʁuje]	-Let me handle this.
2193	**jouet**	**toy; toy**
	adj; m	À l' heure actuelle, la Moldavie est un jouet entre les pattes de l' ours russe.
	[ʒwɛ]	-At present, Moldova is a plaything in the hands of the Russian bear.
2194	**tarder**	**delay**
	vb	Ils condamnaient le gouvernement d'avoir tant tardé à consulter la Chambre.
	[taʁde]	-They then condemned the government for putting it to a vote so late.
2195	**ingénieur**	**engineer**
	m	Jack est ingénieur en électricité.
	[ɛ̃ʒenjœʁ]	-Jack is an electrical engineer.
2196	**chant**	**singing| song**
	m	Le chant est son point fort.
	[ʃɑ̃]	-Singing is her strong point.

2197	**poésie**	**poetry| poem**
	f	La poésie est vieille comme le monde; la poésie est la liberté à l'état pur.
	[pɔezi]	-Poetry is as old as the world; poetry is freedom in its pure state.
2198	**ongle**	**nail**
	m	Mon ongle de pouce s'est cassé.
	[õgl]	-I had my thumbnail torn off.
2199	**trafic**	**traffic**
	m	Le trafic était très important. Les voitures étaient à la file pare-chocs contre pare-chocs.
	[tʁafik]	-The traffic was very heavy. The cars were lined up bumper to bumper.
2200	**activité**	**activity**
	f	Être à bord d'une grande roue est mon activité préférée.
	[aktivite]	-Riding in a Ferris wheel is my favorite thing to do.
2201	**médaille**	**medal**
	f	Il a été récompensé par une médaille d'or une fois.
	[medaj]	-He's been awarded a gold medal once.
2202	**reconnaissance**	**recognition**
	f	L'avion effectuait une reconnaissance aérienne.
	[ʁəkɔnɛsãs]	-The aircraft was conducting aerial reconnaissance.
2203	**foie**	**liver**
	m	Chez les rongeurs (en laboratoire), il provoque une hyperplasie hépatique ainsi que des tumeurs du foie.
	[fwa]	-Alpha-HCH causes liver hyperplasia and liver tumours in (laboratory) rodents.
2204	**cercueil**	**coffin**
	m	Une fois de plus, la Commission vient enfoncer un clou supplémentaire au cercueil.
	[sɛʁkœj]	-Here we are again with the Commission knocking another nail into the coffin.
2205	**gris**	**gray; gray**
	adj; m	Les marchés gris se trouvent à la limite entre transfert licite et trafic illicite.
	[gʁi]	-Grey markets operate at the juncture between licit transfers and illicit trafficking.
2206	**oindre**	**anoint**
	vb	Ils en appellent à Dieu pour les oindre.
	[wɛ̃dʁ]	-They're calling on God to anoint them.
2207	**livraison**	**delivery**
	f	Une livraison accélérée coûtera dix dollars de plus.
	[livʁɛzõ]	-Expedited delivery will cost an additional ten dollars.
2208	**pilule**	**pill**
	f	Toutefois, cette pilule synthétique n'est pas une alternative valable à l'inhalation de THC.
	[pilyl]	-However, this synthetic pill is not a valid alternative to inhaled THC.
2209	**pratiquement**	**virtually**
	adv	La pratique consistant à limiter l'accès aux contraceptifs a pratiquement disparu.
	[pʁatikmã]	-The practice of limiting access to contraceptives has nearly vanished.
2210	**cinquante**	**fifty**
	num	Le salaire minimum en Allemagne est de huit euros cinquante de l'heure.
	[sɛ̃kãt]	-Germany's minimum wage is 8.50 euros an hour.
2211	**armé**	**armed**

	adj [aʁme]	En outre, le terrorisme, en période de conflit armé, sert des objectifs particuliers. -Further, terrorism in armed conflict has a special purpose during armed conflict.
2212	**communiste** adj; m/f [kɔmynist]	**Communist; Communist** Aujourd'hui, le pays le plus polluant est la Chine communiste. -At the moment, the country that is polluting the world most is communist China.
2213	**commissariat** m [kɔmisaʁja]	**police station** Le caractère provisoire du Haut Commissariat des Nations Unies pour les réfugiés. -Time limitation on the Office of the United Nations High Commissioner for Refugees.
2214	**oxygéner** vb [ɔksiʒene]	**oxygenate| bleach** Après tout, le MMT accroît l'indice d'octane de l'essence et augmente aussi les composés oxygénés présents dans l'essence. -After all, MMT raises the octane rating of gasoline, and it rates the oxygenates contained in gasoline, too.
2215	**trouille** f [tʁuj]	**funk** Je déteste ces araignées, elles sont toujours là pour me ficher la trouille quand j'fais le ménage. -I hate those spiders. They're always there to freak me out when I'm cleaning.
2216	**analyser** vb [analize]	**analyze** An HCLD or equivalent analyser for the measurement of the oxides of nitrogen. -Un analyseur HCLD ou appareil équivalent pour la mesure des oxydes d'azote.
2217	**pisse** f [pis]	**piss** Ça te plairait de devoir faire le poirier pour pisser ? -How would you feel if you had to do a fuckin' handstand to take a piss?
2218	**essentiel** adj; m [esɑ̃sjɛl]	**essential; main** Tel est, pour l'essentiel, l'avis de la commission de l'emploi. -That is the main gist of the opinion of the Committee on Employment.
2219	**génération** f [ʒeneʁasjɔ̃]	**generation** Nous n'empêchons plus qu'elle se fasse et se transmette de génération en génération. -We no longer restrict it from being done and carried on from generation to generation.
2220	**adjoindre** vb [adʒwɛ̃dʁ]	**adjoin** Il peut en outre adjoindre à son représentant ou à ses suppléants un ou plusieurs conseillers. -Each such member may also appoint one or more advisers to its representative or alternates.
2221	**écriture** f [ekʁityʁ]	**writing** Il faudrait que je me remette à l'écriture de mon rapport. -I should get back to writing my report.
2222	**annuler** vb [anyle]	**cancel** J'ai dû annuler cette commande car nous ne disposions pas d'assez d'argent pour la payer.

-I had to cancel that order because we didn't have enough money to pay for it.

2223	**massacre**	**massacre**
	m	Le gouvernement chinois contrôlait l'Internet pour empêcher les gens de connaître la vérité du massacre de la place Tian'anmen.
	[masakʁ]	-The Chinese government controlled the internet to prevent the people from knowing the truth of the Tiananmen Square Massacre.
2224	**volontiers**	**willingly**
	adv	Je concède volontiers que la Commission n'est pas responsable de cette situation.
	[vɔlɔ̃tje]	-I gladly admit that the Commission is not responsible for this situation.
2225	**phrase**	**phrase**
	f	J'aimerais entendre la première phrase.
	[fʁaz]	-I'd like to hear the first sentence.
2226	**poème**	**poem| epic**
	m	Je vais vous lire le poème que j'ai écrit à l'instant.
	[pɔɛm]	-I'll read you the poem I wrote just now.
2227	**bail**	**lease| long time**
	m	Ça fait un tel bail !
	[baj]	-It has been such a long time.
2228	**pénis**	**penis**
	m	Elle a reçu une publicité pour l'agrandissement du pénis dans sa boîte de réception.
	[penis]	-She received an ad for penis enlargement in her inbox.
2229	**singe**	**monkey**
	m	As-tu déjà vu un singe ?
	[sɛ̃ʒ]	-Have you ever seen a monkey?
2230	**statuer**	**rule**
	vb	Le tribunal devrait statuer sur la demande d'ajournement présentée par le ministère public.
	[statɥe]	-The Court should rule on the application for an adjournment by the prosecution.
2231	**époux**	**husband| spouse**
	m	Les femmes mariées ne sont pas tenues de prendre la nationalité de leur époux.
	[epu]	-Married women were not obliged to take their husband's nationality.
2232	**automne**	**fall| autumn**
	m	Université de Paris XIII, faculté de droit, automne 1999, printemps et automne 2000.
	[otɔn]	-Université Paris XIII, Faculté de droit, autumn 1999, spring and autumn 2000.
2233	**brigade**	**brigade**
	f	La brigade des pompiers a empêché un incendie.
	[bʁigad]	-The fire brigade prevented a fire.
2234	**éloigner**	**drive away**
	vb	Le défi actuel nous offre une occasion de nous éloigner du bord du gouffre.
	[elwaɲe]	-The present challenge provides us with an opportunity to move away from the brink.
2235	**magicien**	**magician**
	m	Le Président (parle en anglais) : Je ne suis pas sûr d'être magicien; je dois suivre une formation pour cela.
	[maʒisjɛ̃]	

-The Chairman: I am not sure that I am a magician; I will have to go get some training for that.

2236	**survie**	**survival**
f		L'entreprise n'a pas de grandes chances de survie.
[syʁvi]		-The company does not have a good chance of survival.

2237	**batterie**	**battery**
f		La batterie de mon téléphone se décharge rapidement.
[batʁi]		-My phone battery runs out quickly.

2238	**ordonner**	**order	direct**
vb		Si les circonstances le permettent, le tribunal peut ordonner la reprise du travail.
[ɔʁdɔne]		-If the circumstances permit, the court may order the re-establishment of work.

2239	**manche**	**handle; sleeve**
m; f		Son chien a mordu le manche.
[mɑ̃ʃ]		-It'll have the marks of his dog's teeth on the handle.

2240	**creuser**	**dig**
vb		Depuis lors, 23 permis seulement avaient été délivrés pour en creuser de nouveaux.
[kʁøze]		-Since then only 23 permits had been issued to dig new wells.

2241	**mordre**	**bite	snap**
vb		Je n'ai pas peur de mordre et je n'ai pas peur des morsures.
[mɔʁdʁ]		-I am not afraid to bite, and I am not afraid of being bitten back.

2242	**contenir**	**contain	restrain**
vb		Les cartouches doivent contenir au moins 95 % du volume théorique d'hydrogène.
[kɔ̃tniʁ]		-Cartridges shall be contained hydrogen of 95% or more of its designed capacity.

2243	**principe**	**principle**
m		Il tient pour principe de faire une promenade chaque matin.
[pʁɛ̃sip]		-He makes it a rule to take a walk every morning.

2244	**bourrer**	**stuff	fill**
vb		Chaque vendredi soir ils allaient se bourrer la gueule.
[buʁe]		-Every Friday night they went and got liquored up.

2245	**rembourser**	**repay	reimburse**
vb		Il convient également de signaler qu'il sera plus simple de rembourser les dépenses.
[ʁɑ̃buʁse]		-It is also worth mentioning that it will become easier to reimburse expenditure.

2246	**masser**	**massage**
vb		Je vais juste de masser gentiment.
[mase]		-I'm just going to gently massage you.

2247	**luxe**	**luxury**
m		Voyager est un luxe que je ne peux m'accorder.
[lyks]		-Travelling is a luxury I can't allow myself.

2248	**chariot**	**cart	trolley**
m		Une maquette en argile d'un chariot fabriqué en Mésopotamie entre 1900 et 1600 ans av.
[ʃaʁjo]		-A clay model of a chariot that was made in Mesopotamia some time between 1900 and 1600 BC.

| 2249 | **terreur** | **terror** |

	f	Le cœur du garçon effrayé palpitait de terreur.
	[teʁœʁ]	-The frightened boy's heart palpitated with terror.

2250 mobile — mobile

adj
[mɔbil]

Où est mon mobile ?
-Where's my mobile?

2251 sagesse — **wisdom**

f
[saʒɛs]

Une parole (message) de sagesse est une sagesse surnaturelle, non apprise ou acquise.
-A word (i.e. message) of wisdom is supernatural wisdom, not something learned or acquired.

2252 rigoler — **laugh**

vb
[ʁigɔle]

On a juste dit ça pour rigoler.
-We were just flapping our gums.

2253 informer — **inform| advise**

vb
[ɛ̃fɔʁme]

Anyone who believes I'll turn informer for nothing is a fool.
-Quiconque croit que je deviendrai informateur pour rien est idiot.

2254 saluer — **greet**

vb
[salɥe]

Je voudrais également saisir cette occasion pour saluer les autres membres du Bureau.
-I take this opportunity to greet the other officers of the Bureau.

2255 terriblement — **terribly**

adv
[teʁibləmɑ̃]

Le peuple congolais a terriblement souffert pendant de longues années des conflits armés.
-The Congolese people have suffered terribly during long years of armed conflict.

2256 satisfaire — **satisfy| please**

vb
[satisfɛʁ]

Une question évidente concerne les mesures prises pour satisfaire les malvoyants.
-One obvious question is what is being done to cater for the visually impaired.

2257 avaler — **swallow**

vb
[avale]

Les grandes entreprises avaleront les plus petites.
-Large businesses will swallow up smaller ones.

2258 décembre — **December**

m
[desɑ̃bʁ]

Dans certains cas, l'état est arrêté au 31 décembre 2003 ou au 31 décembre 2006.
-In some cases the reporting date is as at 31 December 2003 or 31 December 2006.

2259 planter — **plant**

vb
[plɑ̃te]

Il est donc nécessaire de planter une diversité d'essences.
-It is therefore essential to plant a diverse range of species.

2260 four — **oven**

m
[fuʁ]

Il y a des biscuits au four.
-There are cookies in the oven.

2261 usage — **use| usage**

m
[yzaʒ]

La distinction entre valeurs d'usage indirect et valeurs de non-usage n'est pas très claire.
-The distinction between indirect use values and non-use values is ambiguous.

2262 collège — **college**

m
[kɔlɛʒ]

Un soir, cependant, lorsque Miss Baker revint au collège quelques minutes avant l'heure où tous les étudiants devaient être rentrés, elle trouva une voiture sur sa place de parking.
-One evening, however, when Miss Baker got back to the college a few minutes before the time by which all students had to be in, she found another car in her parking space.

2263 symbole   **symbol**

m
[sɛ̃bɔl]

Supprimer le dernier symbole d'un jeu entraîne également la suppression de ce dernier.
-Deleing the last remaining symbol of a symbol set also deletes the symbol set.

2264 flamme   **flame**

f
[flam]

Je lui ai offert un briquet à double flamme que j'ai acheté aux États-Unis.
-I offered him a double-flame lighter that I bought in the United States.

2265 bloc   **block| unit**

m
[blɔk]

Ces points de l'ordre du jour ont été traités en bloc pour la discussion.
-Those agenda items were taken up en bloc for discussion.

2266 règne   **reign**

m
[ʁɛɲ]

Un étudiant affirme que la purge n'est pas encore terminée en Chine et que la terreur y règne.
-One student says the purge is still going on in China and terror is widespread.

2267 orage   **storm**

m
[ɔʁaʒ]

C'était un sacré orage.
-That was some storm.

2268 destiner   **destine| mean**

vb
[dɛstine]

Nous pouvons destiner les animaux vaccinés en bonne santé au marché intérieur.
-Healthy, vaccinated animals could be kept for the internal market.

2269 renoncer   **renounce| give up**

vb
[ʁənɔ̃se]

Le Parlement est l'endroit qui convient pour prendre ces décisions et je déplore que nous renoncions à notre responsabilité.
-Parliament is the appropriate forum for the making of such decisions, and I eschew the abdication of our responsibility.

2270 royal   **royal**

adj
[ʁwajal]

La Royal Shakespeare Company donne une représentation du Marchand de Venise la semaine prochaine.
-The Royal Shakespeare Company is presenting The Merchant of Venice next week.

2271 texte   **text**

m
[tɛkst]

Pour une raison quelconque, le message texte s'est corrompu. Je l'ai donc restauré avant de le lire.
-For some reason the message text was corrupted, so I restored it before reading.

2272 officiel   **official; official**

adj; m
[ɔfisjɛl]

Si autre document, veuillez indiquer son nom officiel :
-If other document, please give its official name:

2273 pompe   **pump| pomp**

f
[pɔ̃p]

Cette pompe est connectée électriquement à une chaussée.
-The pump is electrically connected to a roadway system electricity grid.

2274 poubelle   **dustbin| rubbish**

	f [pubɛl]		Quelqu'un doit sortir la poubelle. -Someone needs to take the bin out.
2275	**patrouille**	**patrol**	
	f [patʁuj]		Le programme des frégates canadiennes de patrouille est extrêmement important. -The Canadian Patrol Frigate Program is an extremely important program.
2276	**équipement**	**equipment| gear**	
	m [ekipmɑ̃]		L'équipement de son bureau était déductible des impôts. -The furnishing of his work room was tax deductible.
2277	**casino**	**casino**	
	m [kazino]		J'étais au casino Campione d'Italia, un illustre casino bien connu en Europe. -I was at the Campione d'Italia casino, a distinguished casino which is well-known in Europe.
2278	**métal**	**metal**	
	m [metal]		Le nickel est un métal dur, d'une lueur argentée. -Nickel is a hard, bright silver metal.
2279	**destination**	**destination**	
	f [dɛstinasjɔ̃]		Nous traversâmes village après village jusqu'à ce que nous atteignîmes notre destination. -We drove through village after village, until we got to our destination.
2280	**accomplir**	**accomplish**	
	vb [akɔ̃pliʁ]		Nous verrons un changement d'attitude face aux choses que nous pouvons accomplir. -Let us start seeing an attitudinal change and looking at the things we can accomplish.
2281	**pique**	**spade; pike**	
	m; f [pik]		Mou de la tête mais doué avec une pique. -Bit soft in the head but good with a pike.
2282	**accueil**	**welcome**	
	m [akœj]		Jack a reçu un accueil chaleureux. -Jack was given a warm reception.
2283	**rouer**	**cane**	
	vb [ʁwe]		Trois policiers rouent de coups un Africain dans le Barrio Antico (12 novembre 1997). -Three police officers beat up an African in the Barrio Antico (12 November 1997).
2284	**économie**	**economy| economics**	
	f [ekɔnɔmi]		Écouter l'analyse personnel faites par des personnes ne regardant que CCAV à propos de l'économie mondiale a toujours été plutôt amusant. -Listening to the personal analysis about global economy made by people who watch only CCAV has always been kinda funny.
2285	**tombe**	**grave| tomb**	
	f [tɔ̃b]		Travaillons dur ensemble pour trouver la tombe. -Let's work hard together to find the tomb.
2286	**charité**	**charity**	
	f [ʃaʁite]		Ce n'est pas de la charité, car la charité est un acte volontaire. -It is not charity, because charity is voluntary.
2287	**mélanger**	**mix**	
	vb [melɑ̃ʒe]		Mélanger les réformes des politiques avec l'élargissement est une autre erreur. -And to mix up policy reforms with enlargement is another mistake.

2288	**endormir**	**put to sleep**
	vb	Une fois M. Maksimenko endormi, Mlle Podlesnaya a téléphoné à l'auteur puis l'a fait entrer dans l'appartement.
	[ɑ̃dɔʁmiʁ]	-In November 1995 she visited Maksimenko's apartment and slipped a drug, clopheline, into Maksimenko's drink.

2289	**cuisiner**	**cook**
	vb	Madame Roth a déclaré: tous les citoyens veulent cuisiner.
	[kɥizine]	-Mrs Roth declares that all citizens want to cook.

2290	**laboratoire**	**laboratory**
	m	Elles sont dans le laboratoire de sciences.
	[labɔʁatwaʁ]	-They're in the science lab.

2291	**déconner**	**screw| talk rubbish**
	vb	Vous arrêtez de déconner ?
	[dekɔne]	-Look, will you two stop fucking about?

2292	**plaisanterie**	**joke**
	f	Il l'a dit par plaisanterie.
	[plɛzɑ̃tʁi]	-He said it as a joke.

2293	**quitte**	**quits**
	adj	S. qu'elle aurait quitté le MQM et rejoint le PPP.
	[kit]	-Because of his actions, she allegedly quit the MQM party and joined the PPP.

2294	**boisson**	**drink**
	f	Il vous suffit d'acheter une boisson à une station-service et de repartir.
	[bwasɔ̃]	-All you need to do is to buy a drink at a service station and then drive off.

2295	**saut**	**jump| hop**
	m	Vainqueur du saut de grenouilles, Hoppy, avec un saut de 2 mètres et 38 centimètres.
	[so]	-And the winner of the frog-leaping contest was Hoppy, with a jump of seven feet, 10 inches.

2296	**matinée**	**morning**
	f	Comment ta matinée s'est-elle passée ?
	[matine]	-How's your morning been?

2297	**relever**	**raise| pick up**
	vb	Le problème pour le moment est de relever le niveau de compétence de ces hommes.
	[ʁələve]	-Now the challenge will be to raise the level of their abilities.

2298	**otage**	**hostage**
	m	Qui plus est, certaines positions politiques semblent prises en otage par les prises d'otages.
	[ɔtaʒ]	-What is more, some political positions appear to be held hostage by hostage taking.

2299	**ravissant**	**delightful**
	adj	Je souligne au passage à quiconque souhaite s'y rendre en visite que ce pays est ravissant.
	[ʁavisɑ̃]	-For anyone who wants to visit, it is a delightful country.

2300	**fabriquer**	**manufacture| make**
	vb	Il a l'intention de fabriquer ce type d'autobus à grande échelle dans l'avenir.
	[fabʁike]	-The intention is to manufacture these buses on a large scale in the future.

2301	**tireur**	**shooter| drawer**
	m	C'est un tireur d'élite.
	[tiʁœʁ]	-He is a sharp-shooter.

2302	**lave**	**lava**
	f	C'est une rivière de lave.
	[lav]	-It's a river of lava now.
2303	**ambassadeur**	**ambassador; ambassadorial**
	m; adj	Il était ambassadeur aux Nations Unies.
	[ãbasadœʁ]	-He was ambassador to the United Nations.
2304	**atmosphère**	**atmosphere**
	f	L'hôtel a une atmosphère accueillante.
	[atmɔsfɛʁ]	-The hotel has a homey atmosphere.
2305	**menacer**	**threaten| lurk**
	vb	Peut-être devrions-nous le menacer de cette éventualité.
	[mənase]	-Well, perhaps we should threaten him with just that possibility.
2306	**casier**	**locker**
	m	J'ai trouvé ça dans le casier de Jack.
	[kazje]	-This was in Jack's locker.
2307	**capital**	**capital; capital**
	adj; m	Cette approche fonctionnaliste du capital social a aussi été fortement critiquée.
	[kapital]	-And yet this functional approach to social capital has also been heavily criticized.
2308	**cendre**	**ash**
	f	Les retombées de cendre se sont étendues à l'île tout entière gagnant même la Guadeloupe et Antigua.
	[sãdʁ]	-The ash fall covered the entire island and extended to Guadeloupe and Antigua.
2309	**syndicat**	**union| syndicate**
	m	Le désaccord entre le syndicat et la direction pourrait mener à la grève.
	[sɛ̃dika]	-The disagreement between the union and management could lead to a strike.
2310	**suisse**	**Swiss**
	adj	Suisse: En Suisse, il n'y avait pas de sélection de nouvelles variétés.
	[sɥis]	-Switzerland: In Switzerland there is no selection of new varieties.
2311	**énormément**	**enormously**
	adv	Il m'a énormément aidé dans la préparation de mon rapport, tout comme son successeur.
	[enɔʁmemã]	-He was enormously helpful in the preparation of my report, as was his successor.
2312	**outil**	**tool**
	m	La Conférence du désarmement est un outil, et un outil rouille lorsqu'on ne s'en sert pas.
	[uti]	-The CD is a tool, and a tool that is not used gets rusted.
2313	**testament**	**will| device**
	m	La procédure ci-dessus ne s'applique pas aux fondations constituées par testament.
	[tɛstamã]	-The above procedure does not apply for foundations established by testament.
2314	**poète**	**poet**
	m	Un poète peut survivre à tout sauf à une erreur d'impression.
	[pɔɛt]	-A poet can survive everything but a misprint.
2315	**combinaison**	**combination| suit**

f   Quelle est la combinaison du coffre ?
[kɔ̃binɛzɔ̃]   -What's the combination for the safe?

2316 transformer   **transform| change**

vb   Nous devions transformer notre terre en parc national.
[tʁɑ̃sfɔʁme]   -It was necessary for us to transform our land into a national park.

2317 ramasser   **pick up**

vb   Comme le dit un vieil adage chinois, le feu sera plus vif si tous vont
[ʁamase]   ramasser du bois.
                    -As the old Chinese saying goes, joint efforts to collect firewood will build a blazing fire.

2318 avertir   **warn| inform**

vb   En cas de violations moins graves, l'agent de probation peut avertir le mineur
[avɛʁtiʁ]   personnellement.
                    -In the case of less serious breaches, the probation official may warn the juvenile himself.

2319 came   **cam**

f   Un mécanisme à came en spirale vient en prise avec le barillet.
[kam]   -The turret has a spiral cam mechanism engaged thereto.

2320 lecture   **reading**

f   Sa mauvaise capacité de lecture entrave ses progrès scolaires.
[lɛktyʁ]   -His poor reading ability impedes his progress in the class.

2321 processus   **process**

m   Le processus d'élargissement est, en fait, un processus d'intégration de
[pʁɔsesys]   peuples.
                    -The process of enlargement, in fact, is a process of integration of peoples.

2322 vaincre   **overcome| defeat**

vb   Nous savons que nous pouvons vaincre cette terrible épidémie.
[vɛ̃kʁ]   -We know that we can defeat this terrible epidemic.

2323 médical   **medical**

adj   Il ne peut être pratiqué, sur avis médical, que par un personnel médical
[medikal]   agréé.
                    -This must be subject to medical opinion and carried out by approved medical personnel.

2324 atelier   **workshop| studio**

m   J'ai amenagé le garage pour m'en servir d'atelier.
[atəlje]   -I adapted the garage for use as a workshop.

2325 guerrier   **warrior; warlike**

m; adj   Le jouet dont nous discutons aujourd'hui s'appelle le troll guerrier.
[gɛʁje]   -The toy we are debating about today is the warrior troll.

2326 pouce   **inch**

m   J'ai besoin que vous réduisiez l'ourlet d'à peu près un pouce.
[pus]   -I need you to take in the hem by about an inch.

2327 entraîneur   **coach**

m   Lorsque Brian Towriss, l'entraîneur des Huskies, a expliqué la défaite, il n'a
[ɑ̃tʁenœʁ]   pas cherché d'excuses.
                    -Not least, they took this loss with the good grace that is so often lacking in elite athletes today.

2328 peindre   **paint**

vb   Je n'aurais jamais pensé qu'il serait aussi difficile de sélectionner une couleur
[pɛ̃dʁ]   pour peindre la cuisine.
                    -I never thought it'd be this hard to choose a color to paint the kitchen.

2329 panier — **basket**
m
[panje]
Elle souleva un coin de la serviette qui recouvrait son panier et me laissa jeter un rapide coup d'œil.
-She lifted one corner of the napkin which covered her basket and let me have a quick look.

2330 pétrin — **mess| predicament**
m
[petʁɛ̃]
Il est dans le pétrin.
-He is in trouble now.

2331 carrément — **downright**
adv
[kaʁemɑ̃]
Pour dire les choses carrément, les policiers se font rouler par le gouvernement libéral.
-Quite bluntly, police officers are getting the shaft from the Liberal government.

2332 tonnerre — **thunder**
m
[tɔnɛʁ]
Il y eut le bruit d'un claquement de tonnerre à mes oreilles.
-There was the sound of a clap of thunder in my ears.

2333 témoignage — **testimony| witness**
m
[temwaɲaʒ]
Le détective recueillit son témoignage sur place.
-The detective took down his testimony on the spot.

2334 douter — **doubt**
vb
[dute]
Il y a de quoi douter sérieusement de la viabilité du retraitement à long terme.
-Serious doubts are being raised about the long-term viability of reprocessing.

2335 indice — **index**
m
[ɛ̃dis]
Une personne dont l'indice de masse corporelle se situe entre vingt-cinq et vingt-neuf est considérée en surpoids.
-A person with a BMI of 25 to 29 is considered overweight.

2336 création — **creation**
f
[kʁeasjɔ̃]
Le récit de la création, d'une façon symbolique, commence par la création de la lumière.
-The creation account begins symbolically with the creation of light.

2337 environnement — **environment**
m
[ɑ̃viʁɔnmɑ̃]
Cette espèce de papillon de nuit a développé un ingénieux camouflage pour se fondre dans son environnement.
-This species of moth has evolved an ingenious camouflage for blending into its surroundings.

2338 enseigner — **teach| educate**
vb
[ɑ̃seɲe]
Nous devons enseigner les valeurs de
-We need to teach and nurture values of honesty, caring and sharing, and kindness.

2339 dose — **dose| measure**
f
[doz]
Si le médicament ne marche pas, peut-être devrions-nous augmenter la dose.
-If the medicine isn't working, maybe we should up the dosage.

2340 môme — **kid| brat**
m
[mom]
Tu penses encore uniquement à toi... espèce de putain de sale môme !
-Still thinking only about yourself... you fucking child!

2341 curiosité — **curiosity**
f
[kyʁjozite]
C'est cette curiosité qui a engagé Homo sapiens dans la voie de l'évolution.
-It is this curiosity that propelled Homo sapiens up the slope of evolution.

2342 administration — **administration| management**

	f	The Government Commissioner is not a representative of the administration.
	[administʁasjɔ̃]	-Le Commissaire du Gouvernement n'est pas un représentant de l'administration.

2343 misère   **misery**

f

[mizɛʁ]

Le tourisme noir consiste à prendre son pied de la pauvreté et de la misère du monde.

-Dark tourism consists in getting kicks from the world's poverty and misery.

2344 cuir   **leather**

m

[kɥiʁ]

Ils étaient faits de cuir rugeux marron.

-They were made of rough brown leather.

2345 transport   **transport| carriage**

m

[tʁɑ̃spɔʁ]

Le transport de vélos est autorisé.

-The carriage of bicycles is permitted.

2346 prêter   **lend| attribute**

vb

[pʁete]

Parce que les banques ont été encouragées, ou forcées à prêter, à des clients non solvables.

-It is because banks were encouraged to lend or forced to lend to uncreditworthy customers.

2347 trône   **throne**

m

[tʁon]

En fait, le discours du Trône y faisait allusion, ainsi que le dernier budget.

-In fact, it has been mentioned in the Speech from the Throne and in the last budget.

2348 savon   **soap**

m

[savɔ̃]

Il n'y a pas de savon.

-There's no soap.

2349 pirate   **pirate**

m

[piʁat]

La campagne à mener contre la pêche pirate est planétaire et multiforme.

-The campaign that must be waged against pirate fishing is a global and multifaceted one.

2350 pipi   **pee**

m

[pipi]

Il fait pipi au lit.

-He wets his bed.

2351 fouiller   **search| ransack**

vb

[fuje]

Le processus exige que les ministères fouillent dans leurs dossiers.

-There is a process by which the departments have to dig into their files.

2352 plante   **plant**

f

[plɑ̃t]

La plante médicinale est tout ou partie d'une plante délivrée en l'état pour un usage thérapeutique.

-A medicinal plant is all or part of a plant supplied in unprocessed form for therapeutic use.

2353 viol   **rape**

m

[vjɔl]

Le viol est toujours un crime violent.

-Rape is always a crime of violence.

2354 clown   **knockabout**

m

[klun]

Si le mot «clown» n'est pas antiparlementaire, je le réitererai encore une fois.

-If the word ``clown" is not unparliamentary, I will say it again.

2355 douceur   **sweetness| softness**

f

[dusœʁ]

Il m'a poussé avec douceur.

-He pushed me gently.

2356 vain   **vain**

	adj [vɛ̃]	Mais si nous pouvons croire les mouvements écologistes, même cet espoir est vain. -But if we are to believe the environmental movements, even this is vain hope.
2357	**détendre** vb [detɑ̃dʁ]	**loosen** Nous pensons que le déploiement ultérieur d'observateurs internationaux aiderait à détendre sensiblement la situation. -We believe that subsequent deployment of international monitors would help ease the situation in a big way.
2358	**parent** m; adj [paʁɑ̃]	**relative; kin** En ce qui concerne la situation de famille, il existe un lien entre le fait d'être un parent seul et des problèmes multiples. -With respect to family status, being a single parent is related to experiencing multiple problems.
2359	**interrompre** vb [ɛ̃teʁɔ̃pʁ]	**interrupt| stop** Interrompre les relations et les échanges avec un État est toujours une décision importante. -To break off trade and relations with a State is always an important decision.
2360	**etc.** adv [ɛtseteʁa.]	**et cetera** Télécommunications et soutien informatique Télécommunications, etc. 31. -Telecommunication and Computer Support Services Telecommunication, etc. 31.
2361	**écart** m [ekaʁ]	**gap| difference** De toute façon, l'écart est de 130 votes, ce qui est assez considérable. -In any case, there is a difference of 130 votes. It is not a small difference.
2362	**fonction** f [fɔ̃ksjɔ̃]	**function** Mon téléphone a une fonction d'identification de l'appelant qui me permet de filtrer mes appels. -My phone has a caller ID function that lets me screen my calls.
2363	**élire** vb [eliʁ]	**elect** L'Assemblée procède à un troisième tour de scrutin pour élire un juge ad litem. -The Assembly proceeded to a third round of balloting to elect one ad litem judge.
2364	**machin** m [maʃɛ̃]	**gadget| thingy** Peux-tu me passer ce machin ? -Can you pass me that thingamajig?
2365	**fameux** adj [famø]	**famous** La fameuse fracture numérique s'y manifeste de bien des façons. -The much talked about digital divide manifests itself in many ways in Africa.
2366	**talent** m [talɑ̃]	**talent| skill** Je suis convaincu qu'il guidera nos travaux avec beaucoup de sagesse et de talent. -I am sure that he will lead our deliberations with great wisdom and skill.
2367	**nègre** adj; m [nɛgʁ]	**Negro; nigger** Il existe manifestement un nègre quelque part. -There is obviously a Negro out there somewhere.
2368	**catholique**	**Catholic; Catholic**

adj; m/f
[katɔlik]

Il fut le premier Amérindien baptisé selon le rite catholique romain en Amérique.
-He was the first Amerindian baptized as a Roman Catholic in the Americas.

2369 **indiquer**   **indicate| show**

vb
[ɛ̃dike]

Veuillez également indiquer le volume des avoirs saisis et confisqués.
-Please indicate the financial magnitude of the assets seized and confiscated.

2370 **misérable**   **miserable; wretch**

adj; m/f
[mizeʁabl]

"Petite misérable!", s'exclama l'ogre.
-``Ungrateful wretch", shouted the ogre.

2371 **requin**   **shark**

m
[ʁəkɛ̃]

La pratique dite du est connue pour mettre en péril la survie de plusieurs espèces de requin.
-The practice of shark finning is known to endanger the survival of several shark species.

2372 **sincèrement**   **truly| sincerely**

adv
[sɛ̃sɛʁmã]

La Syrie est sincèrement et sérieusement attachée à une paix juste et globale.
-Syria is sincerely and seriously committed to a comprehensive and just peace.

2373 **affection**   **affection| ailment**

f
[afɛksjõ]

Le capitalisme n'est pas un objet de mon affection, c'est simplement un moyen.
-Capitalism is not an object of my affection, it is simply a means to an end.

2374 **porno**   **porn**

m
[pɔʁno]

J'aime regarder du porno lesbien.
-I like watching lesbian porn.

2375 **adversaire**   **opponent; opponent**

adj; m/f
[advɛʁsɛʁ]

Les résultats électoraux préliminaires montrent un très petit écart entre les deux adversaires.
-Preliminary election results show a very small gap between the two contestants.

2376 **actuellement**   **currently| now**

adv
[aktɥɛlmã]

Il y a actuellement 17 programmes sur les mers régionales en cours dans le monde.
-There are currently 17 regional seas programmes currently in operation.

2377 **meuble**   **furniture| charge**

m
[mœbl]

Quel est votre meuble préféré ?
-What's your favorite piece of furniture?

2378 **foutu**   **bloody| damn**

adj
[futy]

On serait à Boston si on zigzaguait pas sur ce foutu Atlantique.
-We'd be in Boston by now if we weren't zigzagging all over the bloody Atlantic.

2379 **dignité**   **dignity**

f
[diɲite]

L'article 1er intitulé « Dignité humaine » énonce : « La dignité humaine est inviolable.
-Article 1, entitled "Human dignity", states that "Human dignity is inviolable.

2380 **ramer**   **row**

vb
[ʁame]

Vous avez dit que nous étions tous dans la même galère et que tout le monde devait ramer; je constate que tout le monde n'a pas encore saisi les rames, mais j'espère qu'ils le feront.

-You said that we are all in the same boat, and that everyone has to row; I do not see everyone bent over the oars just yet, but I hope that will happen.

2381	**rate**	**spleen**
	f	Il a peut-être la rate rompue.
	[ʁat]	-Wait. He could have a ruptured spleen.
2382	**patienter**	**wait**
	vb	Les Bélarussiens forment un peuple exceptionnellement paisible et patient.
	[pasjɑ̃te]	-Belarusians are an exceptionally peaceful and patient people.
2383	**vomir**	**vomit**
	vb	En cas d'ingestion, faire boire une huile végétale, faire vomir et appeler un médecin.
	[vɔmiʁ]	-If ingested, drink plant oil, induce vomiting, call a physician.
2384	**dépression**	**depression**
	f	En 1679, les travaux de Newton se sont arrêtés après qu'il ait souffert d'une dépression nerveuse.
	[depʁesjɔ̃]	-In 1679, Newton's work came to standstill after he suffered a nervous breakdown.
2385	**précisément**	**precisely**
	adv	Selon cette publication, le Royaume-Uni ne compte précisément aucun protestant.
	[pʁesizemɑ̃]	-According to this publication, the United Kingdom has exactly no Protestants.
2386	**circuit**	**circuit**
	m	Je pense que cette lampe a un court-circuit parce que la lumière n'apparait que si je secoue le cordon.
	[siʁkɥi]	-I think this lamp has a short-circuit because the light comes on only if I jiggle the cord.
2387	**télégramme**	**telegram**
	m	À son arrivée à Londres, il m'a envoyé un télégramme.
	[telegʁam]	-On his arrival in London, he sent me a telegram.
2388	**voile**	**veil| sail**
	f	Au XVIIIe siècle, les femmes se déplaçaient plus librement et sans voile au Yémen.
	[vwal]	-In the eighteenth century, women had moved more freely and without a veil in Yemen.
2389	**correctement**	**correctly**
	adv	Il ne suffit pas d'agir correctement mais il faut aussi avoir l'air d'avoir agi correctement.
	[kɔʁɛktəmɑ̃]	-It is not enough for them to act correctly, but they must also appear to be acting correctly.
2390	**fringuer**	**dress**
	vb	Oser fringuer comme ça la gonzesse à Pierrot!
	[fʁɛ̃ge]	-How can they dare dress like this Pierrot's chick!
2391	**améliorer**	**improve| enhance**
	vb	Il a estimé qu'il fallait améliorer la capacité du PNUD à mobiliser des ressources.
	[ameljɔʁe]	-The need to enhance UNDP capacity for resource mobilization was acknowledged.
2392	**observer**	**observe| watch**

vb
[ɔpsɛʁve]

Je pense qu'il vaut la peine d'observer le processus pendant deux années supplémentaires.
-I think it is worth keeping an eye on this process for another two years.

2393 volontaire — **voluntary; voluntary**

adj; m/f
[vɔlɔ̃tɛʁ]

Le bénévolat est une activité volontaire, non rémunérée et destinée aux autres.
-Voluntary activity is voluntary, unpaid and intentional work for others.

2394 fumier — **manure**

m
[fymje]

Il écoulait des montagnes de fumier.
-He could move mountains of manure in spades.

2395 zoo — **zoo**

m
[zo]

Bill a amené son petit frère au zoo.
-Bill took his little brother to the zoo.

2396 égoïste — **selfish; egoist**

adj; m/f
[egɔist]

D'ailleurs, le premier exportateur mondial ne peut pas se permettre un protectionnisme égoïste.
-After all, the world's leading exporter cannot be allowed to operate selfish protectionism.

2397 construction — **construction**

f
[kɔ̃stʁyksjɔ̃]

Les équipes de construction ont travaillé vingt-quatre heures sur vingt-quatre.
-The construction crews worked around the clock.

2398 fillette — **little girl**

f
[fijɛt]

Cessez de pleurer comme une fillette !
-Stop crying like a little girl.

2399 motif — **pattern| ground**

m
[mɔtif]

Ne voyez-vous pas le motif ?
-Don't you see the pattern?

2400 sien — **one's own**

prn
[sjɛ̃]

Il affirme que ce cas est semblable au sien et qu'il subirait le même sort.
-He says that this case is similar to his and that he will face the same fate.

2401 vodka — **vodka**

f
[vɔdka]

La consommation de la vodka a continué comme avant et en plus, on boit du vin.
-Vodka continues to be drunk as before, and on top of that there is wine.

2402 loyauté — **loyalty**

f
[lwajote]

Elle compte également plusieurs îlots inhabités au nord des îles Loyauté.
-There are also several uninhabited islands to the north of the Loyalty Islands.

2403 évidence — **evidence**

f
[evidɑ̃s]

Deuxième évidence : la Côte-d'Ivoire ne fait nullement face à une guerre civile.
-The second obvious fact is that Côte d'Ivoire is in not facing a civil war.

2404 mouton — **sheep**

m
[mutɔ̃]

Nous n'avons aucun mouton.
-We don't have any sheep.

2405 commercial — **commercial**

adj
[kɔmɛʁsjal]

Le succès du dialogue commercial transatlantique et visible.
-The success of the transatlantic business dialogue is obvious.

2406 lier — **link| bind**

	vb	Il est fou à lier.
	[lje]	-He's stark crazy.
2407	**maintenir**	**maintain| sustain**
	vb	Je pense que maintenir le dynamisme actuel, c'est maintenir le policy mix .
	[mɛ̃tniʁ]	-I believe that the way to maintain the current dynamism is to maintain the policy mix.
2408	**dessert**	**dessert**
	m	I 'deserted before dessert', only to find the debate had been cancelled.
	[desɛʁ]	-J'ai "déserté avant le dessert" pour apprendre que le débat avait été annulé.
2409	**catastrophe**	**disaster**
	f	Une catastrophe a été évitée.
	[katastʁɔf]	-A catastrophe has been averted.
2410	**disparition**	**disappearance**
	f	Les forêts pluviales sont actuellement en voie de disparition.
	[dispaʁisjɔ̃]	-The world's rainforests are currently disappearing.
2411	**éternel**	**eternal**
	adj	La vie est une courte promenade avant le sommeil éternel.
	[etɛʁnɛl]	-Life is a short walk before eternal sleep.
2412	**Satan**	**Satan**
	m	Qu'est-ce que le tonnerre ? un éclat de rire de Satan.
	[satã]	-What is thunder? It's Satan's laughter.
2413	**drap**	**sheet**
	m	Le drap est sur le lit.
	[dʁa]	-The sheet is on the bed.
2414	**envelopper**	**envelop| wrap up**
	vb	L'assemblage de réservoirs doit être placé dans une enveloppe de protection.
	[ãvlɔpe]	-The container assembly shall be encased inside a protective housing shell.
2415	**cigare**	**cigar**
	m	Après manger, rien de tel qu'un bon cigare.
	[sigaʁ]	-Well, after a meal... there's nothing like a good cigar.
2416	**éclair**	**lightning**
	m	Un éclair brilla dans les yeux du petit homme.
	[eklɛʁ]	-A bolt of lightning flashed within the eyes of the little man.
2417	**témoigner**	**testify| give evidence**
	vb	Une audience est organisée au deuxième tribunal où le défendeur peut témoigner.
	[temwaɲe]	-A hearing is set in the second court, where the respondent can give evidence.
2418	**feuille**	**sheet| leaf**
	f	Feuille P13W/2, tableau, remplacer le numéro de la feuille CEI par «feuille 7004-147-1».
	[fœj]	-" Sheet P13W/2, the table, correct IEC sheet number, to read: "sheet 7004-147-1".
2419	**embêter**	**bother| worry**
	vb	Je me suis dit, pourquoi t'embêter à signer tous les trois ans ?
	[ãbete]	-I figured, why burden you with signing a contract every three years?
2420	**nichon**	**tit| nipple**
	m	J'ai failli y laisser mon nichon, O.K. ?
	[niʃɔ̃]	-I almost lost a nipple, okay?
2421	**interview**	**interview**

	f	Interview d'un haut responsable du Hezbollah, Financial Times, 26 juin 2007.
	[ɛ̃tɛʁvju]	-Interview with a senior Hizbullah official, Financial Times, 26 June 2007.

2422 partant

adv; m
[paʁtã]

thus; starter

« L'économie en partant du haut vers le bas, ça ne marche jamais, » a dit Obama. « Le pays ne réussit pas lorsque seulement ceux qui sont au sommet s'en sortent bien. Nous réussissons lorsque la classe moyenne s'élargit, lorsqu'elle se sent davantage en sécurité. »
-"Top-down economics never works," said Obama. "The country does not succeed when just those at the very top are doing well. We succeed when the middle class gets bigger, when it feels greater security."

2423 promenade

f
[pʁɔmnad]

walk

Mon père fait une promenade dans le parc.
-My father takes a walk in the park.

2424 extra

adj; m
[ɛkstʁa]

extra; extra

Il croit fermement qu'il a été enlevé par un OVNI et a fait l'objet d'expérimentations par des extra-terrestres.
-He firmly believes that he was abducted by a UFO and experimented on by aliens.

2425 association

f
[asɔsjasjɔ̃]

association

J'ai beaucoup profité de mon association avec lui.
-I benefited much from my association with him.

2426 leader

m
[lidœʁ]

leader| head

Vous gérez un budget et assumez un rôle de leader.
-You will manage a budget and assume a leadership role.

2427 demoiselle

f
[dəmwazɛl]

young lady

La demoiselle est modeste comme une violette.
-The young lady is modest like a violet.

2428 discipline

f
[disiplin]

discipline

Sénateurs, il ne s'agit pas de discipline; il s'agit de formes appropriées de discipline.
-Senators, this is not about discipline; this is about appropriate forms of discipline.

2429 civil

adj
[sivil]

civil

Nos communautés sont disposées à entretenir le dialogue avec les laïques, les responsables politiques, toutes les structures de la société civile et les organisations internationales.
-Our communities are also ready to develop dialogue with the adherents of non-religious views, with politicians, with all civil society structures, with international organizations.

2430 lancement

m
[lãsmã]

launching| start

On décrit également plusieurs fascines combinées avec un dispositif de lancement.
-The invention also provides a plurality of fascines in combination with a launching means.

2431 gras

adj; m
[gʁa]

fat; fat

Elle aimait les hommes gras, elle décida donc de se convertir au Bouddhisme.
-She loved fat men, so she decided to convert to Buddhism.

2432 transfert

transfer

	m [tʁɑ̃sfɛʁ]	Le Général Barranger ordonne votre transfert immédiat. -General Barranger has ordered your immediate transfer.
2433	**satellite** m [satelit]	**satellite** L'ASE a mis un satellite en orbite. -The ESA put a satellite into orbit.
2434	**pompier** m; adj [pɔ̃pje]	**fire-fighter; pompous** Le pompier Lionel Crowther a également été blessé, mais il serait dans un état satisfaisant. -Firefighter Lionel Crowther was also injured, but is in satisfactory condition.
2435	**tennis** m [tenis]	**tennis** Jane joue également au tennis. -Jane plays tennis too.
2436	**toc** int [tɔk]	**knock** Votre "toc toc" a donc été annulé par votre mépris du rituel social qui suit un "toc toc". -So essentially, your knock was negated by your complete lack of adherence to the social etiquette that follows a knock.
2437	**tragique** adj [tʁaʒik]	**tragic** C'est une situation tragique, aux circonstances exceptionnellement tragiques. -This is a tragic state of affairs, particularly tragic in its broad sweep.
2438	**enregistrement** m [ɑ̃ʁəʒistʁəmɑ̃]	**recording** Ses remarques obscènes seront expurgées de l'enregistrement. -His obscene remarks will be expunged from the record.
2439	**pognon** m [pɔɲɔ̃]	**money| dough** Mon oncle préfère claquer son pognon au jeu. -My Uncle would rather blow all of his money at the tables.
2440	**circulation** f [siʁkylasjɔ̃]	**circulation** Cet aquarium est doté d'un système de circulation d'eau en circuit fermé. -This aquarium has a closed loop water circulation system.
2441	**casquer** vb [kaske]	**fork out| pay up** Et qui va casquer ? -And who's going to pay?
2442	**compétition** f [kɔ̃petisjɔ̃]	**competition** Il gagna le premier prix de la compétition. -He got the first prize in the contest.
2443	**caution** f [kosjɔ̃]	**deposit| bail** The approach of both the Commission and the Council was one of extreme caution. -C'est surtout la prudence qui a dicté l'attitude de la Commission et du Conseil.
2444	**opportunité** f [ɔpɔʁtynite]	**oppurtunity** Le prochain sommet UE-Afrique est une opportunité à ne pas manquer à cet égard. -In this connection, the next EU-Africa Summit is an opportunity not to be missed.
2445	**officiellement** adv [ɔfisjɛlmɑ̃]	**officially** Le Conseil de sécurité répondra officiellement au rapport du Secrétaire général. -The Security Council will respond formally to the report of the Secretary-General.

2446 fixé
adj
[fikse]

fixed | appointed
Mais quand vient le terme fixé par Allah, il ne saurait être différé si vous saviez!
-The term appointed by God, when it comes, is never deferred.

2447 fasciner
vb
[fasine]

fascinate
Lls te fascinent.
-They fascinate you.

2448 menu
m; adj
[məny]

menu; small
Activez la commande Remplissage du menu contextuel ou du menu Format.
-From the context menu or under Format on the menu bar, choose Area....

2449 plancher
m; vb
[plãʃe]

floor; floor
J'ai poli le plancher et les meubles.
-I polished up the floor and furniture.

2450 subir
vb
[sybiʁ]

undergo | suffer
L'économie ivoirienne continue de subir les conséquences néfastes de la crise.
-The Ivorian economy continues to suffer the adverse consequences of the crisis.

2451 dentiste
m/f
[dãtist]

dentist
En fait, nous avions le même dentiste et nous nous rencontrions aussi chez le dentiste.
-In fact, we had the same dentist and would meet at the dentist's office too.

2452 légal
adj
[legal]

legal
Obtention préalable d'un passeport et statut de résident légal en Argentine.
-If they have previously held a passport and are legally resident in Argentina.

2453 ticket
m
[tikɛ]

ticket
L'ordinateur acheteur paie le ticket acheté.
-The purchaser computer pays money for the purchased ticket.

2454 civilisation
f
[sivilizasjõ]

civilization
L'exposition propose un aperçu complet de la civilisation antique.
-The exhibition offers profound insights into ancient civilization.

2455 avertissement
m
[avɛʁtismã]

warning
Jack a tenu compte de mon avertissement.
-Jack was mindful of my warning.

2456 tache
f
[taʃ]

spot | stain
J'ai fait une tache d'encre sur la copie.
-I got an ink blot on this form.

2457 balade
f
[balad]

ride | walk
J'avais l'habitude de faire une balade tous les matins.
-I used to take a walk every morning.

2458 nid
m
[ni]

nest
Il y a un nid de vipères à l'édifice Langevin pour aider le premier ministre.
-There is a nest of vipers over at the Langevin Block assisting the Prime Minister.

2459 antenne
f
[ãtɛn]

antenna
Ils sont actuellement à l'antenne.
-They are on the air now.

2460 confier
vb
[kõfje]

entrust
La Commission décide également de confier au Rapporteur la tâche d'achever le rapport.

-The Commission also agreed to entrust the Rapporteur with finalizing the report.

2461	**boxer**	**boxer; box**
	m; vb	En effet, l'organisation tente constamment de boxer dans la catégorie supérieure, avec son tissu d'États, en faveur de la paix.
	[bɔkse]	-Indeed, the organisation is constantly attempting to punch above its weight, with its patchwork of States, for the purposes of peace.
2462	**onde**	**wave**
	f	La compréhension moderne de la dynamique des quanta a pris une tournure non-intuitive avec l'introduction du concept de dualité onde-corpuscule.
	[ɔ̃d]	-Modern understanding of the dynamics of quantum particles took a non-intuitive turn with the introduction of the particle-wave duality concept.
2463	**assaut**	**assault**
	m	Les défenseurs ont arrêté l'assaut des attaquants.
	[aso]	-The defenders checked the onslaught by the attackers.
2464	**fiche**	**plug| card**
	f	Paragraphe 9.2: remplacer «fiche d'homologation» par «fiche de communication».
	[fiʃ]	-Paragrafe 9.2: correct the words "approval form" to read "communication form".
2465	**épisode**	**episode| part**
	m	Il faut espérer que le sommet de Florence mettra un terme à ce navrant épisode.
	[epizɔd]	-Hopefully the Florence Summit will bring an end to this unfortunate episode.
2466	**anneau**	**ring**
	m	Donne-moi un anneau si vous découvrez quelque chose.
	[ano]	-Give me a ring if you find out anything.
2467	**maquillage**	**makeup**
	m	Mon maquillage était ravagé.
	[makijaʒ]	-My makeup was ruined.
2468	**enregistrer**	**register| log**
	vb	Plusieurs indicateurs indirects ont été établis afin d'enregistrer les progrès.
	[ɑ̃ʁəʒistʁe]	-Several proxy indicators of performance have been developed to track progress.
2469	**impact**	**impact**
	m	Il faut savoir que parfois, l'impact psychologique est aussi important que l'impact législatif.
	[ɛ̃pakt]	-Sometimes psychological impact is just as important as legislative impact.
2470	**médias**	**media**
	mpl	Les médias locaux sont censurés et l'accès aux médias internationaux est très limité.
	[medja]	-Local media are censored, and access to international media is extremely limited.
2471	**éléphant**	**elephant**
	m	Un éléphant est un très grand animal.
	[elefɑ̃]	-An elephant is a very large animal.
2472	**déménager**	**move**
	vb	Il perd aussi ses racines puisqu'il doit déménager loin, en ville, pour chercher du travail.
	[demenaʒe]	

-He also loses his roots because he has to move far away to the town to look for work.

2473	**chaussette** f [ʃosɛt]	**sock** Il y a un trou dans cette chaussette. -There's a hole in this sock.
2474	**poker** m [pɔkɛʁ]	**poker** Jack et ses amis jouent au poker presque chaque vendredi soir. -Jack and his friends play poker almost every Friday night.
2475	**ancêtre** m/f [ãsɛtʁ]	**ancestor** Tous les membres de la descendance revendiquent un ancêtre commun et jurent loyauté à cet ancêtre. -All members of the lineage claim a common ancestor and pledge allegiance to this ancestor.
2476	**effacer** vb [efase]	**delete** Le Comité relève que l'amnistie du tribunal de Ponte de Lima du 3 décembre 1999 n'a pas effacé la condamnation de l'auteur au versement de dommages-intérêts. -The Committee notes that the amnesty of the Court of Ponte de Lima dated 3 December 1999 did not expunge the award of damages against the author.
2477	**loger** vb [lɔʒe]	**accommodate| house** D'autres réaménagements sont nécessaires pour loger convenablement les fonctionnaires. -Further upgrades are needed to accommodate Government staff adequately.
2478	**conflit** m [kɔ̃fli]	**conflict** Le juge s'est démis de l'affaire pour cause de conflit d'intérêt. -The judge recused himself from the case because of a conflict of interest.
2479	**hélicoptère** m [elikɔptɛʁ]	**helicopter** Je peux piloter un hélicoptère. -I can pilot a helicopter.
2480	**mâle** adj; m [mal]	**male| masculine; male** Être un mâle est de loin le plus grand facteur de risque de violence. -Maleness is by far the biggest risk factor for violence.
2481	**profit** m [pʁɔfi]	**profit| advantage** Tout ce que vous devez faire, c'est tirer profit de cette occasion rare. -All you have to do is take advantage of this rare opportunity.
2482	**cadre** m [kadʁ]	**framework| frame** « Sors du cadre ! » « Quel cadre ? » -"Think outside the box." "What box?"
2483	**audition** f [odisjɔ̃]	**hearing| performance** Elle souffre d'une mauvaise audition. -She is handicapped by poor hearing.
2484	**pape** m [pap]	**pope** Un rappeur sans bling-bling est comme un pape sans crucifix. -A rapper without bling is like a pope without a crucifix.
2485	**coter** vb [kɔte]	**mark** Veuillez coter le numéro sur la condition aérobie en fonction des éléments suivants (encerclez votre réponse). -Please rate the Aerobic Fitness Issue on the following components (circle your response).
2486	**fragile**	**fragile**

adj
[fʁaʒil]

La Guinée-Bissau demeure un pays fragile dans une sous-région fragile.
-Guinea-Bissau remained a fragile country in a fragile subregion.

2487 **assiette**

f
[asjɛt]

plate| dish

Vous feriez mieux de manger tout ce qui se trouve dans votre assiette.
-You'd better eat everything that's on your plate.

2488 **culpabilité**

f
[kylpabilite]

guilt

Il a confessé sa culpabilité.
-He confessed his guilt.

2489 **foire**

f
[fwaʁ]

fair

Elle a rencontré un garçon à la foire du comté.
-She met a boy at the county fair.

2490 **arabe**

adj; m
[aʁab]

Arab; Arabic

Je ne parle pas l'arabe.
-I don't speak Arabic.

2491 **soutenir**

vb
[sutniʁ]

support| back

Nous soutenons l'objectif des amendements mais nous ne pouvons soutenir leur formulation.
-We support the aim of the amendments but, nevertheless, we cannot support their wording.

2492 **bidon**

m
[bidɔ̃]

can| drum

Dire que vous ne pouvez pas faire le travail parce que vous êtes trop occupées est une excuse bidon.
-Saying you can't do the job because you're too busy is just a cop out.

2493 **république**

f
[ʁepyblik]

republic

S'abstiennent: Guatemala, Honduras, République de Corée, République dominicaine.
-Abstaining: Dominican Republic, Guatemala, Honduras, Republic of Korea.

2494 **saleté**

f
[salte]

dirt| filth

Propre: produit qui est pratiquement exempt de saleté adhérée visible ou d'autre matière étrangère.
-Clean: produce which is practically free from plainly visible adhering dirt or other foreign material.

2495 **quai**

m
[kɛ]

dock| quay

Quand la porte coulissante s'est ouverte, il a failli tomber sur le quai.
-As the door slid open, he almost fell onto the platform.

2496 **funérailles**

adj; fpl
[fyneʁaj]

funeral; funeral

Quand les funérailles ont-elles lieu ?
-When's the funeral?

2497 **pré**

m
[pʁe]

meadow| pasture

Les moutons broutent dans le pré.
-Sheep are feeding in the meadow.

2498 **tristesse**

f
[tʁistɛs]

sadness

aucun de ces mécanismes de défense n'aide l'enfant à échapper à la tristesse.
-importantly, neither of these defences helps children overcome their sadness.

2499 **tribu**

f
[tʁiby]

tribe

Un membre de la tribu Rizeigat a été tué par deux membres de la tribu Mahaliyat.
-One member of the Rizeigat tribe was killed by two members of the Ma'aliyah tribe.

2500	**décès**	**death| demise**
	m	J'ai été surpris par la nouvelle de son décès soudain.
	[desɛ]	-I was surprised at the news of his sudden death.
2501	**établir**	**establish**
	vb	Elle a notamment pu établir que son effectif est actuellement de 6 241 personnes.
	[etabliʁ]	-The current strength of the police force has been established at 6,241 officers.
2502	**touche**	**key**
	f	Maintenez la touche (Option) (Alt) enfoncée et appuyez sur la touche fléchée vers la droite.
	[tuʃ]	-Hold down the (Option) (Alt) key, and press the right arrow key.
2503	**profil**	**profile**
	m	J'essaie de faire profil bas.
	[pʁofil]	-I try to keep a low profile.
2504	**budget**	**budget**
	m	Il faut saluer ce budget, c'est le dernier budget heureux, le dernier budget tranquille.
	[bydʒɛ]	-We must welcome this budget, it is the last easy budget, the last simple budget.
2505	**panneau**	**panel| sign**
	m	La cartouche ne doit pas être plus large que le panneau de signalisation.
	[pano]	-The additional board must be no broader than the signal board.
2506	**lame**	**blade**
	f	Les gardiennes trouvèrent une lame de scie à métaux dans la poche de la prisonnière.
	[lam]	-The guards found a hacksaw blade in the prisoner's pocket.
2507	**disponible**	**available; on call**
	adj; adv	(Le rapport est imprimé en annexe aux pages 913 à 921 (disponible dans le format imprimable PDF).)
	[disponibl]	-(The report is printed as an appendix at pages 913-921 (available in print format PDF).)
2508	**illusion**	**illusion**
	f	Il était possible que tout était une illusion, ou pire, une illusion satanique?
	[ilyzjɔ̃]	-It was possible that everything was illusion, or worse, satanic illusion?
2509	**caravane**	**caravan| trailer**
	f	Une caravane de cinquante chameaux se dirigeait lentement à travers le désert.
	[kaʁavan]	-A caravan of fifty camels slowly made its way through the desert.
2510	**pacifique**	**peaceful| pacific**
	adj	Je suis pacifique.
	[pasifik]	-I am a peace loving person.
2511	**scotch**	**Scotch tape| whisky**
	m	Ce scotch ne colle pas.
	[skɔtʃ]	-This tape isn't sticky.
2512	**mystérieux**	**mysterious**
	adj	Le mystérieux décès d'activistes politiques reste inexpliqué 10 ans après.
	[misteʁjø]	-The mysterious deaths of political activists remain unexplained 10 years later.
2513	**concevoir**	**design| conceive**

vb
[kɔ̃səvwaʁ]

Peut-on concevoir un autre «rêve européen» pour une Europe davantage plurale ?
-Dare one dream a different European dream, a dream of a more pluralistic Europe?

2514 historique — **historical**

adj
[istɔʁik]

L'historique, la structure et le contenu de la nomenclature y étaient expliqués.
-The background, organization and content of the publication were presented.

2515 régiment — **regiment**

m
[ʁeʒimɑ̃]

En 1954 au centre de régiment Secunderabad.
-In 1954... at the Secunderabad Army Regiment Centre.

2516 missile — **missile; missile**

adj; m
[misil]

L'attaque par missile a pris un grand nombre de vies.
-The missile attack took a heavy toll of lives.

2517 boucher — **butcher; plug**

m; vb
[buʃe]

Leur boucher cet horizon, c'est maintenir là une poudrière.
-If we slaughter this prospect, we shall be storing up a powder keg.

2518 niquer — **fuck**

vb
[nike]

Je devrais aussi niquer mon prof d'Anglais...
-Although I might have to bang my English teacher as well.

2519 légitime — **legitimate**

adj
[leʒitim]

Dans la culture de certains peuples, s'est inscrit, de manière indélébile, un sentiment de supériorité tel, qu'il les rend capables de totalement déshumaniser les autres peuples, au point que toute torture, tout viol, tout assassinat de masse leur apparaît légitime.
-In the cultures of certain peoples, a marked feeling of superiority has developed, so much so that it makes them capable of completely dehumanizing other peoples, to the point that that any kind of torture, rape, or mass murder seems acceptable to them.

2520 cuit — **cooked| baked**

adj
[kɥi]

Et pour ce qui est de la préparation, le poisson est déjà cuit.
-And when it comes to cooking, the fish are already cooked.

2521 pilote — **pilot**

m
[pilɔt]

Jack n'a pas l'étoffe d'un pilote de course.
-Jack doesn't have what it takes to be a race car driver.

2522 épuiser — **exhaust| drain**

vb
[epɥize]

Nous savons qu'on a laissé venir de gros chalutiers qui ont épuisé les stocks de poisson.
-We know how the large trawlers have been allowed to come in and deplete the fishing stocks.

2523 former — **form| train**

vb
[fɔʁme]

Michael m'a autorisé à former un commando anti-exhibitionnistes.
-Michael has authorized me to form an emergency anti-flashing task force.

2524 sucer — **suck| suck out**

vb
[syse]

Tu me demandes si j'ai essayé de me sucer moi-même ?
-You're asking me if I ever tried to suck my own penis?

2525 considérer — **consider**

vb
[kɔ̃sideʁe]

La vérité, c'est qu'aujourd'hui, nous pouvons considérer cela comme un succès.
-The truth is that today we can consider this to be a success.

Adjectives

Rank	French-PoS	Translation
9	que-con; prn; prp; adj; adv	that; that; than; which; how
10	un-art; adj; num; prn	a; one; one; one
16	ce-prn; adj	this; that
27	bien-adv; m; adj	well| very; good; right
30	tout-adj; adv; m; prn	all; all; all; all
31	plus-adj; adv; m	more; more; plus
41	comme-con; prp; adj	as; as; such as
52	votre-adj; prn	your; your
56	son-adj; m	its; sound
57	ton-adj; prn; m	your; your; tone
61	bon-adj; m; adv	good| well; voucher; then
64	même-adj; adv	same; even
71	autre-prn; adj; adv	other; another; else
74	peu-adv; m; adj	little; bit; few
81	juste-adj; adv	just| fair; just
83	quelque-adj; adv	some; about
93	sûr-adj	sure| safe
95	avant-adv; prp; adj; m	before; before; front
102	vrai-adj; m	true| real; right
104	mal-m; adv; adj	evil| wrong; amiss; untimely
107	mort-adj; f	dead; death
108	mieux-adv; adj	better; adj
109	petit-adj; m	small| little; child
110	beaucoup-prn; adj; adv	many; much; much
115	quel-adj; prn	what; what
135	seul-adj; m; adv	only; only one; very
147	bas-adj; m	low| base; bottom
154	grand-adj	large| wide
189	vieux-adj; m	old| ancient; old man
202	nouveau-adj; m	new| further; incoming
209	longtemps-adv; adj	for a long time; longtime
210	beau-adj; m	beautiful| nice; beautiful
216	chaque-adj; prn	each; either
224	aucun-adj; prn	no; none
234	fin-f; adj	end; fine
236	jeune-adj; m	young; youth
237	chéri-adj; m	darling| precious; honey
238	premier-adj	first| prime
240	droit-adj; m; adv	right; right; due
242	loin-adv; adj	far; distant
246	gros-adj; m	large| fat; fat man
250	dernier-adj; m	last| latter; last
257	fort-adj; m; adv	strong| loud; fort; highly
262	fou-adj; m	crazy; fool
264	prêt-adj; m	ready| willing; loan
277	haut-adj; m; adv	high; top; in heaven
280	possible-adj; m	possible; possible
282	plein-adj	full| fraught
296	instant-m; adj	moment| while; urgent
301	presque-adv; adj	almost; all but
302	meilleur-m; adj	best; better
307	garde-f; adj	custody| guard; guarding
309	dur-adj	hard| tough
312	important-adj	important
320	ferme-f; adj	farm; firm
324	calme-adj; m	quiet| calm; calm
332	parfait-adj	perfect
334	ceci-prn; adj	this; following
337	pauvre-adj; m	poor; poor person
339	drôle-adj	funny
344	impossible-adj	impossible
345	facile-adj	easy| simple
347	mauvais-adj; m	bad| ill; brute
348	général-adj; m	general; general
359	gentil-adj; m	nice| kind; gentile
362	malade-adj; m	sick| invalid; patient
369	cher-adj; m	expensive| dear; dear
375	plan-m; adj	plan; plane
378	propre-adj; m	own| clean; proper
384	génial-adj	great| brilliant
391	difficile-adj	difficult
394	pire-adj	worse
395	simple-adj	simple; singles
397	sujet-m; adj	subject; prone

403	**sauf**-*prp; adj; con; adv*	except; safe; excepting; short of
409	**noir**-*adj; m*	black; black
416	**inquiet**-*adj*	worried| concerned
418	**sérieux**-*adj; m*	serious; seriousness
425	**grave**-*adj*	serious| grave
427	**courant**-*adj; m*	current| running; current
430	**con**-*m; adj*	cunt| prick; bloody
431	**gauche**-*adj; f*	left; left
432	**content**-*adj*	content| happy
434	**rouge**-*adj; m*	red; red
438	**prochain**-*adj; m*	next| upcoming; next
442	**long**-*adj*	long
444	**idiot**-*m; adj*	idiot; silly
448	**continu**-*adj*	continuous
452	**certain**-*adj*	certain
465	**bizarre**-*adj*	weird| bizarre
473	**froid**-*adj; m*	cold| cool; cold
475	**secret**-*adj; m*	secret| covert; secret
477	**second**-*adj; m*	second; second
478	**cru**-*adj; m*	vintage| raw; vineyard
483	**sœur**-*adj; f*	sister; sister
486	**joli**-*adj*	pretty
489	**agent**-*m; adj*	agent; cooperative
491	**libre**-*adj*	free| open
494	**faux**-*adj*	false| fake
498	**debout**-*adj*	standing
501	**intérieur**-*adj; m*	inside| interior; inside
503	**incroyable**-*adj*	incredible| amazing
505	**présent**-*adj; m*	present; present
506	**absolu**-*adj*	absolute| total
515	**magnifique**-*adj*	magnificent
518	**tranquille**-*adj*	quiet
519	**chaud**-*adj*	hot| warm
522	**pareil**-*adj; prn; m*	such| similar; the same; equal
525	**anniversaire**-*adj; m*	anniversary; anniversary
526	**blanc**-*adj; m*	white| albescent; white
528	**moyen**-*m; adj*	means| medium; medium
531	**clair**-*adj*	clear| bright
543	**médecin**-*m; adj*	doctor; doctoral
544	**midi**-*m; adj*	noon; midday
548	**diable**-*m; adj*	devil; wretched
554	**anglais**-*adj; m|mpl*	English; English
559	**exact**-*adj*	exact
575	**dangereux**-*adj*	dangerous
597	**triste**-*adj*	sad
598	**tel**-*adj*	such
600	**plusieurs**-*adj*	several| divers
604	**étrange**-*adj*	strange
612	**merveilleux**-*adj*	wonderful
617	**sud**-*adj; m*	south; south
624	**public**-*adj; m*	public; public
628	**bête**-*f; adj*	beast| idiot; stupid
632	**amoureux**-*adj; m*	in love; lover
634	**normal**-*adj*	normal
646	**sympa**-*adj*	friendly
650	**clé**-*adj; f*	key; key
651	**nord**-*m; adj*	north; northern
654	**salaud**-*m; adj*	bastard; dirty
657	**terrible**-*adj*	terrible
662	**bonheur**-*m; adj*	happiness; welfare
665	**stupide**-*adj; m*	stupid; stupid
677	**gamin**-*m; adj*	kid; kiddy
686	**dingue**-*adj; m/f*	crazy| wild; loon
687	**inutile**-*adj*	unnecessary| useless
688	**nul**-*adj; m; prn*	no| zero; zero; no one
690	**différent**-*adj*	different
702	**ennemi**-*m; adj*	enemy| hostile; inimical
713	**blessé**-*adj; m*	injured; casualty
714	**humain**-*adj; m*	human; human
716	**coupable**-*adj; m/f*	guilty; culprit
717	**environ**-*adv; prp; adj*	about; around; all but
724	**lâche**-*m; adj*	coward; cowardly
733	**américain**-*adj*	American
741	**riche**-*adj; m/f*	rich; rich person
745	**ridicule**-*adj; m*	ridiculous; ridicule
748	**intéressant**-*adj*	interesting
749	**gosse**-*m/f; adj*	kid| brat; kiddy
750	**rose**-*adj; f*	pink; rose
752	**vide**-*adj; m*	empty; empty
753	**responsable**-*adj; m/f*	responsible; person responsible
755	**capable**-*adj*	capable| competent
761	**fier**-*adj*	proud

771	**longue**-*adj*	long
773	**jeté**-*adj*	thrown
774	**formidable**-*adj*	tremendous| fantastic
783	**monstre**-*m; adj*	monster; monstrous
786	**français**-*adj; m|mpl*	French; French
789	**mien**-*adj*	mine
795	**ouest**-*adj; m*	west; west
800	**prévu**-*adj*	planned
802	**superbe**-*adj*	superb; stunner
804	**horrible**-*adj*	horrible
805	**court**-*adj; m*	short| brief; court
815	**excellent**-*adj*	excellent
827	**animal**-*adj; m*	animal; animal
829	**imbécile**-*m/f; adj*	imbecile; stupid
836	**contraire**-*adj; m*	contrary; contrary
839	**politique**-*f; adj*	policy; political
840	**fait**-*m; adj*	fact; ripe
842	**entier**-*adj*	whole| full
849	**rapide**-*adj; m*	fast| rapid; rapid
851	**frais**-*mpl; adj*	costs; fresh
856	**spécial**-*adj*	special
867	**sacré**-*adj*	sacred
870	**nécessaire**-*adj*	necessary
876	**copain**-*m; adj*	boyfriend| buddy; pally
878	**personnel**-*m; adj*	staff| personnel; personal
880	**mignon**-*adj*	cute| sweet
886	**malin**-*adj; m*	malignant| smart; evil
892	**doux**-*adj*	soft| sweet
900	**enceinte**-*adj; f*	pregnant; enclosure
902	**bleu**-*adj; m*	blue; blue
912	**failli**-*adj; m*	bankrupt
919	**énorme**-*adj*	huge| enormous
925	**moindre**-*adj*	lesser
930	**unique**-*adj*	unique
947	**honnête**-*adj*	honest
951	**aveugle**-*adj; m/f*	blinded; blind
966	**proche**-*adj; adv; m*	near; near; neighbor
969	**ancien**-*adj; m; pfx*	former| ancient; former; ex-
977	**frappé**-*adj*	hit| struck
989	**chinois**-*adj; m*	Chinese; Chinese
995	**étranger**-*adj; m*	foreign| overseas; foreigner
1004	**fantastique**-*adj*	fantastic
1014	**suivant**-*adj; prp; adv*	following; according to; as follows
1017	**passager**-*m; adj*	passenger; passing
1024	**crétin**-*m; adj*	cretin; moronic
1029	**futur**-*adj; m*	future; future
1032	**attendu**-*adj*	expected
1034	**faible**-*adj; m*	low| weak; weakling
1043	**utile**-*adj*	useful
1046	**voleur**-*m; adj*	thief; thievish
1053	**vif**-*adj; m*	bright| lively; quick
1054	**assassin**-*m; adj*	assassin; bloodthirsty
1058	**militaire**-*adj; m*	military; soldier
1065	**puissant**-*adj*	powerful| strong
1066	**vert**-*adj; m*	green| young; putting green
1072	**célèbre**-*adj*	celebrated| popular
1081	**charmant**-*adj; m*	charming| lovely; cunning
1084	**agréable**-*adj*	pleasant| nice
1090	**saint**-*adj; m*	saint; saint; St.
1091	**marrant**-*adj; m*	funny; funny guy
1094	**levé**-*adj*	survey; lifted
1101	**sexy**-*adj*	sexy
1104	**nerveux**-*adj*	nervous
1106	**direct**-*adj; adv*	direct; straight
1111	**aise**-*adj; f*	pleased; pleasure
1117	**champion**-*adj; m*	champion; champion
1121	**extérieur**-*adj; m*	outside| exterior; outside
1123	**intelligent**-*adj*	intelligent
1129	**sage**-*adj; m*	wise; sage
1133	**vache**-*f; adj*	cow; bitchy
1137	**russe**-*adj; m*	Russian; Russian
1139	**amusant**-*adj*	amusing
1141	**ouvert**-*adj*	open
1142	**nombreux**-*adj*	numerous
1144	**mince**-*adj*	thin| slim
1149	**moteur**-*m; adj*	engine; motor
1168	**fantôme**-*m; adj*	ghost; phantom
1173	**japonais**-*adj; m|mpl*	Japanese; Japanese
1191	**allemand**-*adj; m|mpl*	German; German

1194	**innocent**-*adj; m*	innocent; innocent
1195	**véritable**-*adj*	true| real
1198	**patient**-*adj; m*	patient; patient
1199	**menteur**-*m; adj*	liar| lying; lying
1206	**juif**-*adj*	Jewish
1207	**chouette**-*f; adj*	owl; neat
1224	**fini**-*adj; m*	finished| finite; finish
1227	**soudain**-*adv; adj*	suddenly; sudden
1236	**portable**-*adj; m*	portable; portable
1245	**bref**-*adj; adv*	short| brief; in short
1246	**réel**-*adj; m*	real| live; real
1251	**plat**-*adj; m*	flat; flat| dish
1279	**affreux**-*adj*	frightful| dreadful
1282	**prisonnier**-*m; adj*	prisoner; captive
1286	**demi**-*adj; m*	half; half
1288	**alerte**-*adj; f*	alert; alert
1292	**prudent**-*adj*	careful
1294	**donné**-*adj*	given
1297	**propriétaire**-*m/f; adj*	owner| landlord; proprietary
1299	**ténu**-*adj*	tenuous
1303	**sec**-*adj*	dry| dried
1309	**vierge**-*adj; f*	virgin; virgin
1312	**suspect**-*adj; m*	suspect| dubious; suspect
1323	**immeuble**-*m; adj*	building; immovable
1333	**curieux**-*adj; m*	curious; onlooker
1337	**uniforme**-*adj; m*	uniform; uniform
1356	**haine**-*f; adj*	hatred; heating
1364	**brave**-*adj; m*	brave| good; brave
1365	**évident**-*adj*	obvious| evident
1366	**sale**-*adj*	dirty| nasty
1367	**roulé**-*adj*	rolled
1368	**extraordinaire**-*adj*	extraordinary
1375	**gardé**-*adj*	guarded
1376	**net**-*adj; adv*	net| sharp; outright
1377	**vivant**-*adj; m*	living| alive; living
1378	**compliqué**-*adj*	complicated| difficult
1379	**fiancé**-*m; adj*	fiance; engaged
1382	**sombre**-*adj*	dark| gloomy
1385	**voisin**-*m; adj*	neighbor; neighboring
1386	**lourd**-*adj*	heavy
1398	**égal**-*adj; m*	equal| even; equal
1399	**sport**-*m; adj*	sport; sporting
1402	**adorable**-*adj*	adorable
1403	**cinglé**-*adj*	crazy
1412	**commun**-*adj*	common| joint
1420	**délicieux**-*adj*	delicious
1423	**modèle**-*adj; m*	model; model
1432	**débile**-*adj; m/f*	stupid; defective
1436	**liquide**-*adj; m*	liquid| wet; liquid
1438	**marin**-*adj; m*	marine; marine
1441	**jaloux**-*adj*	jealous
1443	**physique**-*adj; f*	physical; physics
1449	**particulier**-*adj; m*	particular| individual; private person
1462	**matériel**-*m; adj*	equipment| material; material
1465	**jaune**-*adj; m*	yellow; yellow
1467	**rare**-*adj*	rare
1469	**magique**-*adj*	magic
1478	**romantique**-*adj; m/f*	romantic; romantic
1483	**inconnu**-*m; adj*	unknown; unfamiliar
1486	**panique**-*adj; f*	panic; panic
1487	**criminel**-*adj; m*	criminal; criminal
1488	**sauvage**-*adj; m*	wild; savage
1490	**complet**-*adj; m*	full| complete; suit
1493	**principal**-*adj; m*	main; principal
1498	**cochon**-*m; adj*	pig| swine; dirty
1507	**profond**-*adj; m*	deep| profound; deep
1508	**malheureux**-*adj; m*	unfortunate| unhappy; unfortunate
1510	**roman**-*m; adj*	novel; Romance
1521	**indien**-*adj*	Indian
1522	**meurtrier**-*m; adj*	murderer; murderous
1531	**logique**-*f; adj*	logic; logical
1536	**courageux**-*adj*	courageous| brave
1554	**pratique**-*f; adj*	practice; practical
1567	**pur**-*adj*	pure| clean
1571	**idéal**-*adj; m*	ideal; ideal
1578	**ordinaire**-*adj; m*	ordinary; ordinary
1582	**naturel**-*adj; m*	natural; nature
1586	**central**-*adj*	central
1590	**chic**-*adj; m*	chic| stylish; chic

1599	**correct**-*adj; adv*	correct; alright	1780	**objectif**-*adj; m*	objective; goal
1601	**national**-*adj; m*	national; national	1788	**copier**-*vb; adj*	copy; copying
1603	**raisonnable**-*adj*	reasonable	1793	**électrique**-*adj*	electric
1607	**étudiant**-*adj; m*	student; student	1800	**las**-*adj*	tired
1611	**nu**-*adj*	naked	1805	**critique**-*adj; f*	critical; review
1614	**couvert**-*adj; m*	covered; place	1807	**cardiaque**-*adj; m/f*	cardiac; heart patient
1618	**doué**-*adj*	gifted| capable	1811	**conférence**-*f; adj*	conference; lecturing
1628	**noble**-*adj; m/f*	noble; noble	1817	**italien**-*adj; m*	Italian; Italian
1629	**large**-*adj*	wide| large	1822	**moral**-*adj; m*	moral; morale
1630	**urgent**-*adj*	urgent	1823	**supérieur**-*adj; m*	upper; superior
1632	**digne**-*adj*	worthy	1825	**tendre**-*adj; vb*	tender; tender
1635	**plaisant**-*adj*	pleasant	1829	**ivre**-*adj*	drunk
1637	**puce**-*f; adj*	chip| flea; puce	1831	**gagnant**-*m; adj*	winner; winning
1641	**absurde**-*adj; m*	absurd; absurd	1838	**assis**-*adj*	seated
1644	**maximum**-*adj; m*	maximum; maximum	1846	**final**-*adj; m*	final| ultimate; finale
1648	**esclave**-*m; adj*	slave; enslaved	1860	**expert**-*adj; m*	expert; expert
1652	**pair**-*adj; m*	even; peer	1866	**moderne**-*adj*	modern
1653	**moche**-*adj*	ugly	1872	**sensible**-*adj*	sensitive
1654	**blond**-*adj; m*	blond; blonde	1900	**sourd**-*adj*	deaf| dull
1659	**scientifique**-*adj; m/f*	scientific; scientist	1904	**injuste**-*adj*	unfair| wrong
1660	**traître**-*m; adj*	traitor; treacherous	1908	**fidèle**-*adj; m/f*	faithful| loyal; stalwart
1662	**cave**-*f; adj*	cellar; hollow	1913	**total**-*adj; m*	total| overall; total
1665	**minable**-*adj; m/f*	shabby| pathetic; piddling	1914	**réservé**-*adj*	reserved
1689	**aimable**-*adj*	friendly| kind	1915	**espagnol**-*adj; m|mpl*	Spanish; Spanish
1692	**adulte**-*adj; m/f*	adult; adult	1916	**solide**-*adj; m*	solid; solid
1698	**vague**-*f; adj*	wave; vague	1918	**habitant**-*m; adj*	inhabitant; resident
1704	**géant**-*adj; m*	giant; giant	1931	**timide**-*adj*	shy
1706	**communauté**-*adj; f*	community; community	1932	**fermé**-*adj*	closed| sealed
1717	**orange**-*adj*	orange	1934	**célibataire**-*adj; m/f*	single| bachelor; single
1729	**professionnel**-*adj; m*	professional; professional	1942	**mondial**-*adj*	global
1730	**incident**-*adj; m*	incident; incident	1944	**généreux**-*adj*	generous| liberal
1736	**exprès**-*adj; adv*	express; on purpose	1962	**pervers**-*adj*	perverse
1738	**rond**-*adj; m*	round; round	1966	**immense**-*adj*	immense| great
1740	**fichu**-*adj; m*	damn| rotten; scarf	1971	**manuel**-*adj; m*	manual; manual
1746	**furieux**-*adj; m*	furious; madman	1972	**cruel**-*adj*	cruel
1751	**classique**-*adj; m*	classic| standard; classic	1974	**méchant**-*adj; m*	wicked| bad; naughty child
1760	**incapable**-*adj*	unable| incapable	1980	**léger**-*adj*	light| lightweight
1768	**précieux**-*adj*	precious| valuable	1989	**nucléaire**-*adj*	nuclear
1778	**précis**-*adj; m*	precise; abstract	1990	**populaire**-*adj*	popular
			2016	**sain**-*adj*	healthy

2021	**impressionnant**-*adj*	impressive| awesome
2027	**chasseur**-*m; adj*	hunter; gunner's
2029	**solitaire**-*adj; m/f*	solitary; loner
2033	**original**-*adj; m*	original; original
2037	**clinique**-*adj; f*	clinical; clinic
2040	**suprême**-*adj; m*	supreme; supreme
2041	**sincère**-*adj*	sincere| genuine
2044	**violent**-*adj*	violent| severe
2046	**coucou**-*adj; m; int*	cuckoo; cuckoo; hello
2047	**franc**-*adj; m*	frank; franc
2050	**excitant**-*adj; m*	exciting; upper
2055	**splendide**-*adj*	splendid
2063	**efficace**-*adj*	effective| efficacious
2066	**gentleman**-*m; adj*	gentleman; gentlemanly
2069	**divin**-*adj*	divine
2071	**négatif**-*adj; m*	negative; negative
2074	**invisible**-*adj*	invisible
2090	**prime**-*f; adj*	premium; incentive
2105	**remarquable**-*adj*	remarkable
2108	**ennuyeux**-*adj*	boring| annoying
2119	**vilain**-*adj; m*	ugly; villein
2120	**complexe**-*adj; m*	complex; complex
2133	**fabuleux**-*adj*	fabulous
2135	**illégal**-*adj*	illegal
2147	**plastique**-*adj; m*	plastic; plastic
2157	**chanceux**-*adj; m*	fortunate; lucky man
2167	**gratuit**-*adj*	free
2168	**britannique**-*adj*	British
2169	**social**-*adj*	social
2178	**noix**-*f; adj*	nut; walnut
2181	**sexuel**-*adj*	sexual
2184	**oublié**-*adj*	forgotten
2188	**reconnaissant**-*adj*	grateful
2190	**bâtard**-*adj; m*	bastard; bastard
2193	**jouet**-*adj; m*	toy; toy
2205	**gris**-*adj; m*	gray; gray
2211	**armé**-*adj*	armed
2212	**communiste**-*adj; m/f*	Communist; Communist
2218	**essentiel**-*adj; m*	essential; main
2250	**mobile**-*adj*	mobile
2270	**royal**-*adj*	royal
2272	**officiel**-*adj; m*	official; official
2293	**quitte**-*adj*	quits
2299	**ravissant**-*adj*	delightful
2303	**ambassadeur**-*m; adj*	ambassador; ambassadorial
2307	**capital**-*adj; m*	capital; capital
2310	**suisse**-*adj*	Swiss
2323	**médical**-*adj*	medical
2325	**guerrier**-*m; adj*	warrior; warlike
2356	**vain**-*adj*	vain
2358	**parent**-*m; adj*	relative; kin
2365	**fameux**-*adj*	famous
2367	**nègre**-*adj; m*	Negro; nigger
2368	**catholique**-*adj; m/f*	Catholic; Catholic
2370	**misérable**-*adj; m/f*	miserable; wretch
2375	**adversaire**-*adj; m/f*	opponent; opponent
2378	**foutu**-*adj*	bloody| damn
2393	**volontaire**-*adj; m/f*	voluntary; voluntary
2396	**égoïste**-*adj; m/f*	selfish; egoist
2405	**commercial**-*adj*	commercial
2411	**éternel**-*adj*	eternal
2424	**extra**-*adj; m*	extra; extra
2429	**civil**-*adj*	civil
2431	**gras**-*adj; m*	fat; fat
2434	**pompier**-*m; adj*	fire-fighter; pompous
2437	**tragique**-*adj*	tragic

Adverbs

Rank	French-PoS	Translation
4	pas-*adv; m*	not; step
9	que-*con; prn; prp; adj; adv*	that; that; than; which; how
15	ne-*adv*	not
17	en-*prp; adv*	in; thereof
24	mais-*con; adv*	but; probably
26	dans-*prp; adv*	in; aboard
27	bien-*adv; m; adj*	well| very; good; right
29	si-*con; adv*	if; so
30	tout-*adj; adv; m; prn*	all; all; all; all
31	plus-*adj; adv; m*	more; more; plus
32	non-*adv; part*	not; no
44	ici-*adv*	here
48	là-*adv*	there
49	rien-*m; prn; adv*	nothing; anything; nix
51	où-*adv; prn; con*	where; that; wherein
53	pourquoi-*adv; con*	why; wherefore
54	quand-*adv; con*	when; when
59	alors-*adv*	then
60	comment-*adv*	how
61	bon-*adj; m; adv*	good| well; voucher; then
63	très-*adv*	very
64	même-*adj; adv*	same; even
66	jamais-*adv*	never| ever
67	aussi-*adv; con*	also| as; and
71	autre-*prn; adj; adv*	other; another; else
72	maintenant-*adv*	now
73	encore-*adv*	still| again
74	peu-*adv; m; adj*	little; bit; few
75	vraiment-*adv*	really| actually
77	toujours-*adv*	always| still
81	juste-*adj; adv*	just| fair; just
83	quelque-*adj; adv*	some; about
86	trop-*adv*	too| too much
95	avant-*adv; prp; adj; m*	before; before; front
101	parce que-*adv*	because
104	mal-*m; adv; adj*	evil| wrong; amiss; untimely
106	après-*adv; prp*	after| next; after
108	mieux-*adv; adj*	better; adj
110	beaucoup-*prn; adj; adv*	many; much; much
112	voilà-*adv*	here
113	depuis-*adv; prp*	since; since
117	déjà-*adv*	already
119	donc-*con; adv*	therefore; consequently
135	seul-*adj; m; adv*	only; only one; very
137	vite-*adv*	quickly| fast
148	moins-*adv; m; prp*	less; minus; wanting
149	entre-*adv; prp*	between; between
152	demain-*adv; m*	tomorrow; tomorrow
160	assez-*adv*	enough| quite
164	puis-*adv*	then
165	tard-*adv*	late
172	combien-*adv*	how many
173	tant-*adv*	so such
182	ni-*con; adv*	or; neither
193	sous-*prp; adv; f*	under; underneath; cash
209	longtemps-*adv; adj*	for a long time; longtime
212	seulement-*adv; con*	only| just; only
221	ensemble-*adv; m; f*	together; ensemble; collection
223	vers-*prp; adv; m*	to| towards; about; verse
228	devant-*adv; prp; m*	before| past; before; front
232	dessus-*adv*	over
240	droit-*adj; m; adv*	right; right; due
242	loin-*adv; adj*	far; distant
253	enfin-*adv*	finally| after all
257	fort-*adj; m; adv*	strong| loud; fort; highly
269	dehors-*adv; m*	outside| out; outside
270	hier-*adv*	yesterday; yesterday
273	près-*adv*	near| by
276	ainsi-*adv; con*	thus| thereby; as
277	haut-*adj; m; adv*	high; top; in heaven
288	plutôt-*adv*	rather| quite
295	bientôt-*adv*	soon| almost
298	tellement-*adv*	so
299	derrière-*adv; m; prp*	behind; behind; behind
301	presque-*adv; adj*	almost; all but
325	dedans-*adv; prp; m*	in; in; inside
340	parfois-*adv*	sometimes
355	exactement-*adv*	exactly| accurately

368	**partout**-*adv*	everywhere| throughout	1128	**pis encore**-*adv*	even worse
373	**sinon**-*con; adv*	otherwise; or else	1143	**également**-*adv*	also| equally
386	**tôt**-*adv*	early| soon	1151	**franchement**-*adv*	honestly| openly
390	**surtout**-*adv*	mainly| above all			
393	**ensuite**-*adv*	then| later	1186	**rapidement**-*adv*	quickly| rapidly
402	**souvent**-*adv*	often	1210	**malheureusement**-*adv*	unfortunately| unhappily
403	**sauf**-*prp; adj; con; adv*	except; safe; excepting; short of	1221	**totalement**-*adv*	totally
405	**sûrement**-*adv*	surely	1227	**soudain**-*adv; adj*	suddenly; sudden
469	**pièce**-*f; adv*	piece| room; apiece	1228	**heureusement**-*adv*	fortunately| happily
471	**ailleurs**-*adv*	somewhere else			
521	**doucement**-*adv*	gently| slowly	1245	**bref**-*adj; adv*	short| brief; in short
530	**complètement**-*adv*	completely| fully	1264	**piano**-*adv; m*	piano; piano
			1273	**évidemment**-*adv*	obviously
556	**moitié**-*adv; f*	half; half	1276	**de là**-*adv*	thence| therefrom
558	**chacun**-*prn; adv*	each; apiece	1283	**directement**-*adv*	directly| right
562	**autour**-*adv*	around	1307	**facilement**-*adv*	easily
566	**simplement**-*adv*	simply	1374	**davantage**-*adv*	further
569	**selon**-*prp; adv*	according to; as follows	1376	**net**-*adj; adv*	net| sharp; outright
584	**tant pis**-*adv*	too bad	1430	**lentement**-*adv*	slowly| leisurely
591	**pourtant**-*con; adv*	yet| however; nevertheless	1440	**auprès**-*adv*	nearby
684	**probablement**-*adv*	probably	1485	**cependant**-*con; adv*	however| yet; though
717	**environ**-*adv; prp; adj*	about; around; all but	1513	**récemment**-*adv*	recently
779	**immédiatement**-*adv*	immediately	1583	**autrefois**-*adv*	once| in the past
			1587	**forcément**-*adv*	necessarily
791	**certainement**-*adv*	definitely	1599	**correct**-*adj; adv*	correct; alright
			1633	**uniquement**-*adv*	only
923	**finalement**-*adv*	finally	1651	**réellement**-*adv*	actually| true
927	**justement**-*adv*	rightly| exactly	1678	**naturellement**-*adv*	naturally
966	**proche**-*adj; adv; m*	near; near; neighbor			
975	**malgré**-*prp; adv*	despite; all the same	1736	**exprès**-*adj; adv*	express; on purpose
981	**lors**-*adv*	then| while	1745	**clairement**-*adv*	clearly
987	**dessous**-*adv; m; prp*	beneath; underside; under it	1764	**auparavant**-*adv*	before
			1782	**profondément**-*adv*	deeply| heavily
1014	**suivant**-*adj; prp; adv*	following; according to; as follows	1786	**entièrement**-*adv*	entirely| quite
1020	**parfaitement**-*adv*	perfectly| thoroughly	1810	**concernant**-*adv; prp*	concerning; concerning
1057	**sérieusement**-*adv*	seriously| gravely	1824	**personnellement**-*adv*	personally
1062	**autrement**-*adv*	otherwise	1880	**extrêmement**-*adv*	extremely
1088	**apparemment**-*adv*	apparently	1957	**suffisamment**-*adv*	enough
1106	**direct**-*adj; adv*	direct; straight	2101	**rarement**-*adv*	rarely| hardly
1120	**désormais**-*adv*	henceforth	2182	**honnêtement**-*adv*	honestly

2189	**particulièrement** *-adv*	particularly
2209	**pratiquement-** *adv*	virtually
2224	**volontiers-***adv*	willingly
2255	**terriblement-***adv*	terribly
2311	**énormément-** *adv*	enormously
2331	**carrément-***adv*	downright
2360	**etc.-***adv*	et cetera
2372	**sincèrement-***adv*	truly| sincerely
2376	**actuellement-** *adv*	currently| now
2385	**précisément-***adv*	precisely
2389	**correctement-** *adv*	correctly
2422	**partant-***adv; m*	thus; starter
2445	**officiellement-** *adv*	officially

Conjunctions

Rank	French-PoS	Translation
9	**que**-*con; prn; prp; adj; adv*	that; that; than; which; how
12	**et**-*con*	and
24	**mais**-*con; adv*	but; probably
29	**si**-*con; adv*	if; so
41	**comme**-*con; prp; adj*	as; as; such as
51	**où**-*adv; prn; con*	where; that; wherein
53	**pourquoi**-*adv; con*	why; wherefore
54	**quand**-*adv; con*	when; when
62	**ou**-*con*	or
67	**aussi**-*adv; con*	also| as; and
119	**donc**-*con; adv*	therefore; consequently
140	**soit**-*con*	whether| either
182	**ni**-*con; adv*	or; neither
212	**seulement**-*adv; con*	only| just; only
276	**ainsi**-*adv; con*	thus| thereby; as
330	**autant**-*con*	as far as
373	**sinon**-*con; adv*	otherwise; or else
403	**sauf**-*prp; adj; con; adv*	except; safe; excepting; short of
591	**pourtant**-*con; adv*	yet| however; nevertheless
863	**puisque**-*con*	since
1485	**cependant**-*con; adv*	however| yet; though

Prepositions

Rank	French-*PoS*	Translation
1	**de**-*prp*	of| from
9	**que**-*con; prn; prp; adj; adv*	that; that; than; which; how
13	**à**-*prp*	to
17	**en**-*prp; adv*	in; thereof
20	**pour**-*prp*	for
26	**dans**-*prp; adv*	in; aboard
35	**avec**-*prp*	with
41	**comme**-*con; prp; adj*	as; as; such as
42	**sur**-*prp*	on
55	**par**-*prp; m*	by; par
82	**sans**-*prp*	without
95	**avant**-*adv; prp; adj; m*	before; before; front
100	**chez**-*prp*	in| by
106	**après**-*adv; prp*	after| next; after
113	**depuis**-*adv; prp*	since; since
148	**moins**-*adv; m; prp*	less; minus; wanting
149	**entre**-*adv; prp*	between; between
183	**contre**-*prp*	against
193	**sous**-*prp; adv; f*	under; underneath; cash
194	**voici**-*prp*	here is
223	**vers**-*prp; adv; m*	to| towards; about; verse
228	**devant**-*adv; prp; m*	before| past; before; front
299	**derrière**-*adv; m; prp*	behind; behind; behind
325	**dedans**-*adv; prp; m*	in; in; inside
381	**dès**-*prp*	from| since
403	**sauf**-*prp; adj; con; adv*	except; safe; excepting; short of
569	**selon**-*prp; adv*	according to; as follows
621	**hors**-*prp*	except
717	**environ**-*adv; prp; adj*	about; around; all but
778	**parmi**-*prp*	among
801	**lorsque**-*prp*	during
938	**durant**-*prp*	during
975	**malgré**-*prp; adv*	despite; all the same
987	**dessous**-*adv; m; prp*	beneath; underside; under it
1014	**suivant**-*adj; prp; adv*	following; according to; as follows
1810	**concernant**-*adv; prp*	concerning; concerning

Pronouns

Rank	French-PoS	Translation
2	**je**-*prn*	I
5	**le**-*art; prn*	the; it
6	**vous**-*prn*	you (form, pl)
7	**la**-*art; prn*	the; it
8	**tu**-*prn*	you (coll)
9	**que**-*con; prn; prp; adj; adv*	that; that; than; which; how
10	**un**-*art; adj; num; prn*	a; one; one; one
11	**il**-*prn*	he, it
16	**ce**-*prn; adj*	this; that
18	**on**-*prn*	we
19	**cela**-*prn*	it| that
21	**moi**-*prn; m*	me; ego
22	**qui**-*prn*	which
23	**nous**-*prn*	we| us
25	**me**-*prn*	me| myself
28	**elle**-*prn*	she| it
30	**tout**-*adj; adv; m; prn*	all; all; all; all
33	**mon**-*prn*	my
34	**te**-*prn*	you
38	**toi**-*prn*	you
40	**se**-*prn*	-self (reflexive marker)
43	**quoi**-*prn*	what
46	**lui**-*prn*	him
49	**rien**-*m; prn; adv*	nothing; anything; nix
51	**où**-*adv; prn; con*	where; that; wherein
52	**votre**-*adj; prn*	your; your
57	**ton**-*adj; prn; m*	your; your; tone
71	**autre**-*prn; adj; adv*	other; another; else
78	**notre**-*prn*	our
94	**leur**-*prn*	their
98	**personne**-*f; prn*	person; nobody
110	**beaucoup**-*prn; adj; adv*	many; much; much
115	**quel**-*adj; prn*	what; what
203	**eux**-*prn*	them
216	**chaque**-*adj; prn*	each; either
224	**aucun**-*adj; prn*	no; none
265	**dont**-*prn*	whose
278	**celui**-*prn*	that
334	**ceci**-*prn; adj*	this; following
522	**pareil**-*adj; prn; m*	such| similar; the same; equal
558	**chacun**-*prn; adv*	each; apiece
688	**nul**-*adj; m; prn*	no| zero; zero; no one
698	**lequel**-*prn*	which
1306	**soi**-*m; prn*	self; self
1413	**tien**-*prn*	yours
1516	**quiconque**-*prn*	whoever
1620	**nôtre**-*prn*	our
2043	**ça**-*prn*	it
2400	**sien**-*prn*	one's own

Nouns

Rank	French-PoS	Translation
4	pas-adv; m	not; step
10	un-art; adj; num; prn	a; one; one; one
14	avoir-vb; m	have; asset
21	moi-prn; m	me; ego
27	bien-adv; m; adj	well| very; good; right
30	tout-adj; adv; m; prn	all; all; all; all
31	plus-adj; adv; m	more; more; plus
36	oui-part; m	yes; yea
45	savoir-vb; m	know; knowledge
49	rien-m; prn; adv	nothing; anything; nix
55	par-prp; m	by; par
56	son-adj; m	its; sound
57	ton-adj; prn; m	your; your; tone
58	pouvoir-m; vb; av	power; can; might
61	bon-adj; m; adv	good| well; voucher; then
65	merci-m; int	thanks; thanks
69	deux-num	two
74	peu-adv; m; adj	little; bit; few
76	temps-m	time
79	vie-f	life
84	monde-m	world
85	accord-m	agreement| deal
89	devoir-m; vb; av	duty; have to; must
90	père-m	father| dad
91	dieu-m	god
92	homme-m	man| person
95	avant-adv; prp; adj; m	before; before; front
96	besoin-m	need
97	femme-f	woman
98	personne-f; prn	person; nobody
102	vrai-adj; m	true| real; right
103	an-m	year
104	mal-m; adv; adj	evil| wrong; amiss; untimely
107	mort-adj; f	dead; death
109	petit-adj; m	small| little; child
111	Monsieur-abr; m	Mr.; sir
114	mère-f	mother
116	fille-f	daughter| girl
118	gens-mpl	people
120	jour-m	day
121	soir-m	evening
123	argent-m	money
124	maison-f	house| home
125	nom-m	name
128	nuit-f	night
129	papa-m	papa
130	maman-f	mom
132	peur-f	fear| scare
134	salut-m; int	salvation; hi
135	seul-adj; m; adv	only; only one; very
141	air-m	air
143	trois-num	three
145	chose-f	thing
147	bas-adj; m	low| base; bottom
148	moins-adv; m; prp	less; minus; wanting
150	passe-f	pass
152	demain-adv; m	tomorrow; tomorrow
155	tête-f	head| top
158	raison-f	reason| why
159	enfant-m	child
161	moment-m	time| moment
162	amour-m	love
163	heure-f	time
170	gars-m	guy
171	chance-f	chance| luck
174	part-f	share| part
175	problème-m	problem| issue
176	coup-m	blow| shot
177	porte-f	door| gate
178	travail-m	work
179	famille-f	family
180	putain-f	whore| bitch
181	idée-f	idea
189	vieux-adj; m	old| ancient; old man
190	attention-f	attention
193	sous-prp; adv; f	under; underneath; cash
195	sang-m	blood
196	histoire-f	history| story
198	question-f	question| issue
199	frère-m	brother
200	ville-f	city
202	nouveau-adj; m	new| further; incoming
204	truc-m	thing| trick
206	œil-m	eye
208	mec-m	guy| dude

210	**beau**-*adj; m*	beautiful| nice; beautiful
211	**police**-*f*	police
214	**eau**-*f*	water
215	**car**-*m*	car
217	**cas**-*m*	case| event
218	**terre**-*f*	earth| land
220	**main**-*f*	hand
221	**ensemble**-*adv; m; f*	together; ensemble; collection
222	**pardon**-*m*	forgiveness
223	**vers**-*prp; adv; m*	to| towards; about; verse
225	**guerre**-*f*	war
226	**suite**-*f*	suite| sequence
228	**devant**-*adv; prp; m*	before| past; before; front
230	**matin**-*m*	morning
231	**aide**-*f*	aid| relief
233	**genre**-*m*	kind| gender
234	**fin**-*f; adj*	end; fine
236	**jeune**-*adj; m*	young; youth
237	**chéri**-*adj; m*	darling| precious; honey
240	**droit**-*adj; m; adv*	right; right; due
241	**côté**-*m*	side
243	**feu**-*m*	fire
245	**train**-*m*	train
246	**gros**-*adj; m*	large| fat; fat man
249	**aura**-*f*	aura
250	**dernier**-*adj; m*	last| latter; last
251	**minute**-*f*	minute
252	**mari**-*m*	husband
254	**Madame**-*f*	madame| Mrs
255	**façon**-*f*	way| method
256	**film**-*m*	film| cinema
257	**fort**-*adj; m; adv*	strong| loud; fort; highly
259	**pays**-*m*	country
260	**endroit**-*m*	place| spot
261	**corps**-*m*	body
262	**fou**-*adj; m*	crazy; fool
264	**prêt**-*adj; m*	ready| willing; loan
267	**cause**-*f*	cause| case
268	**point**-*m*	point| item
269	**dehors**-*adv; m*	outside| out; outside
271	**boulot**-*m*	job| work
272	**garçon**-*m*	boy| lad
274	**cinq**-*num*	five
275	**chef**-*m*	chief| leader
277	**haut**-*adj; m; adv*	high; top; in heaven
279	**bébé**-*m*	baby| kid
280	**possible**-*adj; m*	possible; possible
281	**école**-*f*	school
283	**année**-*f*	year
285	**docteur**-*m*	doctor
286	**tour**-*m; f*	turn; tower
287	**quatre**-*num*	four
290	**semaine**-*f*	week
291	**vérité**-*f*	truth
293	**capitaine**-*m*	captain
294	**affaire**-*f*	case| matter
296	**instant**-*m; adj*	moment| while; urgent
299	**derrière**-*adv; m; prp*	behind; behind; behind
302	**meilleur**-*m; adj*	best; better
303	**numéro**-*m*	number
304	**journée**-*f*	day
305	**dollar**-*m*	dollar| greenback
306	**confiance**-*f*	confidence| faith
307	**garde**-*f; adj*	custody| guard; guarding
308	**souvenir**-*m*	memory| souvenir
310	**bureau**-*m*	office| desk
311	**abord**-*m*	first| start
314	**seigneur**-*m*	lord
316	**route**-*f*	road| way
317	**cul**-*m*	ass
319	**jeu**-*m*	game
320	**ferme**-*f; adj*	farm; firm
321	**plaisir**-*m*	pleasure
322	**mot**-*m*	word
323	**chien**-*m*	dog
324	**calme**-*adj; m*	quiet| calm; calm
325	**dedans**-*adv; prp; m*	in; in; inside
326	**mariage**-*m*	marriage
329	**lit**-*m*	bed
333	**cœur**-*m*	heart| core
335	**service**-*m*	service| serving
337	**pauvre**-*adj; m*	poor; poor person
338	**Mademoiselle**-*abr; f*	Ms.; miss
341	**retour**-*m*	return
342	**verre**-*m*	glass
343	**six**-*num*	six
346	**maître**-*m*	master| teacher
347	**mauvais**-*adj; m*	bad| ill; brute

348	**général**-*adj; m*	general; general	431	**gauche**-*adj; f*	left; left
349	**doute**-*m*	doubt	433	**prix**-*m*	price| prize
350	**prison**-*f*	prison	434	**rouge**-*adj; m*	red; red
352	**faute**-*f*	fault	435	**faim**-*f*	hunger
354	**bras**-*m*	arm	436	**avion**-*m*	aircraft
357	**café**-*m*	cafe| coffee	438	**prochain**-*adj; m*	next| upcoming; next
359	**gentil**-*adj; m*	nice| kind; gentile	440	**voyage**-*m*	travel| trip
361	**lieu**-*m*	place| venue	441	**sorte**-*f*	kind| manner
362	**malade**-*adj; m*	sick| invalid; patient	443	**espèce**-*f*	species| kind
364	**roi**-*m*	king	444	**idiot**-*m; adj*	idiot; silly
366	**président**-*m*	president	446	**début**-*m*	beginning| debut
369	**cher**-*adj; m*	expensive| dear; dear	449	**hôpital**-*m*	hospital
372	**équipe**-*f*	team| crew	450	**grâce**-*f*	grace| favor
374	**esprit**-*m*	mind| spirit	451	**message**-*m*	message
375	**plan**-*m; adj*	plan; plane	453	**patron**-*m*	boss| patron
378	**propre**-*adj; m*	own| clean; proper	456	**oncle**-*m*	uncle
379	**état**-*m*	state| condition	459	**camp**-*m*	camp
380	**bois**-*m*	wood| timber	461	**soleil**-*m*	sun
383	**dix**-*num*	ten	462	**cheveu**-*m*	hair
385	**sécurité**-*f*	security	463	**arme**-*f*	weapon
389	**avis**-*m*	opinion| notice	464	**salle**-*f*	room
396	**paix**-*f*	peace	469	**pièce**-*f; adv*	piece| room; apiece
397	**sujet**-*m; adj*	subject; prone	470	**erreur**-*f*	error| mistake
398	**retard**-*m*	delay	472	**rapport**-*m*	report| ratio
399	**livre**-*m*	book	473	**froid**-*adj; m*	cold| cool; cold
404	**choix**-*m*	choice| selection	474	**scène**-*f*	scene
406	**or**-*m*	gold	475	**secret**-*adj; m*	secret| covert; secret
407	**visage**-*m*	face	476	**sac**-*m*	bag| sack
408	**ordre**-*m*	order	477	**second**-*adj; m*	second; second
409	**noir**-*adj; m*	black; black	478	**cru**-*adj; m*	vintage| raw; vineyard
410	**dîner**-*m; vb*	dinner; dine	481	**hôtel**-*m*	hotel
411	**âge**-*m*	age	482	**soirée**-*f*	evening
412	**chemin**-*m*	path| road	483	**sœur**-*adj; f*	sister; sister
414	**face**-*f*	face| front	484	**pied**-*m*	foot| leg
415	**rue**-*f*	street	485	**carte**-*f*	map| card
417	**photo**-*f*	photo	487	**groupe**-*m*	group| band
418	**sérieux**-*adj; m*	serious; seriousness	489	**agent**-*m; adj*	agent; cooperative
419	**ciel**-*m*	sky| heaven	490	**effet**-*m*	effect
420	**honneur**-*m*	honor| credit	492	**bordel**-*m*	mess| brothel
421	**force**-*f*	force| power	493	**neuf**-*num*	nine
424	**million**-*m*	million	495	**situation**-*f*	situation
426	**voix**-*f*	voice	497	**lumière**-*f*	light| spotlight
427	**courant**-*adj; m*	current| running; current	499	**Noël**-*m*	Christmas
428	**propos**-*m*	talk	500	**cheval**-*m*	horse
429	**bateau**-*m*	boat	501	**intérieur**-*adj; m*	inside| interior; inside
430	**con**-*m; adj*	cunt| prick; bloody	502	**loi**-*f*	law

504	**lettre**-*f*	letter
505	**présent**-*adj; m*	present; present
507	**dame**-*f*	lady
508	**professeur**-*m*	professor| teacher
509	**fric**-*m*	money| cash
511	**coin**-*m*	corner| wedge
512	**colonel**-*m*	colonel
513	**âme**-*f*	soul
514	**dos**-*m*	back| reverse
522	**pareil**-*adj; prn; m*	such| similar; the same; equal
523	**accident**-*m*	accident
524	**appel**-*m*	call| appeal
525	**anniversaire**-*adj; m*	anniversary; anniversary
526	**blanc**-*adj; m*	white| albescent; white
527	**risque**-*m*	risk| hazard
528	**moyen**-*m; adj*	means| medium; medium
532	**meurtre**-*m*	murder
533	**toucher**-*m; vb*	touch; touch
534	**déjeuner**-*vb; m*	lunch; lunch
536	**lire**-*vb; f*	read; lira
537	**avance**-*f*	advance| lead
539	**forme**-*f*	form| shape
540	**bord**-*m*	edge| board
542	**mer**-*f*	sea
543	**médecin**-*m; adj*	doctor; doctoral
544	**midi**-*m; adj*	noon; midday
547	**silence**-*m*	silence| pause
548	**diable**-*m; adj*	devil; wretched
549	**cadeau**-*m*	gift
551	**flic**-*m*	cop
552	**avocat**-*m*	lawyer
554	**anglais**-*adj; m/mpl*	English; English
555	**sept**-*num*	seven
556	**moitié**-*adv; f*	half; half
561	**télé**-*abr; f*	TV; telly
567	**mission**-*f*	mission| assignment
570	**classe**-*f*	class| classroom
571	**pari**-*m*	bet| betting
572	**peuple**-*m*	common people
573	**habitude**-*f*	habit
574	**voie**-*f*	way| track
576	**pote**-*m*	buddy
577	**contrôle**-*m*	control| check
578	**honte**-*f*	shame
579	**impression**-*f*	printing| impression
583	**chanson**-*f*	song
585	**poste**-*m; f*	position; post
586	**huit**-*num*	eight
587	**radio**-*f*	radio
589	**attaque**-*f*	attack
590	**baiser**-*m; vb*	kiss; fuck
592	**réponse**-*f*	response
593	**connard**-*m*	prick
594	**pute**-*f*	bitch
595	**bande**-*f*	band| strip
596	**enfer**-*m*	hell
602	**rire**-*m; vb*	laugh; laugh
603	**compagnie**-*f*	company
605	**exemple**-*m*	example| sample
606	**combat**-*m*	combat
607	**secours**-*m*	relief| help
608	**connerie**-*f*	bullshit
610	**coucher**-*vb; m*	sleep| lay down; sunset
615	**lune**-*f*	moon
616	**bouche**-*f*	mouth
617	**sud**-*adj; m*	south; south
619	**ennui**-*m*	boredom| trouble
620	**but**-*m*	purpose| goal
622	**boîte**-*f*	box| can
623	**vol**-*m*	flight| theft
624	**public**-*adj; m*	public; public
625	**lieutenant**-*m*	lieutenant
626	**système**-*m*	system
627	**époque**-*f*	time| age
628	**bête**-*f; adj*	beast| idiot; stupid
630	**avenir**-*m*	future
631	**santé**-*f*	health
632	**amoureux**-*adj; m*	in love; lover
633	**cuisine**-*f*	kitchen| cuisine
635	**danger**-*m*	danger
636	**gouvernement**-*m*	government| ministry
637	**village**-*m*	village
640	**journal**-*m*	newspaper| journal
641	**approche**-*f*	approach
642	**dommage**-*m*	damage| pity
643	**peau**-*f*	skin
644	**nez**-*m*	nose
647	**mille**-*num*	thousand
648	**banque**-*f*	bank

649	**sergent**-*m*	sergeant
650	**clé**-*adj; f*	key; key
651	**nord**-*m; adj*	north; northern
652	**inspecteur**-*m*	inspector
653	**liberté**-*f*	freedom| liberty
654	**salaud**-*m; adj*	bastard; dirty
655	**cour**-*f*	court
656	**juge**-*m*	judge| beak
659	**crime**-*m*	crime
661	**thé**-*m*	tea
662	**bonheur**-*m; adj*	happiness; welfare
663	**tas**-*m*	pile
664	**travers**-*m*	across
665	**stupide**-*adj; m*	stupid; stupid
666	**blague**-*f*	joke
668	**conseil**-*m*	board| council
670	**rêve**-*m*	dream
671	**pitié**-*f*	pity
672	**vin**-*m*	wine
673	**don**-*m*	gift| donation
674	**sol**-*m*	soil
675	**vent**-*m*	wind
676	**club**-*m*	club
677	**gamin**-*m; adj*	kid; kiddy
678	**tante**-*f*	aunt
679	**bar**-*m*	bar| bass
680	**milieu**-*m*	medium
681	**reine**-*f*	queen
683	**centre**-*m*	center| focus
685	**bière**-*f*	beer
686	**dingue**-*adj; m/f*	crazy| wild; loon
688	**nul**-*adj; m; prn*	no| zero; zero; no one
692	**vêtement**-*m*	garment
693	**liste**-*f*	list
695	**société**-*f*	society| association
696	**soin**-*m*	care| carefulness
699	**parole**-*f*	word| speech
701	**départ**-*m*	departure| starting
702	**ennemi**-*m; adj*	enemy| hostile; inimical
703	**spectacle**-*m*	show| spectacle
704	**recherche**-*f*	research| search
706	**intérêt**-*m*	interest
708	**rôle**-*m*	role
709	**félicitation**-*f*	congratulation
712	**position**-*f*	position
713	**blessé**-*adj; m*	injured; casualty
714	**humain**-*adj; m*	human; human
715	**match**-*m*	match| game
716	**coupable**-*adj; m/f*	guilty; culprit
718	**art**-*m*	art
719	**espoir**-*m*	hope
720	**mur**-*m*	wall
721	**église**-*f*	church
722	**salope**-*f*	slut
723	**beauté**-*f*	beauty
724	**lâche**-*m; adj*	coward; cowardly
727	**colère**-*f*	anger| passion
728	**directeur**-*m*	director
729	**adieu**-*m*	farewell
731	**tort**-*m*	wrong| harm
734	**revenu**-*m*	income
735	**justice**-*f*	justice| law
736	**soldat**-*m*	soldier
737	**expérience**-*f*	experience
738	**cerveau**-*m*	brain| brains
739	**quartier**-*m*	neighborhood| district
740	**prince**-*m*	prince
741	**riche**-*adj; m/f*	rich; rich person
742	**fleur**-*f*	flower
744	**presse**-*f*	press
745	**ridicule**-*adj; m*	ridiculous; ridicule
746	**preuve**-*f*	evidence| proof
749	**gosse**-*m/f; adj*	kid| brat; kiddy
750	**rose**-*adj; f*	pink; rose
751	**nature**-*f*	nature
752	**vide**-*adj; m*	empty; empty
753	**responsable**-*adj; m/f*	responsible; person responsible
754	**courage**-*m*	courage
756	**cinéma**-*m*	cinema
757	**décision**-*f*	decision
758	**taxi**-*m*	taxi
762	**deuxième**-*num*	second
763	**appartement**-*m*	apartment
764	**contact**-*m*	contact
767	**manière**-*f*	way| form
768	**jambe**-*f*	leg
769	**occasion**-*f*	opportunity| occasion
770	**défense**-*f*	defense| prohibition
772	**Jésus**-*m*	Jesus
775	**base**-*f*	base| basis

777	**dent**-*f*	tooth	
780	**paie**-*f*	pay| payroll	
782	**vacance**-*f*	vacancy	
783	**monstre**-*m; adj*	monster; monstrous	
784	**tueur**-*m*	killer	
786	**français**-*adj; m|mpl*	French; French	
787	**course**-*f*	race| running	
788	**majesté**-*f*	majesty	
790	**type**-*m*	type| guy	
794	**importance**-*f*	importance| significance	
795	**ouest**-*adj; m*	west; west	
796	**chat**-*m*	cat	
799	**joie**-*f*	joy	
803	**bain**-*m*	bath	
805	**court**-*adj; m*	short| brief; court	
807	**bombe**-*f*	bomb	
809	**réalité**-*f*	reality	
811	**camion**-*m*	truck| lorry	
813	**cent**-*m; num*	cent| hundred	
814	**rencontre**-*f*	meeting| match	
816	**respect**-*m*	respect	
817	**terrain**-*m*	field| ground	
818	**projet**-*m*	project	
820	**poisson**-*m*	fish	
822	**envers**-*m*	back| against	
823	**kilomètre**-*m*	kilometer	
824	**ange**-*m*	angel	
825	**chaussure**-*f*	shoe	
826	**dossier**-*m*	folder| file	
827	**animal**-*adj; m*	animal; animal	
828	**langue**-*f*	language	
829	**imbécile**-*m/f; adj*	imbecile; stupid	
830	**princesse**-*f*	princess	
832	**charge**-*f*	load| charge	
833	**nourriture**-*f*	food| feed	
834	**pont**-*m*	bridge	
836	**contraire**-*adj; m*	contrary; contrary	
838	**douleur**-*f*	pain	
839	**politique**-*f; adj*	policy; political	
840	**fait**-*m; adj*	fact; ripe	
841	**magasin**-*m*	store| shop	
843	**chapeau**-*m*	hat	
846	**papier**-*m*	paper	
847	**action**-*f*	action| effort	
849	**rapide**-*adj; m*	fast| rapid; rapid	

850	**shérif**-*m*	sheriff
851	**frais**-*mpl; adj*	costs; fresh
852	**réunion**-*f*	meeting| reunion
853	**île**-*f*	island
854	**toilette**-*f*	toilet
855	**opération**-*f*	operation
857	**planète**-*f*	planet
858	**champ**-*m*	field
859	**couleur**-*f*	color
860	**pain**-*m*	bread
861	**destin**-*m*	destiny
865	**vaisseau**-*m*	vessel
866	**sexe**-*m*	sex| gender
868	**repas**-*m*	meal
869	**contrat**-*m*	contract
871	**client**-*m*	customer| client
873	**lait**-*m*	milk
874	**mémoire**-*m; f*	dissertation; memory
876	**copain**-*m; adj*	boyfriend| buddy; pally
877	**reste**-*m*	rest| remainder
878	**personnel**-*m; adj*	staff| personnel; personal
881	**couteau**-*m*	knife
882	**témoin**-*m*	witness
883	**foi**-*f*	faith
885	**direction**-*f*	direction| management
886	**malin**-*adj; m*	malignant| smart; evil
887	**niveau**-*m*	level
891	**procès**-*m*	trial| process
893	**solution**-*f*	solution
895	**goût**-*m*	taste| flavor
897	**différence**-*f*	difference
898	**stop**-*m*	stop
900	**enceinte**-*adj; f*	pregnant; enclosure
901	**université**-*f*	university
902	**bleu**-*adj; m*	blue; blue
903	**mètre**-*m*	meter
907	**officier**-*m*	officer
908	**espace**-*m*	space
909	**sourire**-*m; vb*	smile; smile
910	**mérite**-*m*	merit| worth
912	**failli**-*adj; m*	bankrupt
913	**Angleterre**-*m*	England
914	**vitesse**-*f*	speed
915	**caméra**-*f*	camera
916	**arbre**-*m*	tree| shaft
917	**trésor**-*m*	treasure| treasury

918	**énergie**-*f*	energy
926	**image**-*f*	image
929	**chasse**-*f*	hunting| chase
931	**arrêt**-*m*	stop| stopping
933	**balle**-*f*	ball| bullet
934	**dimanche**-*m*	Sunday
935	**lycée**-*m*	high school
936	**fil**-*m*	thread| lead
937	**morceau**-*m*	piece| track
940	**doigt**-*m*	finger
942	**appareil**-*m*	apparatus
943	**piste**-*f*	track| runway
944	**troisième**-*num*	third
946	**programme**-*m*	program| agenda
948	**voiture**-*f*	car| vehicle
951	**aveugle**-*adj; m/f*	blinded; blind
952	**présence**-*f*	presence
953	**crise**-*f*	crisis| attack
956	**lever**-*vb; m*	lift| raise; rise
958	**pluie**-*f*	rain
961	**souris**-*f*	mouse
963	**regard**-*m*	look| gaze
964	**intention**-*f*	intention| mind
965	**cou**-*m*	neck
966	**proche**-*adj; adv; m*	near; near; neighbor
967	**urgence**-*f*	emergency
968	**folie**-*f*	madness| folly
969	**ancien**-*adj; m; pfx*	former| ancient; former; ex-
970	**relation**-*f*	relation
971	**bouteille**-*f*	bottle
973	**casse**-*f*	case| breakage| robbery
974	**jardin**-*m*	garden
976	**oiseau**-*m*	bird
978	**nombre**-*m*	number
979	**sentiment**-*m*	feeling| sense
980	**toit**-*m*	roof
982	**métier**-*m*	trade| job
983	**maladie**-*f*	disease| illness
986	**succès**-*m*	success
987	**dessous**-*adv; m; prp*	beneath; underside; under it
988	**théâtre**-*m*	theater| stage
989	**chinois**-*adj; m*	Chinese; Chinese
991	**gare**-*f*	station| train station
992	**billet**-*m*	ticket
994	**paradis**-*m*	paradise
995	**étranger**-*adj; m*	foreign| overseas; foreigner
996	**campagne**-*f*	campaign
997	**alcool**-*m*	alcohol
998	**samedi**-*m*	Saturday
1002	**odeur**-*f*	smell| odor
1003	**montagne**-*f*	mountain
1005	**victoire**-*f*	victory| win
1006	**carrière**-*f*	career
1009	**règle**-*f*	rule
1011	**queue**-*f*	tail| queue
1012	**viande**-*f*	meat
1013	**rivière**-*f*	river
1016	**fusil**-*m*	rifle
1017	**passager**-*m; adj*	passenger; passing
1018	**hasard**-*m*	chance| accident
1019	**neige**-*f*	snow
1022	**plage**-*f*	beach
1023	**signal**-*m*	signal
1024	**crétin**-*m; adj*	cretin; moronic
1025	**vidéo**-*f*	video
1027	**pression**-*f*	pressure
1028	**information**-*f*	information
1029	**futur**-*adj; m*	future; future
1030	**univers**-*m*	universe
1031	**volonté**-*f*	will
1033	**excuse**-*f*	excuse
1034	**faible**-*adj; m*	low| weak; weakling
1035	**fiston**-*m*	son
1036	**van**-*m*	van
1040	**gaffe**-*f*	blunder
1041	**ministre**-*m*	minister
1042	**naissance**-*f*	birth| rise
1044	**gaz**-*m*	gas
1045	**bataille**-*f*	battle
1046	**voleur**-*m; adj*	thief; thievish
1047	**poids**-*m*	weight
1049	**star**-*f*	star
1050	**gâteau**-*m*	cake
1051	**ventre**-*m*	belly| stomach
1052	**connaissance**-*f*	knowledge| acquaintance
1053	**vif**-*adj; m*	bright| lively; quick
1054	**assassin**-*m; adj*	assassin; bloodthirsty
1055	**vendredi**-*m*	Friday
1056	**couple**-*m*	couple| pair

1058	**militaire**-*adj; m*	military; soldier
1059	**date**-*f*	date
1060	**titre**-*m*	title| headline
1061	**génie**-*m*	genius| genie
1063	**os**-*m*	bone
1064	**valeur**-*f*	value| worth
1066	**vert**-*adj; m*	green| young; putting green
1067	**fortune**-*f*	fortune| wealth
1068	**major**-*m*	adjutant| matiére principale
1069	**poulet**-*m*	chicken
1071	**genou**-*m*	knee
1074	**cousin**-*m*	cousin
1075	**conscience**-*f*	consciousness| conscience
1077	**article**-*m*	art
1078	**étoile**-*f*	star| blaze
1080	**mine**-*f*	mine| lead
1081	**charmant**-*adj; m*	charming| lovely; cunning
1085	**château**-*m*	castle| chateau
1086	**bal**-*m*	ball
1087	**oreille**-*f*	ear
1089	**zéro**-*m*	zero| nobody
1090	**saint**-*adj; m*	saint; saint; St.
1091	**marrant**-*adj; m*	funny; funny guy
1092	**joue**-*f*	cheek
1093	**salon**-*m*	lounge
1095	**conversation**-*f*	conversation| talk
1097	**fer**-*m*	iron
1098	**gorge**-*f*	throat
1099	**victime**-*f*	victim
1100	**détail**-*m*	detail
1103	**violence**-*f*	violence| force
1105	**aéroport**-*m*	airport
1107	**tribunal**-*m*	court| courthouse
1109	**paquet**-*m*	package| pack
1111	**aise**-*adj; f*	pleased; pleasure
1113	**lance**-*f*	lance| hose
1114	**usine**-*f*	plant| factory
1116	**forêt**-*f*	forest
1117	**champion**-*adj; m*	champion; champion
1118	**horreur**-*f*	horror
1119	**test**-*m*	test
1121	**extérieur**-*adj; m*	outside| exterior; outside
1122	**désert**-*m*	desert
1124	**job**-*m*	job
1125	**compte**-*m*	account
1126	**mode**-*m; f*	mode; fashion
1127	**série**-*f*	series| set
1129	**sage**-*adj; m*	wise; sage
1133	**vache**-*f; adj*	cow; bitchy
1134	**repos**-*m*	rest| pause
1135	**ordinateur**-*m*	computer
1136	**rock**-*m*	rock
1137	**russe**-*adj; m*	Russian; Russian
1138	**minuit**-*m*	midnight
1140	**membre**-*m*	member
1145	**page**-*f*	page
1146	**essence**-*f*	gasoline| essence
1147	**maire**-*m*	mayor
1148	**lundi**-*m*	Monday
1149	**moteur**-*m; adj*	engine; motor
1152	**cigarette**-*f*	cigarette
1154	**puissance**-*f*	power| strength
1155	**hiver**-*m*	winter
1156	**épée**-*f*	sword
1157	**souffle**-*m*	breath| blast
1159	**vingt**-*num*	twenty
1160	**miracle**-*m*	miracle
1162	**artiste**-*m/f*	artist
1164	**lac**-*m*	lake
1165	**sommeil**-*m*	sleep| rest
1167	**leçon**-*f*	lesson
1168	**fantôme**-*m; adj*	ghost; phantom
1169	**acteur**-*m*	actor
1170	**parc**-*m*	park
1171	**chair**-*f*	flesh
1173	**japonais**-*adj; m|mpl*	Japanese; Japanese
1175	**champagne**-*m*	champagne
1176	**semblant**-*m*	semblance
1178	**échange**-*m*	exchange| swap
1183	**gouverneur**-*m*	governor
1184	**chauffeur**-*m*	driver| chauffeur
1187	**unité**-*f*	unit| unity
1189	**souci**-*m*	worry| care
1190	**manteau**-*m*	coat| mantle
1191	**allemand**-*adj; m|mpl*	German; German
1192	**pantalon**-*m*	pants
1193	**policier**-*m*	police officer

1194	**innocent**-*adj; m*	innocent; innocent		1256	**larme**-*f*	tear| drop
1196	**caisse**-*f*	fund| register		1257	**siècle**-*m*	century
1198	**patient**-*adj; m*	patient; patient		1259	**veste**-*f*	jacket
1199	**menteur**-*m; adj*	liar| lying; lying		1260	**couverture**-*f*	coverage| cover
1200	**perte**-*f*	loss| waste		1264	**piano**-*adv; m*	piano; piano
1201	**menace**-*f*	threat		1265	**source**-*f*	source| spring
1202	**émission**-*f*	emission| transmission		1266	**camarade**-*m/f*	comrade| fellow
1204	**permission**-*f*	permission		1267	**couche**-*f*	layer| bed
1205	**front**-*m*	front| forehead		1268	**prêtre**-*m*	priest
1207	**chouette**-*f; adj*	owl; neat		1269	**saison**-*f*	season
1208	**chaise**-*f*	chair		1272	**supporter**-*vb; m*	support| bear; supporter
1209	**sir**-*m*	sir		1274	**distance**-*f*	distance| range
1211	**chocolat**-*m*	chocolate		1278	**somme**-*f*	sum
1212	**whisky**-*m*	whiskey| Scotch		1280	**ours**-*m*	bear
1213	**mouvement**-*m*	movement| stir		1281	**geste**-*m*	gesture| movement
1214	**identité**-*f*	identity		1282	**prisonnier**-*m; adj*	prisoner; captive
1215	**douche**-*f*	shower		1284	**tableau**-*m*	table| picture
1216	**chaleur**-*f*	heat		1286	**demi**-*adj; m*	half; half
1217	**lèvre**-*f*	lip		1287	**commissaire**-*m*	commissioner
1218	**étude**-*f*	study		1288	**alerte**-*adj; f*	alert; alert
1219	**faveur**-*f*	favor		1291	**lunettes**-*fpl*	glasses
1220	**Christ**-*m*	Christ		1296	**aube**-*f*	dawn| blade
1222	**chou**-*m*	cabbage		1297	**propriétaire**-*m/f; adj*	owner| landlord; proprietary
1223	**pause**-*f*	break| rest		1300	**bite**-*f*	cock| knob
1224	**fini**-*adj; m*	finished| finite; finish		1301	**frontière**-*f*	border| frontier
1225	**côte**-*f*	coast		1304	**bosse**-*f*	bump| lump
1226	**mai**-*m*	May		1306	**soi**-*m; prn*	self; self
1229	**choc**-*m*	shock		1308	**porc**-*m*	pork| pig
1230	**note**-*f*	note		1309	**vierge**-*adj; f*	virgin; virgin
1232	**malheur**-*m*	misfortune		1311	**titrage**-*m*	titration
1234	**mars**-*f*	March		1312	**suspect**-*adj; m*	suspect| dubious; suspect
1236	**portable**-*adj; m*	portable; portable		1313	**station**-*f*	station
1237	**secrétaire**-*m/f*	secretary		1316	**jean**-*m*	jeans
1238	**mensonge**-*m*	lie		1317	**bagage**-*m*	luggage
1240	**pistolet**-*m*	gun| pistol		1318	**protection**-*f*	protection
1241	**gloire**-*f*	glory| fame		1319	**tir**-*m*	shot
1242	**accès**-*m*	access		1320	**empereur**-*m*	emperor
1243	**changement**-*m*	change| changing		1321	**océan**-*m*	ocean
1244	**poupée**-*f*	doll| puppet		1322	**concert**-*m*	concert
1246	**réel**-*adj; m*	real| live; real		1323	**immeuble**-*m; adj*	building; immovable
1247	**ballon**-*m*	ball		1325	**chaîne**-*f*	chain| string
1248	**abri**-*m*	shelter| shed		1326	**enfance**-*f*	childhood
1249	**corde**-*f*	rope		1328	**cauchemar**-*m*	nightmare
1251	**plat**-*adj; m*	flat; flat| dish		1329	**amitié**-*f*	friendship
1252	**emploi**-*m*	employment		1330	**magie**-*f*	magic
1254	**attrape**-*f*	catch				

1331	**nana**-*f*	girl| babe
1332	**partenaire**-*m*	partner
1333	**curieux**-*adj; m*	curious; onlooker
1334	**patte**-*f*	tab| leg
1335	**lendemain**-*m*	next day
1336	**souper**-*m; vb*	supper; sup
1337	**uniforme**-*adj; m*	uniform; uniform
1338	**marine**-*f*	navy
1340	**Chine**-*f*	China
1341	**désir**-*m*	desire| wish
1342	**objet**-*m*	object
1346	**humanité**-*f*	humanity
1347	**lapin**-*m*	rabbit
1351	**bâtiment**-*m*	building| vessel
1352	**chèque**-*m*	check
1353	**palais**-*m*	palace
1354	**valise**-*f*	suitcase| case
1356	**haine**-*f; adj*	hatred; heating
1357	**mile**-*m*	mile
1358	**assurance**-*f*	insurance| assurance
1359	**navire**-*m*	ship
1360	**foyer**-*m*	home| fireplace
1361	**printemps**-*m*	spring
1363	**personnage**-*m*	character| figure
1364	**brave**-*adj; m*	brave| good; brave
1370	**explosion**-*f*	explosion| blast
1372	**procureur**-*m*	prosecutor
1373	**opinion**-*f*	opinion
1377	**vivant**-*adj; m*	living| alive; living
1379	**fiancé**-*m; adj*	fiance; engaged
1383	**hâte**-*f*	haste| hastiness
1384	**amen**-*m*	amen
1385	**voisin**-*m; adj*	neighbor; neighboring
1387	**prof**-*m*	prof
1389	**comte**-*m*	count
1391	**réputation**-*f*	reputation| name
1393	**créature**-*f*	creature| being
1397	**soif**-*f*	thirst
1398	**égal**-*adj; m*	equal| even; equal
1399	**sport**-*m; adj*	sport; sporting
1400	**résultat**-*m*	result| product
1401	**siège**-*m*	seat| siege
1404	**canon**-*m*	gun
1405	**gardien**-*m*	keeper| guardian
1407	**terme**-*m*	term
1408	**troupe**-*f*	troop
1409	**théorie**-*f*	theory
1410	**joueur**-*m*	player
1411	**région**-*f*	region| district
1414	**médicament**-*m*	drug| medication
1415	**crâne**-*m*	skull| cranium
1416	**traduction**-*f*	translation
1417	**studio**-*m*	studio
1419	**responsabilité**-*f*	responsibility
1421	**trace**-*f*	trace| track
1423	**modèle**-*adj; m*	model; model
1424	**cellule**-*f*	cell
1425	**gêne**-*f*	discomfort| embarrasment
1426	**pêcher**-*vb; m*	fish; peach
1427	**poule**-*f*	hen
1428	**sénateur**-*m*	senator
1429	**péché**-*m*	sin| trespass
1431	**empire**-*m*	empire
1432	**débile**-*adj; m/f*	stupid; defective
1433	**top**-*m*	top
1435	**imagination**-*f*	imagination
1436	**liquide**-*adj; m*	liquid| wet; liquid
1438	**marin**-*adj; m*	marine; marine
1439	**humeur**-*f*	mood| spirit
1442	**temple**-*m*	temple
1443	**physique**-*adj; f*	physical; physics
1445	**infirmier**-*m*	male nurse
1446	**secteur**-*m*	sector
1448	**cirque**-*m*	circus
1449	**particulier**-*adj; m*	particular| individual; private person
1453	**vision**-*f*	vision
1454	**clocher**-*m*	bell tower
1456	**croix**-*f*	cross
1457	**vente**-*f*	sale
1458	**démon**-*m*	daemon
1460	**aventure**-*f*	adventure
1461	**taule**-*f*	slammer| nick
1462	**matériel**-*m; adj*	equipment| material; material
1463	**surface**-*f*	surface
1464	**télévision**-*f*	television
1465	**jaune**-*adj; m*	yellow; yellow
1468	**journaliste**-*m/f*	journalist| reporter
1470	**rat**-*m*	rat
1471	**cri**-*m*	cry| scream
1472	**patience**-*f*	patience

1473	**ménage-***m*	household| housework	
1474	**comité-***m*	committee| panel	
1477	**Japon-***m*	Japan	
1478	**romantique-***adj; m/f*	romantic; romantic	
1479	**port-***m*	port| harbor	
1480	**crédit-***m*	credit	
1482	**promesse-***f*	promise	
1483	**inconnu-***m; adj*	unknown; unfamiliar	
1484	**ambulance-***f*	ambulance	
1486	**panique-***adj; f*	panic; panic	
1487	**criminel-***adj; m*	criminal; criminal	
1488	**sauvage-***adj; m*	wild; savage	
1489	**royaume-***m*	kingdom	
1490	**complet-***adj; m*	full| complete; suit	
1491	**centaine-***num*	hundred	
1492	**scénario-***m*	scenario	
1493	**principal-***adj; m*	main; principal	
1494	**jus-***m*	juice	
1495	**détective-***m*	detective	
1496	**pot-***m*	pot| jar	
1498	**cochon-***m; adj*	pig| swine; dirty	
1499	**cadavre-***m*	corpse| body	
1500	**tapir-***m*	tapir	
1501	**révolution-***f*	revolution	
1502	**existence-***f*	existence| life	
1504	**lien-***m*	link| connection	
1505	**fromage-***m*	cheese	
1506	**période-***f*	period| term	
1507	**profond-***adj; m*	deep| profound; deep	
1508	**malheureux-***adj; m*	unfortunate| unhappy; unfortunate	
1510	**roman-***m; adj*	novel; Romance	
1511	**poussière-***f*	dust	
1512	**passion-***f*	passion	
1514	**lutte-***f*	fight| struggle	
1517	**cap-***m*	cape| course	
1518	**version-***f*	version	
1519	**entraînement-***m*	training	
1520	**mardi-***m*	Tuesday	
1522	**meurtrier-***m; adj*	murderer; murderous	
1523	**examen-***m*	examination| review	
1524	**septembre-***m*	September	
1527	**serpent-***m*	snake	
1528	**bouton-***m*	button	
1529	**piscine-***f*	swimming pool	

1530	**courrier-***m*	mail| courier
1531	**logique-***f; adj*	logic; logical
1533	**cancer-***m*	cancer
1535	**jeudi-***m*	Thursday
1537	**boss-***m*	boss
1538	**hall-***m*	lobby| lounge
1540	**ascenseur-***m*	elevator| lifter
1541	**garage-***m*	garage
1543	**traitement-***m*	treatment| processing
1544	**sein-***m*	breast| fold
1545	**nation-***f*	nation
1546	**propriété-***f*	property
1547	**labo-***m*	lab
1548	**machine-***f*	machine
1549	**pub-***m; f*	pub; advertising
1551	**commission-***f*	commission| board
1552	**section-***f*	section
1554	**pratique-***f; adj*	practice; practical
1555	**écran-***m*	screen
1557	**ceinture-***f*	belt| waistband
1559	**miel-***m*	honey
1561	**estomac-***m*	stomach
1562	**salaire-***m*	salary
1566	**incendie-***m*	fire
1569	**prénom-***m*	first name
1570	**invité-***m*	guest
1571	**idéal-***adj; m*	ideal; ideal
1572	**condition-***f*	condition
1573	**élève-***m/f*	student
1574	**douze-***num*	twelve
1575	**virus-***m*	virus
1576	**poil-***m*	hair
1577	**jeunesse-***f*	youth
1578	**ordinaire-***adj; m*	ordinary; ordinary
1579	**agence-***f*	agency
1580	**revolver-***m*	revolver
1581	**loup-***m*	wolf
1582	**naturel-***adj; m*	natural; nature
1584	**équipage-***m*	crew
1585	**tempête-***f*	storm
1589	**miroir-***m*	mirror
1590	**chic-***adj; m*	chic| stylish; chic
1591	**jury-***m*	jury
1595	**cérémonie-***f*	ceremony
1596	**tasse-***f*	cup
1597	**absence-***f*	absence

1598	**comportement-** *m*	behavior	
1601	**national-***adj; m*	national; national	
1602	**masque-***m*	mask	
1604	**bijou-***m*	jewel	
1605	**mystère-***m*	mystery	
1606	**cabine-***f*	cabin| cab	
1607	**étudiant-***adj; m*	student; student	
1608	**parfum-***m*	perfume| fragrance	
1610	**vengeance-***f*	vengeance	
1613	**qualité-***f*	quality	
1614	**couvert-***adj; m*	covered; place	
1615	**couloir-***m*	corridor| hallway	
1616	**tape-***f*	slap	
1617	**réaction-***f*	reaction	
1621	**race-***f*	race| breed	
1622	**bêtise-***f*	foolishness	
1624	**colle-***f*	glue	
1625	**poitrine-***f*	chest| bosom	
1626	**enterrement-***m*	burial| funeral	
1628	**noble-***adj; m/f*	noble; noble	
1634	**riz-***m*	rice	
1637	**puce-***f; adj*	chip| flea; puce	
1639	**origine-***f*	origin	
1640	**attitude-***f*	attitude| outlook	
1641	**absurde-***adj; m*	absurd; absurd	
1642	**union-***f*	union	
1643	**bagnole-***f*	wagon| wheel	
1644	**maximum-***adj; m*	maximum; maximum	
1645	**effort-***m*	effort| stress	
1646	**chambre-***f*	room	
1647	**vélo-***m*	bike	
1648	**esclave-***m; adj*	slave; enslaved	
1649	**foot-***m*	football	
1650	**éducation-***f*	education| upbringing	
1652	**pair-***adj; m*	even; peer	
1654	**blond-***adj; m*	blond; blonde	
1655	**boule-***f*	ball	
1656	**déclaration-***f*	declaration	
1658	**site-***m*	site	
1659	**scientifique-***adj; m/f*	scientific; scientist	
1660	**traître-***m; adj*	traitor; treacherous	
1662	**cave-***f; adj*	cellar; hollow	
1663	**cassette-***f*	cassette	
1664	**essai-***m*	test| testing	

1665	**minable-***adj; m/f*	shabby| pathetic; piddling	
1666	**sommet-***m*	top| vertex	
1668	**aile-***f*	wing| blade	
1669	**bagarre-***f*	fight| brawl	
1670	**production-***f*	production	
1671	**rang-***m*	rank| row	
1672	**Bible-***f*	Bible	
1675	**show-***m*	show	
1677	**humour-***m*	humor	
1680	**commandement-***m*	command	
1682	**mandat-***m*	mandate| warrant	
1683	**milliard-***num*	billion	
1684	**fruit-***m*	fruit	
1686	**partage-***m*	sharing| division	
1687	**bourse-***f*	scholarship	
1688	**jungle-***f*	jungle	
1692	**adulte-***adj; m/f*	adult; adult	
1693	**pomme-***f*	apple	
1694	**auteur-***m*	author	
1695	**jugement-***m*	judgment| trial	
1696	**organisation-***f*	organization| setup	
1698	**vague-***f; adj*	wave; vague	
1699	**légende-***f*	legend| caption	
1701	**barbe-***f*	beard	
1702	**territoire-***m*	territory	
1703	**blessure-***f*	injury	
1704	**géant-***adj; m*	giant; giant	
1705	**moto-***f*	motorcycle	
1706	**communauté-***adj; f*	community; community	
1707	**cage-***f*	cage| shaft	
1709	**rayon-***m*	radius| ray	
1710	**sorcier-***m*	sorcerer	
1711	**pile-***f*	battery| pile	
1712	**kilo-***m*	kilo	
1713	**écrivain-***m*	writer	
1716	**limite-***f*	limit	
1720	**quinze-***num*	fifteen	
1722	**conseiller-***m; vb*	advisor| counselor; advise	
1723	**ligne-***f*	line| design	
1724	**escalier-***m*	staircase| stairs	
1725	**explication-***f*	explanation| explication	
1729	**professionnel-***adj; m*	professional; professional	
1730	**incident-***adj; m*	incident; incident	
1731	**colline-***f*	hill	

1732	**junior**-*m*	junior	1802	**loyer**-*m*	rent
1733	**autorisation**-*f*	authorization| permission	1803	**producteur**-*m*	producer
1735	**ministère**-*m*	ministry	1804	**quart**-*m*	quarter
1737	**football**-*m*	football	1805	**critique**-*adj; f*	critical; review
1738	**rond**-*adj; m*	round; round	1806	**acte**-*m*	act| certificate
1739	**exercice**-*m*	exercise| fiscal year	1807	**cardiaque**-*adj; m/f*	cardiac; heart patient
1740	**fichu**-*adj; m*	damn| rotten; scarf	1808	**plateau**-*m*	tray
1741	**vote**-*m*	vote| polling	1809	**auto**-*f*	auto
1742	**domaine**-*m*	field| domain	1811	**conférence**-*f; adj*	conference; lecturing
1744	**religion**-*f*	religion	1812	**baby**-*m*	baby
1746	**furieux**-*adj; m*	furious; madman	1814	**fièvre**-*f*	fever
1748	**bol**-*m; m*	bowl; circumstance	1815	**réception**-*f*	reception| desk
1749	**excellence**-*f*	excellence	1816	**duc**-*m*	duke
1750	**cimetière**-*m*	graveyard	1817	**italien**-*adj; m*	Italian; Italian
1751	**classique**-*adj; m*	classic| standard; classic	1818	**amiral**-*m*	admiral
1752	**baron**-*m*	baron	1819	**fenêtre**-*f*	window
1753	**arrestation**-*f*	arrest| detention	1821	**cervelle**-*f*	brain| brains
1755	**cabinet**-*m*	cabinet	1822	**moral**-*adj; m*	moral; morale
1756	**comédie**-*f*	comedy	1823	**supérieur**-*adj; m*	upper; superior
1757	**bond**-*m*	leap| jump	1826	**discussion**-*f*	discussion| debate
1758	**tunnel**-*m*	tunnel	1827	**sandwich**-*m*	sandwich
1759	**amant**-*m*	lover	1831	**gagnant**-*m; adj*	winner; winning
1761	**drapeau**-*m*	flag	1832	**beurre**-*m*	butter
1762	**do**-*m*	do	1834	**fleuve**-*m*	river| stream
1766	**magazine**-*m*	magazine	1835	**appétit**-*m*	appetite
1769	**éternité**-*f*	eternity| lifetime	1836	**nerf**-*m*	nerve
1772	**proposition**-*f*	proposal| proposition	1840	**liaison**-*f*	link| affair
1773	**soutien**-*m*	support	1841	**document**-*m*	document
1774	**hauteur**-*f*	height| pitch	1842	**place**-*f*	square| spot
1775	**échec**-*m*	failure| check	1843	**nuage**-*m*	cloud
1777	**culture**-*f*	culture	1845	**guitare**-*f*	guitar
1778	**précis**-*adj; m*	precise; abstract	1846	**final**-*adj; m*	final| ultimate; finale
1779	**langage**-*m*	language	1847	**robot**-*m*	robot
1780	**objectif**-*adj; m*	objective; goal	1848	**brise**-*f*	breeze| breath
1781	**onze**-*num*	eleven	1849	**réseau**-*m*	network| grid
1783	**souffrance**-*f*	suffering	1850	**prière**-*f*	prayer
1784	**gang**-*m*	gang	1851	**réalisateur**-*m*	director
1785	**pétrole**-*m*	oil| kerosene	1852	**poison**-*m*	poison
1787	**épreuve**-*f*	test| trial	1853	**surveillance**-*f*	surveillance
1789	**bibliothèque**-*f*	library	1855	**médecine**-*f*	medicine
1791	**altesse**-*f*	highness	1856	**placard**-*m*	cupboard
1792	**trente**-*num*	thirty	1857	**mercredi**-*m*	Wednesday
1794	**ranger**-*m; vb*	ranger; put away	1858	**chiffre**-*m*	figure| number
1797	**vallée**-*f*	valley	1859	**lampe**-*f*	lamp
1798	**pizza**-*f*	pizza	1860	**expert**-*adj; m*	expert; expert
1799	**golf**-*m*	golf			

1861	**autorité**-*f*	authority
1862	**destruction**-*f*	destruction
1863	**congrès**-*m*	conference
1865	**juillet**-*m*	July
1867	**stade**-*m*	stage
1868	**serment**-*m*	oath
1869	**dette**-*f*	debt
1870	**dragon**-*m*	dragon
1874	**expression**-*f*	expression
1875	**métro**-*m*	subway
1878	**balance**-*f*	balance
1879	**lion**-*m*	lion
1881	**séance**-*f*	meeting| session
1882	**collier**-*m*	necklace
1883	**alliance**-*f*	alliance
1884	**congé**-*m*	leave
1885	**portefeuille**-*m*	portfolio| wallet
1888	**terroriste**-*m/f*	terrorist
1889	**clan**-*m*	clan
1890	**exécution**-*f*	execution| implementation
1893	**invitation**-*f*	invitation
1894	**électricité**-*f*	electricity
1897	**avril**-*m*	April
1898	**acier**-*m*	steel
1901	**sire**-*m*	sire
1902	**degré**-*m*	degree
1903	**instruction**-*f*	instruction| education
1905	**division**-*f*	division| split
1906	**fierté**-*f*	pride
1908	**fidèle**-*adj; m/f*	faithful| loyal; stalwart
1910	**mamie**-*f*	granny| nanny
1912	**renseignement**-*m*	inquiry
1913	**total**-*adj; m*	total| overall; total
1915	**espagnol**-*adj; m/mpl*	Spanish; Spanish
1916	**solide**-*adj; m*	solid; solid
1917	**avantage**-*m*	advantage
1918	**habitant**-*m; adj*	inhabitant; resident
1919	**rage**-*f*	rage| rabies
1920	**neveu**-*m*	nephew
1922	**ouverture**-*f*	opening
1923	**blé**-*m*	wheat
1924	**munition**-*f*	munition
1926	**juin**-*m*	June
1930	**bâton**-*m*	stick| baton
1933	**caractère**-*m*	character| nature
1934	**célibataire**-*adj; m/f*	single| bachelor; single
1935	**pasteur**-*m*	pastor| shepherd
1936	**progrès**-*m*	progress
1937	**ordure**-*f*	filth| trash
1938	**matière**-*f*	material
1939	**puits**-*m*	well
1940	**bonté**-*f*	goodness
1943	**intelligence**-*f*	intelligence| intellect
1946	**température**-*f*	temperature
1947	**fête**-*f*	party
1948	**saloperie**-*f*	rubbish
1949	**bonbon**-*m*	candy
1952	**tension**-*f*	voltage| tension
1953	**serviette**-*f*	towel| napkin
1956	**passeport**-*m*	passport
1958	**échelle**-*f*	scale| ladder
1959	**cercle**-*m*	circle| ring
1961	**citoyen**-*m*	citizen
1963	**tentative**-*f*	attempt| bid
1964	**fan**-*m*	fan
1965	**règlement**-*m*	settlement| regulation
1967	**comté**-*m*	county
1968	**crainte**-*f*	fear
1971	**manuel**-*adj; m*	manual; manual
1973	**octobre**-*m*	October
1974	**méchant**-*adj; m*	wicked| bad; naughty child
1975	**bétail**-*m*	livestock| cattle
1976	**dessin**-*m*	drawing| design
1977	**Inde**-*f*	India
1981	**diamant**-*m*	diamond
1982	**dalle**-*f*	slab| flagstone
1984	**asile**-*m*	asylum
1986	**sou**-*m*	cent
1988	**tournage**-*m*	shooting| turning
1992	**couronne**-*f*	crown
1993	**vedette**-*f*	star| launch
1995	**garce**-*f*	bitch
1996	**formation**-*f*	training| formation
1997	**Canada**-*f*	Canada
1998	**audience**-*f*	audience
2000	**procédure**-*f*	procedure
2003	**salade**-*f*	salad
2004	**mouche**-*f*	fly| spot
2005	**conséquence**-*f*	consequence

2007	**espion**-*m*	spy	2081	**possibilité**-*f*	possibility
2009	**objection**-*f*	objection	2082	**réveil**-*m*	alarm clock
2014	**chevalier**-*m*	knight	2084	**ère**-*f*	era
2017	**tradition**-*f*	tradition	2086	**étape**-*f*	step| stage
2019	**département**-*m*	department	2090	**prime**-*f; adj*	premium; incentive
2022	**accusation**-*f*	charge| accusation	2091	**publicité**-*f*	advertising| publicity
2023	**disque**-*m*	disk| discus	2093	**séjour**-*m*	stay| visit
2025	**entretien**-*m*	maintenance| conversation	2094	**tabac**-*m*	tobacco
			2095	**chaos**-*m*	chaos
2027	**chasseur**-*m; adj*	hunter; gunner's	2096	**enfermer**-*f; vb*	lock; confine
2029	**solitaire**-*adj; m/f*	solitary; loner	2097	**tarte**-*f*	pie
2031	**micro**-*f; pfx*	mike; micro-	2098	**frigo**-*m*	fridge
2032	**technologie**-*f*	technology	2099	**traîne**-*f*	train
2033	**original**-*adj; m*	original; original	2106	**exception**-*f*	exception
2034	**ranch**-*m*	ranch	2107	**gant**-*m*	glove
2035	**patrie**-*f*	country| homeland	2109	**ouvrier**-*m*	worker
2036	**tuyau**-*m*	pipe| hose	2111	**record**-*m*	record
2037	**clinique**-*adj; f*	clinical; clinic	2113	**enseigne**-*f*	sign
2038	**régime**-*m*	regime| diet	2114	**angle**-*m*	angle| corner
2039	**album**-*m*	album	2115	**instinct**-*m*	instinct
2040	**suprême**-*adj; m*	supreme; supreme	2116	**impôt**-*m*	tax
2042	**pipe**-*f*	pipe	2119	**vilain**-*adj; m*	ugly; villein
2045	**émotion**-*f*	emotion	2120	**complexe**-*adj; m*	complex; complex
2046	**coucou**-*adj; m; int*	cuckoo; cuckoo; hello	2121	**méthode**-*f*	method
			2123	**motel**-*m*	motel
2047	**franc**-*adj; m*	frank; franc	2124	**tragédie**-*f*	tragedy
2048	**remarque**-*f*	remark| observation	2125	**torture**-*f*	torture
2049	**quatrième**-*num*	fourth	2126	**industrie**-*f*	industry
2050	**excitant**-*adj; m*	exciting; upper	2127	**population**-*f*	population
2051	**sel**-*m*	salt	2128	**adaptation**-*f*	adaptation
2052	**canapé**-*m*	couch	2130	**autoroute**-*f*	highway
2056	**promotion**-*f*	promotion	2131	**pro**-*m/f*	pro
2057	**scandale**-*m*	scandal	2132	**obscurité**-*f*	darkness| obscurity
2058	**cran**-*m*	notch	2134	**linge**-*m*	washing
2060	**élément**-*m*	element	2136	**rigole**-*f*	channel
2064	**événement**-*m*	event	2138	**fauteuil**-*m*	armchair
2065	**personnalité**-*f; abr*	personality; VIP	2139	**vendeur**-*m*	seller| dealer
			2140	**novembre**-*m*	November
2066	**gentleman**-*m; adj*	gentleman; gentlemanly	2141	**collection**-*f*	collection
			2143	**bonhomme**-*m*	fellow| old man
2067	**rumeur**-*f*	rumor	2144	**accent**-*m*	accent
2068	**parking**-*m*	parking	2147	**plastique**-*adj; m*	plastic; plastic
2070	**dégât**-*m*	damage	2148	**marche**-*f*	walking
2071	**négatif**-*adj; m*	negative; negative	2149	**révérend**-*m*	reverend
2075	**signature**-*f*	signature	2150	**commande**-*f*	order
2079	**canard**-*m*	duck	2151	**caporal**-*m*	lance corporal
2080	**stylo**-*m*	pen			

2152	**lot**-*m*	lot| prize	2217	**pisse**-*f*	piss
2153	**trahison**-*f*	treason	2218	**essentiel**-*adj; m*	essential; main
2154	**sensation**-*f*	sensation| feeling	2219	**génération**-*f*	generation
2155	**résistance**-*f*	resistance| strength	2221	**écriture**-*f*	writing
2156	**mesure**-*f*	measure| step	2223	**massacre**-*m*	massacre
2157	**chanceux**-*adj; m*	fortunate; lucky man	2225	**phrase**-*f*	phrase
2158	**boue**-*f*	mud	2226	**poème**-*m*	poem| epic
2159	**merveille**-*f*	wonder| marvel	2227	**bail**-*m*	lease| long time
2160	**poing**-*m*	fist	2228	**pénis**-*m*	penis
2161	**sacrifice**-*m*	sacrifice	2229	**singe**-*m*	monkey
2162	**communication**-*f*	communication	2231	**époux**-*m*	husband| spouse
2164	**chagrin**-*m*	grief| heartache	2232	**automne**-*m*	fall| autumn
2166	**drogue**-*f*	drug	2233	**brigade**-*f*	brigade
2170	**coach**-*m*	trainer	2235	**magicien**-*m*	magician
2171	**coïncidence**-*f*	coincidence	2236	**survie**-*f*	survival
2172	**halte**-*f*	stop| stopover	2237	**batterie**-*f*	battery
2173	**août**-*m*	August	2239	**manche**-*m; f*	handle; sleeve
2174	**malédiction**-*f*	curse	2243	**principe**-*m*	principle
2175	**pension**-*f*	pension	2247	**luxe**-*m*	luxury
2176	**vampire**-*m*	vampire	2248	**chariot**-*m*	cart| trolley
2177	**phase**-*f*	phase	2249	**terreur**-*f*	terror
2178	**noix**-*f; adj*	nut; walnut	2251	**sagesse**-*f*	wisdom
2179	**toast**-*m*	toast	2258	**décembre**-*m*	December
2183	**défi**-*m*	challenge	2260	**four**-*m*	oven
2186	**désastre**-*m*	disaster	2261	**usage**-*m*	use| usage
2190	**bâtard**-*adj; m*	bastard; bastard	2262	**collège**-*m*	college
2191	**solitude**-*f*	solitude| loneliness	2263	**symbole**-*m*	symbol
2193	**jouet**-*adj; m*	toy; toy	2264	**flamme**-*f*	flame
2195	**ingénieur**-*m*	engineer	2265	**bloc**-*m*	block| unit
2196	**chant**-*m*	singing| song	2266	**règne**-*m*	reign
2197	**poésie**-*f*	poetry| poem	2267	**orage**-*m*	storm
2198	**ongle**-*m*	nail	2271	**texte**-*m*	text
2199	**trafic**-*m*	traffic	2272	**officiel**-*adj; m*	official; official
2200	**activité**-*f*	activity	2273	**pompe**-*f*	pump| pomp
2201	**médaille**-*f*	medal	2274	**poubelle**-*f*	dustbin| rubbish
2202	**reconnaissance**-*f*	recognition	2275	**patrouille**-*f*	patrol
2203	**foie**-*m*	liver	2276	**équipement**-*m*	equipment| gear
2204	**cercueil**-*m*	coffin	2277	**casino**-*m*	casino
2205	**gris**-*adj; m*	gray; gray	2278	**métal**-*m*	metal
2207	**livraison**-*f*	delivery	2279	**destination**-*f*	destination
2208	**pilule**-*f*	pill	2281	**pique**-*m; f*	spade; pike
2210	**cinquante**-*num*	fifty	2282	**accueil**-*m*	welcome
2212	**communiste**-*adj; m/f*	Communist; Communist	2284	**économie**-*f*	economy| economics
			2285	**tombe**-*f*	grave| tomb
2213	**commissariat**-*m*	police station	2286	**charité**-*f*	charity
2215	**trouille**-*f*	funk	2290	**laboratoire**-*m*	laboratory

2292	plaisanterie-*f*	joke
2294	boisson-*f*	drink
2295	saut-*m*	jump| hop
2296	matinée-*f*	morning
2298	otage-*m*	hostage
2301	tireur-*m*	shooter| drawer
2302	lave-*f*	lava
2303	ambassadeur-*m; adj*	ambassador; ambassadorial
2304	atmosphère-*f*	atmosphere
2306	casier-*m*	locker
2307	capital-*adj; m*	capital; capital
2308	cendre-*f*	ash
2309	syndicat-*m*	union| syndicate
2312	outil-*m*	tool
2313	testament-*m*	will| device
2314	poète-*m*	poet
2315	combinaison-*f*	combination| suit
2319	came-*f*	cam
2320	lecture-*f*	reading
2321	processus-*m*	process
2324	atelier-*m*	workshop| studio
2325	guerrier-*m; adj*	warrior; warlike
2326	pouce-*m*	inch
2327	entraîneur-*m*	coach
2329	panier-*m*	basket
2330	pétrin-*m*	mess| predicament
2332	tonnerre-*m*	thunder
2333	témoignage-*m*	testimony| witness
2335	indice-*m*	index
2336	création-*f*	creation
2337	environnement-*m*	environment
2339	dose-*f*	dose| measure
2340	môme-*m*	kid| brat
2341	curiosité-*f*	curiosity
2342	administration-*f*	administration| management
2343	misère-*f*	misery
2344	cuir-*m*	leather
2345	transport-*m*	transport| carriage
2347	trône-*m*	throne
2348	savon-*m*	soap
2349	pirate-*m*	pirate
2350	pipi-*m*	pee
2352	plante-*f*	plant
2353	viol-*m*	rape
2354	clown-*m*	knockabout
2355	douceur-*f*	sweetness| softness
2358	parent-*m; adj*	relative; kin
2361	écart-*m*	gap| difference
2362	fonction-*f*	function
2364	machin-*m*	gadget| thingy
2366	talent-*m*	talent| skill
2367	nègre-*adj; m*	Negro; nigger
2368	catholique-*adj; m/f*	Catholic; Catholic
2370	misérable-*adj; m/f*	miserable; wretch
2371	requin-*m*	shark
2373	affection-*f*	affection| ailment
2374	porno-*m*	porn
2375	adversaire-*adj; m/f*	opponent; opponent
2377	meuble-*m*	furniture| charge
2379	dignité-*f*	dignity
2381	rate-*f*	spleen
2384	dépression-*f*	depression
2386	circuit-*m*	circuit
2387	télégramme-*m*	telegram
2388	voile-*f*	veil| sail
2393	volontaire-*adj; m/f*	voluntary; voluntary
2394	fumier-*m*	manure
2395	zoo-*m*	zoo
2396	égoïste-*adj; m/f*	selfish; egoist
2397	construction-*f*	construction
2398	fillette-*f*	little girl
2399	motif-*m*	pattern| ground
2401	vodka-*f*	vodka
2402	loyauté-*f*	loyalty
2403	évidence-*f*	evidence
2404	mouton-*m*	sheep
2408	dessert-*m*	dessert
2409	catastrophe-*f*	disaster
2410	disparition-*f*	disappearance
2412	Satan-*m*	Satan
2413	drap-*m*	sheet
2415	cigare-*m*	cigar
2416	éclair-*m*	lightning
2418	feuille-*f*	sheet| leaf
2420	nichon-*m*	tit| nipple
2421	interview-*f*	interview
2422	partant-*adv; m*	thus; starter

2423	**promenade**-*f*	walk
2424	**extra**-*adj; m*	extra; extra
2425	**association**-*f*	association
2426	**leader**-*m*	leader| head
2427	**demoiselle**-*f*	young lady
2428	**discipline**-*f*	discipline
2430	**lancement**-*m*	launching| start
2431	**gras**-*adj; m*	fat; fat
2432	**transfert**-*m*	transfer
2433	**satellite**-*m*	satellite
2434	**pompier**-*m; adj*	fire-fighter; pompous
2435	**tennis**-*m*	tennis
2438	**enregistrement**-*m*	recording
2439	**pognon**-*m*	money| dough
2440	**circulation**-*f*	circulation
2442	**compétition**-*f*	competition
2443	**caution**-*f*	deposit| bail
2444	**opportunité**-*f*	oppurtunity
2448	**menu**-*m; adj*	menu; small
2449	**plancher**-*m; vb*	floor; floor
2451	**dentiste**-*m/f*	dentist
2453	**ticket**-*m*	ticket
2454	**civilisation**-*f*	civilization
2455	**avertissement**-*m*	warning
2456	**tache**-*f*	spot| stain
2457	**balade**-*f*	ride| walk
2458	**nid**-*m*	nest
2459	**antenne**-*f*	antenna
2461	**boxer**-*m; vb*	boxer; box
2462	**onde**-*f*	wave
2463	**assaut**-*m*	assault
2464	**fiche**-*f*	plug| card
2465	**épisode**-*m*	episode| part
2466	**anneau**-*m*	ring
2467	**maquillage**-*m*	makeup
2469	**impact**-*m*	impact
2470	**médias**-*mpl*	media
2471	**éléphant**-*m*	elephant
2473	**chaussette**-*f*	sock
2474	**poker**-*m*	poker
2475	**ancêtre**-*m/f*	ancestor
2478	**conflit**-*m*	conflict
2479	**hélicoptère**-*m*	helicopter
2480	**mâle**-*adj; m*	male| masculine; male
2481	**profit**-*m*	profit| advantage
2482	**cadre**-*m*	framework| frame
2483	**audition**-*f*	hearing| performance
2484	**pape**-*m*	pope
2487	**assiette**-*f*	plate| dish
2488	**culpabilité**-*f*	guilt
2489	**foire**-*f*	fair
2490	**arabe**-*adj; m*	Arab; Arabic
2492	**bidon**-*m*	can| drum
2493	**république**-*f*	republic
2494	**saleté**-*f*	dirt| filth
2495	**quai**-*m*	dock| quay
2496	**funérailles**-*adj; fpl*	funeral; funeral
2497	**pré**-*m*	meadow| pasture
2498	**tristesse**-*f*	sadness
2499	**tribu**-*f*	tribe
2500	**décès**-*m*	death| demise
2502	**touche**-*f*	key
2503	**profil**-*m*	profile
2504	**budget**-*m*	budget
2505	**panneau**-*m*	panel| sign
2506	**lame**-*f*	blade
2508	**illusion**-*f*	illusion
2509	**caravane**-*f*	caravan| trailer
2511	**scotch**-*m*	Scotch tape| whisky
2515	**régiment**-*m*	regiment
2516	**missile**-*adj; m*	missile; missile
2517	**boucher**-*m; vb*	butcher; plug

Numerals

Rank	Italian-PoS	Translation	
10	un-*art; adj; num; prn*	a; one; one; one	art; adj; num; prn
69	deux-*num*	two	num
143	trois-*num*	three	num
274	cinq-*num*	five	num
287	quatre-*num*	four	num
343	six-*num*	six	num
383	dix-*num*	ten	num
493	neuf-*num*	nine	num
555	sept-*num*	seven	num
586	huit-*num*	eight	num
647	mille-*num*	thousand	num
762	deuxième-*num*	second	num
813	cent-*m; num*	cent| hundred	m; num
944	troisième-*num*	third	num
1159	vingt-*num*	twenty	num
1491	centaine-*num*	hundred	num
1574	douze-*num*	twelve	num
1683	milliard-*num*	billion	num
1720	quinze-*num*	fifteen	num
1781	onze-*num*	eleven	num
1792	trente-*num*	thirty	num
2049	quatrième-*num*	fourth	num
2210	cinquante-*num*	fifty	num

Verbs

Rank	French-PoS	Translation
3	être-*vb*	be| exist
14	avoir-*vb; m*	have; asset
37	aller-*vb*	go| travel
39	faire-*vb*	do
45	savoir-*vb; m*	know; knowledge
47	vouloir-*vb*	want| wish
50	dire-*vb*	say| speak
58	pouvoir-*m; vb; av*	power; can; might
68	voir-*vb*	see| view
70	falloir-*vb*	have to
87	venir-*vb*	come
88	croire-*vb*	believe| think
89	devoir-*m; vb; av*	duty; have to; must
99	aimer-*vb*	love| like
105	parler-*vb*	speak| tell
127	penser-*vb*	think| reflect
131	rester-*vb*	stay| keep
133	désoler-*vb*	distress| grieve
136	arriver-*vb*	arrive| happen
138	prendre-*vb*	take| have
139	regarder-*vb*	look| watch
142	passer-*vb*	pass| spend
144	plaire-*vb*	please
153	appeler-*vb*	call| appeal
156	arrêter-*vb*	stop| quit
157	attendre-*vb*	expect| wait for
166	tuer-*vb*	kill| murder
167	partir-*vb*	depart| leave
168	connaître-*vb*	know
169	aider-*vb*	help| support
184	revoir-*vb*	revise
185	entendre-*vb*	hear
186	comprendre-*vb*	understand| include
187	pendre-*vb*	hang
188	trouver-*vb*	find| get
191	demander-*vb*	request| seek
192	chercher-*vb*	search| try
197	sortir-*vb*	exit| come out
201	finir-*vb*	end| finish
205	tenir-*vb*	hold| keep
207	laisser-*vb*	leave| let
213	importer-*vb*	import
219	placer-*vb*	place| put
227	prier-*vb*	pray
229	mettre-*vb*	put| apply
235	perdre-*vb*	lose| waste
239	donner-*vb*	give| yield
244	jouer-*vb*	play| act
247	compter-*vb*	count| expect
248	mourir-*vb*	die| end
258	écouter-*vb*	listen| hear
263	vivre-*vb*	live
266	espérer-*vb*	hope| expect
284	manger-*vb*	eat| feed
289	marcher-*vb*	walk| work
292	envier-*vb*	envy
297	essayer-*vb*	try| attempt
300	tomber-*vb*	fall| drop
313	peiner-*vb*	labor| pain
315	suffire-*vb*	suffice
327	entrer-*vb*	enter
328	rentrer-*vb*	return
331	revenir-*vb*	return| get back
336	téléphoner-*vb*	call
351	adorer-*vb*	worship
353	oublier-*vb*	forget
356	fêter-*vb*	celebrate| feast
358	chérir-*vb*	cherish
360	valoir-*vb*	be worth
363	changer-*vb*	change| switch
365	commencer-*vb*	start| begin
367	travailler-*vb*	work
370	rendre-*vb*	render| restore
371	écrire-*vb*	write
376	montrer-*vb*	show
377	boire-*vb*	drink
382	sembler-*vb*	seem| sound
387	rêver-*vb*	dream
388	armer-*vb*	arm
392	dormir-*vb*	sleep
400	apprendre-*vb*	learn| teach
401	saler-*vb*	salt
410	dîner-*m; vb*	dinner; dine
413	bouillir-*vb*	boil
422	garder-*vb*	keep| maintain
423	tirer-*vb*	take| draw

437	**devenir**-*vb*	become| be	
439	**acheter**-*vb*	buy| take	
445	**gueuler**-*vb*	yell	
447	**bouger**-*vb*	move| budge	
454	**recevoir**-*vb*	receive| take	
455	**promettre**-*vb*	promise	
458	**occuper**-*vb*	occupy| hold	
460	**manquer**-*vb*	miss	
466	**gagner**-*vb*	win| earn	
467	**fondre**-*vb*	melt| merge	
468	**sauver**-*vb*	save	
480	**battre**-*vb*	beat| fight	
488	**monter**-*vb*	mount| climb	
496	**taire**-*vb*	hush up	
510	**retrouver**-*vb*	find| meet	
516	**rencontrer**-*vb*	meet| encounter	
517	**réussir**-*vb*	succeed| pass	
520	**agir**-*vb*	act	
529	**terminer**-*vb*	finish| conclude	
533	**toucher**-*m; vb*	touch; touch	
534	**déjeuner**-*vb; m*	lunch; lunch	
535	**envoyer**-*vb*	send| forward	
536	**lire**-*vb; f*	read; lira	
538	**détester**-*vb*	hate	
541	**décider**-*vb*	decide| choose	
545	**porter**-*vb*	wear| carry	
546	**ignorer**-*vb*	ignore	
550	**supposer**-*vb*	assume| suppose	
553	**jurer**-*vb*	swear	
557	**surprendre**-*vb*	surprise| catch	
560	**commander**-*vb*	order| command	
563	**disparaître**-*vb*	disappear	
564	**ligner**-*vb*	line	
565	**expliquer**-*vb*	explain	
568	**quitter**-*vb*	leave| quit	
580	**suivre**-*vb*	follow	
581	**retourner**-*vb*	return	
582	**offrir**-*vb*	offer| give	
588	**ressembler**-*vb*	look like	
590	**baiser**-*m; vb*	kiss; fuck	
601	**exister**-*vb*	exist	
602	**rire**-*m; vb*	laugh; laugh	
609	**visiter**-*vb*	visit| view	
610	**coucher**-*vb; m*	sleep| lay down; sunset	
611	**imaginer**-*vb*	imagine	
613	**continuer**-*vb*	continue	
614	**voler**-*vb*	fly| steal	
618	**danser**-*vb*	dance	
629	**vendre**-*vb*	sell	
638	**poser**-*vb*	pose| rest	
639	**ouvrir**-*vb*	open| start	
645	**servir**-*vb*	serve| help	
658	**paraître**-*vb*	seem| appear	
660	**asseoir**-*vb*	sit	
667	**préférer**-*vb; av*	prefer; would rather	
669	**protéger**-*vb*	protect| safeguard	
682	**signer**-*vb*	sign	
689	**sentir**-*vb*	feel	
691	**emmener**-*vb*	drive	
694	**unir**-*vb*	unite	
697	**utiliser**-*vb*	use	
700	**marier**-*vb*	marry	
705	**choisir**-*vb*	choose	
707	**intéresser**-*vb*	interest	
710	**descendre**-*vb*	descend| get off	
711	**tourner**-*vb*	turn| rotate	
725	**adresser**-*vb*	address	
726	**sauter**-*vb*	jump| skip	
730	**parier**-*vb*	bet| gamble	
732	**conduire**-*vb*	lead| drive	
743	**présenter**-*vb*	present| offer	
747	**épouser**-*vb*	marry	
759	**chanter**-*vb*	sing	
760	**excuser**-*vb*	excuse| forgive	
765	**cacher**-*vb*	hide| conceal	
766	**répondre**-*vb*	answer	
776	**glacer**-*vb*	glaze| freeze	
781	**machiner**-*vb*	engineer	
785	**naître**-*vb*	be born	
792	**couper**-*vb*	cut	
797	**dégager**-*vb*	free	
798	**ravir**-*vb*	delight| ravish	
806	**déranger**-*vb*	disturb| disrupt	
808	**ramener**-*vb*	bring back	
810	**enquêter**-*vb*	investigate	
812	**signifier**-*vb*	mean| imply	
819	**éviter**-*vb*	avoid| save	
821	**empêcher**-*vb*	prevent| stop	
831	**droguer**-*vb*	drug	

835	**refuser**-*vb*	refuse	1000	**répéter**-*vb*	repeat| rehearse
837	**enchanter**-*vb*	enchant| rejoice	1001	**souhaiter**-*vb*	wish| hope
844	**raconter**-*vb*	tell	1007	**fatiguer**-*vb*	tire| stress
845	**discuter**-*vb*	discuss	1008	**rater**-*vb*	miss| fail
848	**permettre**-*vb*	allow| enable	1010	**assurer**-*vb*	ensure| insure
862	**découvrir**-*vb*	discover	1015	**obliger**-*vb*	force| oblige
864	**tailler**-*vb*	cut| carve	1021	**échapper**-*vb*	escape
872	**détruire**-*vb*	destroy	1026	**coffrer**-*vb*	put away
875	**pleurer**-*vb*	cry| mourn	1037	**attraper**-*vb*	catch| seize
879	**doubler**-*vb*	double	1038	**inquiéter**-*vb*	worry| alarm
884	**remercier**-*vb*	thank	1039	**cesser**-*vb*	stop| desist
888	**remettre**-*vb*	deliver| return	1048	**discourir**-*vb*	discourse
889	**habiter**-*vb*	live in| inhabit	1070	**embrasser**-*vb*	embrace| kiss
890	**apporter**-*vb*	bring	1073	**cibler**-*vb*	target at
894	**fermer**-*vb*	close	1076	**prévenir**-*vb*	warn| inform
896	**amuser**-*vb*	amuse| entertain	1079	**reprendre**-*vb*	resume| retake
899	**réfléchir**-*vb*	reflect| think	1082	**reposer**-*vb*	rest
904	**mentir**-*vb*	lie	1083	**noter**-*vb*	note
905	**courir**-*vb*	run| race	1096	**piloter**-*vb*	pilot
906	**arranger**-*vb*	arrange	1102	**priver**-*vb*	deprive| deny
909	**sourire**-*m; vb*	smile; smile	1110	**fumer**-*vb*	smoke
911	**accepter**-*vb*	accept	1112	**joindre**-*vb*	join| attach
920	**appartenir**-*vb*	behove	1115	**défendre**-*vb*	defend| uphold
921	**préparer**-*vb*	prepare| make	1130	**concerner**-*vb*	concern
922	**regretter**-*vb*	regret| miss	1131	**grandir**-*vb*	grow| augment
924	**inviter**-*vb*	invite| ask	1132	**pousser**-*vb*	push| drive
928	**enlever**-*vb*	remove| take off	1150	**réparer**-*vb*	repair
932	**filer**-*vb*	spin| run	1153	**partager**-*vb*	share| divide
939	**casser**-*vb*	break| crack	1158	**tenter**-*vb*	try| attempt
941	**vérifier**-*vb*	check| verify	1161	**apprécier**-*vb*	appreciate| appraise
945	**dépendre**-*vb*	depend	1163	**créer**-*vb*	create
949	**régler**-*vb*	adjust| settle	1166	**réveiller**-*vb*	wake| awake
950	**flinguer**-*vb*	shoot| whack	1172	**reculer**-*vb*	back| retreat
954	**amener**-*vb*	bring| lead	1174	**coûter**-*vb*	cost
955	**interdire**-*vb*	prohibit| ban	1177	**annoncer**-*vb*	announce| advertise
956	**lever**-*vb; m*	lift| raise; rise	1179	**payer**-*vb*	pay
957	**obtenir**-*vb*	get| obtain	1180	**débarrasser**-*vb*	rid
959	**récupérer**-*vb*	recover	1181	**fuir**-*vb*	flee| escape
960	**prouver**-*vb*	prove	1182	**supplier**-*vb*	beg| entreat
962	**restaurer**-*vb*	restore	1185	**marquer**-*vb*	mark| tag
972	**rejoindre**-*vb*	rejoin	1188	**fesser**-*vb*	spank
984	**pocher**-*vb*	poach	1197	**monnayer**-*vb*	monetize
985	**frapper**-*vb*	hit| knock	1203	**abandonner**-*vb*	abandon| give up
990	**craindre**-*vb*	fear	1231	**piéger**-*vb*	trap| ensnare
993	**remarquer**-*vb*	notice| note			
999	**produire**-*vb*	produce			

1233	**attaquer**-*vb*	attack
1235	**fonctionner**-*vb*	function
1239	**nettoyer**-*vb*	clean| clear
1250	**respirer**-*vb*	breathe
1253	**ennuyer**-*vb*	bore| annoy
1255	**fouler**-*vb*	tread
1258	**atteindre**-*vb*	reach| achieve
1262	**mener**-*vb*	lead| carry on
1263	**lancer**-*vb*	launch
1270	**mesurer**-*vb*	measure
1271	**entreprendre**-*vb*	undertake| initiate
1272	**supporter**-*vb; m*	support| bear; supporter
1275	**commettre**-*vb*	commit
1277	**laver**-*vb*	wash| launder
1285	**reconnaître**-*vb*	recognize| admit
1289	**plaisanter**-*vb*	joke| fun
1290	**crier**-*vb*	shout| shriek
1293	**ressentir**-*vb*	feel| be affected by
1295	**convaincre**-*vb*	convince
1298	**coincer**-*vb*	jam| catch
1302	**remonter**-*vb*	ascend| reassemble
1305	**diriger**-*vb*	direct| run
1310	**haïr**-*vb*	hate
1314	**tromper**-*vb*	deceive| mislead
1315	**souffrir**-*vb*	suffer| experience
1324	**virer**-*vb*	transfer| turn
1327	**maudire**-*vb*	curse
1336	**souper**-*m; vb*	supper; sup
1339	**réserver**-*vb*	book| reserve
1343	**tracer**-*vb*	draw| mark
1344	**recommencer**-*vb*	restart| start again
1345	**traverser**-*vb*	cross| pass through
1348	**sonner**-*vb*	ring| sound
1349	**baguer**-*vb*	ring
1350	**survivre**-*vb*	survive
1355	**charger**-*vb*	load| charge
1362	**voiler**-*vb*	veil| mask
1369	**piger**-*vb*	understand| get
1371	**sucrer**-*vb*	sweeten
1380	**accuser**-*vb*	accuse| blame
1381	**construire**-*vb*	build| erect
1388	**retirer**-*vb*	withdraw| pull
1390	**contrôler**-*vb*	control| monitor
1392	**exploser**-*vb*	explode
1394	**étudier**-*vb*	study| examine
1395	**brûler**-*vb*	burn| burn off
1396	**surveiller**-*vb*	monitor| watch
1406	**représenter**-*vb*	represent
1418	**libérer**-*vb*	release| liberate
1422	**traiter**-*vb*	treat| deal
1426	**pêcher**-*vb; m*	fish; peach
1434	**deviner**-*vb*	guess| divine
1437	**avancer**-*vb*	advance| forward
1444	**bosser**-*vb*	work
1447	**tâcher**-*vb*	try
1450	**engager**-*vb*	engage
1451	**réaliser**-*vb*	realize| achieve
1455	**empreindre**-*vb*	stamp
1459	**barrer**-*vb*	bar| get ouy
1466	**veiller**-*vb*	watch
1475	**baisser**-*vb*	lower| fall
1476	**combattre**-*vb*	combat| fight
1481	**abrutir**-*vb*	stupefy
1497	**divorcer**-*vb*	divorce
1503	**accompagner**-*vb*	accompany| follow
1509	**nommer**-*vb*	appoint| name
1515	**briser**-*vb*	break| shatter
1525	**élever**-*vb*	raise| elevate
1526	**profiter**-*vb*	benefit| avail
1532	**rythmer**-*vb*	rhythm
1534	**proposer**-*vb*	propose| offer
1539	**figurer**-*vb*	figure
1542	**approcher**-*vb*	hang over
1550	**sabler**-*vb*	sand
1553	**nager**-*vb*	swim
1556	**chuter**-*vb*	tumble
1558	**briller**-*vb*	shine| sparkle
1560	**crever**-*vb*	die| burst
1563	**inventer**-*vb*	invent| make up
1564	**étonner**-*vb*	surprise| wonder
1565	**nourrir**-*vb*	feed| nourish
1568	**refaire**-*vb*	redo| repair
1588	**calmer**-*vb*	calm| soothe
1592	**pardonner**-*vb*	forgive| pardon
1593	**affronter**-*vb*	confront
1594	**lâcher**-*vb*	release| drop

1600	**récompenser-**vb	reward
1609	**avouer-**vb	confess| admit
1612	**presser-**vb	press| squeeze
1619	**attenter-**vb	attempt
1623	**moquer-**vb	mock
1627	**installer-**vb	install| set
1631	**poindre-**vb	dawn
1636	**condamner-**vb	condemn| convict
1657	**chasser-**vb	hunt| expel
1661	**traîner-**vb	drag| trail
1667	**blesser-**vb	hurt| cut
1673	**livrer-**vb	deliver
1674	**venger-**vb	revenge
1676	**flotter-**vb	float| hover
1679	**résoudre-**vb	solve| resolve
1681	**remplacer-**vb	replace| change
1685	**plaindre-**vb	complain| pity
1690	**guider-**vb	guide| steer
1691	**gâcher-**vb	spoil| ruin
1700	**botter-**vb	kick
1708	**désirer-**vb	desire| wish
1714	**forcer-**vb	force| compel
1715	**respecter-**vb	respect| observe
1718	**associer-**vb	associate
1719	**bénir-**vb	bless
1721	**posséder-**vb	have| rejoice
1722	**conseiller-**m; vb	advisor| counselor; advise
1726	**voyager-**vb	travel
1727	**attirer-**vb	attract| bring
1728	**poursuivre-**vb	continue| pursue
1734	**assassiner-**vb	murder
1743	**retenir-**vb	retain| hold
1747	**pisser-**vb	piss
1754	**taper-**vb	type| beat
1763	**échouer-**vb	fail| defeat
1765	**risquer-**vb	risk| venture
1767	**remplir-**vb	fill| fill in
1770	**citer-**vb	quote| mention
1771	**huiler-**vb	oil
1776	**fâcher-**vb	upset
1788	**copier-**vb; adj	copy; copying
1790	**énerver-**vb	annoy| fret
1794	**ranger-**m; vb	ranger; put away
1795	**enterrer-**vb	bury| shelve
1796	**assister-**vb	assist
1801	**soigner-**vb	treat
1813	**charmer-**vb	charm| delight
1820	**couvrir-**vb	cover| coat
1825	**tendre-**adj; vb	tender; tender
1828	**alarmer-**vb	alarm
1830	**héler-**vb	hail
1833	**commercer-**vb	trade| deal
1837	**séparer-**vb	separate| part
1839	**employer-**vb	use| employ
1844	**fiancer-**vb	betroth| fiance
1854	**épauler-**vb	support
1864	**poudrer-**vb	powder
1871	**entraîner-**vb	train| drive
1873	**ajouter-**vb	add
1876	**foncer-**vb	charge
1877	**durer-**vb	last
1886	**trahir-**vb	betray
1887	**repartir-**vb	restart| redivide
1891	**pourrir-**vb	rot| decay
1892	**juger-**vb	judge| assess
1895	**admettre-**vb	admit| allow
1899	**promener-**vb	promenade
1907	**exprimer-**vb	express| voice
1909	**causer-**vb	cause| chat
1911	**couler-**vb	flow| cast
1921	**emprunter-**vb	borrow
1925	**écraser-**vb	crush| overwrite
1927	**dégoûter-**vb	disgust| cause disgust
1928	**démarrer-**vb	start| get started
1929	**louer-**vb	rent| let
1941	**déposer-**vb	deposit| file
1945	**gérer-**vb	manage| run
1950	**rapporter-**vb	report| relate
1951	**filmer-**vb	film| shoot
1954	**guérir-**vb	cure| recover
1955	**rouler-**vb	roll
1960	**exiger-**vb	require| demand
1969	**plaquer-**vb	stick| tackle
1970	**réunir-**vb	gather| reunite
1979	**demeurer-**vb	remain| dwell
1983	**emporter-**vb	take| take away
1985	**organiser-**vb	organize| arrange
1987	**oser-**vb	dare
1991	**orchestrer-**vb	orchestrate

1994	**renvoyer**-*vb*	return| send
1999	**participer**-*vb*	participate| involve
2001	**brancher**-*vb*	connect
2002	**influencer**-*vb*	influence
2006	**grouper**-*vb*	group
2010	**éteindre**-*vb*	turn off| put out
2011	**bouffer**-*vb*	eat
2012	**allumer**-*vb*	turn on| light up
2013	**obéir**-*vb*	obey
2015	**sabrer**-*vb*	cut
2018	**décevoir**-*vb*	disappoint| deceive
2020	**résister**-*vb*	resist
2024	**piquer**-*vb*	prick| sting
2026	**accueillir**-*vb*	welcome| host
2028	**examiner**-*vb*	examine
2030	**goutter**-*vb*	drip
2053	**abattre**-*vb*	down| slaughter
2054	**déclarer**-*vb*	declare
2059	**mêler**-*vb*	mix| mingle
2061	**arracher**-*vb*	snatch| extract
2062	**interroger**-*vb*	question| examine
2072	**éclater**-*vb*	burst| erupt
2073	**viser**-*vb*	aim for
2076	**user**-*vb*	use
2077	**insister**-*vb*	insist
2078	**autoriser**-*vb*	authorize
2083	**pleuvoir**-*vb*	rain
2085	**conclure**-*vb*	conclude
2087	**contacter**-*vb*	contact
2088	**identifier**-*vb*	identify
2089	**attacher**-*vb*	attach| fasten
2096	**enfermer**-*f; vb*	lock; confine
2100	**câbler**-*vb*	wire
2102	**goûter**-*vb*	taste
2103	**disputer**-*vb*	compete| fight
2104	**impliquer**-*vb*	involve| implicate
2110	**être à la traîne**-*vb*	fall behind
2112	**délirer**-*vb*	rave
2117	**rompre**-*vb*	break| break up
2118	**rattraper**-*vb*	catch up| make up
2122	**suggérer**-*vb*	suggest| imply
2129	**admirer**-*vb*	admire
2137	**opérer**-*vb*	operate| carry out
2142	**tonner**-*vb*	thunder
2145	**déplacer**-*vb*	move| travel
2146	**serrer**-*vb*	tighten| clamp
2163	**appuyer**-*vb*	support| press
2165	**concentrer**-*vb*	focus| concentrate
2185	**estimer**-*vb*	estimate
2187	**éliminer**-*vb*	eliminate
2192	**débrouiller**-*vb*	untangle
2194	**tarder**-*vb*	delay
2206	**oindre**-*vb*	anoint
2214	**oxygéner**-*vb*	oxygenate| bleach
2216	**analyser**-*vb*	analyze
2220	**adjoindre**-*vb*	adjoin
2222	**annuler**-*vb*	cancel
2230	**statuer**-*vb*	rule
2234	**éloigner**-*vb*	drive away
2238	**ordonner**-*vb*	order| direct
2240	**creuser**-*vb*	dig
2241	**mordre**-*vb*	bite| snap
2242	**contenir**-*vb*	contain| restrain
2244	**bourrer**-*vb*	stuff| fill
2245	**rembourser**-*vb*	repay| reimburse
2246	**masser**-*vb*	massage
2252	**rigoler**-*vb*	laugh
2253	**informer**-*vb*	inform| advise
2254	**saluer**-*vb*	greet
2256	**satisfaire**-*vb*	satisfy| please
2257	**avaler**-*vb*	swallow
2259	**planter**-*vb*	plant
2268	**destiner**-*vb*	destine| mean
2269	**renoncer**-*vb*	renounce| give up
2280	**accomplir**-*vb*	accomplish
2283	**rouer**-*vb*	cane
2287	**mélanger**-*vb*	mix
2288	**endormir**-*vb*	put to sleep
2289	**cuisiner**-*vb*	cook
2291	**déconner**-*vb*	screw| talk rubbish
2297	**relever**-*vb*	raise| pick up
2300	**fabriquer**-*vb*	manufacture| make
2305	**menacer**-*vb*	threaten| lurk
2316	**transformer**-*vb*	transform| change
2317	**ramasser**-*vb*	pick up
2318	**avertir**-*vb*	warn| inform
2322	**vaincre**-*vb*	overcome| defeat
2328	**peindre**-*vb*	paint

2334	**douter**-*vb*	doubt
2338	**enseigner**-*vb*	teach| educate
2346	**prêter**-*vb*	lend| attribute
2351	**fouiller**-*vb*	search| ransack
2357	**détendre**-*vb*	loosen
2359	**interrompre**-*vb*	interrupt| stop
2363	**élire**-*vb*	elect
2369	**indiquer**-*vb*	indicate| show
2380	**ramer**-*vb*	row
2382	**patienter**-*vb*	wait
2383	**vomir**-*vb*	vomit
2390	**fringuer**-*vb*	dress
2391	**améliorer**-*vb*	improve| enhance
2392	**observer**-*vb*	observe| watch
2406	**lier**-*vb*	link| bind
2407	**maintenir**-*vb*	maintain| sustain
2414	**envelopper**-*vb*	envelop| wrap up
2417	**témoigner**-*vb*	testify| give evidence
2419	**embêter**-*vb*	bother| worry
2441	**casquer**-*vb*	fork out| pay up
2447	**fasciner**-*vb*	fascinate
2449	**plancher**-*m; vb*	floor; floor
2450	**subir**-*vb*	undergo| suffer
2460	**confier**-*vb*	entrust
2461	**boxer**-*m; vb*	boxer; box
2468	**enregistrer**-*vb*	register| log
2472	**déménager**-*vb*	move
2476	**effacer**-*vb*	delete
2477	**loger**-*vb*	accommodate| house
2485	**coter**-*vb*	mark
2491	**soutenir**-*vb*	support| back
2501	**établir**-*vb*	establish
2513	**concevoir**-*vb*	design| conceive
2517	**boucher**-*m; vb*	butcher; plug
2518	**niquer**-*vb*	fuck
2522	**épuiser**-*vb*	exhaust| drain
2523	**former**-*vb*	form| train
2524	**sucer**-*vb*	suck| suck out
2525	**considérer**-*vb*	consider

Alphabetical order

Rank	French-PoS	Translation
1203	abandonner-*vb*	abandon| give up
2053	abattre-*vb*	down| slaughter
311	abord-*m*	first| start
1248	abri-*m*	shelter| shed
1481	abrutir-*vb*	stupefy
1597	absence-*f*	absence
506	absolu-*adj*	absolute| total
1641	absurde-*adj; m*	absurd; absurd
2144	accent-*m*	accent
911	accepter-*vb*	accept
1242	accès-*m*	access
523	accident-*m*	accident
1503	accompagner-*vb*	accompany| follow
2280	accomplir-*vb*	accomplish
85	accord-*m*	agreement| deal
2026	accueillir-*vb*	welcome| host
2282	accueil-*m*	welcome
2022	accusation-*f*	charge| accusation
1380	accuser-*vb*	accuse| blame
439	acheter-*vb*	buy| take
1898	acier-*m*	steel
1806	acte-*m*	act| certificate
1169	acteur-*m*	actor
847	action-*f*	action| effort
2200	activité-*f*	activity
2376	actuellement-*adv*	currently| now
2128	adaptation-*f*	adaptation
729	adieu-*m*	farewell
2220	adjoindre-*vb*	adjoin
1895	admettre-*vb*	admit| allow
2342	administration-*f*	administration| management
2129	admirer-*vb*	admire
1402	adorable-*adj*	adorable
351	adorer-*vb*	worship
725	adresser-*vb*	address
1692	adulte-*adj; m/f*	adult; adult
2375	adversaire-*adj; m/f*	opponent; opponent
1105	aéroport-*m*	airport
294	affaire-*f*	case| matter
2373	affection-*f*	affection| ailment
1279	affreux-*adj*	frightful| dreadful
1593	affronter-*vb*	confront
411	âge-*m*	age
1579	agence-*f*	agency
489	agent-*m; adj*	agent; cooperative
520	agir-*vb*	act
1084	agréable-*adj*	pleasant| nice
146	Ah!-*int*	Ha!
231	aide-*f*	aid| relief
169	aider-*vb*	help| support
2008	Aie!-*int*	Ouch!
1668	aile-*f*	wing| blade
471	ailleurs-*adv*	somewhere else
1689	aimable-*adj*	friendly| kind
99	aimer-*vb*	love| like
276	ainsi-*adv; con*	thus| thereby; as
141	air-*m*	air
1111	aise-*adj; f*	pleased; pleasure
1873	ajouter-*vb*	add
1828	alarmer-*vb*	alarm
2039	album-*m*	album
997	alcool-*m*	alcohol
1288	alerte-*adj; f*	alert; alert
1191	allemand-*adj; m/mpl*	German; German
37	aller-*vb*	go| travel
1883	alliance-*f*	alliance
479	Allô!-*int*	Hello!
2012	allumer-*vb*	turn on| light up
59	alors-*adv*	then
1791	altesse-*f*	highness
1759	amant-*m*	lover
2303	ambassadeur-*m; adj*	ambassador; ambassadorial
1484	ambulance-*f*	ambulance
513	âme-*f*	soul
2391	améliorer-*vb*	improve| enhance
954	amener-*vb*	bring| lead
1384	amen-*m*	amen
733	américain-*adj*	American
1818	amiral-*m*	admiral
1329	amitié-*f*	friendship
632	amoureux-*adj; m*	in love; lover
162	amour-*m*	love
1139	amusant-*adj*	amusing
896	amuser-*vb*	amuse| entertain
2216	analyser-*vb*	analyze

2475	**ancêtre**-*m/f*	ancestor
969	**ancien**-*adj; m; pfx*	former| ancient; former; ex-
824	**ange**-*m*	angel
554	**anglais**-*adj; m/mpl*	English; English
2114	**angle**-*m*	angle| corner
913	**Angleterre**-*m*	England
827	**animal**-*adj; m*	animal; animal
103	**an**-*m*	year
2466	**anneau**-*m*	ring
283	**année**-*f*	year
525	**anniversaire**-*adj; m*	anniversary; anniversary
1177	**annoncer**-*vb*	announce| advertise
2222	**annuler**-*vb*	cancel
2459	**antenne**-*f*	antenna
2173	**août**-*m*	August
942	**appareil**-*m*	apparatus
1088	**apparemment**-*adv*	apparently
763	**appartement**-*m*	apartment
920	**appartenir**-*vb*	behove
153	**appeler**-*vb*	call| appeal
524	**appel**-*m*	call| appeal
1835	**appétit**-*m*	appetite
890	**apporter**-*vb*	bring
1161	**apprécier**-*vb*	appreciate| appraise
400	**apprendre**-*vb*	learn| teach
641	**approche**-*f*	approach
1542	**approcher**-*vb*	hang over
2163	**appuyer**-*vb*	support| press
106	**après**-*adv; prp*	after| next; after
13	**à**-*prp*	to
2490	**arabe**-*adj; m*	Arab; Arabic
916	**arbre**-*m*	tree| shaft
123	**argent**-*m*	money
2211	**armé**-*adj*	armed
463	**arme**-*f*	weapon
388	**armer**-*vb*	arm
2061	**arracher**-*vb*	snatch| extract
906	**arranger**-*vb*	arrange
1753	**arrestation**-*f*	arrest| detention
156	**arrêter**-*vb*	stop| quit
931	**arrêt**-*m*	stop| stopping
136	**arriver**-*vb*	arrive| happen
1077	**article**-*m*	art
1162	**artiste**-*m/f*	artist
718	**art**-*m*	art
1540	**ascenseur**-*m*	elevator| lifter
1984	**asile**-*m*	asylum
1734	**assassiner**-*vb*	murder
1054	**assassin**-*m; adj*	assassin; bloodthirsty
2463	**assaut**-*m*	assault
660	**asseoir**-*vb*	sit
160	**assez**-*adv*	enough| quite
2487	**assiette**-*f*	plate| dish
1838	**assis**-*adj*	seated
1796	**assister**-*vb*	assist
2425	**association**-*f*	association
1718	**associer**-*vb*	associate
1358	**assurance**-*f*	insurance| assurance
1010	**assurer**-*vb*	ensure| insure
2324	**atelier**-*m*	workshop| studio
2304	**atmosphère**-*f*	atmosphere
2089	**attacher**-*vb*	attach| fasten
589	**attaque**-*f*	attack
1233	**attaquer**-*vb*	attack
1258	**atteindre**-*vb*	reach| achieve
157	**attendre**-*vb*	expect| wait for
1032	**attendu**-*adj*	expected
1619	**attenter**-*vb*	attempt
190	**attention**-*f*	attention
1727	**attirer**-*vb*	attract| bring
1640	**attitude**-*f*	attitude| outlook
1254	**attrape**-*f*	catch
1037	**attraper**-*vb*	catch| seize
1296	**aube**-*f*	dawn| blade
224	**aucun**-*adj; prn*	no; none
1998	**audience**-*f*	audience
2483	**audition**-*f*	hearing| performance
1764	**auparavant**-*adv*	before
1440	**auprès**-*adv*	nearby
249	**aura**-*f*	aura
67	**aussi**-*adv; con*	also| as; and
330	**autant**-*con*	as far as
1694	**auteur**-*m*	author
1809	**auto**-*f*	auto
2232	**automne**-*m*	fall| autumn
1733	**autorisation**-*f*	authorization| permission
2078	**autoriser**-*vb*	authorize
1861	**autorité**-*f*	authority
2130	**autoroute**-*f*	highway

562	**autour**-*adv*	around
1583	**autrefois**-*adv*	once| in the past
1062	**autrement**-*adv*	otherwise
71	**autre**-*prn; adj; adv*	other; another; else
2257	**avaler**-*vb*	swallow
537	**avance**-*f*	advance| lead
1437	**avancer**-*vb*	advance| forward
95	**avant**-*adv; prp; adj; m*	before; before; front
1917	**avantage**-*m*	advantage
35	**avec**-*prp*	with
630	**avenir**-*m*	future
1460	**aventure**-*f*	adventure
2318	**avertir**-*vb*	warn| inform
2455	**avertissement**-*m*	warning
951	**aveugle**-*adj; m/f*	blinded; blind
436	**avion**-*m*	aircraft
389	**avis**-*m*	opinion| notice
552	**avocat**-*m*	lawyer
14	**avoir**-*vb; m*	have; asset
1609	**avouer**-*vb*	confess| admit
1897	**avril**-*m*	April

B

1812	**baby**-*m*	baby
1317	**bagage**-*m*	luggage
1669	**bagarre**-*f*	fight| brawl
1643	**bagnole**-*f*	wagon| wheel
1349	**baguer**-*vb*	ring
2227	**bail**-*m*	lease| long time
803	**bain**-*m*	bath
590	**baiser**-*m; vb*	kiss; fuck
1475	**baisser**-*vb*	lower| fall
2457	**balade**-*f*	ride| walk
1878	**balance**-*f*	balance
933	**balle**-*f*	ball| bullet
1247	**ballon**-*m*	ball
1086	**bal**-*m*	ball
595	**bande**-*f*	band| strip
648	**banque**-*f*	bank
1701	**barbe**-*f*	beard
679	**bar**-*m*	bar| bass
1752	**baron**-*m*	baron
1459	**barrer**-*vb*	bar| get ouy

147	**bas**-*adj; m*	low| base; bottom
775	**base**-*f*	base| basis
1045	**bataille**-*f*	battle
2190	**bâtard**-*adj; m*	bastard; bastard
429	**bateau**-*m*	boat
1351	**bâtiment**-*m*	building| vessel
1930	**bâton**-*m*	stick| baton
2237	**batterie**-*f*	battery
480	**battre**-*vb*	beat| fight
210	**beau**-*adj; m*	beautiful| nice; beautiful
110	**beaucoup**-*prn; adj; adv*	many; much; much
723	**beauté**-*f*	beauty
279	**bébé**-*m*	baby| kid
1719	**bénir**-*vb*	bless
96	**besoin**-*m*	need
1975	**bétail**-*m*	livestock| cattle
628	**bête**-*f; adj*	beast| idiot; stupid
1622	**bêtise**-*f*	foolishness
1832	**beurre**-*m*	butter
1672	**Bible**-*f*	Bible
1789	**bibliothèque**-*f*	library
2492	**bidon**-*m*	can| drum
27	**bien**-*adv; m; adj*	well| very; good; right
295	**bientôt**-*adv*	soon| almost
685	**bière**-*f*	beer
1604	**bijou**-*m*	jewel
992	**billet**-*m*	ticket
1300	**bite**-*f*	cock| knob
465	**bizarre**-*adj*	weird| bizarre
666	**blague**-*f*	joke
526	**blanc**-*adj; m*	white| albescent; white
1923	**blé**-*m*	wheat
713	**blessé**-*adj; m*	injured; casualty
1667	**blesser**-*vb*	hurt| cut
1703	**blessure**-*f*	injury
902	**bleu**-*adj; m*	blue; blue
2265	**bloc**-*m*	block| unit
1654	**blond**-*adj; m*	blond; blonde
377	**boire**-*vb*	drink
380	**bois**-*m*	wood| timber
2294	**boisson**-*f*	drink
622	**boîte**-*f*	box| can
1748	**bol**-*m; m*	bowl; circumstance
807	**bombe**-*f*	bomb
61	**bon**-*adj; m; adv*	good| well; voucher; then

1949	**bonbon**-*m*	candy	2100	**câbler**-*vb*	wire
1757	**bond**-*m*	leap| jump	765	**cacher**-*vb*	hide| conceal
662	**bonheur**-*m; adj*	happiness; welfare	1499	**cadavre**-*m*	corpse| body
2143	**bonhomme**-*m*	fellow| old man	549	**cadeau**-*m*	gift
126	**Bonjour!**-*int*	Hello!	2482	**cadre**-*m*	framework| frame
318	**Bonsoir!**-*int*	Good evening!	357	**café**-*m*	cafe| coffee
1940	**bonté**-*f*	goodness	1707	**cage**-*f*	cage| shaft
492	**bordel**-*m*	mess| brothel	1196	**caisse**-*f*	fund| register
540	**bord**-*m*	edge| board	324	**calme**-*adj; m*	quiet| calm; calm
1304	**bosse**-*f*	bump| lump	1588	**calmer**-*vb*	calm| soothe
1444	**bosser**-*vb*	work	1266	**camarade**-*m/f*	comrade| fellow
1537	**boss**-*m*	boss	2319	**came**-*f*	cam
1700	**botter**-*vb*	kick	915	**caméra**-*f*	camera
616	**bouche**-*f*	mouth	811	**camion**-*m*	truck| lorry
2517	**boucher**-*m; vb*	butcher; plug	996	**campagne**-*f*	campaign
2158	**boue**-*f*	mud	459	**camp**-*m*	camp
2011	**bouffer**-*vb*	eat	1997	**Canada**-*f*	Canada
447	**bouger**-*vb*	move| budge	2052	**canapé**-*m*	couch
413	**bouillir**-*vb*	boil	2079	**canard**-*m*	duck
1655	**boule**-*f*	ball	1533	**cancer**-*m*	cancer
271	**boulot**-*m*	job| work	1404	**canon**-*m*	gun
2180	**Boum!**-*int*	Bang!	755	**capable**-*adj*	capable| competent
2244	**bourrer**-*vb*	stuff| fill	293	**capitaine**-*m*	captain
1687	**bourse**-*f*	scholarship	2307	**capital**-*adj; m*	capital; capital
971	**bouteille**-*f*	bottle	1517	**cap**-*m*	cape| course
1528	**bouton**-*m*	button	2151	**caporal**-*m*	lance corporal
2461	**boxer**-*m; vb*	boxer; box	2043	**ça**-*prn*	it
2001	**brancher**-*vb*	connect	1933	**caractère**-*m*	character| nature
354	**bras**-*m*	arm	2509	**caravane**-*f*	caravan| trailer
1364	**brave**-*adj; m*	brave| good; brave	1807	**cardiaque**-*adj; m/f*	cardiac; heart patient
599	**Bravo!**-*int*	Bravo!	215	**car**-*m*	car
1245	**bref**-*adj; adv*	short| brief; in short	2331	**carrément**-*adv*	downright
2233	**brigade**-*f*	brigade	1006	**carrière**-*f*	career
1558	**briller**-*vb*	shine| sparkle	485	**carte**-*f*	map| card
1848	**brise**-*f*	breeze| breath	2306	**casier**-*m*	locker
1515	**briser**-*vb*	break| shatter	2277	**casino**-*m*	casino
2168	**britannique**-*adj*	British	217	**cas**-*m*	case| event
1395	**brûler**-*vb*	burn| burn off	2441	**casquer**-*vb*	fork out| pay up
2504	**budget**-*m*	budget	973	**casse**-*f*	case| breakage| robbery
310	**bureau**-*m*	office| desk	939	**casser**-*vb*	break| crack
620	**but**-*m*	purpose| goal	1663	**cassette**-*f*	cassette
			2409	**catastrophe**-*f*	disaster
	C		2368	**catholique**-*adj; m/f*	Catholic; Catholic
1606	**cabine**-*f*	cabin| cab	1328	**cauchemar**-*m*	nightmare
1755	**cabinet**-*m*	cabinet			

267	**cause**-*f*	cause| case	843	**chapeau**-*m*	hat
1909	**causer**-*vb*	cause| chat	216	**chaque**-*adj; prn*	each; either
2443	**caution**-*f*	deposit| bail	832	**charge**-*f*	load| charge
1662	**cave**-*f; adj*	cellar; hollow	1355	**charger**-*vb*	load| charge
334	**ceci**-*prn; adj*	this; following	2248	**chariot**-*m*	cart| trolley
1557	**ceinture**-*f*	belt| waistband	2286	**charité**-*f*	charity
19	**cela**-*prn*	it| that	1081	**charmant**-*adj; m*	charming| lovely; cunning
1072	**célèbre**-*adj*	celebrated| popular	1813	**charmer**-*vb*	charm| delight
1934	**célibataire**-*adj; m/f*	single| bachelor; single	929	**chasse**-*f*	hunting| chase
1424	**cellule**-*f*	cell	1657	**chasser**-*vb*	hunt| expel
278	**celui**-*prn*	that	2027	**chasseur**-*m; adj*	hunter; gunner's
2308	**cendre**-*f*	ash	1085	**château**-*m*	castle| chateau
1491	**centaine**-*num*	hundred	796	**chat**-*m*	cat
813	**cent**-*m; num*	cent| hundred	519	**chaud**-*adj*	hot| warm
1586	**central**-*adj*	central	1184	**chauffeur**-*m*	driver| chauffeur
683	**centre**-*m*	center| focus	2473	**chaussette**-*f*	sock
1485	**cependant**-*con; adv*	however| yet; though	825	**chaussure**-*f*	shoe
16	**ce**-*prn; adj*	this; that	275	**chef**-*m*	chief| leader
1959	**cercle**-*m*	circle| ring	412	**chemin**-*m*	path| road
2204	**cercueil**-*m*	coffin	1352	**chèque**-*m*	check
1595	**cérémonie**-*f*	ceremony	369	**cher**-*adj; m*	expensive| dear; dear
452	**certain**-*adj*	certain	192	**chercher**-*vb*	search| try
791	**certainement**-*adv*	definitely	237	**chéri**-*adj; m*	darling| precious; honey
738	**cerveau**-*m*	brain| brains	358	**chérir**-*vb*	cherish
1821	**cervelle**-*f*	brain| brains	2014	**chevalier**-*m*	knight
1039	**cesser**-*vb*	stop| desist	500	**cheval**-*m*	horse
558	**chacun**-*prn; adv*	each; apiece	462	**cheveu**-*m*	hair
2164	**chagrin**-*m*	grief| heartache	100	**chez**-*prp*	in| by
1325	**chaîne**-*f*	chain| string	1590	**chic**-*adj; m*	chic| stylish; chic
1171	**chair**-*f*	flesh	323	**chien**-*m*	dog
1208	**chaise**-*f*	chair	1858	**chiffre**-*m*	figure| number
1216	**chaleur**-*f*	heat	1340	**Chine**-*f*	China
1646	**chambre**-*f*	room	989	**chinois**-*adj; m*	Chinese; Chinese
1175	**champagne**-*m*	champagne	1229	**choc**-*m*	shock
1117	**champion**-*adj; m*	champion; champion	1211	**chocolat**-*m*	chocolate
858	**champ**-*m*	field	705	**choisir**-*vb*	choose
171	**chance**-*f*	chance| luck	404	**choix**-*m*	choice| selection
2157	**chanceux**-*adj; m*	fortunate; lucky man	145	**chose**-*f*	thing
1243	**changement**-*m*	change| changing	1207	**chouette**-*f; adj*	owl; neat
363	**changer**-*vb*	change| switch	1222	**chou**-*m*	cabbage
583	**chanson**-*f*	song	1220	**Christ**-*m*	Christ
759	**chanter**-*vb*	sing	1452	**Chut!**-*int*	Hush!
2196	**chant**-*m*	singing| song	1556	**chuter**-*vb*	tumble
2095	**chaos**-*m*	chaos	1073	**cibler**-*vb*	target at
			419	**ciel**-*m*	sky| heaven

2415	**cigare**-*m*	cigar
1152	**cigarette**-*f*	cigarette
1750	**cimetière**-*m*	graveyard
756	**cinéma**-*m*	cinema
1403	**cinglé**-*adj*	crazy
274	**cinq**-*num*	five
2210	**cinquante**-*num*	fifty
2386	**circuit**-*m*	circuit
2440	**circulation**-*f*	circulation
1448	**cirque**-*m*	circus
1770	**citer**-*vb*	quote| mention
1961	**citoyen**-*m*	citizen
2429	**civil**-*adj*	civil
2454	**civilisation**-*f*	civilization
531	**clair**-*adj*	clear| bright
1745	**clairement**-*adv*	clearly
1889	**clan**-*m*	clan
570	**classe**-*f*	class| classroom
1751	**classique**-*adj; m*	classic| standard; classic
650	**clé**-*adj; f*	key; key
871	**client**-*m*	customer| client
2037	**clinique**-*adj; f*	clinical; clinic
1454	**clocher**-*m*	bell tower
2354	**clown**-*m*	knockabout
676	**club**-*m*	club
2170	**coach**-*m*	trainer
1498	**cochon**-*m; adj*	pig| swine; dirty
333	**cœur**-*m*	heart| core
1026	**coffrer**-*vb*	put away
1298	**coincer**-*vb*	jam| catch
2171	**coïncidence**-*f*	coincidence
511	**coin**-*m*	corner| wedge
727	**colère**-*f*	anger| passion
2141	**collection**-*f*	collection
1624	**colle**-*f*	glue
2262	**collège**-*m*	college
1882	**collier**-*m*	necklace
1731	**colline**-*f*	hill
512	**colonel**-*m*	colonel
606	**combat**-*m*	combat
1476	**combattre**-*vb*	combat| fight
172	**combien**-*adv*	how many
2315	**combinaison**-*f*	combination| suit
1756	**comédie**-*f*	comedy
1474	**comité**-*m*	committee| panel
2150	**commande**-*f*	order
1680	**commandement**-*m*	command
560	**commander**-*vb*	order| command
41	**comme**-*con; prp; adj*	as; as; such as
365	**commencer**-*vb*	start| begin
60	**comment**-*adv*	how
1833	**commercer**-*vb*	trade| deal
2405	**commercial**-*adj*	commercial
1275	**commettre**-*vb*	commit
1287	**commissaire**-*m*	commissioner
2213	**commissariat**-*m*	police station
1551	**commission**-*f*	commission| board
1412	**commun**-*adj*	common| joint
1706	**communauté**-*adj; f*	community; community
2162	**communication**-*f*	communication
2212	**communiste**-*adj; m/f*	Communist; Communist
603	**compagnie**-*f*	company
2442	**compétition**-*f*	competition
1490	**complet**-*adj; m*	full| complete; suit
530	**complètement**-*adv*	completely| fully
2120	**complexe**-*adj; m*	complex; complex
1378	**compliqué**-*adj*	complicated| difficult
1598	**comportement**-*m*	behavior
186	**comprendre**-*vb*	understand| include
1125	**compte**-*m*	account
247	**compter**-*vb*	count| expect
1389	**comte**-*m*	count
1967	**comté**-*m*	county
2165	**concentrer**-*vb*	focus| concentrate
1810	**concernant**-*adv; prp*	concerning; concerning
1130	**concerner**-*vb*	concern
1322	**concert**-*m*	concert
2513	**concevoir**-*vb*	design| conceive
2085	**conclure**-*vb*	conclude
1636	**condamner**-*vb*	condemn| convict
1572	**condition**-*f*	condition
732	**conduire**-*vb*	lead| drive
1811	**conférence**-*f; adj*	conference; lecturing
306	**confiance**-*f*	confidence| faith
2460	**confier**-*vb*	entrust
2478	**conflit**-*m*	conflict

1884	**congé**-*m*	leave	716	**coupable**-*adj; m/f*	guilty; culprit
1863	**congrès**-*m*	conference	792	**couper**-*vb*	cut
430	**con**-*m; adj*	cunt| prick; bloody	1056	**couple**-*m*	couple| pair
1052	**connaissance**-*f*	knowledge| acquaintance	176	**coup**-*m*	blow| shot
168	**connaître**-*vb*	know	754	**courage**-*m*	courage
593	**connard**-*m*	prick	1536	**courageux**-*adj*	courageous| brave
608	**connerie**-*f*	bullshit	427	**courant**-*adj; m*	current| running; current
1075	**conscience**-*f*	consciousness| conscience	655	**cour**-*f*	court
1722	**conseiller**-*m; vb*	advisor| counselor; advise	905	**courir**-*vb*	run| race
668	**conseil**-*m*	board| council	1992	**couronne**-*f*	crown
2005	**conséquence**-*f*	consequence	1530	**courrier**-*m*	mail| courier
2525	**considérer**-*vb*	consider	787	**course**-*f*	race| running
2397	**construction**-*f*	construction	805	**court**-*adj; m*	short| brief; court
1381	**construire**-*vb*	build| erect	1074	**cousin**-*m*	cousin
2087	**contacter**-*vb*	contact	881	**couteau**-*m*	knife
764	**contact**-*m*	contact	1174	**coûter**-*vb*	cost
2242	**contenir**-*vb*	contain| restrain	1614	**couvert**-*adj; m*	covered; place
432	**content**-*adj*	content| happy	1260	**couverture**-*f*	coverage| cover
448	**continu**-*adj*	continuous	1820	**couvrir**-*vb*	cover| coat
613	**continuer**-*vb*	continue	990	**craindre**-*vb*	fear
836	**contraire**-*adj; m*	contrary; contrary	1968	**crainte**-*f*	fear
869	**contrat**-*m*	contract	1415	**crâne**-*m*	skull| cranium
183	**contre**-*prp*	against	2058	**cran**-*m*	notch
577	**contrôle**-*m*	control| check	2336	**création**-*f*	creation
1390	**contrôler**-*vb*	control| monitor	1393	**créature**-*f*	creature| being
1295	**convaincre**-*vb*	convince	1480	**crédit**-*m*	credit
1095	**conversation**-*f*	conversation| talk	1163	**créer**-*vb*	create
876	**copain**-*m; adj*	boyfriend| buddy; pally	1024	**crétin**-*m; adj*	cretin; moronic
1788	**copier**-*vb; adj*	copy; copying	2240	**creuser**-*vb*	dig
1249	**corde**-*f*	rope	1560	**crever**-*vb*	die| burst
261	**corps**-*m*	body	1290	**crier**-*vb*	shout| shriek
1599	**correct**-*adj; adv*	correct; alright	1471	**cri**-*m*	cry| scream
2389	**correctement**-*adv*	correctly	659	**crime**-*m*	crime
			1487	**criminel**-*adj; m*	criminal; criminal
1225	**côte**-*f*	coast	953	**crise**-*f*	crisis| attack
241	**côté**-*m*	side	1805	**critique**-*adj; f*	critical; review
2485	**coter**-*vb*	mark	88	**croire**-*vb*	believe| think
1267	**couche**-*f*	layer| bed	1456	**croix**-*f*	cross
610	**coucher**-*vb; m*	sleep| lay down; sunset	478	**cru**-*adj; m*	vintage| raw; vineyard
2046	**coucou**-*adj; m; int*	cuckoo; cuckoo; hello	1972	**cruel**-*adj*	cruel
			2344	**cuir**-*m*	leather
1911	**couler**-*vb*	flow| cast	633	**cuisine**-*f*	kitchen| cuisine
859	**couleur**-*f*	color	2289	**cuisiner**-*vb*	cook
1615	**couloir**-*m*	corridor| hallway	2520	**cuit**-*adj*	cooked| baked
965	**cou**-*m*	neck	317	**cul**-*m*	ass

2488	**culpabilité**-*f*	guilt
1777	**culture**-*f*	culture
1333	**curieux**-*adj; m*	curious; onlooker
2341	**curiosité**-*f*	curiosity

D

1982	**dalle**-*f*	slab| flagstone
507	**dame**-*f*	lady
575	**dangereux**-*adj*	dangerous
635	**danger**-*m*	danger
618	**danser**-*vb*	dance
26	**dans**-*prp; adv*	in; aboard
1059	**date**-*f*	date
1374	**davantage**-*adv*	further
1	**de**-*prp*	of| from
1276	**de là**-*adv*	thence| therefrom
1180	**débarrasser**-*vb*	rid
1432	**débile**-*adj; m/f*	stupid; defective
498	**debout**-*adj*	standing
2192	**débrouiller**-*vb*	untangle
446	**début**-*m*	beginning| debut
2258	**décembre**-*m*	December
2500	**décès**-*m*	death| demise
2018	**décevoir**-*vb*	disappoint| deceive
541	**décider**-*vb*	decide| choose
757	**décision**-*f*	decision
1656	**déclaration**-*f*	declaration
2054	**déclarer**-*vb*	declare
2291	**déconner**-*vb*	screw| talk rubbish
862	**découvrir**-*vb*	discover
325	**dedans**-*adv; prp; m*	in; in; inside
1115	**défendre**-*vb*	defend| uphold
770	**défense**-*f*	defense| prohibition
2183	**défi**-*m*	challenge
797	**dégager**-*vb*	free
2070	**dégât**-*m*	damage
1927	**dégoûter**-*vb*	disgust| cause disgust
1902	**degré**-*m*	degree
269	**dehors**-*adv; m*	outside| out; outside
117	**déjà**-*adv*	already
534	**déjeuner**-*vb; m*	lunch; lunch
1420	**délicieux**-*adj*	delicious
2112	**délirer**-*vb*	rave
152	**demain**-*adv; m*	tomorrow; tomorrow

191	**demander**-*vb*	request| seek
1928	**démarrer**-*vb*	start| get started
2472	**déménager**-*vb*	move
1979	**demeurer**-*vb*	remain| dwell
1286	**demi**-*adj; m*	half; half
2427	**demoiselle**-*f*	young lady
1458	**démon**-*m*	daemon
777	**dent**-*f*	tooth
2451	**dentiste**-*m/f*	dentist
2019	**département**-*m*	department
701	**départ**-*m*	departure| starting
945	**dépendre**-*vb*	depend
1978	**dé**-*pfx*	un-| in-
2145	**déplacer**-*vb*	move| travel
1941	**déposer**-*vb*	deposit| file
2384	**dépression**-*f*	depression
113	**depuis**-*adv; prp*	since; since
806	**déranger**-*vb*	disturb| disrupt
250	**dernier**-*adj; m*	last| latter; last
299	**derrière**-*adv; m; prp*	behind; behind; behind
2186	**désastre**-*m*	disaster
710	**descendre**-*vb*	descend| get off
1122	**désert**-*m*	desert
1708	**désirer**-*vb*	desire| wish
1341	**désir**-*m*	desire| wish
133	**désoler**-*vb*	distress| grieve
1120	**désormais**-*adv*	henceforth
381	**dès**-*prp*	from| since
2408	**dessert**-*m*	dessert
1976	**dessin**-*m*	drawing| design
987	**dessous**-*adv; m; prp*	beneath; underside; under it
232	**dessus**-*adv*	over
2279	**destination**-*f*	destination
2268	**destiner**-*vb*	destine| mean
861	**destin**-*m*	destiny
1862	**destruction**-*f*	destruction
1100	**détail**-*m*	detail
1495	**détective**-*m*	detective
2357	**détendre**-*vb*	loosen
538	**détester**-*vb*	hate
872	**détruire**-*vb*	destroy
1869	**dette**-*f*	debt
762	**deuxième**-*num*	second
69	**deux**-*num*	two

228	**devant**-*adv; prp; m*	before| past; before; front
437	**devenir**-*vb*	become| be
1434	**deviner**-*vb*	guess| divine
89	**devoir**-*m; vb; av*	duty; have to; must
548	**diable**-*m; adj*	devil; wretched
1981	**diamant**-*m*	diamond
91	**dieu**-*m*	god
897	**différence**-*f*	difference
690	**différent**-*adj*	different
391	**difficile**-*adj*	difficult
1632	**digne**-*adj*	worthy
2379	**dignité**-*f*	dignity
934	**dimanche**-*m*	Sunday
410	**dîner**-*m; vb*	dinner; dine
686	**dingue**-*adj; m/f*	crazy| wild; loon
1106	**direct**-*adj; adv*	direct; straight
1283	**directement**-*adv*	directly| right
728	**directeur**-*m*	director
885	**direction**-*f*	direction| management
50	**dire**-*vb*	say| speak
1305	**diriger**-*vb*	direct| run
2428	**discipline**-*f*	discipline
1048	**discourir**-*vb*	discourse
1826	**discussion**-*f*	discussion| debate
845	**discuter**-*vb*	discuss
563	**disparaître**-*vb*	disappear
2410	**disparition**-*f*	disappearance
2507	**disponible**-*adj; adv*	available; on call
2103	**disputer**-*vb*	compete| fight
2023	**disque**-*m*	disk| discus
1274	**distance**-*f*	distance| range
2069	**divin**-*adj*	divine
1905	**division**-*f*	division| split
1497	**divorcer**-*vb*	divorce
383	**dix**-*num*	ten
285	**docteur**-*m*	doctor
1841	**document**-*m*	document
940	**doigt**-*m*	finger
305	**dollar**-*m*	dollar| greenback
1762	**do**-*m*	do
1742	**domaine**-*m*	field| domain
642	**dommage**-*m*	damage| pity
119	**donc**-*con; adv*	therefore; consequently
673	**don**-*m*	gift| donation
1294	**donné**-*adj*	given
239	**donner**-*vb*	give| yield
265	**dont**-*prn*	whose
392	**dormir**-*vb*	sleep
2339	**dose**-*f*	dose| measure
514	**dos**-*m*	back| reverse
826	**dossier**-*m*	folder| file
879	**doubler**-*vb*	double
521	**doucement**-*adv*	gently| slowly
2355	**douceur**-*f*	sweetness| softness
1215	**douche**-*f*	shower
1618	**doué**-*adj*	gifted| capable
838	**douleur**-*f*	pain
349	**doute**-*m*	doubt
2334	**douter**-*vb*	doubt
892	**doux**-*adj*	soft| sweet
1574	**douze**-*num*	twelve
1870	**dragon**-*m*	dragon
1761	**drapeau**-*m*	flag
2413	**drap**-*m*	sheet
2166	**drogue**-*f*	drug
831	**droguer**-*vb*	drug
240	**droit**-*adj; m; adv*	right; right; due
339	**drôle**-*adj*	funny
1816	**duc**-*m*	duke
309	**dur**-*adj*	hard| tough
938	**durant**-*prp*	during
1877	**durer**-*vb*	last

E

214	**eau**-*f*	water
2361	**écart**-*m*	gap| difference
1178	**échange**-*m*	exchange| swap
1021	**échapper**-*vb*	escape
1775	**échec**-*m*	failure| check
1958	**échelle**-*f*	scale| ladder
1763	**échouer**-*vb*	fail| defeat
2416	**éclair**-*m*	lightning
2072	**éclater**-*vb*	burst| erupt
281	**école**-*f*	school
2284	**économie**-*f*	economy| economics
258	**écouter**-*vb*	listen| hear
1555	**écran**-*m*	screen
1925	**écraser**-*vb*	crush| overwrite
371	**écrire**-*vb*	write

2221	écriture-*f*	writing	1450	engager-*vb*	engage
1713	écrivain-*m*	writer	928	enlever-*vb*	remove| take off
1650	éducation-*f*	education| upbringing	702	ennemi-*m; adj*	enemy| hostile; inimical
2476	effacer-*vb*	delete	619	ennui-*m*	boredom| trouble
490	effet-*m*	effect	1253	ennuyer-*vb*	bore| annoy
2063	efficace-*adj*	effective| efficacious	2108	ennuyeux-*adj*	boring| annoying
1645	effort-*m*	effort| stress	919	énorme-*adj*	huge| enormous
1398	égal-*adj; m*	equal| even; equal	2311	énormément-*adv*	enormously
1143	également-*adv*	also| equally	17	en-*prp; adv*	in; thereof
721	église-*f*	church	810	enquêter-*vb*	investigate
2396	égoïste-*adj; m/f*	selfish; egoist	2438	enregistrement-*m*	recording
1894	électricité-*f*	electricity	2468	enregistrer-*vb*	register| log
1793	électrique-*adj*	electric	2113	enseigne-*f*	sign
2060	élément-*m*	element	2338	enseigner-*vb*	teach| educate
2471	éléphant-*m*	elephant	221	ensemble-*adv; m; f*	together; ensemble; collection
1573	élève-*m/f*	student	393	ensuite-*adv*	then| later
1525	élever-*vb*	raise| elevate	185	entendre-*vb*	hear
2187	éliminer-*vb*	eliminate	1626	enterrement-*m*	burial| funeral
2363	élire-*vb*	elect	1795	enterrer-*vb*	bury| shelve
28	elle-*prn*	she| it	842	entier-*adj*	whole| full
2234	éloigner-*vb*	drive away	1786	entièrement-*adv*	entirely| quite
2419	embêter-*vb*	bother| worry	1519	entraînement-*m*	training
1070	embrasser-*vb*	embrace| kiss	1871	entraîner-*vb*	train| drive
1202	émission-*f*	emission| transmission	2327	entraîneur-*m*	coach
691	emmener-*vb*	drive	149	entre-*adv; prp*	between; between
2045	émotion-*f*	emotion	1271	entreprendre-*vb*	undertake| initiate
821	empêcher-*vb*	prevent| stop	327	entrer-*vb*	enter
1320	empereur-*m*	emperor	2025	entretien-*m*	maintenance| conversation
1431	empire-*m*	empire	2414	envelopper-*vb*	envelop| wrap up
1252	emploi-*m*	employment	822	envers-*m*	back| against
1839	employer-*vb*	use| employ	292	envier-*vb*	envy
1983	emporter-*vb*	take| take away	717	environ-*adv; prp; adj*	about; around; all but
1455	empreindre-*vb*	stamp	2337	environnement-*m*	environment
1921	emprunter-*vb*	borrow	535	envoyer-*vb*	send| forward
900	enceinte-*adj; f*	pregnant; enclosure	1854	épauler-*vb*	support
837	enchanter-*vb*	enchant| rejoice	1156	épée-*f*	sword
73	encore-*adv*	still| again	2465	épisode-*m*	episode| part
2288	endormir-*vb*	put to sleep	627	époque-*f*	time| age
260	endroit-*m*	place| spot	747	épouser-*vb*	marry
918	énergie-*f*	energy	2231	époux-*m*	husband| spouse
1790	énerver-*vb*	annoy| fret	1787	épreuve-*f*	test| trial
1326	enfance-*f*	childhood			
159	enfant-*m*	child			
596	enfer-*m*	hell			
2096	enfermer-*f; vb*	lock; confine			
253	enfin-*adv*	finally| after all			

2522	**épuiser**-*vb*	exhaust| drain	819	**éviter**-*vb*	avoid| save
1584	**équipage**-*m*	crew	559	**exact**-*adj*	exact
372	**équipe**-*f*	team| crew	355	**exactement**-*adv*	exactly| accurately
2276	**équipement**-*m*	equipment| gear	1523	**examen**-*m*	examination| review
2084	**ère**-*f*	era	2028	**examiner**-*vb*	examine
470	**erreur**-*f*	error| mistake	1749	**excellence**-*f*	excellence
1724	**escalier**-*m*	staircase| stairs	815	**excellent**-*adj*	excellent
1648	**esclave**-*m; adj*	slave; enslaved	2106	**exception**-*f*	exception
908	**espace**-*m*	space	2050	**excitant**-*adj; m*	exciting; upper
1915	**espagnol**-*adj; m/mpl*	Spanish; Spanish	1033	**excuse**-*f*	excuse
443	**espèce**-*f*	species| kind	760	**excuser**-*vb*	excuse| forgive
266	**espérer**-*vb*	hope| expect	1890	**exécution**-*f*	execution| implementation
2007	**espion**-*m*	spy	605	**exemple**-*m*	example| sample
719	**espoir**-*m*	hope	1739	**exercice**-*m*	exercise| fiscal year
374	**esprit**-*m*	mind| spirit	1960	**exiger**-*vb*	require| demand
1664	**essai**-*m*	test| testing	1502	**existence**-*f*	existence| life
297	**essayer**-*vb*	try| attempt	601	**exister**-*vb*	exist
1146	**essence**-*f*	gasoline| essence	737	**expérience**-*f*	experience
2218	**essentiel**-*adj; m*	essential; main	1860	**expert**-*adj; m*	expert; expert
2185	**estimer**-*vb*	estimate	1638	**ex-**-*pfx*	ex-
1561	**estomac**-*m*	stomach	1725	**explication**-*f*	explanation| explication
2501	**établir**-*vb*	establish	565	**expliquer**-*vb*	explain
2086	**étape**-*f*	step| stage	1392	**exploser**-*vb*	explode
379	**état**-*m*	state| condition	1370	**explosion**-*f*	explosion| blast
2360	**etc.**-*adv*	et cetera	1736	**exprès**-*adj; adv*	express; on purpose
12	**et**-*con*	and	1874	**expression**-*f*	expression
2010	**éteindre**-*vb*	turn off| put out	1907	**exprimer**-*vb*	express| voice
2411	**éternel**-*adj*	eternal	1121	**extérieur**-*adj; m*	outside| exterior; outside
1769	**éternité**-*f*	eternity| lifetime	2424	**extra**-*adj; m*	extra; extra
1078	**étoile**-*f*	star| blaze	1368	**extraordinaire**-*adj*	extraordinary
1564	**étonner**-*vb*	surprise| wonder	1880	**extrêmement**-*adv*	extremely
604	**étrange**-*adj*	strange			
995	**étranger**-*adj; m*	foreign| overseas; foreigner			
2110	**être à la traîne**-*vb*	fall behind		**F**	
3	**être**-*vb*	be| exist	2300	**fabriquer**-*vb*	manufacture| make
1218	**étude**-*f*	study	2133	**fabuleux**-*adj*	fabulous
1607	**étudiant**-*adj; m*	student; student	1261	**fac**-*abr*	uni
1394	**étudier**-*vb*	study| examine	414	**face**-*f*	face| front
457	**Euh!**-*int*	Haw!	1776	**fâcher**-*vb*	upset
203	**eux**-*prn*	them	345	**facile**-*adj*	easy| simple
2064	**événement**-*m*	event	1307	**facilement**-*adv*	easily
1273	**évidemment**-*adv*	obviously	255	**façon**-*f*	way| method
2403	**évidence**-*f*	evidence	1034	**faible**-*adj; m*	low| weak; weakling
1365	**évident**-*adj*	obvious| evident	912	**failli**-*adj; m*	bankrupt

435	**faim**-*f*	hunger
39	**faire**-*vb*	do
840	**fait**-*m; adj*	fact; ripe
70	**falloir**-*vb*	have to
2365	**fameux**-*adj*	famous
179	**famille**-*f*	family
1964	**fan**-*m*	fan
1004	**fantastique**-*adj*	fantastic
1168	**fantôme**-*m; adj*	ghost; phantom
2447	**fasciner**-*vb*	fascinate
1007	**fatiguer**-*vb*	tire| stress
352	**faute**-*f*	fault
2138	**fauteuil**-*m*	armchair
494	**faux**-*adj*	false| fake
1219	**faveur**-*f*	favor
709	**félicitation**-*f*	congratulation
97	**femme**-*f*	woman
1819	**fenêtre**-*f*	window
1097	**fer**-*m*	iron
1932	**fermé**-*adj*	closed| sealed
320	**ferme**-*f; adj*	farm; firm
894	**fermer**-*vb*	close
1188	**fesser**-*vb*	spank
1947	**fête**-*f*	party
356	**fêter**-*vb*	celebrate| feast
2418	**feuille**-*f*	sheet| leaf
243	**feu**-*m*	fire
1379	**fiancé**-*m; adj*	fiance; engaged
1844	**fiancer**-*vb*	betroth| fiance
2464	**fiche**-*f*	plug| card
1740	**fichu**-*adj; m*	damn| rotten; scarf
1908	**fidèle**-*adj; m/f*	faithful| loyal; stalwart
761	**fier**-*adj*	proud
1906	**fierté**-*f*	pride
1814	**fièvre**-*f*	fever
1539	**figurer**-*vb*	figure
932	**filer**-*vb*	spin| run
116	**fille**-*f*	daughter| girl
2398	**fillette**-*f*	little girl
936	**fil**-*m*	thread| lead
1951	**filmer**-*vb*	film| shoot
256	**film**-*m*	film| cinema
1846	**final**-*adj; m*	final| ultimate; finale
923	**finalement**-*adv*	finally
234	**fin**-*f; adj*	end; fine
1224	**fini**-*adj; m*	finished| finite; finish
201	**finir**-*vb*	end| finish
1035	**fiston**-*m*	son
2446	**fixé**-*adj*	fixed| appointed
2264	**flamme**-*f*	flame
742	**fleur**-*f*	flower
1834	**fleuve**-*m*	river| stream
551	**flic**-*m*	cop
950	**flinguer**-*vb*	shoot| whack
1676	**flotter**-*vb*	float| hover
2203	**foie**-*m*	liver
883	**foi**-*f*	faith
2489	**foire**-*f*	fair
968	**folie**-*f*	madness| folly
1876	**foncer**-*vb*	charge
2362	**fonction**-*f*	function
1235	**fonctionner**-*vb*	function
467	**fondre**-*vb*	melt| merge
1737	**football**-*m*	football
1649	**foot**-*m*	football
421	**force**-*f*	force| power
1587	**forcément**-*adv*	necessarily
1714	**forcer**-*vb*	force| compel
1116	**forêt**-*f*	forest
1996	**formation**-*f*	training| formation
539	**forme**-*f*	form| shape
2523	**former**-*vb*	form| train
774	**formidable**-*adj*	tremendous| fantastic
257	**fort**-*adj; m; adv*	strong| loud; fort; highly
1067	**fortune**-*f*	fortune| wealth
262	**fou**-*adj; m*	crazy; fool
2351	**fouiller**-*vb*	search| ransack
1255	**fouler**-*vb*	tread
2260	**four**-*m*	oven
2378	**foutu**-*adj*	bloody| damn
1360	**foyer**-*m*	home| fireplace
2486	**fragile**-*adj*	fragile
851	**frais**-*mpl; adj*	costs; fresh
2047	**franc**-*adj; m*	frank; franc
786	**français**-*adj; m/mpl*	French; French
1151	**franchement**-*adv*	honestly| openly
977	**frappé**-*adj*	hit| struck
985	**frapper**-*vb*	hit| knock
199	**frère**-*m*	brother
509	**fric**-*m*	money| cash

2098	**frigo**-*m*	fridge
2390	**fringuer**-*vb*	dress
473	**froid**-*adj; m*	cold| cool; cold
1505	**fromage**-*m*	cheese
1301	**frontière**-*f*	border| frontier
1205	**front**-*m*	front| forehead
1684	**fruit**-*m*	fruit
1181	**fuir**-*vb*	flee| escape
1110	**fumer**-*vb*	smoke
2394	**fumier**-*m*	manure
2496	**funérailles**-*adj; fpl*	funeral; funeral
1746	**furieux**-*adj; m*	furious; madman
1016	**fusil**-*m*	rifle
1029	**futur**-*adj; m*	future; future

G

1691	**gâcher**-*vb*	spoil| ruin
1040	**gaffe**-*f*	blunder
1831	**gagnant**-*m; adj*	winner; winning
466	**gagner**-*vb*	win| earn
677	**gamin**-*m; adj*	kid; kiddy
1784	**gang**-*m*	gang
2107	**gant**-*m*	glove
1541	**garage**-*m*	garage
1995	**garce**-*f*	bitch
272	**garçon**-*m*	boy| lad
1375	**gardé**-*adj*	guarded
307	**garde**-*f; adj*	custody| guard; guarding
422	**garder**-*vb*	keep| maintain
1405	**gardien**-*m*	keeper| guardian
991	**gare**-*f*	station| train station
170	**gars**-*m*	guy
1050	**gâteau**-*m*	cake
431	**gauche**-*adj; f*	left; left
1044	**gaz**-*m*	gas
1704	**géant**-*adj; m*	giant; giant
1425	**gêne**-*f*	discomfort| embarrasment
348	**général**-*adj; m*	general; general
2219	**génération**-*f*	generation
1944	**généreux**-*adj*	generous| liberal
384	**génial**-*adj*	great| brilliant
1061	**génie**-*m*	genius| genie
1071	**genou**-*m*	knee
233	**genre**-*m*	kind| gender

118	**gens**-*mpl*	people
359	**gentil**-*adj; m*	nice| kind; gentile
2066	**gentleman**-*m; adj*	gentleman; gentlemanly
1945	**gérer**-*vb*	manage| run
1281	**geste**-*m*	gesture| movement
776	**glacer**-*vb*	glaze| freeze
1241	**gloire**-*f*	glory| fame
1799	**golf**-*m*	golf
1098	**gorge**-*f*	throat
749	**gosse**-*m/f; adj*	kid| brat; kiddy
2102	**goûter**-*vb*	taste
895	**goût**-*m*	taste| flavor
2030	**goutter**-*vb*	drip
636	**gouvernement**-*m*	government| ministry
1183	**gouverneur**-*m*	governor
450	**grâce**-*f*	grace| favor
154	**grand**-*adj*	large| wide
1131	**grandir**-*vb*	grow| augment
2431	**gras**-*adj; m*	fat; fat
2167	**gratuit**-*adj*	free
425	**grave**-*adj*	serious| grave
2205	**gris**-*adj; m*	gray; gray
246	**gros**-*adj; m*	large| fat; fat man
487	**groupe**-*m*	group| band
2006	**grouper**-*vb*	group
1954	**guérir**-*vb*	cure| recover
225	**guerre**-*f*	war
2325	**guerrier**-*m; adj*	warrior; warlike
445	**gueuler**-*vb*	yell
1690	**guider**-*vb*	guide| steer
1845	**guitare**-*f*	guitar

H

793	**Ha!**-*int*	Ha!
1918	**habitant**-*m; adj*	inhabitant; resident
889	**habiter**-*vb*	live in| inhabit
573	**habitude**-*f*	habit
1356	**haine**-*f; adj*	hatred; heating
1310	**haïr**-*vb*	hate
1538	**hall**-*m*	lobby| lounge
2172	**halte**-*f*	stop| stopover
1018	**hasard**-*m*	chance| accident
1383	**hâte**-*f*	haste| hastiness

277	**haut**-*adj; m; adv*	high; top; in heaven
1774	**hauteur**-*f*	height| pitch
151	**Hé!**-*int*	Hey!
1830	**héler**-*vb*	hail
2479	**hélicoptère**-*m*	helicopter
163	**heure**-*f*	time
1228	**heureusement**-*adv*	fortunately| happily
270	**hier**-*adv*	yesterday; yesterday
196	**histoire**-*f*	history| story
2514	**historique**-*adj*	historical
1155	**hiver**-*m*	winter
92	**homme**-*m*	man| person
947	**honnête**-*adj*	honest
2182	**honnêtement**-*adv*	honestly
420	**honneur**-*m*	honor| credit
578	**honte**-*f*	shame
1896	**Hop!**-*int*	Poof!
449	**hôpital**-*m*	hospital
1118	**horreur**-*f*	horror
804	**horrible**-*adj*	horrible
621	**hors**-*prp*	except
481	**hôtel**-*m*	hotel
1771	**huiler**-*vb*	oil
586	**huit**-*num*	eight
714	**humain**-*adj; m*	human; human
1346	**humanité**-*f*	humanity
1439	**humeur**-*f*	mood| spirit
1677	**humour**-*m*	humor

I

44	**ici**-*adv*	here
1571	**idéal**-*adj; m*	ideal; ideal
181	**idée**-*f*	idea
2088	**identifier**-*vb*	identify
1214	**identité**-*f*	identity
444	**idiot**-*m; adj*	idiot; silly
546	**ignorer**-*vb*	ignore
853	**île**-*f*	island
2135	**illégal**-*adj*	illegal
2508	**illusion**-*f*	illusion
11	**il**-*prn*	he, it
926	**image**-*f*	image
1435	**imagination**-*f*	imagination

611	**imaginer**-*vb*	imagine
829	**imbécile**-*m/f; adj*	imbecile; stupid
779	**immédiatement**-*adv*	immediately
1966	**immense**-*adj*	immense| great
1323	**immeuble**-*m; adj*	building; immovable
2469	**impact**-*m*	impact
2104	**impliquer**-*vb*	involve| implicate
794	**importance**-*f*	importance| significance
312	**important**-*adj*	important
213	**importer**-*vb*	import
344	**impossible**-*adj*	impossible
2116	**impôt**-*m*	tax
579	**impression**-*f*	printing| impression
2021	**impressionnant**-*adj*	impressive| awesome
1760	**incapable**-*adj*	unable| incapable
1566	**incendie**-*m*	fire
1730	**incident**-*adj; m*	incident; incident
1483	**inconnu**-*m; adj*	unknown; unfamiliar
503	**incroyable**-*adj*	incredible| amazing
1977	**Inde**-*f*	India
2335	**indice**-*m*	index
1521	**indien**-*adj*	Indian
2369	**indiquer**-*vb*	indicate| show
2126	**industrie**-*f*	industry
1445	**infirmier**-*m*	male nurse
2002	**influencer**-*vb*	influence
1028	**information**-*f*	information
2253	**informer**-*vb*	inform| advise
2195	**ingénieur**-*m*	engineer
1904	**injuste**-*adj*	unfair| wrong
1194	**innocent**-*adj; m*	innocent; innocent
1108	**in--**-*pfx*	un-
416	**inquiet**-*adj*	worried| concerned
1038	**inquiéter**-*vb*	worry| alarm
2077	**insister**-*vb*	insist
652	**inspecteur**-*m*	inspector
1627	**installer**-*vb*	install| set
296	**instant**-*m; adj*	moment| while; urgent
2115	**instinct**-*m*	instinct
1903	**instruction**-*f*	instruction| education
1943	**intelligence**-*f*	intelligence| intellect
1123	**intelligent**-*adj*	intelligent
964	**intention**-*f*	intention| mind
955	**interdire**-*vb*	prohibit| ban

748	**intéressant**-*adj*	interesting		656	**juge**-*m*	judge| beak
707	**intéresser**-*vb*	interest		1695	**jugement**-*m*	judgment| trial
706	**intérêt**-*m*	interest		1892	**juger**-*vb*	judge| assess
501	**intérieur**-*adj; m*	inside| interior; inside		1206	**juif**-*adj*	Jewish
2062	**interroger**-*vb*	question| examine		1865	**juillet**-*m*	July
2359	**interrompre**-*vb*	interrupt| stop		1926	**juin**-*m*	June
2421	**interview**-*f*	interview		1688	**jungle**-*f*	jungle
687	**inutile**-*adj*	unnecessary| useless		1732	**junior**-*m*	junior
1563	**inventer**-*vb*	invent| make up		553	**jurer**-*vb*	swear
2074	**invisible**-*adj*	invisible		1591	**jury**-*m*	jury
1893	**invitation**-*f*	invitation		1494	**jus**-*m*	juice
1570	**invité**-*m*	guest		81	**juste**-*adj; adv*	just| fair; just
924	**inviter**-*vb*	invite| ask		927	**justement**-*adv*	rightly| exactly
1817	**italien**-*adj; m*	Italian; Italian		735	**justice**-*f*	justice| law
1829	**ivre**-*adj*	drunk				

J

K

				1712	**kilo**-*m*	kilo
1441	**jaloux**-*adj*	jealous		823	**kilomètre**-*m*	kilometer
66	**jamais**-*adv*	never| ever				
768	**jambe**-*f*	leg				
1173	**japonais**-*adj; m|mpl*	Japanese; Japanese		**L**		
1477	**Japon**-*m*	Japan		48	**là**-*adv*	there
974	**jardin**-*m*	garden		7	**la**-*art; prn*	the; it
1465	**jaune**-*adj; m*	yellow; yellow		1547	**labo**-*m*	lab
2	**je**-*prn*	I		2290	**laboratoire**-*m*	laboratory
1316	**jean**-*m*	jeans		724	**lâche**-*m; adj*	coward; cowardly
772	**Jésus**-*m*	Jesus		1594	**lâcher**-*vb*	release| drop
773	**jeté**-*adj*	thrown		1164	**lac**-*m*	lake
1535	**jeudi**-*m*	Thursday		207	**laisser**-*vb*	leave| let
319	**jeu**-*m*	game		873	**lait**-*m*	milk
236	**jeune**-*adj; m*	young; youth		2506	**lame**-*f*	blade
1577	**jeunesse**-*f*	youth		1859	**lampe**-*f*	lamp
1124	**job**-*m*	job		1113	**lance**-*f*	lance| hose
799	**joie**-*f*	joy		2430	**lancement**-*m*	launching| start
1112	**joindre**-*vb*	join| attach		1263	**lancer**-*vb*	launch
486	**joli**-*adj*	pretty		1779	**langage**-*m*	language
1092	**joue**-*f*	cheek		828	**langue**-*f*	language
244	**jouer**-*vb*	play| act		1347	**lapin**-*m*	rabbit
2193	**jouet**-*adj; m*	toy; toy		1629	**large**-*adj*	wide| large
1410	**joueur**-*m*	player		1256	**larme**-*f*	tear| drop
120	**jour**-*m*	day		1800	**las**-*adj*	tired
1468	**journaliste**-*m/f*	journalist| reporter		2302	**lave**-*f*	lava
640	**journal**-*m*	newspaper| journal		1277	**laver**-*vb*	wash| launder
304	**journée**-*f*	day		2426	**leader**-*m*	leader| head
				5	**le**-*art; prn*	the; it

1167	**leçon**-*f*	lesson		1581	**loup**-*m*	wolf
2320	**lecture**-*f*	reading		1386	**lourd**-*adj*	heavy
2452	**légal**-*adj*	legal		2402	**loyauté**-*f*	loyalty
1699	**légende**-*f*	legend| caption		1802	**loyer**-*m*	rent
1980	**léger**-*adj*	light| lightweight		46	**lui**-*prn*	him
2519	**légitime**-*adj*	legitimate		497	**lumière**-*f*	light| spotlight
1335	**lendemain**-*m*	next day		1148	**lundi**-*m*	Monday
1430	**lentement**-*adv*	slowly| leisurely		615	**lune**-*f*	moon
698	**lequel**-*prn*	which		1291	**lunettes**-*fpl*	glasses
504	**lettre**-*f*	letter		1514	**lutte**-*f*	fight| struggle
94	**leur**-*prn*	their		2247	**luxe**-*m*	luxury
1094	**levé**-*adj*	survey; lifted		935	**lycée**-*m*	high school
956	**lever**-*vb; m*	lift| raise; rise				
1217	**lèvre**-*f*	lip			**M**	
1840	**liaison**-*f*	link| affair				
1418	**libérer**-*vb*	release| liberate		1548	**machine**-*f*	machine
653	**liberté**-*f*	freedom| liberty		781	**machiner**-*vb*	engineer
491	**libre**-*adj*	free| open		2364	**machin**-*m*	gadget| thingy
1504	**lien**-*m*	link| connection		254	**Madame**-*f*	madame| Mrs
2406	**lier**-*vb*	link| bind		338	**Mademoiselle**-*abr; f*	Ms.; miss
361	**lieu**-*m*	place| venue		841	**magasin**-*m*	store| shop
625	**lieutenant**-*m*	lieutenant		1766	**magazine**-*m*	magazine
1723	**ligne**-*f*	line| design		2235	**magicien**-*m*	magician
564	**ligner**-*vb*	line		1330	**magie**-*f*	magic
1716	**limite**-*f*	limit		1469	**magique**-*adj*	magic
2134	**linge**-*m*	washing		515	**magnifique**-*adj*	magnificent
1879	**lion**-*m*	lion		1226	**mai**-*m*	May
1436	**liquide**-*adj; m*	liquid| wet; liquid		220	**main**-*f*	hand
536	**lire**-*vb; f*	read; lira		72	**maintenant**-*adv*	now
693	**liste**-*f*	list		2407	**maintenir**-*vb*	maintain| sustain
329	**lit**-*m*	bed		1147	**maire**-*m*	mayor
2207	**livraison**-*f*	delivery		24	**mais**-*con; adv*	but; probably
399	**livre**-*m*	book		124	**maison**-*f*	house| home
1673	**livrer**-*vb*	deliver		346	**maître**-*m*	master| teacher
2477	**loger**-*vb*	accommodate| house		788	**majesté**-*f*	majesty
1531	**logique**-*f; adj*	logic; logical		1068	**major**-*m*	adjutant| matiére principale
502	**loi**-*f*	law				
242	**loin**-*adv; adj*	far; distant		362	**malade**-*adj; m*	sick| invalid; patient
442	**long**-*adj*	long		983	**maladie**-*f*	disease| illness
209	**longtemps**-*adv; adj*	for a long time; longtime		2480	**mâle**-*adj; m*	male| masculine; male
771	**longue**-*adj*	long		2174	**malédiction**-*f*	curse
981	**lors**-*adv*	then| while		975	**malgré**-*prp; adv*	despite; all the same
801	**lorsque**-*prp*	during		1210	**malheureusement**-*adv*	unfortunately| unhappily
2152	**lot**-*m*	lot| prize		1508	**malheureux**-*adj; m*	unfortunate| unhappy; unfortunate
1929	**louer**-*vb*	rent| let				

1232	**malheur**-*m*	misfortune
886	**malin**-*adj; m*	malignant| smart; evil
104	**mal**-*m; adv; adj*	evil| wrong; amiss; untimely
130	**maman**-*f*	mom
1910	**mamie**-*f*	granny| nanny
2239	**manche**-*m; f*	handle; sleeve
1682	**mandat**-*m*	mandate| warrant
284	**manger**-*vb*	eat| feed
767	**manière**-*f*	way| form
460	**manquer**-*vb*	miss
1190	**manteau**-*m*	coat| mantle
1971	**manuel**-*adj; m*	manual; manual
2467	**maquillage**-*m*	makeup
2148	**marche**-*f*	walking
289	**marcher**-*vb*	walk| work
1520	**mardi**-*m*	Tuesday
326	**mariage**-*m*	marriage
700	**marier**-*vb*	marry
252	**mari**-*m*	husband
1438	**marin**-*adj; m*	marine; marine
1338	**marine**-*f*	navy
1185	**marquer**-*vb*	mark| tag
1091	**marrant**-*adj; m*	funny; funny guy
1234	**mars**-*f*	March
1602	**masque**-*m*	mask
2223	**massacre**-*m*	massacre
2246	**masser**-*vb*	massage
715	**match**-*m*	match| game
1462	**matériel**-*m; adj*	equipment| material; material
1938	**matière**-*f*	material
2296	**matinée**-*f*	morning
230	**matin**-*m*	morning
1327	**maudire**-*vb*	curse
347	**mauvais**-*adj; m*	bad| ill; brute
1644	**maximum**-*adj; m*	maximum; maximum
1974	**méchant**-*adj; m*	wicked| bad; naughty child
208	**mec**-*m*	guy| dude
2201	**médaille**-*f*	medal
1855	**médecine**-*f*	medicine
543	**médecin**-*m; adj*	doctor; doctoral
2470	**médias**-*mpl*	media
2323	**médical**-*adj*	medical
1414	**médicament**-*m*	drug| medication
302	**meilleur**-*m; adj*	best; better
2287	**mélanger**-*vb*	mix
2059	**mêler**-*vb*	mix| mingle
1140	**membre**-*m*	member
64	**même**-*adj; adv*	same; even
874	**mémoire**-*m; f*	dissertation; memory
1201	**menace**-*f*	threat
2305	**menacer**-*vb*	threaten| lurk
1473	**ménage**-*m*	household| housework
1262	**mener**-*vb*	lead| carry on
1238	**mensonge**-*m*	lie
1199	**menteur**-*m; adj*	liar| lying; lying
904	**mentir**-*vb*	lie
2448	**menu**-*m; adj*	menu; small
25	**me**-*prn*	me| myself
65	**merci**-*m; int*	thanks; thanks
1857	**mercredi**-*m*	Wednesday
114	**mère**-*f*	mother
542	**mer**-*f*	sea
910	**mérite**-*m*	merit| worth
2159	**merveille**-*f*	wonder| marvel
612	**merveilleux**-*adj*	wonderful
451	**message**-*m*	message
2156	**mesure**-*f*	measure| step
1270	**mesurer**-*vb*	measure
2278	**métal**-*m*	metal
2121	**méthode**-*f*	method
982	**métier**-*m*	trade| job
903	**mètre**-*m*	meter
1875	**métro**-*m*	subway
229	**mettre**-*vb*	put| apply
2377	**meuble**-*m*	furniture| charge
532	**meurtre**-*m*	murder
1522	**meurtrier**-*m; adj*	murderer; murderous
2031	**micro**-*f; pfx*	mike; micro-
544	**midi**-*m; adj*	noon; midday
1559	**miel**-*m*	honey
789	**mien**-*adj*	mine
108	**mieux**-*adv; adj*	better; adj
880	**mignon**-*adj*	cute| sweet
1357	**mile**-*m*	mile
680	**milieu**-*m*	medium
1058	**militaire**-*adj; m*	military; soldier
647	**mille**-*num*	thousand
1683	**milliard**-*num*	billion
424	**million**-*m*	million
1665	**minable**-*adj; m/f*	shabby| pathetic; piddling

1144	**mince**-*adj*	thin| slim
1080	**mine**-*f*	mine| lead
1735	**ministère**-*m*	ministry
1041	**ministre**-*m*	minister
1138	**minuit**-*m*	midnight
251	**minute**-*f*	minute
1160	**miracle**-*m*	miracle
1589	**miroir**-*m*	mirror
2370	**misérable**-*adj; m/f*	miserable; wretch
2343	**misère**-*f*	misery
2516	**missile**-*adj; m*	missile; missile
567	**mission**-*f*	mission| assignment
2250	**mobile**-*adj*	mobile
1653	**moche**-*adj*	ugly
1423	**modèle**-*adj; m*	model; model
1126	**mode**-*m; f*	mode; fashion
1866	**moderne**-*adj*	modern
925	**moindre**-*adj*	lesser
148	**moins**-*adv; m; prp*	less; minus; wanting
21	**moi**-*prn; m*	me; ego
556	**moitié**-*adv; f*	half; half
2340	**môme**-*m*	kid| brat
161	**moment**-*m*	time| moment
84	**monde**-*m*	world
1942	**mondial**-*adj*	global
1197	**monnayer**-*vb*	monetize
33	**mon**-*prn*	my
111	**Monsieur**-*abr; m*	Mr.; sir
783	**monstre**-*m; adj*	monster; monstrous
1003	**montagne**-*f*	mountain
488	**monter**-*vb*	mount| climb
376	**montrer**-*vb*	show
1623	**moquer**-*vb*	mock
1822	**moral**-*adj; m*	moral; morale
937	**morceau**-*m*	piece| track
2241	**mordre**-*vb*	bite| snap
107	**mort**-*adj; f*	dead; death
2123	**motel**-*m*	motel
1149	**moteur**-*m; adj*	engine; motor
2399	**motif**-*m*	pattern| ground
322	**mot**-*m*	word
1705	**moto**-*f*	motorcycle
2004	**mouche**-*f*	fly| spot
248	**mourir**-*vb*	die| end
2404	**mouton**-*m*	sheep
1213	**mouvement**-*m*	movement| stir
528	**moyen**-*m; adj*	means| medium; medium
1924	**munition**-*f*	munition
720	**mur**-*m*	wall
1605	**mystère**-*m*	mystery
2512	**mystérieux**-*adj*	mysterious

N

1553	**nager**-*vb*	swim
1042	**naissance**-*f*	birth| rise
785	**naître**-*vb*	be born
1331	**nana**-*f*	girl| babe
1601	**national**-*adj; m*	national; national
1545	**nation**-*f*	nation
751	**nature**-*f*	nature
1582	**naturel**-*adj; m*	natural; nature
1678	**naturellement**-*adv*	naturally
1359	**navire**-*m*	ship
15	**ne**-*adv*	not
870	**nécessaire**-*adj*	necessary
2071	**négatif**-*adj; m*	negative; negative
2367	**nègre**-*adj; m*	Negro; nigger
1019	**neige**-*f*	snow
1836	**nerf**-*m*	nerve
1104	**nerveux**-*adj*	nervous
1376	**net**-*adj; adv*	net| sharp; outright
1239	**nettoyer**-*vb*	clean| clear
493	**neuf**-*num*	nine
1920	**neveu**-*m*	nephew
644	**nez**-*m*	nose
2420	**nichon**-*m*	tit| nipple
182	**ni**-*con; adv*	or; neither
2458	**nid**-*m*	nest
2518	**niquer**-*vb*	fuck
887	**niveau**-*m*	level
1628	**noble**-*adj; m/f*	noble; noble
499	**Noël**-*m*	Christmas
409	**noir**-*adj; m*	black; black
2178	**noix**-*f; adj*	nut; walnut
978	**nombre**-*m*	number
1142	**nombreux**-*adj*	numerous
125	**nom**-*m*	name
1509	**nommer**-*vb*	appoint| name

32	**non**-*adv; part*	not; no		2198	**ongle**-*m*	nail
651	**nord**-*m; adj*	north; northern		18	**on**-*prn*	we
634	**normal**-*adj*	normal		1781	**onze**-*num*	eleven
1230	**note**-*f*	note		855	**opération**-*f*	operation
1083	**noter**-*vb*	note		2137	**opérer**-*vb*	operate| carry out
78	**notre**-*prn*	our		1373	**opinion**-*f*	opinion
1620	**nôtre**-*prn*	our		2444	**opportunité**-*f*	oppurtunity
1565	**nourrir**-*vb*	feed| nourish		2267	**orage**-*m*	storm
833	**nourriture**-*f*	food| feed		1717	**orange**-*adj*	orange
23	**nous**-*prn*	we| us		1991	**orchestrer**-*vb*	orchestrate
202	**nouveau**-*adj; m*	new| further; incoming		1578	**ordinaire**-*adj; m*	ordinary; ordinary
2140	**novembre**-*m*	November		1135	**ordinateur**-*m*	computer
1611	**nu**-*adj*	naked		2238	**ordonner**-*vb*	order| direct
1843	**nuage**-*m*	cloud		408	**ordre**-*m*	order
1989	**nucléaire**-*adj*	nuclear		1937	**ordure**-*f*	filth| trash
128	**nuit**-*f*	night		1087	**oreille**-*f*	ear
688	**nul**-*adj; m; prn*	no| zero; zero; no one		1696	**organisation**-*f*	organization| setup
303	**numéro**-*m*	number		1985	**organiser**-*vb*	organize| arrange
				2033	**original**-*adj; m*	original; original
				1639	**origine**-*f*	origin
	O			406	**or**-*m*	gold
				1987	**oser**-*vb*	dare
1697	**Ô!**-*int*	Oh!		1063	**os**-*m*	bone
2013	**obéir**-*vb*	obey		2298	**otage**-*m*	hostage
1780	**objectif**-*adj; m*	objective; goal		51	**où**-*adv; prn; con*	where; that; wherein
2009	**objection**-*f*	objection		122	**ouais**-*part*	yeah
1342	**objet**-*m*	object		2184	**oublié**-*adj*	forgotten
1015	**obliger**-*vb*	force| oblige		353	**oublier**-*vb*	forget
2132	**obscurité**-*f*	darkness| obscurity		62	**ou**-*con*	or
2392	**observer**-*vb*	observe| watch		795	**ouest**-*adj; m*	west; west
957	**obtenir**-*vb*	get| obtain		36	**oui**-*part; m*	yes; yea
769	**occasion**-*f*	opportunity| occasion		1280	**ours**-*m*	bear
458	**occuper**-*vb*	occupy| hold		2312	**outil**-*m*	tool
1321	**océan**-*m*	ocean		1141	**ouvert**-*adj*	open
1973	**octobre**-*m*	October		1922	**ouverture**-*f*	opening
1002	**odeur**-*f*	smell| odor		2109	**ouvrier**-*m*	worker
206	**œil**-*m*	eye		639	**ouvrir**-*vb*	open| start
2272	**officiel**-*adj; m*	official; official		2214	**oxygéner**-*vb*	oxygenate| bleach
2445	**officiellement**-*adv*	officially				
907	**officier**-*m*	officer			**P**	
582	**offrir**-*vb*	offer| give				
80	**Oh!**-*int*	Oh!		2510	**pacifique**-*adj*	peaceful| pacific
2206	**oindre**-*vb*	anoint		1145	**page**-*f*	page
976	**oiseau**-*m*	bird		780	**paie**-*f*	pay| payroll
456	**oncle**-*m*	uncle		860	**pain**-*m*	bread
2462	**onde**-*f*	wave		1652	**pair**-*adj; m*	even; peer

396	**paix**-*f*	peace
1353	**palais**-*m*	palace
2329	**panier**-*m*	basket
1486	**panique**-*adj; f*	panic; panic
2505	**panneau**-*m*	panel| sign
1192	**pantalon**-*m*	pants
129	**papa**-*m*	papa
2484	**pape**-*m*	pope
846	**papier**-*m*	paper
1109	**paquet**-*m*	package| pack
994	**paradis**-*m*	paradise
658	**paraître**-*vb*	seem| appear
101	**parce que**-*adv*	because
1170	**parc**-*m*	park
222	**pardon**-*m*	forgiveness
1592	**pardonner**-*vb*	forgive| pardon
522	**pareil**-*adj; prn; m*	such| similar; the same; equal
2358	**parent**-*m; adj*	relative; kin
332	**parfait**-*adj*	perfect
1020	**parfaitement**-*adv*	perfectly| thoroughly
340	**parfois**-*adv*	sometimes
1608	**parfum**-*m*	perfume| fragrance
730	**parier**-*vb*	bet| gamble
571	**pari**-*m*	bet| betting
2068	**parking**-*m*	parking
105	**parler**-*vb*	speak| tell
778	**parmi**-*prp*	among
699	**parole**-*f*	word| speech
55	**par**-*prp; m*	by; par
1686	**partage**-*m*	sharing| division
1153	**partager**-*vb*	share| divide
2422	**partant**-*adv; m*	thus; starter
1332	**partenaire**-*m*	partner
174	**part**-*f*	share| part
1999	**participer**-*vb*	participate| involve
1449	**particulier**-*adj; m*	particular| individual; private person
2189	**particulièrement**-*adv*	particularly
167	**partir**-*vb*	depart| leave
368	**partout**-*adv*	everywhere| throughout
4	**pas**-*adv; m*	not; step
1017	**passager**-*m; adj*	passenger; passing
150	**passe**-*f*	pass
1956	**passeport**-*m*	passport
142	**passer**-*vb*	pass| spend
1512	**passion**-*f*	passion
1935	**pasteur**-*m*	pastor| shepherd
1472	**patience**-*f*	patience
1198	**patient**-*adj; m*	patient; patient
2382	**patienter**-*vb*	wait
2035	**patrie**-*f*	country| homeland
453	**patron**-*m*	boss| patron
2275	**patrouille**-*f*	patrol
1334	**patte**-*f*	tab| leg
1223	**pause**-*f*	break| rest
337	**pauvre**-*adj; m*	poor; poor person
1179	**payer**-*vb*	pay
259	**pays**-*m*	country
643	**peau**-*f*	skin
1429	**péché**-*m*	sin| trespass
1426	**pêcher**-*vb; m*	fish; peach
2328	**peindre**-*vb*	paint
313	**peiner**-*vb*	labor| pain
187	**pendre**-*vb*	hang
2228	**pénis**-*m*	penis
127	**penser**-*vb*	think| reflect
2175	**pension**-*f*	pension
235	**perdre**-*vb*	lose| waste
90	**père**-*m*	father| dad
1506	**période**-*f*	period| term
848	**permettre**-*vb*	allow| enable
1204	**permission**-*f*	permission
1363	**personnage**-*m*	character| figure
2065	**personnalité**-*f; abr*	personality; VIP
98	**personne**-*f; prn*	person; nobody
1824	**personnellement**-*adv*	personally
878	**personnel**-*m; adj*	staff| personnel; personal
1200	**perte**-*f*	loss| waste
1962	**pervers**-*adj*	perverse
109	**petit**-*adj; m*	small| little; child
2330	**pétrin**-*m*	mess| predicament
1785	**pétrole**-*m*	oil| kerosene
74	**peu**-*adv; m; adj*	little; bit; few
572	**peuple**-*m*	common people
132	**peur**-*f*	fear| scare
2177	**phase**-*f*	phase
417	**photo**-*f*	photo
2225	**phrase**-*f*	phrase

1443	**physique**-*adj; f*	physical; physics		958	**pluie**-*f*	rain
1264	**piano**-*adv; m*	piano; piano		31	**plus**-*adj; adv; m*	more; more; plus
469	**pièce**-*f; adv*	piece| room; apiece		600	**plusieurs**-*adj*	several| divers
484	**pied**-*m*	foot| leg		288	**plutôt**-*adv*	rather| quite
1231	**piéger**-*vb*	trap| ensnare		984	**pocher**-*vb*	poach
1369	**piger**-*vb*	understand| get		2226	**poème**-*m*	poem| epic
1711	**pile**-*f*	battery| pile		2197	**poésie**-*f*	poetry| poem
2521	**pilote**-*m*	pilot		2314	**poète**-*m*	poet
1096	**piloter**-*vb*	pilot		2439	**pognon**-*m*	money| dough
2208	**pilule**-*f*	pill		1047	**poids**-*m*	weight
2042	**pipe**-*f*	pipe		1576	**poil**-*m*	hair
2350	**pipi**-*m*	pee		1631	**poindre**-*vb*	dawn
2281	**pique**-*m; f*	spade; pike		2160	**poing**-*m*	fist
2024	**piquer**-*vb*	prick| sting		268	**point**-*m*	point| item
2349	**pirate**-*m*	pirate		1852	**poison**-*m*	poison
394	**pire**-*adj*	worse		820	**poisson**-*m*	fish
1128	**pis encore**-*adv*	even worse		1625	**poitrine**-*f*	chest| bosom
1529	**piscine**-*f*	swimming pool		2474	**poker**-*m*	poker
2217	**pisse**-*f*	piss		211	**police**-*f*	police
1747	**pisser**-*vb*	piss		1193	**policier**-*m*	police officer
943	**piste**-*f*	track| runway		839	**politique**-*f; adj*	policy; political
1240	**pistolet**-*m*	gun| pistol		1693	**pomme**-*f*	apple
671	**pitié**-*f*	pity		2273	**pompe**-*f*	pump| pomp
1798	**pizza**-*f*	pizza		2434	**pompier**-*m; adj*	fire-fighter; pompous
1856	**placard**-*m*	cupboard		834	**pont**-*m*	bridge
1842	**place**-*f*	square| spot		1990	**populaire**-*adj*	popular
219	**placer**-*vb*	place| put		2127	**population**-*f*	population
1022	**plage**-*f*	beach		1308	**porc**-*m*	pork| pig
1685	**plaindre**-*vb*	complain| pity		2374	**porno**-*m*	porn
144	**plaire**-*vb*	please		1236	**portable**-*adj; m*	portable; portable
1635	**plaisant**-*adj*	pleasant		177	**porte**-*f*	door| gate
2292	**plaisanterie**-*f*	joke		1885	**portefeuille**-*m*	portfolio| wallet
1289	**plaisanter**-*vb*	joke| fun		545	**porter**-*vb*	wear| carry
321	**plaisir**-*m*	pleasure		1479	**port**-*m*	port| harbor
2449	**plancher**-*m; vb*	floor; floor		638	**poser**-*vb*	pose| rest
857	**planète**-*f*	planet		712	**position**-*f*	position
375	**plan**-*m; adj*	plan; plane		1721	**posséder**-*vb*	have| rejoice
2352	**plante**-*f*	plant		2081	**possibilité**-*f*	possibility
2259	**planter**-*vb*	plant		280	**possible**-*adj; m*	possible; possible
1969	**plaquer**-*vb*	stick| tackle		585	**poste**-*m; f*	position; post
2147	**plastique**-*adj; m*	plastic; plastic		576	**pote**-*m*	buddy
1251	**plat**-*adj; m*	flat; flat| dish		1496	**pot**-*m*	pot| jar
1808	**plateau**-*m*	tray		2274	**poubelle**-*f*	dustbin| rubbish
282	**plein**-*adj*	full| fraught		2326	**pouce**-*m*	inch
875	**pleurer**-*vb*	cry| mourn		1864	**poudrer**-*vb*	powder
2083	**pleuvoir**-*vb*	rain		1427	**poule**-*f*	hen

1069	**poulet**-*m*	chicken	1361	**printemps**-*m*	spring
1244	**poupée**-*f*	doll| puppet	350	**prison**-*f*	prison
20	**pour**-*prp*	for	1282	**prisonnier**-*m*; *adj*	prisoner; captive
53	**pourquoi**-*adv*; *con*	why; wherefore	1102	**priver**-*vb*	deprive| deny
1891	**pourrir**-*vb*	rot| decay	433	**prix**-*m*	price| prize
1728	**poursuivre**-*vb*	continue| pursue	684	**probablement**-*adv*	probably
591	**pourtant**-*con*; *adv*	yet| however; nevertheless	175	**problème**-*m*	problem| issue
1132	**pousser**-*vb*	push| drive	2000	**procédure**-*f*	procedure
1511	**poussière**-*f*	dust	891	**procès**-*m*	trial| process
58	**pouvoir**-*m*; *vb*; *av*	power; can; might	2321	**processus**-*m*	process
1554	**pratique**-*f*; *adj*	practice; practical	438	**prochain**-*adj*; *m*	next| upcoming; next
2209	**pratiquement**-*adv*	virtually	966	**proche**-*adj*; *adv*; *m*	near; near; neighbor
1768	**précieux**-*adj*	precious| valuable	1372	**procureur**-*m*	prosecutor
1778	**précis**-*adj*; *m*	precise; abstract	1803	**producteur**-*m*	producer
2385	**précisément**-*adv*	precisely	1670	**production**-*f*	production
667	**préférer**-*vb*; *av*	prefer; would rather	999	**produire**-*vb*	produce
2497	**pré**-*m*	meadow| pasture	508	**professeur**-*m*	professor| teacher
238	**premier**-*adj*	first| prime	1729	**professionnel**-*adj*; *m*	professional; professional
138	**prendre**-*vb*	take| have	2503	**profil**-*m*	profile
1569	**prénom**-*m*	first name	1526	**profiter**-*vb*	benefit| avail
921	**préparer**-*vb*	prepare| make	2481	**profit**-*m*	profit| advantage
273	**près**-*adv*	near| by	1387	**prof**-*m*	prof
952	**présence**-*f*	presence	1507	**profond**-*adj*; *m*	deep| profound; deep
505	**présent**-*adj*; *m*	present; present	1782	**profondément**-*adv*	deeply| heavily
743	**présenter**-*vb*	present| offer	946	**programme**-*m*	program| agenda
366	**président**-*m*	president	1936	**progrès**-*m*	progress
301	**presque**-*adv*; *adj*	almost; all but	818	**projet**-*m*	project
744	**presse**-*f*	press	2131	**pro**-*m/f*	pro
1612	**presser**-*vb*	press| squeeze	2423	**promenade**-*f*	walk
1027	**pression**-*f*	pressure	1899	**promener**-*vb*	promenade
264	**prêt**-*adj*; *m*	ready| willing; loan	1482	**promesse**-*f*	promise
2346	**prêter**-*vb*	lend| attribute	455	**promettre**-*vb*	promise
1268	**prêtre**-*m*	priest	2056	**promotion**-*f*	promotion
746	**preuve**-*f*	evidence| proof	1534	**proposer**-*vb*	propose| offer
1076	**prévenir**-*vb*	warn| inform	1772	**proposition**-*f*	proposal| proposition
800	**prévu**-*adj*	planned	428	**propos**-*m*	talk
1850	**prière**-*f*	prayer	378	**propre**-*adj*; *m*	own| clean; proper
227	**prier**-*vb*	pray	1297	**propriétaire**-*m/f*; *adj*	owner| landlord; proprietary
2090	**prime**-*f*; *adj*	premium; incentive	1546	**propriété**-*f*	property
740	**prince**-*m*	prince	1318	**protection**-*f*	protection
830	**princesse**-*f*	princess	669	**protéger**-*vb*	protect| safeguard
1493	**principal**-*adj*; *m*	main; principal			
2243	**principe**-*m*	principle			

960	**prouver**-*vb*	prove
1292	**prudent**-*adj*	careful
624	**public**-*adj; m*	public; public
2091	**publicité**-*f*	advertising| publicity
1549	**pub**-*m; f*	pub; advertising
1637	**puce**-*f; adj*	chip| flea; puce
164	**puis**-*adv*	then
863	**puisque**-*con*	since
1154	**puissance**-*f*	power| strength
1065	**puissant**-*adj*	powerful| strong
1939	**puits**-*m*	well
1567	**pur**-*adj*	pure| clean
180	**putain**-*f*	whore| bitch
594	**pute**-*f*	bitch

Q

2495	**quai**-*m*	dock| quay
1613	**qualité**-*f*	quality
54	**quand**-*adv; con*	when; when
739	**quartier**-*m*	neighborhood| district
1804	**quart**-*m*	quarter
287	**quatre**-*num*	four
2049	**quatrième**-*num*	fourth
9	**que**-*con; prn; prp; adj; adv*	that; that; than; which; how
115	**quel**-*adj; prn*	what; what
83	**quelque**-*adj; adv*	some; about
198	**question**-*f*	question| issue
1011	**queue**-*f*	tail| queue
1516	**quiconque**-*prn*	whoever
1720	**quinze**-*num*	fifteen
22	**qui**-*prn*	which
2293	**quitte**-*adj*	quits
568	**quitter**-*vb*	leave| quit
43	**quoi**-*prn*	what

R

1621	**race**-*f*	race| breed
844	**raconter**-*vb*	tell
587	**radio**-*f*	radio
1919	**rage**-*f*	rage| rabies
158	**raison**-*f*	reason| why
1603	**raisonnable**-*adj*	reasonable
2317	**ramasser**-*vb*	pick up

808	**ramener**-*vb*	bring back
2380	**ramer**-*vb*	row
2034	**ranch**-*m*	ranch
1794	**ranger**-*m; vb*	ranger; put away
1671	**rang**-*m*	rank| row
849	**rapide**-*adj; m*	fast| rapid; rapid
1186	**rapidement**-*adv*	quickly| rapidly
1950	**rapporter**-*vb*	report| relate
472	**rapport**-*m*	report| ratio
1467	**rare**-*adj*	rare
2101	**rarement**-*adv*	rarely| hardly
2381	**rate**-*f*	spleen
1008	**rater**-*vb*	miss| fail
1470	**rat**-*m*	rat
2118	**rattraper**-*vb*	catch up| make up
798	**ravir**-*vb*	delight| ravish
2299	**ravissant**-*adj*	delightful
1709	**rayon**-*m*	radius| ray
1617	**réaction**-*f*	reaction
1851	**réalisateur**-*m*	director
1451	**réaliser**-*vb*	realize| achieve
809	**réalité**-*f*	reality
1513	**récemment**-*adv*	recently
1815	**réception**-*f*	reception| desk
454	**recevoir**-*vb*	receive| take
704	**recherche**-*f*	research| search
1344	**recommencer**-*vb*	restart| start again
1600	**récompenser**-*vb*	reward
2202	**reconnaissance**-*f*	recognition
2188	**reconnaissant**-*adj*	grateful
1285	**reconnaître**-*vb*	recognize| admit
2111	**record**-*m*	record
1172	**reculer**-*vb*	back| retreat
959	**récupérer**-*vb*	recover
1246	**réel**-*adj; m*	real| live; real
1651	**réellement**-*adv*	actually| true
1568	**refaire**-*vb*	redo| repair
899	**réfléchir**-*vb*	reflect| think
835	**refuser**-*vb*	refuse
139	**regarder**-*vb*	look| watch
963	**regard**-*m*	look| gaze
2038	**régime**-*m*	regime| diet
2515	**régiment**-*m*	regiment
1411	**région**-*f*	region| district
1009	**règle**-*f*	rule

1965	**règlement**-*m*	settlement| regulation
949	**régler**-*vb*	adjust| settle
2266	**règne**-*m*	reign
922	**regretter**-*vb*	regret| miss
681	**reine**-*f*	queen
972	**rejoindre**-*vb*	rejoin
970	**relation**-*f*	relation
2297	**relever**-*vb*	raise| pick up
1744	**religion**-*f*	religion
2105	**remarquable**-*adj*	remarkable
2048	**remarque**-*f*	remark| observation
993	**remarquer**-*vb*	notice| note
2245	**rembourser**-*vb*	repay| reimburse
884	**remercier**-*vb*	thank
888	**remettre**-*vb*	deliver| return
1302	**remonter**-*vb*	ascend| reassemble
1681	**remplacer**-*vb*	replace| change
1767	**remplir**-*vb*	fill| fill in
814	**rencontre**-*f*	meeting| match
516	**rencontrer**-*vb*	meet| encounter
370	**rendre**-*vb*	render| restore
2269	**renoncer**-*vb*	renounce| give up
1912	**renseignement**-*m*	inquiry
328	**rentrer**-*vb*	return
1994	**renvoyer**-*vb*	return| send
1150	**réparer**-*vb*	repair
1887	**repartir**-*vb*	restart| redivide
868	**repas**-*m*	meal
1000	**répéter**-*vb*	repeat| rehearse
766	**répondre**-*vb*	answer
592	**réponse**-*f*	response
1082	**reposer**-*vb*	rest
1134	**repos**-*m*	rest| pause
1079	**reprendre**-*vb*	resume| retake
1406	**représenter**-*vb*	represent
2493	**république**-*f*	republic
1391	**réputation**-*f*	reputation| name
2371	**requin**-*m*	shark
1849	**réseau**-*m*	network| grid
1914	**réservé**-*adj*	reserved
1339	**réserver**-*vb*	book| reserve
2155	**résistance**-*f*	resistance| strength
2020	**résister**-*vb*	resist
1679	**résoudre**-*vb*	solve| resolve
1715	**respecter**-*vb*	respect| observe
816	**respect**-*m*	respect
1250	**respirer**-*vb*	breathe
1419	**responsabilité**-*f*	responsibility
753	**responsable**-*adj; m/f*	responsible; person responsible
588	**ressembler**-*vb*	look like
1293	**ressentir**-*vb*	feel| be affected by
962	**restaurer**-*vb*	restore
877	**reste**-*m*	rest| remainder
131	**rester**-*vb*	stay| keep
1400	**résultat**-*m*	result| product
398	**retard**-*m*	delay
1743	**retenir**-*vb*	retain| hold
1388	**retirer**-*vb*	withdraw| pull
341	**retour**-*m*	return
581	**retourner**-*vb*	return
510	**retrouver**-*vb*	find| meet
852	**réunion**-*f*	meeting| reunion
1970	**réunir**-*vb*	gather| reunite
517	**réussir**-*vb*	succeed| pass
1166	**réveiller**-*vb*	wake| awake
2082	**réveil**-*m*	alarm clock
670	**rêve**-*m*	dream
331	**revenir**-*vb*	return| get back
734	**revenu**-*m*	income
2149	**révérend**-*m*	reverend
387	**rêver**-*vb*	dream
184	**revoir**-*vb*	revise
1501	**révolution**-*f*	revolution
1580	**revolver**-*m*	revolver
741	**riche**-*adj; m/f*	rich; rich person
745	**ridicule**-*adj; m*	ridiculous; ridicule
49	**rien**-*m; prn; adv*	nothing; anything; nix
2136	**rigole**-*f*	channel
2252	**rigoler**-*vb*	laugh
602	**rire**-*m; vb*	laugh; laugh
527	**risque**-*m*	risk| hazard
1765	**risquer**-*vb*	risk| venture
1013	**rivière**-*f*	river
1634	**riz**-*m*	rice
1847	**robot**-*m*	robot
1136	**rock**-*m*	rock
364	**roi**-*m*	king
708	**rôle**-*m*	role
1510	**roman**-*m; adj*	novel; Romance

1478	**romantique**-*adj; m/f*	romantic; romantic
2117	**rompre**-*vb*	break| break up
1738	**rond**-*adj; m*	round; round
750	**rose**-*adj; f*	pink; rose
2283	**rouer**-*vb*	cane
434	**rouge**-*adj; m*	red; red
1367	**roulé**-*adj*	rolled
1955	**rouler**-*vb*	roll
316	**route**-*f*	road| way
2270	**royal**-*adj*	royal
1489	**royaume**-*m*	kingdom
415	**rue**-*f*	street
2067	**rumeur**-*f*	rumor
1137	**russe**-*adj; m*	Russian; Russian
1532	**rythmer**-*vb*	rhythm

S

1550	**sabler**-*vb*	sand
2015	**sabrer**-*vb*	cut
476	**sac**-*m*	bag| sack
867	**sacré**-*adj*	sacred
2161	**sacrifice**-*m*	sacrifice
1129	**sage**-*adj; m*	wise; sage
2251	**sagesse**-*f*	wisdom
2016	**sain**-*adj*	healthy
1090	**saint**-*adj; m*	saint; saint; St.
1269	**saison**-*f*	season
2003	**salade**-*f*	salad
1562	**salaire**-*m*	salary
654	**salaud**-*m; adj*	bastard; dirty
1366	**sale**-*adj*	dirty| nasty
401	**saler**-*vb*	salt
2494	**saleté**-*f*	dirt| filth
464	**salle**-*f*	room
1093	**salon**-*m*	lounge
722	**salope**-*f*	slut
1948	**saloperie**-*f*	rubbish
2254	**saluer**-*vb*	greet
134	**salut**-*m; int*	salvation; hi
998	**samedi**-*m*	Saturday
1827	**sandwich**-*m*	sandwich
195	**sang**-*m*	blood
82	**sans**-*prp*	without
631	**santé**-*f*	health

2412	**Satan**-*m*	Satan
2433	**satellite**-*m*	satellite
2256	**satisfaire**-*vb*	satisfy| please
403	**sauf**-*prp; adj; con; adv*	except; safe; excepting; short of
726	**sauter**-*vb*	jump| skip
2295	**saut**-*m*	jump| hop
1488	**sauvage**-*adj; m*	wild; savage
468	**sauver**-*vb*	save
45	**savoir**-*vb; m*	know; knowledge
2348	**savon**-*m*	soap
2057	**scandale**-*m*	scandal
1492	**scénario**-*m*	scenario
474	**scène**-*f*	scene
1659	**scientifique**-*adj; m/f*	scientific; scientist
2511	**scotch**-*m*	Scotch tape| whisky
1881	**séance**-*f*	meeting| session
1303	**sec**-*adj*	dry| dried
477	**second**-*adj; m*	second; second
607	**secours**-*m*	relief| help
475	**secret**-*adj; m*	secret| covert; secret
1237	**secrétaire**-*m/f*	secretary
1446	**secteur**-*m*	sector
1552	**section**-*f*	section
385	**sécurité**-*f*	security
314	**seigneur**-*m*	lord
1544	**sein**-*m*	breast| fold
2093	**séjour**-*m*	stay| visit
2051	**sel**-*m*	salt
569	**selon**-*prp; adv*	according to; as follows
290	**semaine**-*f*	week
1176	**semblant**-*m*	semblance
382	**sembler**-*vb*	seem| sound
1428	**sénateur**-*m*	senator
2154	**sensation**-*f*	sensation| feeling
1872	**sensible**-*adj*	sensitive
979	**sentiment**-*m*	feeling| sense
689	**sentir**-*vb*	feel
1837	**séparer**-*vb*	separate| part
40	**se**-*prn*	-self (reflexive marker)
1524	**septembre**-*m*	September
555	**sept**-*num*	seven
649	**sergent**-*m*	sergeant
1127	**série**-*f*	series| set
1057	**sérieusement**-*adv*	seriously| gravely

418	**sérieux**-*adj; m*	serious; seriousness
1868	**serment**-*m*	oath
1527	**serpent**-*m*	snake
2146	**serrer**-*vb*	tighten| clamp
335	**service**-*m*	service| serving
1953	**serviette**-*f*	towel| napkin
645	**servir**-*vb*	serve| help
135	**seul**-*adj; m; adv*	only; only one; very
212	**seulement**-*adv; con*	only| just; only
866	**sexe**-*m*	sex| gender
2181	**sexuel**-*adj*	sexual
1101	**sexy**-*adj*	sexy
850	**shérif**-*m*	sheriff
1675	**show**-*m*	show
29	**si**-*con; adv*	if; so
1257	**siècle**-*m*	century
1401	**siège**-*m*	seat| siege
2400	**sien**-*prn*	one's own
1023	**signal**-*m*	signal
2075	**signature**-*f*	signature
682	**signer**-*vb*	sign
812	**signifier**-*vb*	mean| imply
547	**silence**-*m*	silence| pause
395	**simple**-*adj*	simple; singles
566	**simplement**-*adv*	simply
2041	**sincère**-*adj*	sincere| genuine
2372	**sincèrement**-*adv*	truly| sincerely
2229	**singe**-*m*	monkey
373	**sinon**-*con; adv*	otherwise; or else
1901	**sire**-*m*	sire
1209	**sir**-*m*	sir
1658	**site**-*m*	site
495	**situation**-*f*	situation
343	**six**-*num*	six
2169	**social**-*adj*	social
695	**société**-*f*	society| association
483	**sœur**-*adj; f*	sister; sister
1397	**soif**-*f*	thirst
1801	**soigner**-*vb*	treat
1306	**soi**-*m; prn*	self; self
696	**soin**-*m*	care| carefulness
482	**soirée**-*f*	evening
121	**soir**-*m*	evening
140	**soit**-*con*	whether| either
736	**soldat**-*m*	soldier
461	**soleil**-*m*	sun
1916	**solide**-*adj; m*	solid; solid
2029	**solitaire**-*adj; m/f*	solitary; loner
2191	**solitude**-*f*	solitude| loneliness
674	**sol**-*m*	soil
893	**solution**-*f*	solution
1382	**sombre**-*adj*	dark| gloomy
1278	**somme**-*f*	sum
1165	**sommeil**-*m*	sleep| rest
1666	**sommet**-*m*	top| vertex
56	**son**-*adj; m*	its; sound
1348	**sonner**-*vb*	ring| sound
1710	**sorcier**-*m*	sorcerer
441	**sorte**-*f*	kind| manner
197	**sortir**-*vb*	exit| come out
1189	**souci**-*m*	worry| care
1227	**soudain**-*adv; adj*	suddenly; sudden
1157	**souffle**-*m*	breath| blast
1783	**souffrance**-*f*	suffering
1315	**souffrir**-*vb*	suffer| experience
1001	**souhaiter**-*vb*	wish| hope
1986	**sou**-*m*	cent
1336	**souper**-*m; vb*	supper; sup
1265	**source**-*f*	source| spring
1900	**sourd**-*adj*	deaf| dull
909	**sourire**-*m; vb*	smile; smile
961	**souris**-*f*	mouse
193	**sous**-*prp; adv; f*	under; underneath; cash
2491	**soutenir**-*vb*	support| back
1773	**soutien**-*m*	support
308	**souvenir**-*m*	memory| souvenir
402	**souvent**-*adv*	often
856	**spécial**-*adj*	special
703	**spectacle**-*m*	show| spectacle
2055	**splendide**-*adj*	splendid
1399	**sport**-*m; adj*	sport; sporting
1867	**stade**-*m*	stage
1049	**star**-*f*	star
1313	**station**-*f*	station
2230	**statuer**-*vb*	rule
898	**stop**-*m*	stop
1417	**studio**-*m*	studio
665	**stupide**-*adj; m*	stupid; stupid
2080	**stylo**-*m*	pen
2450	**subir**-*vb*	undergo| suffer
986	**succès**-*m*	success

2524	**sucer**-*vb*	suck| suck out
1371	**sucrer**-*vb*	sweeten
617	**sud**-*adj; m*	south; south
315	**suffire**-*vb*	suffice
1957	**suffisamment**-*adv*	enough
2122	**suggérer**-*vb*	suggest| imply
2310	**suisse**-*adj*	Swiss
226	**suite**-*f*	suite| sequence
1014	**suivant**-*adj; prp; adv*	following; according to; as follows
580	**suivre**-*vb*	follow
397	**sujet**-*m; adj*	subject; prone
802	**superbe**-*adj*	superb; stunner
1823	**supérieur**-*adj; m*	upper; superior
1182	**supplier**-*vb*	beg| entreat
1272	**supporter**-*vb; m*	support| bear; supporter
550	**supposer**-*vb*	assume| suppose
2040	**suprême**-*adj; m*	supreme; supreme
93	**sûr**-*adj*	sure| safe
405	**sûrement**-*adv*	surely
1463	**surface**-*f*	surface
557	**surprendre**-*vb*	surprise| catch
42	**sur**-*prp*	on
390	**surtout**-*adv*	mainly| above all
1853	**surveillance**-*f*	surveillance
1396	**surveiller**-*vb*	monitor| watch
2236	**survie**-*f*	survival
1350	**survivre**-*vb*	survive
1312	**suspect**-*adj; m*	suspect| dubious; suspect
2263	**symbole**-*m*	symbol
646	**sympa**-*adj*	friendly
2309	**syndicat**-*m*	union| syndicate
626	**système**-*m*	system

T

2094	**tabac**-*m*	tobacco
1284	**tableau**-*m*	table| picture
2456	**tache**-*f*	spot| stain
1447	**tâcher**-*vb*	try
864	**tailler**-*vb*	cut| carve
496	**taire**-*vb*	hush up
2366	**talent**-*m*	talent| skill
584	**tant pis**-*adv*	too bad
173	**tant**-*adv*	so such
678	**tante**-*f*	aunt
1616	**tape**-*f*	slap
1754	**taper**-*vb*	type| beat
1500	**tapir**-*m*	tapir
165	**tard**-*adv*	late
2194	**tarder**-*vb*	delay
2097	**tarte**-*f*	pie
663	**tas**-*m*	pile
1596	**tasse**-*f*	cup
1461	**taule**-*f*	slammer| nick
758	**taxi**-*m*	taxi
2032	**technologie**-*f*	technology
598	**tel**-*adj*	such
561	**télé**-*abr; f*	TV; telly
2387	**télégramme**-*m*	telegram
336	**téléphoner**-*vb*	call
1464	**télévision**-*f*	television
298	**tellement**-*adv*	so
2333	**témoignage**-*m*	testimony| witness
2417	**témoigner**-*vb*	testify| give evidence
882	**témoin**-*m*	witness
1946	**température**-*f*	temperature
1585	**tempête**-*f*	storm
1442	**temple**-*m*	temple
76	**temps**-*m*	time
1825	**tendre**-*adj; vb*	tender; tender
205	**tenir**-*vb*	hold| keep
2435	**tennis**-*m*	tennis
1952	**tension**-*f*	voltage| tension
1963	**tentative**-*f*	attempt| bid
1158	**tenter**-*vb*	try| attempt
1299	**ténu**-*adj*	tenuous
34	**te**-*prn*	you
1407	**terme**-*m*	term
529	**terminer**-*vb*	finish| conclude
817	**terrain**-*m*	field| ground
218	**terre**-*f*	earth| land
2249	**terreur**-*f*	terror
657	**terrible**-*adj*	terrible
2255	**terriblement**-*adv*	terribly
1702	**territoire**-*m*	territory
1888	**terroriste**-*m/f*	terrorist
2313	**testament**-*m*	will| device
1119	**test**-*m*	test
155	**tête**-*f*	head| top
2271	**texte**-*m*	text

988	**théâtre**-*m*	theater| stage	245	**train**-*m*	train
661	**thé**-*m*	tea	1543	**traitement**-*m*	treatment| processing
1409	**théorie**-*f*	theory	1422	**traiter**-*vb*	treat| deal
2453	**ticket**-*m*	ticket	1660	**traître**-*m; adj*	traitor; treacherous
1413	**tien**-*prn*	yours	518	**tranquille**-*adj*	quiet
1931	**timide**-*adj*	shy	2432	**transfert**-*m*	transfer
423	**tirer**-*vb*	take| draw	2316	**transformer**-*vb*	transform| change
2301	**tireur**-*m*	shooter| drawer	2345	**transport**-*m*	transport| carriage
1319	**tir**-*m*	shot	367	**travailler**-*vb*	work
1311	**titrage**-*m*	titration	178	**travail**-*m*	work
1060	**titre**-*m*	title| headline	1345	**traverser**-*vb*	cross| pass through
2179	**toast**-*m*	toast	664	**travers**-*m*	across
2436	**toc**-*int*	knock	1792	**trente**-*num*	thirty
854	**toilette**-*f*	toilet	63	**très**-*adv*	very
38	**toi**-*prn*	you	917	**trésor**-*m*	treasure| treasury
980	**toit**-*m*	roof	2499	**tribu**-*f*	tribe
2285	**tombe**-*f*	grave| tomb	1107	**tribunal**-*m*	court| courthouse
300	**tomber**-*vb*	fall| drop	597	**triste**-*adj*	sad
57	**ton**-*adj; prn; m*	your; your; tone	2498	**tristesse**-*f*	sadness
2332	**tonnerre**-*m*	thunder	944	**troisième**-*num*	third
2142	**tonner**-*vb*	thunder	143	**trois**-*num*	three
1433	**top**-*m*	top	1314	**tromper**-*vb*	deceive| mislead
731	**tort**-*m*	wrong| harm	2347	**trône**-*m*	throne
2125	**torture**-*f*	torture	86	**trop**-*adv*	too| too much
386	**tôt**-*adv*	early| soon	2215	**trouille**-*f*	funk
1913	**total**-*adj; m*	total| overall; total	1408	**troupe**-*f*	troop
1221	**totalement**-*adv*	totally	188	**trouver**-*vb*	find| get
2502	**touche**-*f*	key	204	**truc**-*m*	thing| trick
533	**toucher**-*m; vb*	touch; touch	166	**tuer**-*vb*	kill| murder
77	**toujours**-*adv*	always| still	784	**tueur**-*m*	killer
286	**tour**-*m; f*	turn; tower	1758	**tunnel**-*m*	tunnel
1988	**tournage**-*m*	shooting| turning	8	**tu**-*prn*	you (coll)
711	**tourner**-*vb*	turn| rotate	2036	**tuyau**-*m*	pipe| hose
30	**tout**-*adj; adv; m; prn*	all; all; all; all	790	**type**-*m*	type| guy
1421	**trace**-*f*	trace| track			
1343	**tracer**-*vb*	draw| mark		**U**	
2017	**tradition**-*f*	tradition			
1416	**traduction**-*f*	translation	10	**un**-*art; adj; num; prn*	a; one; one; one
2199	**trafic**-*m*	traffic	1337	**uniforme**-*adj; m*	uniform; uniform
2124	**tragédie**-*f*	tragedy	1642	**union**-*f*	union
2437	**tragique**-*adj*	tragic	930	**unique**-*adj*	unique
1886	**trahir**-*vb*	betray	1633	**uniquement**-*adv*	only
2153	**trahison**-*f*	treason	694	**unir**-*vb*	unite
2099	**traîne**-*f*	train	1187	**unité**-*f*	unit| unity
1661	**traîner**-*vb*	drag| trail	901	**université**-*f*	university

1030	**univers**-*m*	universe		1099	**victime**-*f*	victim
967	**urgence**-*f*	emergency		1005	**victoire**-*f*	victory| win
1630	**urgent**-*adj*	urgent		752	**vide**-*adj; m*	empty; empty
2261	**usage**-*m*	use| usage		1025	**vidéo**-*f*	video
2076	**user**-*vb*	use		79	**vie**-*f*	life
1114	**usine**-*f*	plant| factory		1309	**vierge**-*adj; f*	virgin; virgin
1043	**utile**-*adj*	useful		189	**vieux**-*adj; m*	old| ancient; old man
697	**utiliser**-*vb*	use		1053	**vif**-*adj; m*	bright| lively; quick
				2119	**vilain**-*adj; m*	ugly; villein
	V			637	**village**-*m*	village
				200	**ville**-*f*	city
782	**vacance**-*f*	vacancy		1159	**vingt**-*num*	twenty
1133	**vache**-*f; adj*	cow; bitchy		672	**vin**-*m*	wine
1698	**vague**-*f; adj*	wave; vague		1103	**violence**-*f*	violence| force
2356	**vain**-*adj*	vain		2044	**violent**-*adj*	violent| severe
2322	**vaincre**-*vb*	overcome| defeat		2353	**viol**-*m*	rape
865	**vaisseau**-*m*	vessel		1324	**virer**-*vb*	transfer| turn
1064	**valeur**-*f*	value| worth		1575	**virus**-*m*	virus
1354	**valise**-*f*	suitcase| case		407	**visage**-*m*	face
1797	**vallée**-*f*	valley		2073	**viser**-*vb*	aim for
360	**valoir**-*vb*	be worth		1453	**vision**-*f*	vision
2176	**vampire**-*m*	vampire		609	**visiter**-*vb*	visit| view
1036	**van**-*m*	van		137	**vite**-*adv*	quickly| fast
1993	**vedette**-*f*	star| launch		914	**vitesse**-*f*	speed
1466	**veiller**-*vb*	watch		1377	**vivant**-*adj; m*	living| alive; living
1647	**vélo**-*m*	bike		263	**vivre**-*vb*	live
2139	**vendeur**-*m*	seller| dealer		2401	**vodka**-*f*	vodka
1055	**vendredi**-*m*	Friday		194	**voici**-*prp*	here is
629	**vendre**-*vb*	sell		574	**voie**-*f*	way| track
1610	**vengeance**-*f*	vengeance		112	**voilà**-*adv*	here
1674	**venger**-*vb*	revenge		2388	**voile**-*f*	veil| sail
87	**venir**-*vb*	come		1362	**voiler**-*vb*	veil| mask
1457	**vente**-*f*	sale		68	**voir**-*vb*	see| view
675	**vent**-*m*	wind		1385	**voisin**-*m; adj*	neighbor; neighboring
1051	**ventre**-*m*	belly| stomach		948	**voiture**-*f*	car| vehicle
941	**vérifier**-*vb*	check| verify		426	**voix**-*f*	voice
1195	**véritable**-*adj*	true| real		614	**voler**-*vb*	fly| steal
291	**vérité**-*f*	truth		1046	**voleur**-*m; adj*	thief; thievish
342	**verre**-*m*	glass		623	**vol**-*m*	flight| theft
1518	**version**-*f*	version		2393	**volontaire**-*adj; m/f*	voluntary; voluntary
223	**vers**-*prp; adv; m*	to| towards; about; verse		1031	**volonté**-*f*	will
1066	**vert**-*adj; m*	green| young; putting green		2224	**volontiers**-*adv*	willingly
1259	**veste**-*f*	jacket		2383	**vomir**-*vb*	vomit
692	**vêtement**-*m*	garment		1741	**vote**-*m*	vote| polling
1012	**viande**-*f*	meat		52	**votre**-*adj; prn*	your; your

47	**vouloir**-*vb*	want| wish
6	**vous**-*prn*	you (form, pl)
440	**voyage**-*m*	travel| trip
1726	**voyager**-*vb*	travel
102	**vrai**-*adj; m*	true| real; right
75	**vraiment**-*adv*	really| actually

W

1212	**whisky**-*m*	whiskey| Scotch

Z

1089	**zéro**-*m*	zero| nobody
2395	**zoo**-*m*	zoo
2092	**Zut!**-*int*	Heck!

Contact, Further Reading and Resources

For more tools, tips & tricks visit our site www.mostusedwords.com. We publish various language learning resources.

If you have a great idea you want to pitch us, please send an e-mail to info@mostusedwords.com.

Frequency Dictionaries

Frequency Dictionaries in this series:

French Frequency Dictionary 1 – Essential Vocabulary – 2500 Most Common French Words
French Frequency Dictionary 2 - Intermediate Vocabulary – 2501-5000 Most Common French Words
French Frequency Dictionary 3 - Advanced Vocabulary – 5001-7500 Most Common French Words
French Frequency Dictionary 4 - Master Vocabulary – 7501-10000 Most Common French Words

Please visit our website www.mostusedwords.com/frequency-dictionary/french-english for more information.

Our goal is to provide language learners with frequency dictionaries for every major and minor language worldwide. You can view our selection on www.mostusedwords.com/frequency-dictionary

Bilingual books

We're creating a selection of parallel texts, and our selection is ever expanding.

To help you in your language learning journey, all our bilingual books come with a dictionary included, created for that particular book.

Current bilingual books available are English, Spanish, Portuguese, Italian, German, and French.

For more information, check www.mostusedwords.com/parallel-texts. Check back regularly for new books and languages.

Other language learning methods

You'll find reviews of other 3rd party language learning applications, software, audio courses, and apps. There are so many available, and some are (much) better than others.

Check out our reviews at www.mostusedwords.com/reviews.

Contact

If you have any questions, you can contact us through e-mail info@mostusedwords.com.